D1572278

Research, Education, and
American Indian Partnerships at the
Crow Canyon Archaeological Center

Research, Education,
and American Indian
Partnerships at the
**Crow Canyon
Archaeological Center**

EDITED BY **SUSAN C. RYAN**

UNIVERSITY PRESS OF COLORADO
Denver

Published by University Press of Colorado
1580 North Logan Street, Suite 660
PMB 39883
Denver, Colorado 80203-1942

 The University Press of Colorado is a proud member of
the Association of University Presses.

The University Press of Colorado is a cooperative publishing enterprise supported, in part, by Adams State University, Colorado State University, Fort Lewis College, Metropolitan State University of Denver, University of Alaska Fairbanks, University of Colorado, University of Denver, University of Northern Colorado, University of Wyoming, Utah State University, and Western Colorado University.

∞ This paper meets the requirements of the ANSI/NISO Z39.48-1992 (Permanence of Paper).

ISBN: 978-1-64642-458-0 (hardcover)
ISBN: 978-1-64642-459-7 (ebook)
https://doi.org/10.5876/9781646424597

Library of Congress Cataloging-in-Publication Data

Names: Ryan, Susan C., (Archaeologist), editor.
Title: Research, education, and American Indian partnerships at the Crow Canyon Archaeological
    Center / edited by Susan C. Ryan.
Description: Denver : University Press of Colorado, [2023] | Includes bibliographical references
    and index.
Identifiers: LCCN 2023012265 (print) | LCCN 2023012266 (ebook) | ISBN 9781646424580 (hard-
    cover) | ISBN 9781646424597 (ebook)
Subjects: LCSH: Crow Canyon Archaeological Center—History. | Archaeology—Research—
    Southwest, New. | Archaeology—Study and teaching—Southwest, New. | Indians of North
    America—Southwest, New—Antiquities. | Indians of North America—Research—Southwest,
    New. | Multicultural education—Southwest, New. | Southwest, New—Antiquities—Study and
    teaching—Colorado.
Classification: LCC E78.S7 R455 2023 (print) | LCC E78.S7 (ebook) | DDC 979/.01—dc23/
    eng/20230407
LC record available at https://lccn.loc.gov/2023012265
LC ebook record available at https://lccn.loc.gov/2023012266

This book was supported in part by the Crow Canyon Archaeological Center and the Arizona
Archaeological and Historical Society.

Cover photograph courtesy of the Crow Canyon Archaeological Center.

Photos courtesy of the Crow Canyon Archaeological Center.

This book is dedicated to Dr. Stuart Struever (left) and Dylan Schwindt (right). We are forever grateful for the impact you both had on Crow Canyon and the world.

Contents

Part II: Indigenous Archaeology

Part III: Archaeology and Public Education

Part IV: Community and Regional Studies

Figures

Tables

Research, Education, and
American Indian Partnerships
at the Crow Canyon Archaeological Center

I

Forty Years of Integrating American Indian Knowledge, Public Education, and Archaeological Research in the Central Mesa Verde Region

SUSAN C. RYAN

The Crow Canyon Archaeological Center (Crow Canyon), founded in 1983, is a nonprofit organization whose mission is to empower present and future generations by making the human past accessible and relevant through archaeological research, experiential education, and American Indian knowledge. As a core value, we believe the study of the past is an intrinsically worthwhile endeavor that creates more informed and sustainable societies. Through a better understanding of human history, we shed light on how the past can teach us about the challenges societies face throughout the world and strive to create change for the betterment of humanity.

For the past four decades, the focus of Crow Canyon's mission-based initiatives has been the Indigenous occupation of the central Mesa Verde region in southwestern Colorado. As defined here, the central Mesa Verde archaeological region is an area of approximately 10,000 square miles bounded by the Colorado, Piedra, and San Juan Rivers. It is located within the larger physiographic region known as the Colorado Plateau, a vast area of geologic uplift encompassing much of western Colorado, eastern Utah, northern Arizona, and northwestern New

https://doi.org/10.5876/9781646424597.c001

3

Mexico. The Mesa Verde region is a land of spectacular contrasts, where sandstone canyons divide sage-covered plains and juniper and pine woodlands, against the distant backdrop of the San Juan Mountains, a part of the Rocky Mountains. Cold winters give way to hot, dry summers, and periods of precipitation are punctuated by sporadic—but sometimes prolonged—periods of drought.

Living on this landscape has, at times throughout the centuries, been challenging—peoples in the past and present have met these challenges with extraordinary ingenuity and resilience. From the arrival of Paleolithic hunters to the first farmers who transitioned to sedentism, the story of how people have adapted to, and flourished on, this landscape is one of the most fascinating stories in human history. And flourish they did. The central Mesa Verde region has one of the densest concentrations of archaeological sites in North America. At present, Montezuma County, Colorado—where the Crow Canyon Archaeological Center campus is located—has over 21,000 archaeological sites recorded in the state database. This is a mere fraction of those present on the landscape as numerous parcels located on private, Tribal, public, and federal lands have not been fully surveyed. Some researchers note the population of the county today, approximately 26,000 people, is what the ancestral population was at its height during the thirteenth century AD. The central Mesa Verde region provides endless opportunities to study the past to better serve present and future generations.

Assisted by thousands of participants engaged in citizen science, Crow Canyon has generated one of the largest archaeological datasets in North America. At the time of this publication, eleven long-term research projects (table 1.1), five "Occasional Papers," four manuals and guides, and a substantial photographic database have been published on Crow Canyon's website (www.crowcanyon.org). In addition, countless books, journal articles, book chapters in edited volumes, dissertations, theses, and conference proceedings utilizing Crow Canyon data have been authored in the last forty years, many of which are referenced throughout this volume. The practice of publishing online began in 1997, when a revolutionary decision was made to make our work available and relevant to those outside of Crow Canyon. As a result, archaeological data, educational curricula, and other resources are free and accessible to Tribal communities, cross-disciplinary researchers, and a global public on Crow Canyon's website. The publications and data we share are perpetually growing as we continue to shed new light on the ancient past and its relevance to modern societies throughout the world.

Crow Canyon's educational philosophy is grounded in the belief that everyone's history matters. Our K–12, college, and adult research, education, and travel programs include place-based, experiential learning activities that bring the past to life and articulate with all areas of our mission. Many research and education programs actively engage participants in authentic scientific research

TABLE 1.1. Major Crow Canyon Archaeological Center projects, their dates, and associated major publications.

Major Projects, Crow Canyon	Project Dates	Major Publications
Duckfoot Site	1983–1997	Lightfoot (1994); Lightfoot and Etzkorn (1993);
Sand Canyon Archaeological Project	1983–1993	Adler (1992); Huber (1993); Kuckelman (2007); Lipe (1992); Varien (1999)
Castle Rock Pueblo Project	1992–1994	Kuckelman (2000)
Village Mapping Project	1993–1995	Lipe and Ortman (2000)
Village Testing Project	1994–1997	Churchill (2002) (Woods Canyon Pueblo); Kuckelman (2003) (Yellow Jacket Pueblo); Ortman et al. (2000) (Hedley Ruin)
Communities through Time: Migration, Cooperation, and Conflict	1997–2004	Ryan (2015a) (Shields Pueblo); Ryan (2015b) (Albert Porter Pueblo)
Village Ecodynamics I Project	2001–2006	Glowacki and Ortman (2012); Kohler and Varien (2012); Varien et al. (2007);
Goodman Point Archaeological Project	2005–2010	Kuckelman (2017) (Goodman Point Pueblo); Coffey (2018) (Goodman Point Community Testing)
Village Ecodynamics II Project	2009–2014	Reese et al. (2019); Schwindt et al. (2016)
Basketmaker Communities Project	2011–2020	Diederichs (2020)
Northern Chaco Outliers Project	2016–present	To be determined

Source: Table created by author.

in the field and/or the laboratory and are aligned with state standards. The Crow Canyon curriculum was developed in consultation with Indigenous partners, ensuring that multicultural perspectives are represented and respected. Crow Canyon remains a recognized leader in education for K–12 teachers, providing them with the knowledge, skills, and abilities to teach students—often from diverse backgrounds—multicultural perspectives on science, technology, engineering, art, and math (STEAM) and humanities curricula.

Crow Canyon partners with American Indians to enrich our understanding of past and present Indigenous cultures and to assist with cultural preservation initiatives. Working closely with our Native American Advisory Group, Tribal governments, and scholars, Crow Canyon seeks to broaden and enhance the perspectives gained through archaeological research, incorporate Indigenous science and perspectives into our educational curricula, and initiate projects that are culturally relevant and directly benefit Indigenous communities. Through well-designed mission-based projects and collaborations with descendant community members,

Crow Canyon has contributed to some of the most significant understandings in southwestern archaeology and is a leader in place-based, experiential education.

THIS VOLUME

The primary goal of this volume is to celebrate Crow Canyon in the past, present, and future by providing a backdrop to our humble beginnings and highlighting key mission accomplishments in American Indian initiatives, education, and research over the past four decades. It is our hope that future directions presented here will guide southwestern archaeology and public education beyond current practices—particularly regarding Indigenous archaeology and Indigenous partnerships—and provide strategic directions to guide Crow Canyon into the mid-twenty-first century and beyond.

The authors in this volume know Crow Canyon and the central Mesa Verde region well; they are current and former Crow Canyon researchers, educators, and cultural specialists, Indigenous scholars, and current research associates. All have been inspired by the organization's mission and have made it their life's work to further and share knowledge of the human past for the betterment of societies today and in the future.

VOLUME THEMES AND SECTIONS

This volume is comprised of individual chapters that serve as distinct contributions, yet they are grouped into parts according to overarching themes including (1) "History of the Crow Canyon Archaeological Center," (2) "Indigenous Archaeology," (3) "Archaeology and Public Education," (4) "Community and Regional Studies," and (5) "Human-Environment Relationship Research." These parts are representative of Crow Canyon's well-rounded mission work that has taken place over the last four decades.

Part I examines the origins and early history of the Crow Canyon Archaeological Center. In chapter 2, Lightfoot and Lipe discuss how the "Crow Canyon School" merged with two organizations: the Interdisciplinary Supplemental Education Programs, Inc., and the Center for American Archaeology, an affiliate of Northwestern University. In 1983, the Crow Canyon Archaeological Center was launched and dedicated to long-term archaeological research in the central Mesa Verde region while expanding public involvement to include data collection-based programs in the field and laboratory. In chapter 3, Kohler, Lightfoot, Varien, and Lipe explore Crow Canyon's emergence as a nonprofit research and education institution as the Dolores Archaeological Program (DAP) came to an end and how the DAP contributed researchers, archaeological methodologies, theoretical underpinnings, and inspiration for decades to come.

In part II, authors focus on Crow Canyon's contributions to Indigenous archaeology and projects and partnerships codeveloped with tribes and individuals. In chapter 4, Ermigiotti, Varien, Coffey, Bocinsky, Kuwanwisiwma, and Koyiyumptewa summarize the Pueblo Farming Project, an experimental maize garden program initiated in 2008 with the Hopi Tribe. By examining temperature, moisture, soil composition, and frost-free growing days, they discuss how environmental variables affect modern-day maize yields and apply these data to contribute to our understanding of regional depopulation in the late thirteenth century AD. In chapter 5, Kuwanwisiwma and Bernardini provide a summary of the importance of Mesa Verde in Hopi migrations for twenty-seven clans. This unique perspective on Hopi history provides a multivocal interpretation of the past and supports the role of the Mesa Verde region as a "convergence place" for coalescent communities. In chapter 6, Ortman suggests the future of Indigenous archaeology lies in reframing Western scientific inquiries similar to those of Indigenous ones. Recognizing that Indigenous peoples have traditionally learned from ancestral sites in ways different from Western scientists, Ortman urges us to explore the past with Indigenous partners to expand knowledge and benefit societies throughout the world. In chapter 7, Suina explores the history of colonization and the role of Indigenous knowledge in cultural preservation within the eastern Pueblos. Noting how knowledge is intended for subsets of the population—both Indigenous and non-Indigenous—Suina discusses how archaeologists can forge mutually beneficial relationships with tribes and Indigenous partners.

In part III, contributors examine the role of education at Crow Canyon and within STEAM-focused public archaeology. Like the archaeological research-focused chapters following this section, education contributions utilize various scales of inquiry including the examination of measurable outcomes and impacts of lesson plans within the discipline of public archaeology. In chapter 8, Franklin presents a synthesis of Crow Canyon's education initiatives and contextualizes them within the constructs of cognitive theory and social semiotics. Included in this summary are essential aspects of educational practices that have characterized Crow Canyon's public education programs for four decades, including experiential education and inquiry pedagogy, situated learning, multivocality, and the inclusion of descendant communities. In chapter 9, Patterson, Franklin, and Hammond explore the role of archaeology within K–12 education and demonstrate how science, technology, engineering, art, math, and other subjects are naturally aligned with archaeological studies. Additionally, they explore new directions in archaeological education to foster a greater understanding of our shared humanity in young learners.

Part IV, the largest section of the volume, examines archaeological research focused on community and regional studies within the central Mesa Verde region. Like much of our work over the past four decades, the scholarship in this section is presented at various analytical and interpretive scales. Some of the chapters explore households and villages at the residential level, while others focus on longer periods of time and incorporate regional and interregional data. Contributions in this section are organized primarily by time, beginning with the Basketmaker III period (AD 500–750) and ending with the depopulation of the region at the end of the Pueblo III period (AD 1150–1280).

In chapter 10, Schleher, Diederichs, Hughes, and Lyle explore how the social structure of a newly formed Basketmaker III period community comprised of diverse migrants shifted over the generations into a cohesive group dominated by long-standing family lineages and recognizable communities of practice. In chapter 11, Throgmorton, Wilshusen, and Coffey discuss a notable gap in archaeological knowledge around the "Long Tenth Century," a 140-year period beginning in AD 890 and a time when aggregated villages began to transition into great house communities and when Chaco Canyon reached its northernmost extent. In chapter 12, Glowacki, Coffey, and Varien discuss one of Crow Canyon's most impactful contributions to southwestern archaeology: the emergence and nature of community centers from the dawn of sedentism to the final depopulation of the region. Their contribution describes four decades of community center research at Crow Canyon, the importance of the Community Center Database, and the long-term impacts of this research, as well as offering suggestions to guide future research endeavors. In chapter 13, Potter, Varien, Coffey, and Bocinsky examine the formation of three, late thirteenth-century AD community centers, Yucca House, Moqui Springs Pueblo, and Cowboy Wash Pueblo, located on the "frontier" of the central Mesa Verde region. They argue differences in community organization were the result of social, environmental, and demographic factors, including the persistent threat of violence. In chapter 14, Schleher, Linford, Coffey, Kuckelman, Ortman, Till, Varien, and Merewether examine patterns in pottery production to infer cultural dynamics in the socially and spatially related Goodman Point and Sand Canyon communities from AD 900 to 1280. Applying a communities of practice approach, they argue for greater social stability in the Goodman Point community versus the Sand Canyon community, where there is greater evidence of migrants and diversity in pottery production practices. In chapter 15, Arakawa, Merewether, and Hughes summarize Crow Canyon's contributions to lithic analyses methods and research for the past four decades. They address mobility, territoriality, and trade to explore the development of political autonomy in the thirteenth century AD. In chapter 16, Adler and Hegmon study two late-AD 1200s villages—Sand Canyon Pueblo, located in the central Mesa Verde region, and Pot Creek Pueblo, located in the northern Rio Grande region—to examine behavioral similarities and differences in community coalescence, occupation, and depopulation. Their data suggest shared behaviors provide avenues to broaden our understanding of how people negotiated conflict, resource scarcity, and socially mediated strategies that became foundational to descendant community members living in the

Southwest today. In chapter 17, Lekson explores bi-wall, tri-wall, and quadri-wall structures and their role in the development of the Aztec regional system as power shifted from Chaco Canyon to the middle San Juan region at the end of the AD 1000s. Marking the locations of elites and nobles, these "symbols of power" imbued vernacular architectural elements while signaling a noticeable shift in social, political, and ritual frameworks. In chapter 18, Bellorado and Windes provide new insights into late thirteenth-century AD depopulation behaviors in the greater Cedar Mesa area of present-day southeastern Utah's Bears Ears National Monument. By collecting and examining tree-ring data, they provide new evidence for late (AD 1250–1270) construction activities in canyon sites with defensive attributes and how these activities articulate with those taking place to the east of Comb Ridge. In chapter 19, Kuckelman considers the push-pull factors that led to regional depopulation in the mid-to-late AD 1200s. Examining data collected from numerous villages throughout the region, Kuckelman argues environmental challenges, warfare, and other social disruptions were powerful deterrents to the continued occupation of the region.

Part V of the volume focuses on human-environment relationships and resource availability from the Basketmaker III period to the Pueblo III period in the central Mesa Verde region. In chapter 20, Badenhorst, Driver, and Wolverton examine the role of rodents in the diet of ancestral peoples utilizing data from numerous Crow Canyon Archaeological Center long-term research projects. Although they note there is little evidence of increased rodent consumption through time, they suggest the rise of turkey production may have reduced the need for intensified garden hunting, where rodents may have been captured. In chapter 21, Schollmeyer and Driver utilize Crow Canyon's unusually fine-grained temporal assignments of faunal datasets from villages throughout the region to examine the impacts of human hunting and land use on lagomorph, artiodactyl, and turkey through time and argue that local changes in human population density and distribution influenced the relative abundance of local animals. In chapter 22, Oas and Adams undertake one of the largest studies of consistently acquired, examined, and reported archaeological flora assemblages to assess stability and change in plant use from the Basketmaker III period to the Pueblo III period. Through archaeological and ethnobotanical research, they provide insights into the history of various foods, fuels, and other economically important plants to Indigenous populations living in the central Mesa Verde region.

In the final chapter, chapter 23, Perry offers insights that guide the discipline and Crow Canyon's mission work into the future as we strategically create impactful and meaningful work alongside Indigenous partners, cross-disciplinary researchers, students of all ages, and citizen scientists from across the world. Noting that the future of our discipline is rooted in the recognition of privilege, Perry suggests that our work include reparations for the behaviors of the founders of our discipline and that we provide compensation to Indigenous peoples for the benefits we have received, and will receive, in the past, present, and future.

On behalf of the Crow Canyon Archaeological Center and all authors in this volume, we are extremely grateful, honored, and privileged to produce a body of work celebrating Indigenous cultures in the northern Southwest and humbly recognize that our mission-related work would not be possible without Indigenous peoples in the past, present, and future. The authors in this volume respectfully acknowledge ancestral and descendant Indigenous communities for their contributions to all humankind, and we are grateful for the opportunity to partner with them to create more-informed societies worldwide. I hope you enjoy this volume, and may it provide thought-provoking discourse and subsequent actions for the betterment of all humankind.

REFERENCES

Adler, Michael A. 1992. "The Upland Survey." In *The Sand Canyon Archaeological Project: A Progress Report*, edited by William D. Lipe, 11–23. Occasional Papers, no. 2. Cortez, CO: Crow Canyon Archaeological Center.

Churchill, Melissa J., ed. 2002. *The Archaeology of Woods Canyon Pueblo: A Canyon-Rim Village in Southwestern Colorado*. Cortez, CO: Crow Canyon Archaeological Center. https://www.crowcanyon.org/resources/the_archaeology_of_woods_canyon _pueblo_a_canyon_rim_village_in_southwestern_colorado/.

Coffey, Grant D., ed. 2018. *The Goodman Point Archaeological Project: Goodman Point Community Testing*. Cortez, CO: Crow Canyon Archaeological Center. Accessed May 20, 2022. https://core.tdar.org/document/447957/the-goodman-point-archaeological -project-community-testing (tDAR id: 447957), https://doi.org/10.6067/XCV8447957.

Diederichs, Shanna R. 2020. "Basketmaker Communities Project Synthesis." In *The Basketmaker Communities Project*, edited by Shanna R. Diederichs, 862–894. Accessed May 20, 2022. https://www.crowcanyon.org/resources/the_basketmaker _communities_project_2020_final_interpretive_report/.

Glowacki, Donna M., and Scott G. Ortman 2012. "Characterizing Community Center (Village) Formation in the VEP Study Area, A.D. 600–1280." In *Emergence and Collapse of Early Villages: Models of Central Mesa Verde Archaeology*, edited by Timothy A. Kohler and Mark D. Varien, 219–246. Berkeley: University of California Press.

Huber, Edgar K. 1993. "Thirteenth Century Pueblo Aggregation and Organizational Change in Southwestern Colorado." PhD diss., Department of Anthropology, Washington State University, Pullman.

Kohler, Timothy A., and Mark D. Varien. 2012. *Emergence and Collapse of Early Villages: Models of Central Mesa Verde Archaeology*. Berkeley: University of California Press.

Kuckelman, Kristin A., ed. 2000. *The Archaeology of Castle Rock Pueblo: A Late-Thirteenth-Century Village in Southwestern Colorado*. Cortez, CO: Crow Canyon Archaeological

Center. https://www.crowcanyon.org/resources/the_archaeology_of_castle_rock
_pueblo_a_thirteenth_century_village_in_southwestern_colorado/.

Kuckelman, Kristin A., ed. 2003. *The Archaeology of Yellow Jacket Pueblo (Site 5MT5):
Excavations at a Large Community Center in Southwestern Colorado.* Cortez, CO: Crow
Canyon Archaeological Center. http://www.crowcanyon.org/yellowjacket.

Kuckelman, Kristin A., ed. 2007. *The Archaeology of Sand Canyon Pueblo: Intensive Excavations at a Late-Thirteenth-Century Village in Southwestern Colorado.* Cortez, CO: Crow
Canyon Archaeological Center. http://www.crowcanyon.org/sandcanyon.

Kuckelman, Kristin A., ed. 2017. *The Goodman Point Archaeological Project: Goodman Point
Pueblo Excavations.* Cortez, CO: Crow Canyon Archaeological Center. https://www
.crowcanyon.org/projects/goodman_point_community_project/.

Lightfoot, Ricky R. 1994. *The Duckfoot Site.* Vol. 2, *Archaeology of the House and Household.*
Occasional Papers, no. 4. Cortez, CO: Crow Canyon Archaeological Center.

Lightfoot, Ricky R., and Mary C. Etzkorn, eds. 1993. *The Duckfoot Site.* Vol. 1, *Descriptive
Archaeology.* Occasional Papers, no. 3. Cortez, CO: Crow Canyon Archaeological Center.

Lipe, William D., ed. 1992. "The Sand Canyon Archaeological Project: A Progress
Report." Crow Canyon Archaeological Center, Cortez, CO. https://institute
.crowcanyon.org/occasional_papers/Sand_Canyon_Progress_Report.pdf.

Lipe, William D., and Scott G. Ortman. 2000. "Spatial Patterning in Northern San Juan
Villages, A.D. 1050–1300." *Kiva* 66 (1): 91–122.

Ortman, Scott G., Donna M. Glowacki, Melissa J. Churchill, and Kristin A. Kuckelman.
2000. "Pattern and Variation in Northern San Juan Village Histories." *Kiva* 66 (1):
123–146.

Reese, Kelsey M., Donna M. Glowacki, and Timothy A. Kohler. 2019. "Dynamic Communities on the Mesa Verde Cuesta." *American Antiquity* 84 (4): 728–747.

Ryan, Susan C., ed. 2015a. "The Archaeology of Shields Pueblo (Site 5MT3807): Excavations at a Mesa-Top Community Center in Southwestern Colorado." Crow Canyon
Archaeological Center, Cortez, CO. http://www.crowcanyon.org/shieldspueblo.

Ryan, Susan C., ed. 2015b. "The Archaeology of Albert Porter Pueblo (Site 5MT123):
Excavations at a Great House Community Center in Southwestern Colorado." Crow
Canyon Archaeological Center, Cortez, CO. Accessed January 6, 2021. http://www
.crowcanyon.org/albertporter.

Schwindt, Dylan M., R. Kyle Bocinsky, Scott G. Ortman, Donna M. Glowacki, Mark D.
Varien, and Timothy A. Kohler. 2016. "The Social Consequences of Climate Change
in the Central Mesa Verde Region." *American Antiquity* 81 (1): 74–96.

Varien, Mark D. 1999. *Sedentism and Mobility in a Social Landscape: Mesa Verde and Beyond.*
Tucson: University of Arizona Press.

Varien, Mark D., Scott G. Ortman, Timothy A. Kohler, Donna M. Glowacki, and
C. David Johnson. 2007. "Historical Ecology in the Mesa Verde Region: Results from
the Village Ecodynamics Project." *American Antiquity* 72 (2): 273–299.

History of the Crow Canyon Archaeological Center

2

The Early History of Crow Canyon's Archaeology, Education, and American Indian Programs

RICKY R. LIGHTFOOT AND WILLIAM D. LIPE

This volume celebrates the fortieth anniversary of the organization we know today as the Crow Canyon Archaeological Center. Crow Canyon did not just appear out of thin air but rather has its roots in two nonprofit organizations that merged in 1982 and a large contract archaeology program that ended in 1985. The large contract archaeology project was the Dolores Archaeological Program (DAP), which conducted reservoir mitigation survey and excavations approximately 10 mi. north of the Crow Canyon campus. The story of the impact that the DAP had on Crow Canyon is told in another chapter of this volume (Kohler et al., chapter 3 in this volume). This chapter will focus on the two nonprofit organizations, which had very different missions and different identities, but each had a founding leader who devoted his life to building an organization and on achieving the organization's mission. One organization was the Interdisciplinary Supplemental Education Programs (I-SEP), founded in Colorado in 1972 by educator Edward F. Berger and known locally as the Crow Canyon School. The second organization was the Center for American Archaeology (CAA), founded in 1969 by archaeologist Stuart Struever and originally named the Foundation

https://doi.org/10.5876/9781646424597.c002

for Illinois Archaeology. This chapter presents an abbreviated history of these two organizations and their leaders and how they came together to form the nascent stage of the Crow Canyon Archaeological Center.

EDWARD F. BERGER AND THE CHERRY CREEK HIGH SCHOOL PROGRAMS 1968–1977

In 1968, Ed Berger, a history teacher at Cherry Creek High School (CCHS) in the Denver metro area, began bringing small groups of students to the Cortez area every summer for educational programs (Berger 1993, 2009; Berger and Berger 2016). These were designed to help students become self-motivated learners through participating in a variety of activities, including community involvement, tutoring other students, developing a personal understanding of the area's natural environment, and immersing themselves in understanding the area's history, with emphasis on visiting and interpreting archaeological sites. In 1970, Berger purchased a house in Arriola, Colorado, which he called the "Cherry Creek House," to provide accommodations for the students who participated in his summer programs. In 1972, Berger incorporated his educational initiative as a nonprofit organization called Interdisciplinary Supplemental Education Programs, Incorporated (I-SEP).

In 1969, Berger was introduced to prominent southwestern archaeologist Arthur Rohn, who agreed to help Berger and his CCHS students gain hands-on experience in archaeological excavation. Thus, participation in archaeological fieldwork was added to the supplemental and enrichment programs offered to students. During the summer programs of 1971 through 1973, the CCHS students assisted in excavations alongside Rohn's Wichita State University graduate students at the Lee Scott site near Arriola. The results of this work were never published, and apparently a report of the excavations was not written. In the summers of 1974 through 1977, I-SEP employed Ronald Gould, a PhD student at the University of Texas at Austin who had been one of Rohn's graduate students at Wichita State University, to work as an "archaeo-educator." His responsibilities included directing CCHS summer program students in the excavation of the Mustoe site in the Goodman Point area. Gould's (1982) dissertation, which used neutron activation analysis of pottery from the Mustoe site, is available from the University of Texas library and is the only report of the excavations.

In 1974, Ed Berger purchased 80 acres of land in Crow Canyon, where he began to develop a permanent home for his I-SEP programs. The following year, he completed his doctorate in education at the University of Northern Colorado based on the educational concepts that he had developed and put into practice in his CCHS programs (see Franklin, chapter 8 in this volume). Ed began operating his CCHS summer programs from the new Crow Canyon property. In the spring of 1975 Ed moved three state-surplus trailers to the property, linked them together, and remodeled them to provide classrooms, a kitchen, and student housing. The cluster of trailers was covered on the outside with rough-cut lumber, which gave it a rustic western look, and it soon became known among the students as "The Fort." Ed set up a large water storage tank, which had to be filled with water hauled from town, to provide gravity-fed water to the buildings. He also installed a septic system for sewage treatment. During the summer of 1975, Berger continued offering his summer programs for CCHS students housed in their new accommodations at Crow Canyon. In 1976, Ed married Joanne Hindlemann, and the couple moved into a travel trailer on the property, where they stayed until they built a small apartment adjoining the Fort in 1979. Ed Berger resigned from the Cherry Creek High School faculty in 1976 but was contracted to continue offering summer programs for the school during the summers of 1976 and 1977, which included excavating at the Mustoe site. After the 1977 program season, there were no more archaeological excavation programs conducted by I-SEP until after the merger with CAA was completed.

THE I-SEP / CROW CANYON SCHOOL PROGRAMS 1976–1982

Between 1976 and 1981, educational programs offered by I-SEP and what was by then known as the Crow Canyon School diversified and increased in enrollment. Ed Berger began offering continuing education programs for teachers through an agreement with Colorado State University (Berger 1993, 2009). From 1977 through 1979, job training programs for students from the Ute Mountain Ute Tribe were implemented with funding through the federal Comprehensive Employment and Training Act (CETA); one emphasis was preparing students for anticipated jobs with the newly formed Ute Mountain Ute Tribal Park. In 1979, a new set of field programs, in what was called the Interpretive Services Division, was added to the Crow Canyon repertoire; prominent rock art researcher Sally Cole led river trips on which groups from the Denver Museum of Natural History visited and helped record the San Juan Canyon's outstanding petroglyph and pictograph panels. Fred Blackburn, former head of the Bureau of Land Management Grand Gulch Ranger program in southeastern Utah, led groups on educational expeditions to a variety of natural history and archaeological locations in the Four Corners area. In 1979 and 1980, with funding from the Colorado Endowment for the Humanities, fourteen public seminars led by archaeologists and cultural resource managers were presented in venues in surrounding local communities. A 120-page book containing a summary of each presentation and titled *Insights into the Ancient Ones* was published with Jo Berger as the senior editor (Berger and Berger 1981). A second edition in 1984 (Berger and Berger 1984), which also included statements from E. Charles Adams and Bruce Bradley, was distributed free to libraries. Enlisting community support for the preservation of archaeological sites was also promoted through "Chuckwagon" dinners and evening stage shows that involved talks by Ed Berger about local history and the value of the area's archaeological resources, as well as musical performances by Jo Berger and other local musicians.

STUART STRUEVER AND THE CENTER FOR AMERICAN ARCHAEOLOGY

Stuart Struever was born and raised in central Illinois and had a lifelong interest in archaeology. Stuart was a student of Lewis Binford at the University of Chicago, where he earned his PhD in 1968. After a brief stint on the faculty of the University of Chicago, he took a position at Northwestern University, where he was allowed to pursue his vision of establishing a network of privately funded nonprofit institutions that were positioned to conduct long-term regional research in archaeology (Struever 1968). While at Northwestern, Struever developed a long-term archaeological research program in southern Illinois, centered at the small town of Kampsville, owned and operated by the nonprofit Foundation for Illinois Archaeology (FIA). Excavations, supported by National Science Foundation and other grants between 1969 and 1978, revealed a long sequence of prehistoric occupations at the deeply stratified Koster site near Kampsville (Struever and Holton 1979). Fieldwork and discoveries at Koster promoted the growth of FIA's scientific capabilities and also attracted much public interest through well-attended interpretive tours of the excavations and public speaking engagements by Struever. At Koster, Struever developed the model of using public educational programs to generate funding to support a large multidisciplinary archaeology research center. The education programs included field programs for K–12 students and adults, as well as a university-level field school operated in conjunction with Northwestern University. In 1979, the FIA began publishing a magazine titled *Early Man*, composed of articles about archaeology that were oriented to general audiences. In 1981, the FIA board developed an affiliated satellite campus at Fox River near Chicago and changed the organization's name to the Center for American Archaeology—a move that set the stage for adding new campuses beyond Illinois.

THE MERGER OF I-SEP AND CENTER FOR AMERICAN ARCHAEOLOGY

Also in 1981, Struever met with Ed and Jo Berger to discuss the possibility that Crow Canyon might become affiliated with CAA as the home of its next campus—one in the American Southwest (figure 2.1). Negotiations continued in 1982, and the Bergers spent much of that summer attending educational programs at Kampsville, while Washington State University (WSU) rented the Crow Canyon facilities to house a WSU field school being led by William Lipe and Tim Kohler (see Kohler et al., chapter 3 in this volume); it was conducted

FIGURE 2.1. *Jo and Ed Berger. Courtesy of the Crow Canyon Archaeological Center.*

in conjunction with the nearby Dolores Archaeological Program. Jo Berger worked on a master's degree in planning and community development from the University of Colorado, which she completed in August 1982.

On the face of things, a merger between the two organizations was an ideal match. Both organizations were conducting outdoor experiential education programs involving archaeological themes. CAA's education programs were integrated with a fully developed multidisciplinary archaeological research program in Illinois, and the Bergers were interested in once again offering archaeology excavation programs that contributed to I-SEP's educational goals. Ed Berger perceived that an affiliation with CAA offered the possibility of much-needed funding, national recognition, and the opportunity for the growth in his Crow Canyon School programs. Struever perceived that the Crow Canyon School's proximity to Mesa Verde National Park with its well preserved and visually appealing ruins was the ideal place to locate a regional research center in the American Southwest. In late 1982, an agreement was reached in which the two organizations merged, establishing Crow Canyon as an affiliate of CAA. At first it was named the Crow Canyon Campus of the Center for American Archaeology. CAA acquired 70 acres of the 80-acre campus owned by Ed Berger, and Berger donated $101,000 of the appraised value of the land and improvements to help launch the success of the new merger.

ESTABLISHING THE NEW RESEARCH AND EDUCATION
CENTER AT CROW CANYON, 1983–1986

The merger of I-SEP and CAA at the end of 1982 set in motion a series of changes at Crow Canyon that amplified the goals of creating a major independent archaeological research program and integrating campus-based education programs with the research. By early 1983, a new lodge—with a kitchen, dining hall, and dormitory rooms—replaced one of the old trailers in the Fort (figure 2.2). PhD archaeologists E. Charles Adams and Bruce Bradley were hired to develop and lead a comprehensive research program based on current archaeological method and theory, as incorporated in Struever's research and the goals of the Center for American Archaeology. Ed Berger became the Center's executive director with Jo Berger as associate director. In the spring of 1983, excavations were launched at the Duckfoot site under the direction of newly hired Crow Canyon staff archaeologists Adams and Bradley (Lightfoot 1994; Lightfoot and Etzkorn 1993), and by the summer of 1983, a detailed multiyear regional research design was written (Adams 1983). Several hundred students and adults participated in nationally advertised education programs built around fieldwork at the nearby Duckfoot site and analyses of the artifacts from those excavations (see Kohler et al., chapter 3 in this volume). Also in 1983, Bradley and Adams mapped the large Sand Canyon Pueblo, located approximately 12 mi. west of Cortez. In 1984, an excavation program that would ultimately last twelve years was launched at Sand Canyon Pueblo, led by Adams and Bradley (Kuckelman 2007), and DAP veteran archaeologist Lightfoot was hired to lead the excavation program at Duckfoot (see Kohler et al., chapter 3 in this volume).

Between 1982 and 1985, Ed Berger oversaw the construction of the new lodge and ten new cabins, styled after Navajo hogans, to accommodate more adult program participants on campus. Ed and Jo were hands-on leaders in directing the developments and transitions that emerged from the merger with CAA, but by the winter of 1985–1986, the differences in the visions of Struever and the Bergers began to strain the leadership of the organization. CAA was also finding it difficult to manage a satellite campus in Colorado from its offices in Illinois. Developing, maintaining, and operating two major research and education centers created a serious financial strain. The board and staff in Illinois perceived that Struever was putting more energy and resources into developing the facilities and programs at Crow Canyon at the expense of the campus and programs in Illinois. By the end of 1985 the merger between CAA and the Crow Canyon School began to deteriorate. Rather than allow the developments he had worked to build at Crow Canyon to collapse, Struever recruited his lifelong friend and Denver entrepreneur Ray Duncan to chair and populate a new Colorado-based board of trustees.

FIGURE 2.2. *Photo from 1984 of chuck wagon and newly constructed lodge in the background. Courtesy of the Crow Canyon Archaeological Center.*

EXPANSION OF FACILITIES, PROGRAMS, AND STAFF AT CROW CANYON, 1986–1996

In early 1986, further dramatic changes at Crow Canyon were underway. Ed and Joanne Berger resigned to focus their attention on the needs of their newly growing family and to pursue new professional opportunities in educational consulting, planning, and community development. Adams moved to a new job at the Arizona State Museum, and Professor Bill Lipe of Washington State University took on Adams's research director position part-time. Struever severed his relationship with CAA and retained the title of president of Crow Canyon, but his principal responsibility was fundraising. At Duncan's request, Struever also resigned from his tenured position at Northwestern to devote his full attention to continue building Crow Canyon. Writer, editor of the *Durango Herald*, and former mayor of Durango Ian (Sandy) Thompson, a longtime friend and associate of Crow Canyon, was appointed as the new executive director.

Under the leadership of Thompson as executive director and Lipe as research director, the research and education programs continued to grow and diversify. In 1986, former DAP staffers Megg Heath and Angela Schwab were hired as full-time directors of education and the laboratory, respectively. Karen Adams was hired to launch and lead a new environmental archaeology program focused on analyzing plant and animal remains from the excavations. Mike Adler and Carla Van West were brought on to conduct archaeological survey in the Sand Canyon and Goodman Point localities, which provided data for their dissertations, as well as moving Crow Canyon Research out of the single-site excavation mode and into broader studies of the locality and region (see Kohler et al., chapter 3, Adler and Hegmon, chapter 16, and Glowacki et al., chapter 12 in this volume). An internship program for university undergraduate and graduate students was launched, including internships in archaeological excavation, survey, laboratory analysis, environmental archaeology, and education.

As executive director, Thompson profoundly shaped the continued development of Crow Canyon for the next decade. He believed that Crow Canyon had a moral responsibility to engage in dialogues with American Indians living in the Four Corners region, and particularly the Pueblo Indian people, who were the descendants of those whose settlements were being studied archaeologically. He traveled to the Indian Pueblos of New Mexico to meet with Tribal leaders to tell them about Crow Canyon and invite them to visit. As a result, anthropologist Alfonso Ortiz, a member of the Pueblo of Ohkay Owingeh, brought a group of Pueblo Indian leaders to Crow Canyon in 1989 for a meeting in which they visited the sites and lab and talked with Crow Canyon staff. In 1986, Thompson recruited Rina Swentzell, a member of the Pueblo of Santa Clara with a doctorate in American Studies, to lead a weeklong seminar at Crow Canyon. That same year, Crow Canyon launched the Cultural Exploration program led by archaeologists that increasingly included American Indians as lead scholars alongside archaeologists to present multiple ways of knowing the past. Thompson led the effort to create the board of American Indian advisors, and with the help of a grant from the Dr. Scholl Foundation, a Native American Advisory Group (NAAG) was formed in 1995. The advisory group members reviewed and commented on all of Crow Canyon's education and research program activities. This oversight led to an increase in the inclusion of more information regarding the connection between the archaeological sites being studied with the modern descendants who still live in the Southwest.

Also in 1995, Thompson led an initiative to host the first Native American Graves Protection and Repatriation Act (NAGPRA) consultations in Colorado between the Bureau of Land Management (BLM) and American Indian tribes throughout the Southwest. Crow Canyon had conducted excavations from 1990 to 1994 in which human remains were found at Castle Rock Pueblo, a site on BLM land. NAGPRA, which was passed by the US Congress in 1990, required federal agencies overseeing archaeology projects on federal land to consult with American Indian tribes regarding the treatment and disposition of human remains. By 1995, the law was still not being enforced, so Thompson secured grant funding to host the BLM consultations at Crow Canyon. From that time forward, Crow Canyon staff made a commitment to comply not only with the letter of the law but also the spirit of the law, regardless of whether the sites they worked on were on federal or private land. A detailed policy statement on treatment of human remains was adopted by the Crow Canyon board in 1998, and a revised and updated version was adopted in 2013.

SUMMARY

This volume celebrates the fortieth anniversary of the Crow Canyon Archaeological Center. Some might say that the organization has a much deeper history based on the origins of the two organizations, the Crow Canyon School / I-SEP and CAA, that merged in 1982. Although the organization maintained the same location where the Crow Canyon School had operated since 1975, the mission, programs, staff, and vision of the program changed dramatically in 1983 and the years following. While Ed Berger's CCHS students had participated in summer programs between 1969 and 1977 that included site excavations led by qualified archaeologists, those excavations were not a part of any larger I-SEP research design or project, and I-SEP did not assume responsibility for analysis and reporting the results. Unfortunately, these excavations were never adequately reported. For Berger's CCHS students, archaeology was one of many subjects taught in the summer school programs. Ed Berger correctly perceived that archaeology was a valuable educational theme because it crosscuts the natural sciences, such as biology and geology, with the social sciences, such as anthropology, sociology, history, and geography. Also, Ed Berger could see that hands-on participation in archaeology could inspire students and cause "accelerated learning," to use his phrase. But neither he nor I-SEP were ever positioned to initiate and conduct large-scale regional research projects and follow through with the analysis, reporting, and curation that are the ethical obligations that go along with excavating sites.

Through the merger, CAA and Struever brought to Crow Canyon a vision of developing a world-class archaeological research center that could sustain long-term interdisciplinary research in the region. Therein lies an important distinction between an organization that provides interdisciplinary education programs versus an organization that initiates and conducts interdisciplinary scientific research projects. Struever was one of the academic leaders in changing the paradigm in American archaeology from a single-scholar approach to an interdisciplinary scientific-team approach. That shift is a key part of the transformation that began to happen in 1983. CAA provided an infusion of capital that allowed Crow Canyon to build new facilities and expand its staff to include, for the first time, two full-time PhD archaeologists, E. Charles Adams and Bruce A. Bradley. In subsequent years, the facilities and the research staff continued to grow, and the diversity of the research team expanded.

From 1983 forward, Crow Canyon has maintained a commitment to long-term archaeological research, including excavation, survey, and environmental studies to address problem-oriented regional and interregional research designs. Crow Canyon has consistently fulfilled its legal and ethical obligation for analyzing the artifacts, faunal remains, and botanical remains, as well as soil, pollen, and other environmental samples; curating the collections and records in federal repositories; publishing descriptive reports and databases; and presenting the methods of field and laboratory data collection from all its projects. In addition, Crow Canyon has progressively included all its field and laboratory data in larger problem-oriented studies at regional, national, and international scales.

The Crow Canyon website now provides public access to an unbroken chain of detailed research reports and databases for a dozen multiyear projects conducted in southwestern Colorado, starting with the Duckfoot site (https://www.crow canyon.org/index.php/access-our-research/site-reports-databases). These site reports and databases are accessible free of charge to anyone in the world with an internet connection. In addition to the online reports and databases, numerous books, journal articles, and chapters in edited volumes have been published by the Crow Canyon staff and its research associates over this forty-year history.

The Bergers and the Crow Canyon School / I-SEP laid a foundation for Native American involvement at Crow Canyon by developing programs for local Ute Mountain Ute youth and with their individual relationships and friendships with members of other Southwestern Indian tribes. As executive director, Ian Thompson greatly expanded Crow Canyon's deeper and more focused partnerships with American Indians from many tribes and invited their participation in detailed and formal reviews of the Center's education programs, collaborative involvement with the research programs, and contributing Native interpretations of the past alongside archaeological understandings. His efforts paved the way for even stronger relationships and partnerships that are presented in many chapters in this volume (see Ermigiotti et al., chapter 4, Kuwanwisiwma and Bernardini, chapter 5, Ortman, chapter 6, Suina, chapter 7, and Perry, chapter 23, in this volume).

While the Crow Canyon Archaeological Center emerged from deeper roots that were established fifteen years earlier in two different organizations, what resulted in 1983 and after was profoundly different than what came before. The transformation that happened after 1983 at Crow Canyon was influenced by the fact that one of the largest interdisciplinary archaeology projects in America was taking place at the exact same time about 10 mi. away. The Dolores Archaeological Program required that hundreds of professional archaeologists be deployed each year from 1978 to 1985 to conduct excavation, analysis, special projects, report writing, and publication (Breternitz 1993). The impact of that synchronicity is the subject of chapter 3 in this volume by Kohler and others.

REFERENCES

Adams, E. Charles. 1983. "Archeological Research Design." Unpublished report on file, Crow Canyon Archaeological Center, Cortez, CO.

Berger, Edward F. 1993. *Crow Canyon: Pioneering Education and Archaeology on the Southwestern Colorado Frontier*. Sedona, AZ: Southwest Research and Educational Services.

Berger, Edward F. 2009. *Crow Canyon: Pioneering Education and Archaeology on the Southwestern Colorado Frontier*. 2nd ed. https://millennialbooks.com.

Berger, Edward F., and Joanne H. Berger. 2016. *Crow Canyon Education and Archaeology Research Center: The Early Years, 1968–1986*. https://millennialbooks.com.

Berger, Joanne H., and Edward F. Berger, eds. 1981. *Insights into the Ancient Ones*. Cortez, CO: Cortez Printers.

Berger, Joanne H., and Edward F. Berger, eds. 1984. *Insights into the Ancient Ones*. 2nd ed. Interdisciplinary Supplemental Education Programs. Cortez, CO.

Breternitz, David A. 1993. "The Dolores Archaeological Program: In Memoriam." *American Antiquity* 58 (1): 118–125.

Gould, Ronald R. 1982. *The Mustoe Site: The Application of Neutron Activation Analysis in the Interpretation of a Multi-Component Archaeological Site*. Unpublished PhD diss., University of Texas, Austin.

Kuckelman, Kristin A. 2007. "The Archaeology of Sand Canyon Pueblo: Intensive Excavations at a Late-Thirteenth-Century Village in Southwestern Colorado." https://www.crowcanyon.org/ResearchReports/SandCanyon/Text/scpw_contentsvolume.asp.

Lightfoot, Ricky R. 1994. *The Duckfoot Site*. Vol. 2, *Archaeology of the House and Household*. Cortez, CO: Occasional Papers, no. 4. Cortez, CO: Crow Canyon Archaeological Center.

Lightfoot, Ricky R., and Mary C. Etzkorn, eds. 1993. *The Duckfoot Site*. Vol. 1, *Descriptive Archaeology*. Cortez, CO: Occasional Papers, no. 3. Cortez, CO: Crow Canyon Archaeological Center.

Struever, Stuart, 1968. Problems, "Methods and Organization: A Disparity in the Growth of Archaeology." In *Anthropological Archeology in the Americas*, edited by Betty J. Meggers, 131–151. Washington, DC: Anthropological Society of Washington.

Struever, Stuart, and Felicia Antonelli Holton. 1979. *Koster: Americans in Search of Their Prehistoric Past*. New York. Anchor Press / Doubleday.

3

From DAP Roots to Crow Canyon and VEP Shoots

Some Recollections

TIMOTHY A. KOHLER, RICKY R. LIGHTFOOT,
MARK D. VARIEN, AND WILLIAM D. LIPE

The 1970s were an exciting time in American archaeology. Processualism (or the New Archaeology), with its optimistic view that scientific approaches would unlock all aspects of the archaeological record, was ascendant. Legislation including the Reservoir Salvage Act of 1960 as amended (16 U.S.C. 469—often informally referred to as the "Moss-Bennett legislation") and the National Historic Preservation Act of 1966 as amended (16 U.S.C. 470) was making possible projects of a scale not seen in the United States since the Works Progress Administration of the 1930s (Knudson et al. 1986; Lipe 2018).

One such large-scale project was the Dolores Archaeological Program (DAP), mitigating the damage to the archaeological record of a reservoir and irrigation system being built on a 10 mi. stretch of the Dolores River and surrounding lands in southwestern Colorado in the late 1970s and early 1980s (Voggesser 2001). A later part of the project dealt with building and mitigating the effects of the water delivery system, which we don't address here. As the DAP wound down, the nearby Crow Canyon Archaeological Center was emerging as a private, non-profit research and education institution, affiliated at the time with the Center

https://doi.org/10.5876/9781646424597.c003

for American Archaeology based in Illinois (see Lightfoot and Lipe, chapter 2 in this volume). Our goal in this chapter is to show how the DAP contributed significant momentum, staff, methods, a firm local chronology, and theoretical inspiration to the Center and how the Center contributed to and interacted with the National Science Foundation–funded Village Ecodynamics Project (VEP).

THE DOLORES ARCHAEOLOGICAL PROGRAM

The DAP (figure 3.1) began in June 1978, was completed in December 1985, and had a total cost of nearly $10 million (Breternitz 1993), or some 31 million in 2020 dollars. In addition, the Bureau of Reclamation project provided funding for the construction of the Bureau of Land Management's Canyons of the Ancients Visitor Center and Museum (CAVM), formerly the Anasazi Heritage Center, a state-of-the-art curation facility and museum near Dolores, Colorado. During six field seasons, DAP archaeologists surveyed and recorded 1,626 archaeological sites on more than 16,000 acres in the project area. In addition, field crews excavated all or part of 125 sites, collecting more than 1.5 million artifacts. The project produced a bookshelf of thirteen published volumes and 286 technical reports. These reports in turn gave rise to several theses, dissertations, and numerous publications in academic journals and edited volumes. Many of these publications and the DAP's datasets are conveniently available online through the Digital Archaeological Record (https://core.tdar .org/project/5398/the-dolores-archaeological-program). The DAP was performed under the overall direction of David Breternitz, University of Colorado, with Washington State University (WSU) as a principal subcontractor.

The DAP was one of the largest contract archaeology projects ever conducted in the US, at its height employing more than 200 archaeologists in the field and lab and more than 540 people altogether over its seven and a half years. There were not enough archaeologists with experience in the local area to fill the required positions in the field, lab, publications, and administration sectors. The authors of this chapter are only a few of the many who gained their first experience in the archaeology of southwestern Colorado through the DAP. As the project began, William Lipe, a co-principal investigator on the DAP, was the only established researcher among the four authors here. In 1978, Lipe was an associate professor at WSU with experience in ancestral Pueblo societies west of the DAP in the Red Rock Plateau / Glen Canyon (Fowler 2006; Lipe 1970) and Cedar Mesa (Matson et al. 1988) areas of southeastern Utah. Tim Kohler, who eventually became a DAP co-principal investigator, came to the project in 1979 as an adjunct professor at WSU with a one-year-old PhD from the University of Florida and experience in Woodland-period villages in north-central and gulf coastal Florida. Mark Varien and Ricky Lightfoot began their careers in Texas, with Varien having worked in Mesoamerica and Oklahoma and Lightfoot in Alaska before coming to the DAP in 1979 and 1980, respectively. They both

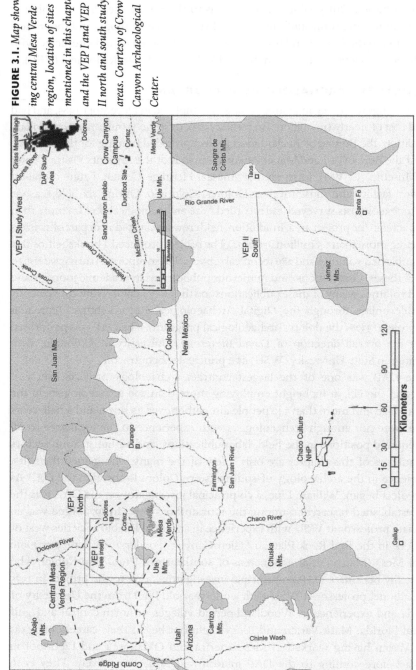

FIGURE 3.1. *Map showing central Mesa Verde region, location of sites mentioned in this chapter, and the VEP I and VEP II north and south study areas. Courtesy of Crow Canyon Archaeological Center.*

became crew chiefs and wrote or contributed to numerous DAP site reports, including the two-volume report on Grass Mesa Village (Lipe et al. 1988).

If the DAP had begun two decades earlier or later, its fundamental goals and methods would likely have been quite different (Lipe 2018). As it was, the general research design (Kane et al. 1983), also summarized in the implementation plan (Knudson et al. 1986), emphasized five problem domains: economy and adaptation, paleodemography, social organization, extraregional relationships, and cultural process. These concerns were solidly in the processual archaeology tradition. The DAP derived its explanatory goals and probabilistic sampling component from Lewis Binford (1964). More important to the project, though (and much more fun to read), was Kent Flannery's *Early Mesoamerican Village* (1976), with its sparkling dialogue on the issues encountered in putting a processual approach on the ground in a Formative Stage society having many analogies with the Pueblo I period sites in the Dolores area. Michael Schiffer's (1976) views on how archaeological assemblages and sites formed also deeply influenced DAP field procedures, forms, and the way we approached our analyses.

The DAP spatial, temporal, and sociocultural systematics were developed by Al Kane (1983), who was partly inspired by taxonomic schemes in Gordon Willey and Philip Phillips (1958). The spatial systematics began with activity areas and use areas and proceeded through household clusters, interhousehold clusters, habitations, intercommunity clusters, localities, sectors, districts, and regions. There was also a detailed typology of formal site types that included limited activity loci, seasonal loci, and habitations of various scales. These and other categories, and the provenience forms used in the field that also required considering assemblage formation processes, were crucial to the standardization essential to DAP's success. Back at the lab, enforcement of these data-quality standards by lab director Paul Farley was a much-feared obstacle to assistant-crew-chief happiness. The attention to detail and standardization in field and lab data were essential to making data digitally accessible and useful for comparative analyses. More than for any other large project of its time, the DAP field-provenience and laboratory-recording methods were structured around use of computers (Udick and Wilshusen 1999).

Reflecting on the project fifteen years after its close, Lipe (1999) considered the main substantive and methodological contributions of the DAP to be the following:

- an improved understanding of Pueblo culture from AD 650 to AD 900;
- more attention to the environmental and climatic conditions during this period than was typical in archaeological projects;
- an increased understanding of processes of sociocultural change (especially those underlying formation of large villages from small hamlets);

- development of archaeological methods;
- great attention to data comparability and quality control that accompanied data computerization, starting with the project's elaborate recording forms that were designed to make this possible (see also Schlanger and Kohler 2006).

The contractual nature of the DAP also demanded prompt publication of all field and lab results, inculcating good habits in all participants.

Connected with Lipe's last two points, we would add that the ability to work on problems using large datasets potentially spanning dozens of sites and employing data from several material categories was revolutionary in the context of world archaeology in that era. Later research of both Crow Canyon and the VEP would build on these advances. While contractual obligations guided DAP work, the project aspired to be more than a good CRM project as evidenced by the many publications produced by DAP researchers. Their problem-oriented research addressed some 300 years of change using a highly resolved chronology, imparting a clear sense of how a number of variables changed through time in a linked fashion. The many possible examples of these studies include Allen Kane (1986), William Lipe (1986), Timothy Kohler et al. (1986), Sarah Schlanger (1987, 1988) and Richard Wilshusen (1986, 1987). These and other publications powerfully illustrate the utility of large datasets in which various types of information confront each other, sometimes using computational approaches including simulation to derive or test hypotheses.

CROW CANYON ARCHAEOLOGICAL CENTER'S EARLY YEARS

Merger with the Center for American Archaeology

The DAP's final full-scale field season was in 1983, though lab work and report writing continued until December 1985. As the DAP was winding down, the Interdisciplinary Supplemental Education Programs (I-SEP), popularly known as the Crow Canyon School, had become the southwestern branch campus of the Center for American Archaeology (CAA) based in Illinois (see Lightfoot and Lipe, chapter 2 in this volume). In 1985, Crow Canyon became independent of CAA and in 1986 changed its name to the Crow Canyon Archaeological Center. With the start of excavations at the Duckfoot site in 1983 (see figure 3.1), Crow Canyon became committed to conducting long-term archaeological research projects, designed and managed by resident professional staff, with campus-based education programs closely integrated with the research (Varien and Lightfoot 2006). As we describe throughout the rest of this chapter, the coincidence of the ending of DAP and the transition at Crow Canyon created a significant long-term advantage for Crow Canyon.

A doctoral student of Binford's at the University of Chicago, Stuart Struever was one of the leading proponents of processual archaeology in the 1960s, as well as the founder and president of the CAA, which acquired the Crow Canyon campus in 1983 and funded the expansion of its facilities and programs. Struever (1968) argued that to truly advance knowledge of past cultural systems, archaeology requires parent organizations to provide funding and facilities to sustain multidisciplinary teams to engage in long-term regional research programs, conduct excavations and surveys, and employ the full range of available methods in attacking explanatory problems.

The DAP successfully implemented the large-scale, multidisciplinary program of research advocated by Struever, but as a publicly funded data recovery project, it could not sustain the effort beyond its contractual dates. Fortunately, Crow Canyon emerged as a private, nonprofit institution just at the right moment to develop the facilities, capacity, and funding to maintain a long-term regional research program. Crow Canyon built upon and expanded the knowledge gained at DAP and has so far sustained the research effort for four decades beyond the end of DAP. (For more on Crow Canyon's education programs and collaboration with American Indian advisors and partners, see Franklin and Patterson et al., chapter 9 in this volume.) Crow Canyon's field and lab recording systems and forms were modeled on those developed by the DAP, making it easy to incorporate DAP veterans into its staff (table 3.1). In addition, Crow Canyon employed Art Rohr and Lynn Udick, former directors of the DAP information technology and database management, to set up the information technology systems at Crow Canyon to be consistent with those at DAP.

From 1983 on, Crow Canyon assumed the professional obligation of publishing detailed reports, written largely by its own staff, that summarized both field observations and laboratory analyses of its excavations. The DAP provided a model for this, with its large "descriptive" reports, sometimes running to hundreds of pages, made available to libraries, scholars, students, and the general public. In the 1980s, however, the ambitious goals of processual archaeology were promoting methods that produced ever-more-fine-grained types of data both in field recording and analysis, and hence ever-larger reports. Lipe, in his part-time role as Crow Canyon's research director, was committed to the principle stated by Jesse Jennings, Lipe's former boss on the Glen Canyon Project, endorsed by Dave Breternitz and observed throughout Lipe's career, that *unreported excavations are philosophically indistinguishable from pothunting*. Lipe's entreaties to Crow Canyon donors bore fruit, especially in the form of significant gifts from Peggy and Steve Fossett, for funding the Occasional Papers of the Crow Canyon Archaeological Center "hard-copy" publications. Two volumes reporting Duckfoot site excavations and interpretations were eventually published in that series. In the mid-1990s, however, Executive Director Ian "Sandy" Thompson correctly perceived that data production in archaeology had outpaced the capacity of paper volumes and led the Center to develop ways

TABLE 3.1. People who worked at both the DAP and Crow Canyon, and their main roles.

Name	DAP Role(s)	CCAC Role(s)	CCAC Years
Mary Etzkorn	Field archaeologist	Lab archaeologist; publications editor	1987–2015
Betty Havers	Field volunteer	Field volunteer	1985–1994
George Havers	Field volunteer	Field volunteer	1985–1994
Megg Heath	Educational consultant	Director of education	1986–1992
Carla Hoehn	Publication / administration assistant	Chief financial officer	2019–present
Mark Hovezak	Field archaeologist	Assistant director: environmental archaeology	1990–1995
Tim Hovezak	Field archaeologist	Field archaeologist	2003–2004
Ed Huber	Field archaeologist	Project director: Green Lizard Site	1987–1988
Jim Kleidon	Crew chief / author	Assistant project director: Sand Canyon Pueblo	1986–1991
Tim Kohler	Locality supervisor: Grass Mesa; co-principal investigator; author	Research associate; Principal investigator: VEP; board member	2000–present
Kristin Kuckelman	Crew chief / author	Project director: Yellow Jacket, Goodman Point Pueblos; publications editor	1989–2019
Patricia Flint Lacey	Lab archaeologist/analyst	Educator	1985
Ricky Lightfoot	Crew chief / author	Project director; president & CEO; board member/chair	1984–present
Carrie Lipe	Field archaeologist	Assistant project director: Duckfoot Site	1985–1986
William Lipe	Co-principal investigator (WSU) / senior staff author	Advisory board; director of research; board member	1982–present
Tom May	Draftsman	Draftsman	1985–1993
Neal Morris	Crew chief / author	Field assistant; draftsman	1985–present
Art Rohr	IT director	IT director	1990–1999
Angela Schwab	Lab staff	Lab director; IT staff; campus manager	1985–2005
Louise Schmidlap	Lab director	Lab archaeologist; publications director	1985–2015
Leslie Sesler	Field archaeologist	Field archaeologist	2003–2004; 2007–2008
Lynn Udick	Environmental archaeology field staff; IT staff; Publications staff	IT staff; publications director	1990–1999

continued on next page

TABLE 3.1.—*continued*

Name	DAP Role(s)	CCAC Role(s)	CCAC Years
Mark Varien	Crew chief / author	Project director; research director; co-PI: VEP; VP Programs; executive VP Research Institute	1987–present
Roger Walkenhorst	Field archaeologist	Educator	1987
Richard Wilshusen	Crew chief / author	Survey crew chief; director of research; research associate	1987–present

Note: The authors tried to remember everyone who worked at DAP and Crow Canyon and apologize if they missed anyone who should have been included.

to publish its work on the internet. The result has been an unbroken series of digital reports that cover all of Crow Canyon's multiyear field projects, coupled with regulated access to the digital databases that were inspired by the pioneering work of the DAP. See https://www.crowcanyon.org/index.php/access-our-research/site-reports-databases.

The Duckfoot Site Project

Crow Canyon's first excavation project, beginning in 1983, was at the Duckfoot site, a well-preserved Pueblo I period hamlet conveniently located about a mile northwest of the Crow Canyon campus (Lightfoot 1994; Lightfoot and Etzkorn 1993). The site provided an ideal opportunity for Crow Canyon to investigate a site contemporaneous with the Pueblo I period settlements in the DAP area but located in a different environment. This was also the opportunity for Crow Canyon archaeologists to employ the field and lab methods used at DAP and to build upon the DAP's knowledge gains. Crow Canyon archaeologists spent five years supervising groups of students and adult volunteers in excavating this small habitation using mainly trowels and whisk brooms. A comparable site at the DAP would have been excavated in a few months using not just trowels and whisk brooms but also backhoes and shovels.

The Duckfoot Site provided an ideal opportunity to evaluate the DAP model of household organization, because Crow Canyon archaeologists excavated all of the twenty surface rooms, four pit structures, and the entire midden. (In light of Crow Canyon's commitment to conservation goals in field archaeology, we point out that the sampling frame here was the locality's population of Pueblo I period sites, which included a large number of unexcavated sites.) Excavation revealed the skeletal remains of seven people—including men, women, and children—on the floors of the four pit structures. Three of the four pit structure roofs burned and collapsed at the time of depopulation, resulting in charring of the human remains. The fourth pit structure did not burn, but a partial human skeleton was placed on the floor prior to the dismantling of the roof, which was deposited in the structure. The abundant usable tools and containers on structure floors and the human remains on pit structure floors indicate that the entire site was rapidly and simultaneously depopulated, with the pit structures being deliberately and ritually closed—leaving no possibility for the departing residents to return and reuse the settlement. While there are no clear indications why so many people died in such a brief time, there are hints elsewhere that some violence surrounded the termination of the Pueblo I period (e.g., Kohler et al. 2020). Burned roof timbers sealed the artifact assemblages and human remains and provided 375 tree-ring dates, more than half of which were cutting dates.

Ricky Lightfoot (1994) applied Michael Schiffer's (1976) approach to the study of site-formation processes and evaluated the DAP models of household organization (Lightfoot 1994; Lightfoot et al. 2014). He used rim sherds to reconstruct the total discard assemblage of gray ware pottery in the midden, applying estimates of vessel use-lives to evaluate the rate of gray ware pottery discard and to model a typical household assemblage of pottery. With these results he could compare the structure floor assemblages to the expected household assemblage based on the midden accumulations. The floor artifact assemblages, activity area distribution, refitting of floor sherds between structures, and doorway connections between structures combined to form a model of household organization that differed from that developed at the DAP. In Lightfoot's model, each pit structure and its associated suite of living and storage rooms represented the space occupied by one extended household. This model built on Stephen Lekson's (1988) argument that the post-Basketmaker period small pit structures traditionally called "kivas" by southwestern archaeologists should be interpreted as domestic structures—an approach also adopted by Lipe (1989). (The DAP had interpreted each such suite as occupied by an aggregate of multiple households, with each living room representing a separate household.) Lightfoot's alternative model was eventually adopted by the VEP as well (e.g., Kohler and Higgins 2016) and formed the basis for VEP population reconstructions (e.g., Ortman et al. 2007).

The nearly complete excavation of Duckfoot and its precise dating allowed Varien to develop studies that examined how artifacts accumulate at residential sites (Varien 1999a, 1999b; Varien and Mills 1987; Varien and Potter 1997), inspired in part by Kohler's (1978) early work on accumulations and analysis of artifact accumulations at the DAP (Kohler and Blinman 1987). Using Duckfoot data, Varien developed an annual accumulation rate for cooking pottery at residential sites in the central Mesa Verde region (Varien 1999b, 73–80). He combined this accumulation rate with estimates of the total discard of cooking pottery at residential sites, obtained through probability sampling, refining approaches Kohler developed on the DAP (Kohler and Gross 1984; Varien 1999a). Varien used the annual accumulation rate and the estimates of total cooking pottery discard to calculate how long households occupied their residential sites, documenting how occupation span changed over time in the central Mesa Verde region (Varien 1999b; Varien and Ortman 2007). He then used the occupation span estimates to discuss how length of occupation affected architectural change (Varien 1999b) and site structure and organization of activities (Varien 2012) at residential sites in the region.

The Sand Canyon Archaeological Project

In 1983, Crow Canyon staff mapped Sand Canyon Pueblo (SCP), a large Pueblo III period village at the head of Sand Canyon (see figure 3.1), launching a twelve-year excavation project there the following year. The Sand Canyon Archaeological Project used survey and excavations at selected sites to characterize the social and environmental history of the 200 km² Sand Canyon locality (SCL). A three-year survey program began in 1985, supervised by Carla Van West during the first two years and Michael Adler in the final year (Adler 1992). This block survey covered 6,400 acres (26 km²) surrounding the large Pueblo III period Sand Canyon and Goodman Point Pueblos and identified 429 archaeological sites with 696 components. Additional block surveys were subsequently conducted in the southern portion of SCL (Adler and Metcalf 1991; Gleichman and Gleichman 1992; Ortman and Varien 2007). This work provided a locality-level social and demographic context for the intensive excavation-based studies of late Pueblo II and Pueblo III period occupation in the SCL, similar to the role of survey on the DAP (Schlanger 1987). This research provided a basis for defining communities in the SCL (Adler 1994, 2002; Adler and Varien 1994).

Almost incredibly, the excavations at SCP provided the first in-depth look at canyon-head villages since the much-less-detailed work by Sylvanus Morley (1908). Fieldwork included the complete excavation of seven kiva suites (a kiva and its associated rooms), intensive testing of the great kiva and D-shaped bi-wall structure, and limited testing in other contexts. The short occupation, affirmed by many tree-ring dates, surprised many archaeologists. Among the many important publications on this site are those evaluating its role as a planned community center (Bradley 1993; Ortman and Bradley 2002) and considering its abundant public architecture (Ortman and Bradley 2002) and how feasting related to this architecture (Potter and Ortman 2004). Others weigh the relationship between Chaco Canyon and Sand Canyon Pueblo (Bradley 1996; Kuckelman 2008) and reconstruct the violence surrounding the depopulation of the site and region (Kuckelman 2010; Kuckelman et al. 2002).

Excavation also began at several late Pueblo II and Pueblo III period sites identified by the SCL survey to assess their relationship to Sand Canyon Pueblo. Edgar Huber excavated part of the Green Lizard site, a small residential site located on a bench in Sand Canyon in 1987 and 1988. Huber showed that its occupation overlapped with the initial period of Sand Canyon Pueblo's rapid growth (Huber 1993; Huber and Lipe 1992). In 1988, under Varien's direction, Crow Canyon began a four-year site-testing program that employed a stratified random sampling approach to provide statistically comparable assemblage data from thirteen sites in the SCL, including initial excavations at Castle Rock Pueblo (Varien 1999a). The Sand Canyon Archaeological Project Site Testing Program anchored Varien's dissertation and subsequent book (Varien 1999b). The testing program demonstrated that small residential sites located on the mesa tops dated to the early Pueblo III period and suggested that their households moved to Sand Canyon Pueblo when its settlement began. Surface rooms at these mesa top sites continued to be used as field houses during the late Pueblo III period. In contrast, occupation at small residential sites in canyon settings dated to the late Pueblo III period and overlapped with the occupation of Sand Canyon Pueblo. Occupation-span estimates from these sites and the probabilistically sampled sites in the DAP were fundamental to building later VEP population estimates (e.g., Schwindt et al. 2016; Varien et al. 2007).

A major contribution of the DAP in the 1980s was to document the rise and subsequent collapse of large, late Pueblo I period villages. In some cases, evidence was found of episodes of violence at or near the end of village occupation (see Kuckelman, chapter 19 in this volume; Orcutt et al. 1990). Crow Canyon's investigation of the Pueblo III period in the Sand Canyon locality also encountered evidence of violence, most dramatically at Castle Rock Pueblo (Kuckelman et al. 2002). These findings have pushed archaeologists to develop interpretive (Martin 2021) and explanatory (Kohler et al. 2014) accounts of violence in the northern Southwest.

Survey, testing, and excavation by the DAP and then by Crow Canyon in the SCL produced a clearer understanding of settlement pattern changes in the Pueblo I and in the late Pueblo II and III periods. Cycles of settlement aggregation and dispersion were recognized in both areas. In addition to investigating Pueblo III period residential aggregates such as Sand Canyon Pueblo, Crow Canyon archaeologists documented the predominance of dispersed settlement characterized by numerous small homesteads or hamlets in much of the Pueblo II–III period. They recognized that some sites were serving as focal points or "community centers" for such dispersed patterns, as indicated by their larger size (fifty or more total structures, nine or more pit structures, and public buildings such as great kivas or small Chaco-style great houses; see Adler and Hegmon chapter 16, Arakawa et al., chapter 15, Potter et al., chapter 13, Schleher et al., chapter 10, and Glowacki et al., chapter 12 in this volume).

In the 1980s Steve Lekson and some other "big picture" archaeologists argued that even though most of the small sites in an area had never been recorded, and many had been destroyed, most of the "big sites" were still present or had been recorded or described in the literature, or at least remained known locally. Thus, these could be used as indicators of the locations of both dispersed and aggregated communities. In 1990, Crow Canyon hosted a conference titled "Pueblo Cultures in Transition" in which the participants created lists and compiled maps of big sites and used them to synthesize the culture histories of a dozen areas that covered most of the US Southwest from AD 1150 to 1350. In the published conference proceedings (Adler 1996), the chapter on the Mesa Verde region (Varien et al. 1996) was one of the most detailed, thanks in part to the contributions of Crow Canyon archaeologists. (See Glowacki et al., chapter 12 in this volume, for a discussion of Crow Canyon community center research).

Also in 1990, building on her experience in the SCL survey, Van West completed a dissertation at WSU that developed a model of prehistoric agricultural productivity for a large area of southwestern Colorado (published as Van West 1994). Her model, as well as the "big site" database that Crow Canyon archaeologists continued to develop after the "Pueblo Cultures in Transition" conference, were essential starting points for the VEP.

The Village Ecodynamics Project

While Lipe, Varien, Lightfoot, and others were building the program at Crow Canyon through the mid-1980s and 1990s, Kohler was getting to know the archaeology of the northern Rio Grande at Bandelier National Monument. This led to work with researchers at the Santa Fe Institute (SFI) on simulating aspects of Pueblo settlement and subsistence using agent-based modeling software then under development at SFI. These models built on Van West's (1994) estimates for potential maize productivity for every year from AD 900 to AD 1300 for every 4 ha within a 1,816 km² area in the heart of the central Mesa Verde region.

Van West's work made it possible to demonstrate that the villages in this area tended to build up during periods, and in places, of high agricultural production, and tended to decline or disperse when production turned unfavorable, as predicted by a model of household economic self-interest (Kohler and Van West 1996). Partly on the strength of these results, the National Science Foundation (NSF) funded the collaboration between WSU, Crow Canyon, and scientists at Wayne State University and the Colorado School of Mines in 2002 that is called VEP I (for Village Ecodynamics Project, Phase 1).

The VEP had roots in both Crow Canyon research and in earlier DAP work. Both VEP I and the follow-on VEP II drew on Crow Canyon's in-depth knowledge of its research area and on DAP paleoenvironmental and paleoclimatic research (e.g., Petersen 1982) and simulation approaches (e.g., Orcutt 1987).

After twenty years of research in southwestern Colorado, Crow Canyon had amassed a vast amount of primary information about the human history and the past environment of southwestern Colorado, organized in research databases derived from its surveys, excavations, and problem-oriented studies. In addition to the survey databases developed by the DAP and the early Crow Canyon work, there was also a very large amount of survey data generated as a result of federal agency compliance with the mandates of Section 106 of the National Historic Preservation Act. Development of oil, gas, and carbon dioxide resources in southwestern Colorado, as well as construction of an extensive canal and ditch network to deliver water from McPhee Reservoir to farms in a large portion of southwestern Colorado, all required survey and in some cases excavation.

The VEP would draw extensively from these surveys via the cooperation of the Office of Archaeology and Historic Preservation in Denver to provide standardized archaeological data from tens of thousands of site forms from hundreds of individual cultural resource management surveys, ranging from coverage of areas of less than an acre to many hundreds of acres. Scott Ortman and colleagues (2007) developed a method to make systematic use of these data to synthesize a great deal of existing knowledge about the archaeology of the central Mesa Verde region (Varien et al. 2007) (figure 3.1). Under the field direction of Donna Glowacki, the VEP also conducted new mapping and characterization of surface ceramics at several more poorly known community centers (Glowacki et al., chapter 12 in this volume; Glowacki and Ortman 2012).

VEP I studies were focused on paleodemography, on understanding why villages (or community centers) periodically formed and dissolved in this area, and on discovering what we could learn by juxtaposing the behavior of the agent-based model (ABM; Kohler and Varien 2012) with what we knew about the empirical data. The ABM ("Village") was a unique feature of VEP research and proved useful in several ways. For example, we could make a comparison between the degree of aggregation (population concentration) expected by the model—in which it primarily results from resource concentration and to a smaller extent from exchange among households—and compare that with what we reconstructed empirically for the VEP I area. This comparison revealed that variability in violence (Cole 2012) and number of households through time helped explain the differences between the degree of aggregation in the Village ABM, and that actually seen in the VEP I area (Kohler 2012). The conclusion, at that point, was that villages do form when and where resources are concentrated but dissolve as resources become less concentrated and population decreases; these conditions are accompanied by lower violence.

In 2008 the NSF funded an expansion of the study area to encompass most of the central Mesa Verde region in southwestern Colorado, and another region in the northern Rio Grande, collectively referred to as Village Ecodynamics Project, Phase 2 (VEP II) (figure 3.1). The VEP II retained all the interests and approaches of VEP I but added a larger view of the Southwest and more focus on how social groups (and not just their constituent households) interacted. Products of this more expansive view included a refinement of earlier work on the Neolithic (or Agricultural) Demographic Transition in the US Southwest (Kohler and Reese 2014) and development of a new method for estimating whether any specific portion of the upland Southwest had enough warmth and precipitation to have supported maize dryland farming in any year beginning in AD 1 (Bocinsky and Kohler 2014). Kyle Bocinsky's new approach allowed estimates of maize paleoproductivity to expand far beyond the area first studied by Van West while retaining the spatial and temporal precision achieved by Van West. The ABM also expanded in several directions under the leadership of Ziad Kobti, a VEP II co-principal investigator at the University of Windsor, for example, by developing methods for modeling social and economic specialization (Cockburn et al. 2013) and for modeling the emergence of corporate groups competing for prime agricultural land, through violence if necessary (Crabtree et al. 2017).

One of the problems tackled in both phases of the VEP was the famous depopulation of the northern Southwest in the late AD 1200s (see also Adler and Hegmon, chapter 16, Bellorado and Windes, chapter 18, Ermigiotti et al., chapter 4, Glowacki et al., chapter 12, and Kuckelman, chapter 19 in this volume). In VEP I, Varien and colleagues (2007) introduced a revised estimate for spatialized maize productivity that lowered Van West's estimates considerably by introducing several corrections, including disallowing any production above 7,900 ft. and reducing production above 7,054. ft. in years that were colder than average. Even with these revisions, it seemed unlikely that shortfalls in maize were common in the thirteenth century AD, unless conflict dramatically limited access to fields. Most contributors to an Amerind conference volume growing out of a symposium in the 2007 Society for American Archaeology meetings (Kohler et al. 2010) downplayed the importance of deteriorating climates in causing the depopulation. Varien (2010), for example, pointed out that the process of depopulation likely began not long after AD 1225—an interpretation proposed earlier by Andrew Duff and Richard Wilshusen (2000)—and continued until AD 1285, spanning years of both high and low production. Moreover, it seemed a stretch to use cold and drought to explain why locations along the San Juan River (normally both warm and wet) were depopulated simultaneously with the cool highlands of Mesa Verde National Park. Kohler (2010), though, noted that the VEP productivity reconstructions were trained on conditions from 1931 to 1960 and that many years in the thirteenth century AD (as well as some earlier) were colder than any years in the training dataset, raising the possibility that the VEP reconstructions for the thirteenth century were too high (see also Wright 2010).

Pueblo Farming Project

Examining such issues was one goal of the Pueblo Farming Project (PFP). The PFP was codeveloped by Crow Canyon and the Hopi Tribe, and partly supported in its early years by the VEP (see Ermigiotti et al., chapter 4 in this volume). Results from these experimental gardens so far demonstrate that the VEP production estimates are on average similar to those obtained in the experimental fields but that variation in yields due to annual changes in precipitation and temperature resulted in much greater variation in yields in the experimental plots than in the VEP model estimates (Bocinsky and Varien 2017). Ermigiotti and colleagues (chapter 4 in this volume) point out that one of the plots added recently (the Mike Coffey Garden, a plot near Dove Creek, Colorado, that at 7,300 ft. is almost 1,200 ft. higher than the plots on the Crow Canyon campus) has been exceptionally productive, even in very dry years when other PFP plots produced little or failed completely. This result suggests that some production could have been obtained on this landscape even in very dry years, so long as they were not too cold.

At this point it seems reasonable to say that reduced production of maize during portions of the period between AD 600 and 1300 was probably extremely important to social dynamics. Whether complete or near failure of maize production was a key factor in the depopulation of the mid to late AD 1200s, though, is not resolved. Such failure would likely have required conjunctures of cold and dry conditions that at present are very unusual. The eruption of the Samalas Volcano in Java in AD 1257—one of the largest eruptions during the Holocene—likely contributed to cold conditions noted in tree-ring records from the San Francisco Peaks from AD 1258 to 1272 and, perhaps, to the final depopulation of northern Southwest shortly thereafter (Salzer 2000; Windes and Van West 2021).

Although NSF funding terminated in 2014, publications partly funded or inspired by VEP II have continued to appear, making additional contributions to understanding the final depopulation of the northern Southwest (Kohler et al. 2020; Schwindt et al. 2016); making sense of large-scale patterning in tree-cutting for construction in the upland Southwest (Bocinsky et al. 2016); tracing the dynamics of community size and placement on the Mesa Verde cuesta (Reese et al. 2019); and disentangling the overlapping timing of violence, climate variability, and wealth inequality in the northern Southwest (Ellyson et al. 2019; Kohler et al. 2020). In sum, as the second phase of the VEP looked beyond the central Mesa Verde region, it also considered more aspects of the social experience of living in the northern Southwest prior to the arrival of the Spanish than did VEP I, while continuing to seek characterizations of elusive social processes in ways that allow quantification (e.g., Scheffer et al. 2021).

CONCLUSIONS

Knowledge making in archaeology is highly cumulative. It is connected to the way archaeologists produce knowledge, which requires "scaffolding" to build elaborate edifices in which (figuratively speaking) support for one part helps support the rest (Chapman and Wylie 2016). Excavation is slow, expensive, and usually unglamorous, but only problem-oriented excavation can provide hard data on chronology, subsistence, and technology that—in conjunction with supports from tree-ring and other forms of dating and other archaeometric inputs—form the foundation for much of what we know in archaeology.

Excavation and survey are not just cumulative but are also necessarily place based. Although we began this chapter with the DAP, it too built on much prior research in the northern Southwest. As we have seen, the DAP jumpstarted Crow Canyon by providing an infusion of personnel, research experience, directions of inquiry, and a wealth of local excavation data. The VEP complemented the empirical work of Crow Canyon by encouraging wider spatial perspectives and more use of computation. These in turn have helped to develop a more comparative perspective on the research that Crow Canyon continues to pursue.

One of the reasons for the success of the VEP is that it was also a Crow Canyon project, energized by additional outside funding and personnel with overlapping, but slightly different, sets of skills and interests. Given archaeology's fundamental nature as a hybrid discipline, with strong connections to both the natural and social sciences including history (Preston 2013), we should perhaps continue to look for hybrid entities such as the Crow Canyon / VEP combination to generate research advances. Crow Canyon's new Research Institute seeks to fill this role.

Established in 2014, the Research Institute was modeled, in part, on VEP projects in which Crow Canyon's researchers team with interdisciplinary networks of scholars—archaeologists, economists, geographers, sociologists, educators, and Indigenous culture specialists, among others—whose collaborative approach to research is especially suited to addressing big questions with large and complex datasets. Projects conducted under the aegis of the Research Institute address a wide variety of interrelated issues relevant not only to archaeologists but also to educators, policy makers, advocacy groups, and Indigenous peoples. These include human-environment relationships, economic systems, social complexity, Indigenous archaeology, and cultural and scientific literacy.

The potential exists for archaeology—long regarded as simply the study of antiquity—to provide fresh perspectives on some of the most intransigent and controversial issues of our time. One way to do this is to consider prehistory and modernity as two portions of a single historical continuum that is considered in such a way as to allow equivalent measurements to be made, and appropriately contextualized, in both arenas. Crow Canyon and VEP alumni have been prominent exponents of such studies (e.g., Kohler and Rockman 2020; Ortman 2019), and examples can be found in applications of settlement scaling theory (Ortman and Lobo 2020), evaluation of wealth inequality through time (Kohler et al. 2017), and demonstrations that the experiment in global climate change on which we have embarked will likely take humanity well outside of the temperature niche to which we have been accustomed for at least 6,000 years (Xu et al. 2020). To us these seem a fitting vindication of Struever's foundational aspirations for what archaeology can achieve.

Acknowledgments. We thank our many colleagues over the four decades recounted here for their energy, intellectual contributions—far too numerous to mention—and companionship. We are particularly grateful to Richard Wilshusen for the very helpful suggestions on this chapter that only he, as an insider to so many of the events related here, could make.

REFERENCES

Adler, Michael A. 1992. "The Upland Survey." In *The Sand Canyon Archaeological Project: A Progress Report*, edited by William D. Lipe, 11–23. Occasional Papers, no. 2. Cortez, CO: Crow Canyon Archaeological Center.

Adler, Michael A. 1994. "Population Aggregation and the Anasazi Social Landscape: A View from the Four Corners." In *The Ancient Southwestern Community: Models and Methods for the Study of Prehistoric Social Organization*, edited by Wirt H. Wills and Robert D. Leonard, 85–101. Albuquerque: University of New Mexico Press.

Adler, Michael A., ed. 1996. *The Prehistoric Pueblo World, A.D. 1150–1350.* Tucson: University of Arizona Press.

Adler, Michael A. 2002. "The Ancestral Pueblo Community as Structure and Strategy." In *Seeking the Center Place: Archaeology and Ancient Communities in the Mesa Verde Region*, edited by Mark D. Varien and Richard H. Wilshusen, 25–39. Salt Lake City: University of Utah Press.

Adler, Michael A., and Maripat Metcalf. 1991. "Draft Report on Archaeological Survey of Lower East Rock and Sand Canyons, Montezuma County, Colorado." Report Submitted to the Bureau of Land Management, San Juan Resource Area Office, Durango, Colorado. Cortez, CO: Crow Canyon Archaeological Center.

Adler, Michael A., and Mark D. Varien. 1994. "The Changing Face of the Community in the Mesa Verde Region A.D. 1000–1300." In *Proceedings of the Anasazi Symposium, 1991*, compiled by Art Hutchinson and Jack E. Smith, 83–97. Mesa Verde, CO: Mesa Verde Museum Association,

Binford, Lewis R. 1964. "A Consideration of Archaeological Research Design." *American Antiquity* 29 (4): 425–441.

Bocinsky, R. Kyle, and Timothy A. Kohler. 2014. "A 2,000-Year Reconstruction of the Rain-Fed Maize Agricultural Niche in the US Southwest." *Nature Communications* 5 (5618).

Bocinsky, R. Kyle, Jonathan Rush, Keith W. Kintigh, and Timothy A. Kohler. 2016. "Exploration and Exploitation in the Macrohistory of the Pre-Hispanic Pueblo Southwest." *Science Advances* 2, no. 4: e1501532.

Bocinsky, R. Kyle, and Mark D. Varien. 2017. "Comparing Maize Paleoproduction Models with Experimental Data." *Journal of Ethnobiology* 37 (2): 282–307.

Bradley, Bruce A. 1993. "Planning, Growth, and Functional Differentiation at a Prehistoric Pueblo: A Case Study from Southwestern Colorado." *Journal of Field Archaeology* 20 (1): 32–42.

Bradely, Bruce A. 1996. "Pitchers to Mugs: Chacoan Revival at Sand Canyon Pueblo." *The Kiva* 61 (3): 241–255.

Breternitz, David A. 1993. "The Dolores Archaeological Program: In Memoriam." *American Antiquity* 58 (1): 118–125.

Chapman, Robert, and Alison Wylie. 2016. *Evidential Reasoning in Archaeology*. London: Bloomsbury.

Cockburn, Denton, Stefani A. Crabtree, Ziad Kobti, Timothy A. Kohler, and R. Kyle Bocinsky. 2013. "Simulating Social and Economic Specialization in Small-Scale Agricultural Societies." *Journal of Artificial Societies and Social Simulation* 16 (4): 4.

Cole, Sarah M. 2012. "Population Dynamics and Warfare in the Central Mesa Verde Region." In *Emergence and Collapse of Early Villages: Models of Central Mesa Verde Archaeology*, edited by Timothy A. Kohler and Mark D. Varien, 197–218. Berkeley: University of California Press.

Crabtree, Stefani A., R. Kyle Bocinsky, Paul L. Hooper, Susan C. Ryan, and Timothy A. Kohler. 2017. "How to Make a Polity (in the Central Mesa Verde Region)." *American Antiquity* 82 (1): 71–95.

Duff, Andrew I., and Richard H. Wilshusen. 2000. "Prehistoric Population Dynamics in the Northern San Juan Region, A.D. 900–1300." *Kiva* 66 (1): 167–190.

Ellyson, Laura J., Timothy A. Kohler, and Catherine M. Cameron. 2019. "How Far from Chaco to Orayvi? Quantifying Inequality Among Pueblo Households." *Journal of Anthropological Archaeology* 55 (September 1): 101073.

Flannery, Kent V., ed. 1976. *The Early Mesoamerican Village*. New York: Academic Press.

Fowler, Don D. 2006. "The Archaeology of Glen Canyon: 'The Place No One Knew.'" In *Tracking Ancient Footsteps: William D. Lipe's Contributions to Southwestern Prehistory and Public Archaeology*, edited by R. G. Matson and Timothy A. Kohler, 21–28. Pullman: Washington State University Press.

Gleichman, Carol L., and Peter J. Gleichman. 1992. "The Lower Sand Canyon Survey." In *The Sand Canyon Archaeological Project: A Progress Report*, edited by William D. Lipe, 25–31. Occasional Papers, no. 2. Cortez, CO: Crow Canyon Archaeological Center.

Glowacki, Donna M., and Scott G. Ortman. 2012. "Characterizing Community Center (Village) Formation in the VEP Study Area, AD 600–1280." In *Emergence and Collapse* of *Early Villages: Models of Central Mesa Verde Archaeology*, edited by Timothy A. Kohler and Mark D. Varien, 219–246. Berkeley: University of California Press.

Huber, Edgar K. 1993. "Thirteenth Century Pueblo Aggregation and Organizational Change in Southwestern Colorado." PhD diss., Department of Anthropology, Washington State University, Pullman.

Huber, Edgar K., and William D. Lipe. 1992. "Excavations at the Green Lizard Site." In *The Sand Canyon Archaeological Project: A Progress Report*, edited by William D. Lipe, 69–77. Occasional Papers, no. 2. Cortez, CO: Crow Canyon Archaeological Center.

Kane, Allen E. 1983. "Introduction to Field Investigations and Analysis." In *Dolores Archaeological Program: Field Investigations and Analysis—1978*, edited by David A. Breternitz, 1–38. Denver: USDI Bureau of Reclamation.

Kane, Allen E. 1986. "Prehistory of the Dolores River Valley." In *Dolores Archaeological Program: Final Synthetic Report*, edited by David A. Breternitz, Christine K. Robinson, and G. Timothy Gross, 353–435. Denver: USDI Bureau of Reclamation.

Kane, Allen E., William D. Lipe, Ruthann Knudson, Timothy A. Kohler, Steven E. James, Patrick Hogan, and Lynne Sebastian. 1983. "The Dolores Archaeological Program Research Design." In *Dolores Archaeological Program: Field Investigations and Analysis—1978*, edited by David A. Breternitz, 39–60. Denver: USDI Bureau of Reclamation.

Knudson, Ruthann, Steven E. James, Allen E. Kane, William D. Lipe, and Timothy A. Kohler. 1986. "The Dolores Project Cultural Resources Mitigation Design." In *Dolores Archaeological Program: Research Designs and Initial Survey Results*, edited by Allen E. Kane, William D. Lipe, Timothy A. Kohler, and Christine K. Robinson, 13–42. Denver: USDI Bureau of Reclamation.

Kohler, Timothy A. 1978. "Ceramic Breakage Rate Simulation: Population Size and the Southeastern Chiefdom." *Newsletter of Computer Archaeology* 14 (1): 1–18.

Kohler, Timothy A. 2010. "A New Paleoproductivity Reconstruction for Southwestern Colorado, and Its Implications for Understanding the Thirteenth Century Depopulation." In *Leaving Mesa Verde: Peril and Change in the Thirteenth Century Southwest*, edited by Timothy A. Kohler, Mark D. Varien, and Aaron M. Wright, 102–127. Tucson: Amerind Foundation and University of Arizona Press.

Kohler, Timothy A. 2012. "The Rise and Collapse of Villages in the Central Mesa Verde Region." In *Emergence and Collapse of Early Villages: Models of Central Mesa Verde Archaeology*, edited by Timothy A. Kohler and Mark D. Varien, 247–262. Berkeley: University of California Press.

Kohler, Timothy A., and Eric Blinman. 1987. "Solving Mixture Problems in Archaeology: Analysis of Ceramic Materials for Dating and Demographic Reconstruction." *Journal of Anthropological Archaeology* 6 (1): 1–28.

Kohler, Timothy A., Laura J. Ellyson, and R. Kyle Bocinsky. 2020. "Beyond One-Shot Hypotheses: Explaining Three Increasingly Large Collapses in the Northern

Pueblo Southwest." In *Going Forward by Looking Back: Archaeological Perspectives on Socio-ecological Crisis, Response and Collapse*, edited by Felix Reide and Payson Sheets, 304–332. New York: Berghahn Books.

Kohler, Timothy A., and G. Timothy Gross. 1984. "Probability Sampling in Excavation: A Program Review." In *Dolores Archaeological Program: Synthetic Report, 1978–1981*, compiled by David A. Breternitz, 72–76. Denver: USDI Bureau of Reclamation.

Kohler, Timothy A., and Rebecca Higgins. 2016. "Quantifying Household Inequality in Early Pueblo Villages." *Current Anthropology* 57 (5): 690–697.

Kohler, Timothy A., Janet D. Orcutt, Eric Blinman, and Kenneth L. Petersen. 1986. "Anasazi Spreadsheets: The Cost of Doing Agricultural Business in Prehistoric Dolores." In *Dolores Archaeological Program: Final Synthetic Report*, edited by David A. Breternitz, Christine K. Robinson, and G. Timothy Gross, 525–538. Denver: USDI Bureau of Reclamation.

Kohler, Timothy A., Scott G. Ortman, Katie E. Grundtisch, Carla M. Fitzpatrick, and Sarah M. Cole. 2014. "The Better Angels of Their Nature: Declining Violence through Time among Prehispanic Farmers of the Pueblo Southwest." *American Antiquity* 79 (3): 444–464.

Kohler, Timothy A., and Kelsey M. Reese. 2014. "Long and Spatially Variable Neolithic Demographic Transition in the North American Southwest." *Proceedings of the National Academy of Sciences* 111 (28): 10101–10106.

Kohler, Timothy A., and Marci Rockman. 2020. "The IPCC: A Primer for Archaeologists." *American Antiquity* 85 (4): 627–651.

Kohler, Timothy A., Michael E. Smith, Amy Bogaard, Gary M. Feinman, Christian E. Peterson et al. 2017. "Greater Post-Neolithic Wealth Disparities in Eurasia than in North America and Mesoamerica." *Nature* 551 (November 30): 619–622.

Kohler, Timothy A., and Carla R. Van West. 1996. "The Calculus of Self-Interest in the Development of Cooperation: Sociopolitical Development and Risk among the Northern Anasazi." In *Evolving Complexity and Environmental Risk in the Prehistoric Southwest*, edited by Joseph A. Tainter and Bonnie B. Tainter, 169–196. Santa Fe Institute Studies in the Sciences of Complexity, Proceedings Volume XXIV. Reading, MA: Addison-Wesley.

Kohler, Timothy A., and Mark D. Varien. 2012. "Emergence and Collapse of Early Villages in the Central Mesa Verde." In *Emergence and Collapse of Early Villages: Models of Central Mesa Verde Archaeology*, edited by Timothy A. Kohler and Mark D. Varien, 1–14. Berkeley: University of California Press.

Kohler, Timothy A., Mark D. Varien, and Aaron M. Wright, eds. 2010. *Leaving Mesa Verde: Peril and Change in the Thirteenth-Century Southwest*. Tucson: Amerind Foundation and University of Arizona Press.

Kuckelman, Kristin A. 2008. "An Agent-Centered Case Study of the Depopulation of Sand Canyon Pueblo." In *The Social Construction of Communities: Agency, Structure, and*

Identity in the Prehispanic Southwest, edited by Mark D. Varien and James M. Potter, 75–101. Boulder: AltaMira Press.

Kuckelman, Kristin A. 2010. "The Depopulation of Sand Canyon Pueblo: A Large Ancestral Pueblo Village in Southwestern Colorado." *American Antiquity* 75 (3): 497–526.

Kuckelman, Kristin A., Ricky R. Lightfoot, and Debra L. Martin. 2002. "The Bioarchaeology and Taphonomy of Violence at Castle Rock and Sand Canyon Pueblos, Southwestern Colorado." *American Antiquity* 67 (3): 486–513.

Lekson, Stephen H. 1988. "The Idea of the Kiva in Anasazi Archaeology." *Kiva* 53 (3): 213–234.

Lightfoot, Ricky R. 1994. *The Duckfoot Site*. Vol. 2, *Archaeology of the House and Household*. Occasional Papers, no. 4. Cortez, CO: Crow Canyon Archaeological Center.

Lightfoot, Ricky R., and Mary C. Etzkorn, eds. 1993. *The Duckfoot Site*. Vol. 1, *Descriptive Archaeology*. Occasional Papers, no. 3. Cortez, CO: Crow Canyon Archaeological Center.

Lightfoot, Ricky R., Richard H. Wilshusen, and Mark D. Varien. 2014. "Defining and Using Households in Archaeological Analysis." In *Bulletin of the Texas Archaeological Society*, Volume 85 (2014), edited by Tamra L. Walter, Timothy K. Perrtula, and Nancy A. Kenmotsu, 225–234. Austin: Texas Archaeological Society.

Lipe, William D. 1970. "Anasazi Communities in the Red Rock Plateau, Southeastern Utah." In *Reconstructing Prehistoric Pueblo Societies*, edited by William Longacre, 84–139. Albuquerque: University of New Mexico Press.

Lipe, William D. 1986. "Modeling Dolores Area Cultural Dynamics." In *Dolores Archaeological Program: Final Synthetic Report*, edited by David A. Breternitz, Christine K. Robinson, and G. Timothy Gross, 439–468. Denver: USDI Bureau of Reclamation.

Lipe, William D. 1989. "Social Scale of Mesa Verde Anasazi Kivas." In *The Architecture of Social Integration in Prehistoric Pueblos*, edited by William D. Lipe and Michelle Hegmon, 53–71. Occasional Papers, no. 1. Cortez, CO: Crow Canyon Archaeological Center.

Lipe, William D. 1999. "View from the Lake: Legacies of the Dolores Archaeological Program, SW Colorado." In *The Dolores Legacy: A User's Guide to the Dolores Archaeological Program Data*, edited by Richard H. Wilshusen, Karin Burd, Jonathan Till, Christine G. Ward, and Brian Yunker, 135–144. https://core.tdar.org/document/6243/the-dolores-legacy-a-users-guide-to-the-dolores-archaeological-program-data.

Lipe, William D. 2018. "Glen Canyon, Dolores, and Animas–La Plata: Big Projects and Big Changes in Public Archaeology." In *New Perspectives in Cultural Resource Management*, edited by Francis McManamon, 61–84. New York: Routledge.

Lipe, William D., Mark D. Varien, J. Neal Morris, Ricky R. Lightfoot, and Timothy A. Kohler. 1988. "Synthesis." In *Dolores Archaeological Program: Anasazi Communities at Dolores: Grass Mesa Village*, edited by William D. Lipe, J. Neal Morris, and Timothy A. Kohler, 1213–1302. Denver: USDI Bureau of Reclamation.

Martin, Debra L. 2021. "Violence and Masculinity in Small-Scale Societies." *Current Anthropology* 62 (supp. 23) (February). https://doi.org/10.1086/711689.

Matson, R. G., William D. Lipe, and William R. Haase. 1988. "Adaptational Continuities and Occupational Discontinuities: The Cedar Mesa Anasazi." *Journal of Field Archaeology* 15 (3): 245–263.

Morley, Sylvanus G. 1908. "The Excavation of the Cannonball Ruins in Southwestern Colorado." *American Anthropologist* (n.s.) 10: 596–610.

Orcutt, Janet D. 1987. "Modeling Prehistoric Agricultural Ecology in the Dolores Area." In *Dolores Archaeological Program: Supporting Studies: Settlement and Environment*, edited by Kenneth L. Petersen and Janet D. Orcutt, 649–677. Denver: USDI Bureau of Reclamation.

Orcutt, Janet D., Eric Blinman, and Timothy A. Kohler. 1990. "Explanations of Population Aggregation in the Mesa Verde Region Prior to A.D. 900." In *Perspectives on Southwestern Prehistory*, edited by Charles Redman and Paul Minnis, 196–212. Boulder: Westview Press.

Ortman, Scott G. 2019. "A New Kind of Relevance for Archaeology." *Frontiers in Digital Humanities* 6 (October). https://doi.org/10.3389/fdigh.2019.00016.

Ortman, Scott G., and Bruce A. Bradley. 2002. "Sand Canyon Pueblo: The Container in the Center." In *Seeking the Center Place: Archaeology and Ancient Communities in the Mesa Verde Region*, edited by Mark D. Varien and Richard H. Wilshusen, 41–80. Salt Lake City: University of Utah Press.

Ortman, Scott G., and José Lobo. 2020. "Smithian Growth in a Non-industrial Society." *Science Advances* 6 (25). https://doi.org/10.1126/sciadv.aba5694.

Ortman, Scott G., and Mark D. Varien. 2007. "Settlement Patterns in the McElmo Dome Study Area." In *The Archaeology of Sand Canyon Pueblo: Intensive Excavations at a Late-Thirteenth-Century Village in Southwestern Colorado*, edited by Kristin A. Kuckelman. http://www.crowcanyon.org/sandcanyon.

Ortman, Scott G., Mark D. Varien, and T. Lee Gripp. 2007. "Empirical Bayesian Methods for Archaeological Survey Data: An Application from the Mesa Verde Region." *American Antiquity* 72 (2): 241–272.

Petersen, Kenneth L. 1982. *Climatic Reconstruction*. Dolores Archaeological Program Technical Reports DAP-014. Denver: USDI Bureau of Reclamation.

Potter, James M., and Scott G. Ortman. 2004. "Community and Cuisine in the Prehispanic Southwest." In *Identity, Feasting, and the Archaeology of the Greater Southwest: Proceedings of the 2002 Southwest Symposium*, edited by Barbara J. Mills, 173–191. Boulder: University Press of Colorado.

Preston, John. 2013. "Positivist and Post-Positivist Philosophy of Science." In *The Oxford Handbook of Archaeological Theory*, edited by Andrew Gardner, Mark Lake, and Ulrike Sommer, n.p. New York: Oxford University Press.

Reese, Kelsey M., Donna M. Glowacki, and Timothy A. Kohler. 2019. "Dynamic Communities on the Mesa Verde Cuesta." *American Antiquity* 84 (4): 728–747.

Salzer, Matthew W. 2000. "Temperature Variability and the Northern Anasazi: Possible Implications for Regional Abandonment." *Kiva* 65 (4): 295–318.

Scheffer, Marten, Egbert H. van Nes, Darcy Bird, R. Kyle Bocinsky, and Timothy A. Kohler. 2021. "Instability Preceded Transformations of Prehispanic Pueblo Societies." *PNAS* 118 (18): e2024397118.

Schiffer, Michael B. 1976. *Behavioral Archeology*. New York: Academic Press.

Schlanger, Sarah H. 1987. "Population Measurement, Size, and Change, AD 600–1175." In *Dolores Archaeological Program: Supporting Studies: Settlement and Environment*, edited by Kenneth L. Petersen and Janet D. Orcutt, 568–613. Denver: USDI Bureau of Reclamation.

Schlanger, Sarah H. 1988. "Patterns of Population Movement and Long-Term Population Growth in Southwestern Colorado." *American Antiquity* 53 (4): 773–793.

Schlanger, Sarah H., and Timothy A. Kohler. 2006. "Basketmaker III, Pueblo I, and the Dolores Archaeological Project." In *Tracking Ancient Footsteps: William D. Lipe's Contributions to Southwestern Prehistory and Public Archaeology*, edited by R. G. Matson and Timothy A. Kohler, 63–79. Pullman: Washington State University Press.

Schwindt, Dylan M., R. Kyle Bocinsky, Scott G. Ortman, Donna M. Glowacki, Mark D. Varien, and Timothy A. Kohler. 2016. "The Social Consequences of Climate Change in the Central Mesa Verde Region." *American Antiquity* 81 (1): 74–96.

Struever, Stuart. 1968. "Problems, Methods and Organization: A Disparity in the Growth of Archeology." *Anthropological Archeology in the Americas*, edited by Betty J. Meggars, 131–151. Washington, DC: Anthropological Society of Washington.

Udick, Lynn L., and Richard H. Wilshusen. 1999. "The DAP Data Files: A Short History of Their Original Design, Past Uses, and Possible Importance in the Near Future." In *The Dolores Legacy: A User's Guide to the Dolores Archaeological Program Data*, compiled by Richard H. Wilshusen with contributions from Karin Burd, Jonathan Till, Christine G. Ward, and Brian Yunker, 13–22. Accessed March 30, 2021. (tDAR id: 6243), https://doi.org/10.6067/XCV84F1PQQ.

Van West, Carla R. 1994. *Modeling Prehistoric Agricultural Productivity in Southwestern Colorado: A GIS Approach*. Vol. 67. Reports of Investigations. Pullman, WA, and Cortez, CO: Department of Anthropology, Washington State University and Crow Canyon Archaeological Center.

Varien, Mark D. ed. 1999a. *The Sand Canyon Archaeological Project: Site Testing*. Cortez, CO: Crow Canyon Archaeological Center. https://www.crowcanyon.org/Research Reports/SiteTesting/start.asp.

Varien, Mark D. 1999b. *Sedentism and Mobility in a Social Landscape: Mesa Verde and Beyond*. Tucson: University of Arizona Press.

Varien, Mark D. 2010. "Depopulation of the Northern San Juan Region: Historical Review and Archaeological Context." In *Leaving Mesa Verde: Peril and Change in the Thirteenth Century Southwest*, edited by Timothy A. Kohler, Mark D. Varien, and Aaron Wright, 1–33. Tucson: Amerind Foundation and University of Arizona Press.

Varien, Mark D. 2012. "Occupation Span and the Organization of Activities at Residential Sites: A Case Study from the Mesa Verde Region." In *Ancient Households of the Americas: Conceptualizing What Households Do*, edited by John G. Douglass and Nancy Gonlin, 47–78. Boulder: University Press of Colorado.

Varien, Mark D., and Ricky R. Lightfoot. 2006. "Research, Public Education, and Native American Collaboration." In *Tracking Ancient Footsteps: William D. Lipe's Contributions to Southwestern Prehistory and Public Archaeology*, edited by R. G. Matson and Timothy A. Kohler, 81–96. Pullman: Washington State University Press.

Varien, Mark D., William D. Lipe, Michael A. Adler, Ian M. Thompson, and Bruce A. Bradley. 1996. "Southwestern Colorado and Southeastern Utah Settlement Patterns: A.D. 1100 to 1300." In *The Prehistoric Pueblo World, A.D. 1150–1350*, edited by Michael A. Adler, 86–113. Tucson: University of Arizona Press.

Varien, Mark D., and Barbara J. Mills. 1997. "Accumulations Research: Problems and Prospects for Estimating Site Occupation Span." *Journal of Archaeological Method and Theory* 4 (2): 141–191.

Varien, Mark D., and Scott G. Ortman. 2007. "Accumulations Research in the Southwestern United States: Middle Range Research for Big-Picture Problems." *World Archaeology* 37 (1): 132–155.

Varien, Mark D., Scott G. Ortman, Timothy A. Kohler, Donna M. Glowacki, and Charles D. Johnson. 2007. "Historical Ecology in the Mesa Verde Region: Results from the Village Ecodynamics Project." *American Antiquity* 72 (2): 273–300.

Varien, Mark D., and James M. Potter. 1997. "Unpacking the Discard Equation: Simulating the Accumulation of Artifacts in the Archaeological Record." *American Antiquity* 62 (2): 194–213.

Voggesser, Garrit. 2001. "Dolores Project History. Bureau of Reclamation History." https://www.usbr.gov/projects/index.php?id=453.

Willey, Gordon R., and Phillip Phillips. 1958. *Method and Theory in American Archaeology.* Chicago: University of Chicago Press.

Wilshusen, Richard H. 1986. "The Relationship between Abandonment Mode and Ritual Use in Pueblo I Anasazi Protokivas." *Journal of Field Archaeology* 13 (2): 245–254.

Wilshusen, Richard H. 1987. "Sipapus, Ceremonial Vaults, and Foot Drums (or, a Resounding Argument for Protokivas)." In *Dolores Archaeological Program: Supporting Studies: Additive and Reductive Technologies*, edited by Eric Blinman, Carl J. Phagan, and Richard H. Wilshusen, 649–671. Denver: USDI Bureau of Reclamation.

Windes, Thomas C., and Carla R. Van West. 2021. "Landscapes, Horticulture, and the Early Chacoan Bonito Phase." In *The Greater Chacoan Landscape: Ancestors, Scholarship, and Advocacy*, edited by Ruth M. Van Dyke and Carrie C. Heitman, 41–92. Louisville: University Press of Colorado.

Wright, Aaron M. 2010. "The Climate of the Depopulation of the Northern Southwest." In *Leaving Mesa Verde: Peril and Change in the Thirteenth Century Southwest*, edited by Timothy A. Kohler, Mark D. Varien, and Aaron Wright, 75–101. Tucson: Amerind Foundation and University of Arizona Press.

Xu, Chi, Timothy A. Kohler, Timothy M. Lenton, Jens-Christian Svenning, and Marten Scheffer. 2020. "Future of the Human Climate Niche." *PNAS* 117 (21): 11350–11355. https://doi.org/10.1073/pnas.1910114117.

Indigenous Archaeology

Indigenous Archaeology

4

The Pueblo Farming Project

Research, Education, and Native American Collaboration

PAUL ERMIGIOTTI, MARK D. VARIEN, GRANT D. COFFEY,
R. KYLE BOCINSKY, LEIGH KUWANWISIWMA, AND
STEWART B. KOYIYUMPTEWA

Maize farming represents a fundamental aspect of Pueblo people's identity. As noted by Denis Wall and Virgil Masayesva (2004, 436), "For traditional Hopis corn is the central bond. Its essence, physically, spiritually, and symbolically, pervades their existence." This relationship between people and maize extends back for millennia in the US Southwest (see Kuwanwisiwma and Bernardini, chapter 5 and Suina, chapter 7 in this volume).

This chapter focuses on an experimental farming program conducted as one part of the Pueblo Farming Project (PFP). We begin by discussing how Hopi perspectives shaped the PFP. Next, we present a brief review of experimental garden projects in the region, then we compare the experimental gardens located on Crow Canyon's campus near Cortez, Colorado, with a garden located about 50 km north, near Dove Creek, Colorado (figure 4.1). This comparison examines how a suite of environmental and ecological factors affects maize yields. We show how differences between these gardens result in much higher yields at the garden near Dove Creek. We evaluate one of the primary Hopi goals for the project: whether Hopi seed and farming techniques would produce yields in an

https://doi.org/10.5876/9781646424597.c004

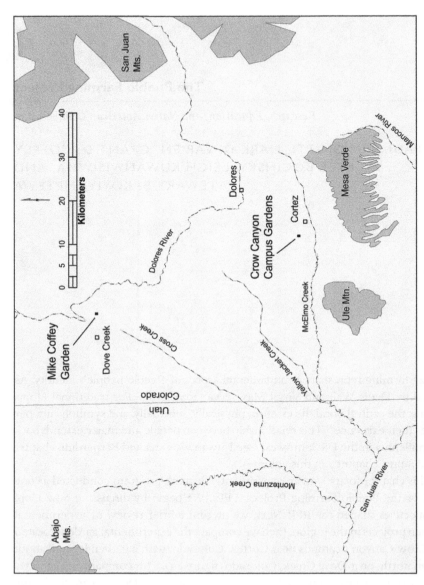

FIGURE 4.1. Locations of Pueblo Farming Project Gardens. *Courtesy of Crow Canyon Archaeological Center.*

FIGURE 4.2. *Lee Wayne Lomayestewa speaks with students about the importance of maize in Hopi culture in an experimental garden on Crow Canyon's campus. Courtesy of Crow Canyon Archaeological Center.*

area they view as their ancestral homeland. Finally, we discuss how our results contribute to understanding the depopulation of the central Mesa Verde region at the end of the thirteenth century AD.

The PFP represents one of Crow Canyon's longest-running projects and one of the Center's most important collaborations with American Indian partners. The experimental farming component serves as the centerpiece of the PFP, but the project also develops and delivers educational curricula, publishes research results, and pursues Hopi interests in maize and maize farming. A journal article (Bocinsky and Varien 2017) and book chapter (Varien et al. 2018) report PFP research results, and an e-book, *The Pueblo Farming Project*, provides the most thorough description of the PFP and updates the results of the experimental farming program each year (Ermigiotti et al. 2020). On the education front, students attending Crow Canyon's campus-based programs visit PFP experimental gardens to learn about the role of maize agriculture in Pueblo life (figure 4.2). The PFP team also created and published five lesson plans aligned to the state of Colorado academic standards (Ermigiotti et al. 2020) and produced a documentary film *More than Planting a Seed* (Simon 2016), which can be accessed in the e-book. At the request of the Hopi Cultural Preservation Office (HCPO), the PFP also conducted DNA analysis of sixteen varieties of modern Hopi maize (Swarts 2017). Finally, the HCPO hosted a meeting at Kykotsmovi, Arizona, in

2018, where the PFP team shared the results of the project and a meal with the Hopi community.

BACKGROUND

We present a detailed history of the PFP elsewhere (Bocinsky and Varien 2017; Ermigiotti et al. 2020; Varien et al. 2018), and the reader should consult those sources for an account of how the experimental farming program developed and the individuals who contributed to the project. Here, we summarize details of the project to provide a background for this chapter.

The idea for the PFP emerged from a 2004 Native American Graves Protection and Repatriation Act (NAGPRA) consultation with Crow Canyon, the HCPO, and the National Park Service to discuss the Goodman Point Archaeological Project. At the end of the meeting, Crow Canyon researchers asked whether there were other studies HCPO would like Crow Canyon to conduct; they requested that Crow Canyon research ancestral Pueblo maize farming and link that to modern Pueblo farming. Their request led the HCPO and Crow Canyon to codesign the PFP, along with input from other eastern Pueblo farmers and researchers who study Pueblo maize agriculture. In 2005, Crow Canyon hosted a meeting of Pueblo farmers, scholars, and HCPO staff. The farmers came from Hopi, Jemez, Ohkay Owingeh, and Tesuque/Zuni Pueblos, and they recommended we initiate an experimental farming program focused on direct-precipitation maize farming (also known as dryland farming). They also agreed the Hopi farmers should lead the project since they continue to use direct-precipitation maize farming today.

Hopi farmers returned to Crow Canyon's campus in 2007 to select the locations for the gardens. We began with five gardens on campus but eventually abandoned two of those plots due to modern site disturbance and poor yields. In 2015, we added a mesa top garden on farmland about 50 km (31 miles) north of Crow Canyon near Dove Creek, Colorado (figure 4.1).

Farmers from the HCPO and several members from the Cultural Resources Advisory Task Team (CRATT) visited CCAC each year between 2008 and 2017. They instructed Crow Canyon staff on how to plant, gave advice on tending plants throughout the growing season, and returned to supervise the harvest. Crow Canyon staff and volunteers have continued to plant and harvest the gardens from 2018 to the present. The Hopi farmers provided seed for the initial 2008 planting. Several different varieties of corn seed (*poshumi*) were planted between 2008 and 2010. Since 2011 only Hopi blue (*sakwapqà ö*) and white corn (*qotsaqá ö*) have been planted, using seed from previous harvests. During each growing season, CCAC staff made weekly visits to the gardens to measure maize vegetative and reproductive growth. They also recorded environmental data and documented yields for each harvest. During the PFP, Hopi farmers shared their perspectives on maize farming and corn culture. These insights shaped our understanding of how the ancestral Pueblo people may have similarly been sustained, physically and spiritually, by maize.

HOPI KNOWLEDGE

The HPCO staff and farmers who participated in in the PFP stated that one of their primary objectives was learning whether Hopi seed and farming practices would succeed in the central Mesa Verde region. Some clans view this area as a part of their traditional homeland (see Kuwanwisiwma and Bernardini, chapter 5 in this volume). Leigh Kuwanwisiwma notes, this connection remains important to Hopi people. "A corn culture that we see today in Hopi is shaped by a corn culture from a millennium ago." Stewart Koyiyumptewa states that the values of the "corn culture" pervade every aspect of Hopi life. "From when we enter the world to our end life, all of that is involved using corn. They are the primary source for our prayer offerings."

Throughout the PFP, Hopi farmers shared their knowledge about the fundamental importance of maize and maize farming to Hopi people and Hopi culture. Without exception, each emphasized that success goes far beyond the technical details of planting, tending, and harvesting. "Agriculture is an act of faith for the Hopi that serves as a religious focus as well as an economic activity. The themes of humility, cooperation, respect and universal earth stewardship became the way of life for all Hopis" (Kuwanwisiwma 2005, 15–16). This viewpoint enhanced the understanding of Pueblo farming for the non-Hopi members of our team, and, where appropriate, we include their knowledge and perspectives in the outreach and educational materials advanced by the PFP.

All crops, especially maize, necessitate nurturing. "They are your children," our advisors repeatedly informed us. "They need encouragement, sing to them each time you approach."

The phrases for each stage of development of the maize plants, loosely translated, are equivalent to terms used for the stages of a human development, for example, crawling, standing upright, sexual maturity (Ermigiotti et al. 2020). This kinship with corn, along with the belief that a (Hopi) farmer needs to have a good heart and prayers, represents the most important factor leading to a good harvest and agricultural sustainability.

One point of contrast between the Hopi farmers who worked on the PFP and the Western scientific researchers was that the Hopi never look at the crops as statistics or data. In our efforts to collect data and to accurately quantify yields, Hopi advisors felt that we were reluctant to step further into the process and fully understand corn farming because we were not eating some of the fresh corn, *sami*, at the milky kernel stage. They pointed out that this may affect yields because when corn is not used for the purpose it was intended, it pouts and will not grow to its full potential. Stewart Koyiyumptewa uses the word *motsiwngwa* to refer to a time to indulge in the fruits of one's labor ensuring future success. We hope to better address this concern. Over the duration of the PFP the Hopi participants have come to accept our need to document and record all aspects of the process throughout the project.

EXPERIMENTAL MAIZE FARMING AND THE PUEBLO FARMING PROJECT

Ethnographic observations and scientific interests in Indigenous farming practices date to the late nineteenth and early twentieth centuries (e.g., Beaglehole 1937; Clark 1928; Cushing [1974] 1920; Forde 1931; Hack 1942; Whiting 1966). Researchers rely on experimental gardening to supplement our understanding of pre-Hispanic agricultural practices (Bellorado 2007). Experimental maize farming at Mesa Verde National Park, conducted from 1918 to 1936, began as a demonstration garden to facilitate public education (Franke and Watson 1936). Navajo Park Service employees planted this garden using traditional deep-planting and wide-spacing methods. The longevity of this program demonstrated the sustainability of ancient garden plots in climatic conditions not unlike those today.

Their repeated planting of maize in the same garden addressed questions surrounding soil depletion. Experimenters learned that soil fertility is maintained through the wide-spacing of plants and by interspacing the plants to different locations within the garden each year. Additionally, the project addressed the importance of winter precipitation in maintaining adequate soil moisture for the successful germination of seeds and the subsequent growing season (Franke and Watson 1936).

In 1975, The Southwestern Archaeological Program at San José State University established five experimental gardens at Hovenweep National Monument (Hammett and Hornbeck 1984; Litzinger 1976; Winter 1976). Each garden tested a different variable to investigate agricultural production. Two plots compared water control devices: one a check dam and the other canyon bottom terraces. A third garden, located on the mesa top, determined the effects of supplemental watering on growth. A fourth garden, previously set up for food production, used a variety of cultivated plants to establish their potential under current climatic conditions. A fifth garden, established near Pleasant View, Colorado, was not weeded to assess competition from invasive plant species. The experimental gardens yielded poor harvests but demonstrated that successful gardens need adequate soil depth to maintain moisture, protection from herbivores, and reduced-or-no competition from weeds (Litzinger 1976).

In 1979 and 1980, Dolores Archaeological Program (DAP) researchers planted two large experimental farming gardens using twelve varieties of southwestern maize and an assortment of beans and squash species to document variation in growth rates and productivity. They noted that maize development and yield were affected by plant spacing and density. The gardens were affected by topography, and cold air drainage increased the possibility of crop failure (Bellorado 2007; Bye and Shuster 1984; Shuster 1981, 1983).

Karen Adams, Deborah Muenchrath, and Dylan Schwindt (1999) examined the morphology, phenology, and physiology of a Southwest US maize cultivar in a two-year (1992, 1993) controlled garden experiment. Their analysis of the yields helped refine methods used to interpret archaeological maize remains (Bellorado 2007). Adams and others (2006) conducted another two-year (2004, 2005) experimental farming project, Maize of American Indigenous Societies (MAÍS), a grow-out of 123 maize accessions curated by the USDA. The USDA originally collected most of these accessions from American Indian farmers in the mid-1900s. The MAÍS project crops were irrigated to provide optimal growing conditions. These data helped define distinctive morphological groups and field traits within the accessions (Adams et al. 2006; Bellorado 2007).

In 2003 and 2004 the Animas–La Plata Archaeological Project (ALP) supported a program to assess connections between settlement locations and farming catchments. Benjamin Bellorado (2007, 2009) created several experimental gardens. Using traditional direct precipitation agricultural methods, including deep-planting and wide-spacing (Dominguez and Kolm 2005), several different Indigenous maize varieties were grown to assess variability in yields. Hand pollination maintained the genetic distinctness of the maize varieties. Weather station and a temperature monitor transects recorded the length of the frost-free growing season and the effects of cold-air drainage. These experiments demonstrated that simple water management practices, combined with an adequate frost-free growing season, and the accumulation of sufficient growing season heat units, or Growing Degree Days (GDDs), resulted in sustainable maize yields (Bellorado 2007, 2009).

These projects largely laid the foundation for Crow Canyon's Pueblo Farming Project. Bellorado helped set up the research design for the PFP using methodology incorporated by the ALP studies. Record keeping of temperature, precipitation, soil moisture, weekly vegetative, and reproductive growth stages; monitoring the effects of cold air drainage on the length of the growing season; and the assessment of yields helped create a long-term dataset for the PFP that can now provide a valuable baseline for future studies (Bellorado 2007, 2009; Bocinsky and Varien 2017; Ermigiotti et al. 2020).

COMPARING CROW CANYON CAMPUS GARDENS TO THE DOVE CREEK GARDEN

Pueblo settlement during most of the AD 600 to 1280 period occurred predominantly in mesa top settings (Glowacki et al., chapter 12 in this volume). Deep aeolian soil, called Mesa Verde loess, covers these mesa tops. Researchers believe ancestral Pueblo farmers focused on these rich soils for maize agriculture (Van West 1994), just as modern farming occurs on these soils.

In 2015, Mike Coffey, a local farmer from Dove Creek, Colorado, provided us with a space on his land that he thought would be ideal for maize. We call this plot the "Mike Coffey Garden" (MCG) and have farmed it from 2015 to the present. Next, we compare the environmental and ecological characteristics of the MCG plot with three plots on Crow Canyon's campus: Paul's Old Garden (POG), the Pueblo Learning Center Garden (PLC), and the Check Dam Garden (CDG).

SETTING: LANDFORM, ELEVATION, AND ASPECT

The settings of the gardens discussed here vary in several important ways. Those located on the Crow Canyon campus—the POG, PLC, and CDG—are a maximum of 153 m apart across an area of about 12,300 m². All these gardens lie between 6,120 and 6,140 ft. in elevation. The gardens are located along the east-central part of Crow Canyon, a south-flowing tributary to McElmo Canyon, and have either flat or west-southwest exposures. The POG is located on level ground near the bottom of Crow Canyon, and both the PLC and CDG are situated in small, westerly flowing drainages on the east side of Crow Canyon, about 4 to 6 m above the POG. Due to their location in small drainages, the PLC and CDG capture runoff events while the POG typically does not. Although the elevations of gardens vary slightly, their location within the canyon has increased impacts from cold air drainage that shortened the growing season in some years (Ermigiotti et al. 2020).

In contrast, the MCG garden lies at a higher elevation, about 50 km northwest of the Crow Canyon campus in an upland setting east of Dove Creek, Colorado. Located along the southern flank of a small, southwestern-flowing drainage, the garden sits at an elevation of about 7,300 ft. This elevation typically results in larger winter snow accumulations compared to the campus gardens, and the topography immediately around this field allows cold air to drain away from the field into major nearby canyons (Gillreath-Brown et al. 2019). The northern aspect of the field helps retain soil moisture from reduced sun and wind exposure. Unlike other fields discussed here, the MCG is situated within an existing agricultural field in which beans and wheat have been grown in rotation for at least the past forty years.

SOILS

All gardens located on the Crow Canyon campus are situated on soils classified by The Natural Resources Conservation Service (NRCS) as Wetherill loam with 3–6 percent slopes. The POG is also partially located on Ackmen Loam with 1–3 percent slopes (Soil Survey Geographic Database [Soil Survey Staff 2020]). Despite general similarities, significant variation exists in the soils present in the gardens (Fadem and Diederichs 2019). For instance, soils in the PLC garden are sandier given its location in an ephemeral, narrow drainage where eroding upslope sediments are deposited, whereas the composition of the POG soils suggests the presence of more clay and less aggradation of colluvial sediments (Utah State University Analytical Laboratories 2009). Slight differences, like those above, influence infiltration rates and water-holding capacity, and the topographic locations of the fields also impacts their ability to capture runoff events. All these factors influence the amount of moisture that gets on, and remains in, the gardens.

The NRCS designated soils present in the MCG as Illex-Granath complex with 6 to 12 percent slopes (Soil Survey Staff 2020). These soils are a clay loam with good infiltration and water retention properties. This field has the deepest soil of any field discussed here, and it has darker sediment; this is likely an indication of remnant organic material possibly from a stand of Gambel oak (*Quercus gambelii*) that was cleared, burned, or removed when the field was created in the early 1900s. The small drainage just to the north of the field is also one of the wettest areas in the surrounding landscape during the spring, suggesting the presence of a perched water table or some other subsurface water.

GROWING SEASON: TEMPERATURE AND MOISTURE

There is no debate that water and temperature are two of the greatest environmental factors influencing maize development and yields (Adams et al. 2006; Benson 2010, 2011; Muenchrath and Salvador 1995). Precipitation delivered as rain or snow is stored in the soil. Soil moisture can be increased by water run-on, diversion, or irrigation, or by capturing water and soil using check dams.

Precipitation in the Mesa Verde region comes mainly as winter snow (December to March) and summer (July to September) monsoonal rains. Average annual precipitation varies widely across the landscape and is affected by elevation and proximity to local landforms (Benson 2010; Van West and Dean 2000). The National Corn Handbook, Purdue University Cooperative Extension Service, states, "with dryland farming, corn is generally not grown in areas receiving less than 25 inches (60 cm) of annual precipitation" (Neild and Newman n.d.). Suggested lower threshold requirements for Southwest maize productivity are 11.8 inches (30 cm) of precipitation and 1,800 GDD (Benson 2011; Shaw 1988). The annual precipitation for the PFP study area averaged 12 inches (30.48 cm) of precipitation during a twelve-year period (2008–2019), which is close to the thirty-year (1981–2010) average for nearby Cortez, Colorado (J. Andrus, NOAA, NWS Cooperative weather observer, personal communication, November 2021). The timing of precipitation and the availability of soil moisture are as important as total annual precipitation (Adams et al. 1999; Van West and Dean 2000). The plant's access to nutrients also depends on sufficient soil moisture, since nutrients in the soil are available to the plant in solution and cannot be absorbed without it. Inadequate soil moisture may result in nutrient deficiencies (Muenchrath and Salvador 1995).

Soil moisture and air temperatures influence both vegetative growth and reproductive development. Stress during stages of development can reduce yields, impacting seedling emergence, anthesis (tasseling), and silking (Adams et al. 1999; Adams et al. 2006).

The length of the growing season for maize is more nuanced than the number of frost-free days in any given location or year. In the spring, maize can survive a frost of about 28°F (−2°C) because the growing point (apical meristem) of the plant remains below the ground surface. Some southwestern landraces can emerge from deeper planting depths, up to 40 cm, due to the development of a significantly elongated mesocotyl. This adaptation allows for earlier planting while insulating the growing point of the plant (Adams et al. 2006; Bousselot et al. 2017; Collins 1914; Muenchrath and Salvador 1995; Troyer 1997).

Plant development and kernel maturity depend on accumulated heat units or cumulative GDDs, which are not the same as solar days. The ideal temperature for maize growth is between 50°F and 86°F (10 to 30°C). Beyond these thresholds, maize growth and development are limited. The accumulation of GDDs is calculated based on these thresholds.[1] Many modern hybrids require an average of 2,400 to 3,200 GDD (Adams et al. 2006). Growing season may be influenced by environmental adaptations of the cultivar. Bellorado's (2007, 2009) experimental studies in Ridges Basin have demonstrated—and PFP results confirm (Ermigiotti et al. 2020)—that the GDD requirements for some Indigenous maize varieties to produce yields are far below the above range (table 4.1). Further, variation in the length of the frost-free season is not always directly correlated to elevation but is dramatically influenced by cold air drainage (Adams 1979; Bellorado 2007).

SOIL MOISTURE AND YIELDS

A water year (WY) refers to the amount of precipitation that occurs from October 1 to September 30 of the following year. The WY year is used to account for moisture that accumulates in the soil after harvest but before the start of the calendar year. Precipitation that falls during the growing season is critical for maize growth and maturation. Table 4.1 illustrates the Daymet (Thornton et al. 2020) environmental data for the gardens and suggests the MCG received more cumulative moisture during the water year than the PLC, POG, or CDG. Although some individual summer storms did provide more moisture to the campus gardens than to the MCG, the MCG received more moisture during the growing season, allowing for more moisture to enter the soil column when the maize was growing and maturing. In some years, such as 2015, the precipitation

TABLE 4.1. Environmental data and yields for the PFP Gardens.

Growing Season Precipitation (May 24–September 24) in Centimeters						
Year	2015	2016	2017	2018	2019	Average
Mike Coffey Garden	28.1	20.9	11.2	8.9	7.3	15.28
Campus Gardens	16.0	13.9	9.4	8.4	4.6	10.46

Water Year Precipitation (October 1—September 30) in Centimeters						
Year	2014–2015	2015–2016	2016–2017	2017–2018	2018–2019	Average
Mike Coffey Garden	53.7	58.5	40.8	17.4	51.7	44.42
Campus Gardens	37.9	39.5	40.2	14.7	40.2	34.5

Cumulative GDDs (Degrees Fahrenheit)						
Year	2015	2016	2017	2018	2019	Average
Mike Coffey Garden	1,772.55	1,863.45	1,973.70	2,097.90	1,872.45	1,916.01
Campus Gardens	2,263.05	2,303.1	2,346.75	2,425.95	2,249.55	2,317.68

Yields per Garden kg/ha						
Year	2015	2016	2017	2018	2019	Average
CDG	355	897	1,461	0	1,259	794.40
MCG	2,567	708	1,817	1,032	2,520	1,728.80
PLC	305	302	154	0	79	168.00
POG	674	94	498	13	149	258.60

Source: Table by authors.

difference was especially pronounced, and the difference resulted in higher yields for the MCG compared to campus gardens.

Precipitation that falls after the previous harvest, and prior to the next planting, influences overall soil moisture and yields. This precipitation provides soil moisture for seed germination and early-stage growth until summer monsoons arrive. The importance of this moisture can be seen in 2018 data. In that year, both the MCG and campus gardens received similar (and scant) overall precipitation during the growing season, with only about 5 mm of precipitation separating the two garden locations (table 4.1). In terms of the entire WY however, the MCG received 27 mm more precipitation, and most of that fell prior to planting outside of the growing season. Yields from the MCG outperformed any of the campus gardens, which produced little-to-no yields. Greater winter moisture accumulations in the upland garden area, though not the only factor influencing greater yields at the MCG in 2018, allowed for better conditions at the time of planting and through the early growing season.

Differences in soil composition between the MCG and campus gardens influence how they absorb and retain available moisture. The MCG soils have more clay at every level of the rooting column, grading from clay loam at shallower depths to clay at around 37 to 60 inches of depth. Due to the high clay content, water permeability is slow, but these sediments hold more moisture in the root zone allowing for increased maize production (Benson 2011; Dominguez and Kolm 2005).

Soils in the campus gardens possess less clay and are classified as loams with slightly better water permeability. More site-specific analysis of sediments in the POG, PLC, and CDG also suggest that although there are broad similarities in attributes, subtle—but important—differences are also present in the campus gardens. For instance, the sandier soils in the PLC allow for increased water permeability; however, these soils retain less moisture than the POG, which has higher clay content and potentially deeper sediments (Fadem and Diederichs 2019).

The importance of overall precipitation and soil characteristics is reflected in the cumulative soil moisture data shown in figure 4.3. Beginning in 2015, and in partnership with the University of North Texas, and specifically Dr. Steve Wolverton and Dr. Lisa Nagaoka, soil temperature and moisture sensors were placed in three of the PFP gardens (CDG, PLC, and MCG) and have comparable data through 2019. A moisture monitor was also added to the POG in 2020. Sensors were deployed at three depths: 15 cm, 30 cm, and 45 cm below the modern ground surface. We used Decagon Devices 5TM soil temperature and moisture sensors in tandem with Em50 series data loggers to collect data. These sensors recorded the temperature (°C) and the amount of water vapor (expressed in m^3 of vapor water content per m^3 of soil) every hour over the course of their deployment. These data are depicted in figure 4.3, with the teal line representing the MCG at each depth, the solid red line representing the average of the campus gardens at each depth, and the light red bars indicating the high and low values across the campus gardens.

The primary difference between the MCG and the campus is the stable and relatively high level of moisture retained at 45 cm at the MCG. The values for the 15 cm and 30 cm depths are broadly similar across all gardens, although they do fluctuate in response to specific storms or precipitation events. At 45 cm of depth, the MCG retains much more moisture, and that level is remarkably stable throughout the year compared to the other gardens. This is at least partly a function of more precipitation at the MCG, the higher clay content of the soils, and the depth of soils in the field.

In addition to precipitation and soil characteristics, differences in ambient temperature between the MCG and the campus gardens affect the amount of soil moisture present, which, in turn, influences the rate of evapotranspiration in the plants. The previous section on GDDs suggests that temperatures are slightly cooler at the MCG compared to the campus gardens. Maximum growth rates for maize occur at about 30°C (86°F), higher temperatures increase soil

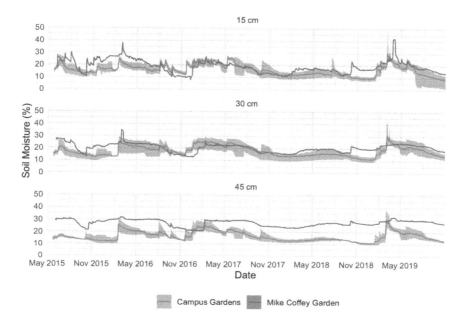

FIGURE 4.3. *Soil moisture measurements at the PFP gardens at 15, 30, and 45 cm depths. Soil moisture is measured as volumetric water content, m³/m³. The lighter ribbon represents the range of soil moisture values at the campus gardens, the darker line represents the average soil moisture value across the campus gardens, and the teal line represents the soil moisture value for the MCG. Data are shown from May 23, 2015, through May 2019. Courtesy of Crow Canyon Archaeological Center.*

evaporation, reduce stored moisture, and cause the plant to wilt. Finally, the northern aspect of the MCG also reduces exposure to wind and solar radiation, further helping to retain soil moisture.

DISCUSSION

Determining whether Hopi seed and Hopi farming practices would succeed in the central Mesa Verde region represents an important goal of the PFP and something especially meaningful for the Hopi members of the team. Our experimental farming project demonstrates that Hopi seed and farming techniques indeed do produce yields, and in the case of the MCG garden exceptionally abundant yields. A heuristic example illustrates just how exceptional. Ethnographic accounts estimate a desirable goal of producing 160 kg of maize per person per year (Adams et al. 2006, 52; Van West 1994, 125), or 1,120 kg for a family of seven. We can also assume that to buffer years with poor production, Pueblo farmers likely planted a field large enough to feed that family for three years, or 3,360 kg of maize. The average MCG yields (1,728.80 kg/hectare) would require a field size of about 1.9 hectares to meet this need. The average yield from most productive campus garden—the Check Dam Garden—would require a field of 4.2 hectares to produce a three-year supply of maize for a family of seven. These figures can be compared to Ernest Beaglehole's (1937, 37) observation that Hopi families in the early 1900s typically planted fields about 2.8 hectares in size.

In the preceding sections we described the differences between the MCG and campus gardens in terms of setting, soils, temperature, growing season, and precipitation. These differences result in the MCG garden having greater and more stable soil moisture, especially moisture deep in the soil profile. The difference in soil moisture translates into MCG yields that are four times greater than those from the combined average of the campus gardens. Hopi farmers noted that another factor that could contribute to higher MCG garden productivity is that this field had been rotated, with beans planted every third year, before we started planting there. Quantifying these variables and their effect on yields represents an important contribution of the PFP. But the dramatic differences in yields documented by the PFP also contribute to our understanding of ancestral Pueblo maize farming in the central Mesa Verde region and whether drought alone forced farmers to migrate from the region. We focus on three points here.

First, the consistently high yields from the MCG support an important point made by the computer models that estimate agricultural productivity in the central Mesa Verde region (Schwindt et al. 2016; Van West 1994). The best lands would have produced yields even during years when environmental conditions were significantly below average, including the late AD 1200s, when ancestral Pueblo people migrated from the region (see Kuckelman, chapter 19 in this volume for a discussion of environmental downturn and regional depopulation). For example, the summer of 2018 was among the driest on record in the Four Corners region. In fact, the ongoing megadrought since the year 2000 ranks as the driest period over the last 1,200+ years (Williams, Cook, Smerdon et al. 2022; Williams, Cook, Smerdon, Cook et al. 2020). Even during the 2018 drought, the MCG still produced significant yields (median: 1,019 kg/ha; mean: 1,032 kg/ha), whereas the Crow Canyon campus gardens produced only negligible yields. Even unprecedented drought—clearly the most important climate hazard for ancestral Pueblo maize farmers in the central Mesa Verde region—could not eliminate production on the best lands for maize farming.

Second, the central Mesa Verde region population peaked in the mid-AD 1200s, and this forced some farmers to cultivate areas with below-average productivity (Schwindt et al. 2016). Researchers argue that differences in productivity increased conflict and contributed to the depopulation of the region (Kuckelman 2010, 2016, chapter 19 in this volume; Schwindt et al. 2016). The MCG clearly represents exceptional agricultural land, and we believe farming occurred there during earlier periods because a large, late Pueblo I and early Pueblo II (AD 880 to 980) village, named the Gillota-Johnson site, lies just 650 m to the west. Reliable springs, abundant wild resources, and easy access to hunting in the uplands east of the Dolores River also characterize the locale. Yet virtually no thirteenth-century AD settlement occurs in this area. If competition for land forced some to cultivate marginal areas, why did ancestral Pueblo farmers avoid the prime lands around MCG that had been previously farmed? Was there some other factor that kept ancestral Pueblo farmers from cultivating this area? Answering these questions will be a focus of future research.

Finally, Hopi oral traditions provide information on the migrations that left the central Mesa Verde region depopulated at the end of the thirteenth century AD (Kuwanwisiwma and Bernardini, chapter 5 in this volume). Stewart Koyiyumptewa is a member of the Badger Clan, and clan history identifies the central Mesa Verde region as the clan's homeland; he notes that when the Badger Clan migrated from the region, they were one of the last clans to arrive at the Hopi mesas. When asked about this migration, Stewart said, "You know, there's theories about famine and drought. I think we could have survived here. We weren't necessarily forced to go. It was a choice, to be part of this much bigger cultural group. They moved to join this one religious culture where the ceremonial calendar is divided by the ceremonies of the northern clans and those of the clans that migrated to Hopi from the south. That was why they left this area, to form this unique cultural system that combined the different clan groups from the south and the north" (Zoom meeting, March 17, 2021).

Initiated by the Hopi Cultural Preservation Office, the PFP investigates maize and maize farming as one of the central features of what Hopis call their "corn culture." That corn culture also characterizes the other Pueblo nations, and corn is important to most Indigenous cultures of the Southwestern United States. For Crow Canyon, the PFP represents an important project that advances the Center's mission by integrating research, education, and American Indian partnerships. The experimental farming component of the PFP has become the most thoroughly documented long-term experiment of its kind. The ability to sustain this project for fifteen years exemplifies Crow Canyon's founding vision of supporting long-term research and education programs.

NOTE

1. We report GDD in Fahrenheit units here. To convert to Celsius GDD, simply divide by 1.8.

REFERENCES

Adams, Charles E. 1979. "Cold Air Drainage and the Length of Growing Season in the Hopi Mesas Area." *Kiva* 44 (4): 285–296.

Adams, Karen R., Cathryn M. Meegan, Scott G. Ortman, R. Emerson Howell, Lindsay C. Werth, Deborah A. Muenchrath, Michael K. O'Neill, and Candice A. C. Gardner. 2006. "MAÍS (Maize of American Indigenous Societies) Southwest: Ear Descriptions and Traits that Distinguish 27 Morphologically Distinct Groups of 123 Historic USDA Maize (Zea mays L. Mays)." Accessions and Data Relevant to Archaeological Subsistence models. JSMF Grant #21002035. Research Report to the James S. McDonnell Foundation.

Adams, Karen R., Deborah A. Muenchrath, and Dylan M. Schwindt. 1999. "Moisture Effects on the Morphology of Ears, Cobs and Kernels of a North American Maize Cultivar, and Implications for the Interpretation of Archaeological Maize." *Journal of Archaeological Sciences* 26.5 (May): 483–496.

Beaglehole, Ernest. 1937. "Notes on Hopi Economic Life." Yale University Publications in Anthropology No. 15. Yale University Press, New Haven, CT.

Bellorado, Benjamin A. 2007. "Breaking Down the Models: Reconstructing Prehistoric Subsistence Agriculture in the Durango District of Southwestern Colorado." MA thesis, Department of Anthropology, Northern Arizona University, Flagstaff.

Bellorado, Benjamin A. 2009. "Reconstruction of Prehistoric Subsistence Agriculture in Ridges Basin." In *Animas-La Plata Project*. Vol 13, Special Studies, edited by James M. Potter, 215–233. Phoenix: SWCA Environmental Consultants.

Benson, Larry V. 2010. "Factors Controlling Pre-Columbian and Early Historic Maize Productivity in the American Southwest." Part 1: "The Southern Colorado Plateau and Rio Grande Regions." U.S. Geological Survey, Boulder, CO.

Benson, Larry V. 2011. "Factors Controlling Pre-Columbian and Early Historic Maize Productivity in the American Southwest." Part 2: "The Chaco Halo, Mesa Verde, Pajarito Plateau / Bandelier, and Zuni Archaeological Regions." U.S. Geological Survey, Boulder, CO.

Bocinsky, R. Kyle, and Mark D. Varien. 2017. "Comparing Maize Paleoproduction Models with Experimental Data." *Journal of Ethnobiology* 37 (2): 282–307. (Published by the Society of Ethnobiology.)

Bousselot, Jennifer M., D. Muenchrath, A. D. Knapp, and J. D. Reeder. 2017. "Emergence and Seedling Characteristics of Maize Native to the Southwestern US." *American Journal of Plant Sciences* 8 (06): 1304–1318.

Bye, Robert A., Jr., and Rita Shuster. 1984. "Developing an Integrated Model for Contemporary and Archaeological Agricultural Subsistence Systems." In *Prehistoric Agricultural Strategies in the Southwest*, edited by Suzanne K. Fish and Paul R. Fish, 125–146. Arizona State University Anthropological Research Papers No. 33, Tempe.

Clark, S. P. 1928. "Lesson from Southwestern Indian Agriculture." University of Arizona College of Agriculture, Agricultural Experiment Station. Bulletin No. 125. University Station, Tucson.

Cushing, Frank, S. (1974) 1920. *Zuni Breadstuff.* Indian Notes and Monographs No. 8. Museum of the American Indian, Heye Foundation, New York.

Collins, G. N. 1914. "A Drought-Resisting Adaptation in Seedlings of Hopi Maize." *Journal of Agricultural Research* 1 (January): 293–307.

Dominguez, Steven, and Kenneth Kolm. 2005. "Beyond Water Harvesting: Perspective on Traditional Southwestern Agricultural Technology." *American Antiquity* 70 (4): 732–765.

Ermigiotti, Paul, Mark Varien, Erin Bohm, Kyle Bocinsky, the Hopi Cultural Preservation Office, and the Hopi Cultural Resources Advisory Team. 2020. "The Pueblo Farming Project: A Collaboration between Hopi Farmers and the Crow Canyon Archaeological Center." http://pfp.crowcanyon.org.

Fadem, Cynthia M., and Shanna R. Diederichs. 2019. "Farming the Great Sage Plain: Experimental Agroarchaeology and the Basketmaker III Soil Record." *Culture, Agriculture, Food and Environment* 42 (1): 4–15. https://doi.org/10.1111/CUAG.12241.

Forde, C. Daryll 1931. "Hopi Agriculture and Land Ownership." *The Journal of the Royal Anthropological Institute of Great Britain and Ireland* 61 (July–December): 357–405.

Franke, Paul R., and Don Watson. 1936. *An Experimental Garden in Mesa Verde National Park.* Symposium on Prehistoric Agriculture, University of New Mexico, Albuquerque.

Gillreath-Brown, Andrew, Lisa Nagaoka, and Steve S. Wolverton. 2019. "A Geospatial Method for Estimating Soil Moisture Variability in Prehistoric Agricultural Landscapes." *PLoS ONE* 14 (8): e0220457.

Hack, John T. 1942. "The Changing Physical Environment of the Hopi Indians of Arizona." *Papers of the Peabody Museum of American Archaeology and Ethnology* 35 (1). Harvard University, Cambridge.

Hammett, Julia E., and Anita B. Hornback. 1984. "The 1977 Garden Experiments at Hovenweep." In *Hovenweep 1977.* Archaeological Report No. 4, edited by Julia Hammett and Nancy Olsen, 35–52. San Jose, CA: Anthropology Department, San José State University.

Kuckelman, Kristin A. 2010. "The Depopulation of Sand Canyon Pueblo, a Large Ancestral Pueblo Village in Southwestern Colorado." *American Antiquity* 75 (3): 497–525.

Kuckelman Kristin A. 2016. "Cycles of Subsistence Stress, Warfare, and Population Movement in the Northern San Juan." In *The Archaeology of Food and Warfare,* edited by A. VanDerwarker and A. G. Wilson. Cham, Germany: Springer. https://doi.org/10.1007/978-3-319-18506-4_6.

Kuwanwisiwma, Leigh J. 2005. "The Hopi Way: Dry Farming." In *Thirst for Survival: The Hopi Struggle to Preserve the Past, Ensure the Future.* A publication of the Hopi Tribe and Ascend Media. Spring 2005.

Litzinger, William J. 1976. "The Experimental Garden Project, 1975." In *Hovenweep 1975.* Archaeological Report No. 2, edited by Joseph Winter, 177–190. San Jose, CA: Anthropology Department, San José State University.

Muenchrath, Deborah A., and Ricardo J. Salvador. 1995. "Maize Productivity and Agro-ecology: Effects of Environment and Agricultural Practices on the Biology of Maize." In *Soil, Water, Biology and Belief in Prehistoric and Traditional Southwestern Agriculture*, edited by H. Wolcott Toll, 303–333. Albuquerque: New Mexico Archaeological Council Special Publication 2.

Neild, Ralph E., and James E. Newman. n.d. NCH-40 (National Corn Handbook). Purdue University Cooperative Extension Service, West Lafayette, IN. ag.purdue.edu.

Schwindt, Dylan M., R. Kyle Bocinsky, Scott G. Ortman, Donna M. Glowacki, Mark D. Varien, and Timothy A. Kohler. 2016. "The Social Consequences of Climate Change in the Central Mesa Verde Region." *American Antiquity* 81 (1): 74–96.

Shaw, R. H. 1988. Climate Requirement. In *Corn and Corn Improvement*, edited by G. F. Sprague and J. W. Dudley, 609–638. Madison: American Society of Agronomy.

Shuster, Rita. 1981. "Factors Affecting Productivity in Subsistence Agriculture." MA thesis, Department of Environmental, Population, and Organismic Biology, University of Colorado, Boulder.

Shuster, Rita. 1983. *Preliminary Report: Demonstration and Experimental Garden Studies 1979 and 1980*. Dolores Archaeological Program Technical Report. Submitted to Cultural Resources Mitigation Program: Dolores Project Bureau of Reclamation, Upper Colorado Region, Contract No. 8-07-40-S0562.

Simon, Chris, dir. 2016. *More than Planting a Seed*. DVD. Produced by Shirley Powell and Marjorie Connolly. Cortez, CO: Crow Canyon Archaeological Center. DVD. Accessed January 26, 2021. https://www.youtube.com/watch?v=2x23FF_kUyo.

Soil Survey Staff, Natural Resources Conservation Service, United States Department of Agriculture. 2020. Soil Survey Geographic (SSURGO) Database for [Cortez Area, Parts of Dolores and Montezuma Counties, Colorado]. https://websoilsurvey.nrcs.usda.gov/.

Swarts, Kelly. 2017. "GBS Genotyping and Analysis of In Situ Hopi Germplasm." Manuscript on file, Crow Canyon Archaeological Center and the Hopi Cultural Preservation Office.

Thornton, M. M., R. Shrestha, Y. Wei, P. E. Thornton, S. Kao, and B. E. Wilson. 2020. "Daymet: Daily Surface Weather Data on a 1-km Grid for North America, Version 4." ORNL DAAC, Oak Ridge, TN. https://doi.org/10.3334/ORNLDAAC/1840.

Troyer, Forrest A. 1997. "The Location of Genes Governing Long First Internode of Corn." *Genetics* 145 (4): 1149–1154.

Utah State University Analytical Laboratories. 2009. Soil Testing Report. On file, Crow Canyon Archaeological Center, Cortez, CO.

Van West, C. R. 1994. "Modeling Prehistoric Agricultural Productivity in Southwestern Colorado: A GIS Approach." Reports of Investigations 67. Department of Anthropology, Washington State University, Pullman, WA, and Crow Canyon, Cortez, CO.

Van West, Carla R., and Dean, Jeffery S. 2000. "Environmental Characteristics of the A.D. 900–1300 Period in the Central Mesa Verde Region." *Kiva* 66 (1): 19–44.

Varien, Mark D., Shirley Powell, and Leigh Kuwanwisiwma. 2018. "The Genetic Diversity of Hopi Corn." In *Footprints of Hopi History: Hopihiniwtiput Kukveni'at*, edited by L. J. Kuwanwisiwma, T. J. Ferguson, and C. Colwell, 157–177. Tucson: University of Arizona Press.

Wall, Dennis, and Virgil Masayesva. 2004. "People of the Corn." In *American Indian Quarterly* 28 (3 and 4): 435–453.

Whiting, Alfred F. 1966. *Ethnobotany of the Hopi.* Reprint. New York: AMS Press. Originally published 1939, by Northern Arizona Society of Science and Art, Bulletin No.15, Museum of Northern Arizona, Flagstaff.

Williams, A. Park, Benjamin I. Cook, and Jason E. Smerdon. 2022. "Rapid Intensification of the Emerging Southwestern North American Megadrought in 2020–2021." *Nature Climate Change* 12 (February 14): 232–234.

Williams, A. Park, Edward R. Cook, Jason E. Smerdon, Benjamin I. Cook, John T. Abatzoglou, Kasey Bolles, Seung H. Baek, Andrew M. Badger, and Ben Livneh. 2020. "Large Contribution from Anthropogenic Warming to an Emerging North American Megadrought." *Science* 368 (6488): 314–318.

Winter, Joseph C., L. Casjens, P. Hogan, B. Noisat, and J. Hammet. 1977. *Hovenweep 1976.* Archeological Report, no. 2. San Jose, CA: San José State University.

5

Place of the Songs

Hopi Connections to the Mesa Verde Region

LEIGH KUWANWISIWMA AND WESLEY BERNARDINI

Hopi connections to the Mesa Verde region have been noted by anthropologists and archaeologists for more than a century (see Anyon 1999; Steinbrecher and Hopkins 2019). Anthropologist Florence Hawley Ellis (1967, 36), for example, identified Keresan words and influences in Hopi ceremonies, leading her to connect Hopi clans with a Keresan homeland in the Four Corners area (see Ortman 2012 for a recent perspective on Keresan origins). Almost a century ago, archaeologist Jesse Walter Fewkes (1924, 378) commented on continuities between the ancient inhabitants of Mesa Verde and the Hopi people, noting that "several idols are peculiar to certain clans (Snake and others) and . . . those Walpi idols that were reputed to have been brought from the north are identical with idols of the cliff dwellers. We may interpret this similarity as one more evidence, supporting many others, that the ancestors of certain clans of the Hopi were cliff dwellers."

Somewhat surprisingly, Mesa Verde is not explicitly mentioned by name in some of the older, commonly cited collections of Hopi clan migration traditions (e.g., Fewkes 1900; Stephen 1936; Voth 1905). These omissions can be explained in part by considering when, and how, Hopi clan traditions have come to be

https://doi.org/10.5876/9781646424597.c005

documented, and by recognizing that narrators and recorders did not always use the same geographic labels that archaeologists use today. The earliest researchers who documented Hopi clan traditions, such as Fewkes and Alexander Stephen, worked at a time when archaeologists had very few techniques to establish the ages of the ancient sites they studied. At Mesa Verde National Park, Fewkes correctly (if vaguely) interpreted the lack of historical objects in the cliff dwellings to mean that the sites dated to the "stone age," with an estimated antiquity of 500 to 1000 years before present (Fewkes 1911, 80–81). But he misinterpreted Spanish historical documents to indicate that the Homol'ovi Pueblos were occupied into the AD 1600s (Fewkes 1900, 598). When Hopi consultants told Fewkes that clans "from the east" arrived *after* those that passed through the Homol'ovi villages, Fewkes may have concluded that the occupation of Mesa Verde greatly predated the period of Hopi clan migrations documented in oral traditions. Fewkes's time living in Hopi villages also preceded his excavations in Mesa Verde cliff dwellings by about a decade, perhaps explaining his failure to overtly query Hopi consultants about ancestral ties to Mesa Verde. Finally, "eastern" Hopi clans were often discussed in connection with the Tewa region and language, leading Fewkes to conclude they originated in the Tewa region of the Rio Grande Valley. More recent research (Ortman 2012) indicates that for at least some eastern clans, the Rio Grande was a point on a longer migration pathway that stretches back to the Mesa Verde region in the AD 1200s.

Contemporary Hopi people are unambiguous about the strong connections between Hopi and the Mesa Verde region. Hopi Tribal member Leroy Lewis (as quoted in Anyon 1999, 31), for example, noted that the Hopi name for Mesa Verde proper is included in sacred Hopi songs, a fact that demonstrates that "we are deeply affiliated with these sites." Interviews with Hopi people have documented at least twenty-seven clans with traditional connections to the Mesa Verde region (Anyon 1999; Steinbrecher and Hopkins 2019) (table 5.1).

HOPI CONNECTIONS TO THE MESA VERDE REGION

The remainder of this chapter presents an interview with Leigh Kuwanwisiwma, a Greasewood Clan member from the village of Paaqavi on Third Mesa, about Hopi connections to the Mesa Verde region. The interview was conducted with Wesley Bernardini on December 2, 2020, in Leigh's home in Paaqavi. Leigh Kuwanwisiwma was the founding director of the Hopi Cultural Preservation Office (HCPO), which he led for twenty-eight years until his retirement in 2017. In Hopi society, traditional knowledge is held within individual clans and ceremonial societies, but Leigh's role as HCPO director enabled him to interact with a wide range of knowledgeable Hopi people and these interactions provide him with a uniquely broad perspective on Hopi history that complements information passed on to Mr. Kuwanwisiwma within the Greasewood Clan and its

TABLE 5.1. Hopi clans with connections to the Mesa Verde region.

Hopi Name	English Gloss	Associated Hopi Village(s)
Kwanngyam	Agave Clan	Orayvi
Hoongyam	Arrow	Orayvi
Honangyam	Badger Clan	Orayvi, Wàlpi, Musangnuvi
Honngyam	Bear Clan	Songòopavi
Piqösngyam	Bearstrap Clan	Songòopavi
Aawatngyam	Bow Clan	Orayvi
Kokongyam	Burrowing Owl Clan	Orayvi
Poovolngyam	Butterfly Clan	Songòopavi
Tsaakwaynangyam	Chakwaina Clan	Songòopavi
Isngyam	Coyote Clan	Orayvi
Angwusngyam	Crow Clan	Wàlpi
Alngyam	Deer Clan	Wàlpi
Kwaangyam	Eagle Clan	Songòopavi
Kookopngyam	Fire Clan	Orayvi
Lenngyam	Flute Clan	Wàlpi
Tepngyam	Greasewood Clan	Orayvi
Honangyam	Gray Badger	Unspecified
Katsinngyam	Katsina Clan	Orayvi, Songòopavi, Musangnuvi, Wàlpi
Kuukutsngyam	Lizard Clan	Unspecified
Tapngyam	Rabbit Clan	Unspecified
Tsu'ngyam	Rattlesnake Clan	Orayvi, Musangnuvi, Wàlpi
Paaqapngyam	Reed (Bamboo) Clan	Orayvi, Wàlpi
Hospo'ngyam	Roadrunner Clan	Orayvi
Hospo'ngyam	Roadrunner Clan	Wàlpi
Tuwangyam	Sand Clan	Orayvi
Pipnmgyam	Tobacco Clan	Unspecified
Piikyasngyam	Young Corn	Munqapi

phratry members, the Bow and Bamboo Clans. Leigh Kuwanwisiwma's willingness to share selected traditional knowledge for the purpose of documenting Hopi history exemplifies the contrast between Western and eastern Pueblo stances on secrecy as discussed by Joe Suina, chapter 7 in this volume. The unedited interview transcript has been annotated to provide additional information, clarifications, and references.

The history of the Hopi people is far reaching, if you take all the traditions, the clan traditions and later the collected Tribal traditions. It really teaches the Hopi knowledge way back into prehistory, going into what the people refer to as the final or "fourth way" of life. The essence of this history really centers around the Southwest particularly. The Hopis went through three prior worlds and then finally into South and North America and then focusing on the Southwest, where the Hopis are really prominent in terms of habitation and where their traditions are the strongest.

Mesa Verde is one of the areas in the Southwest with strong Hopi traditions. Over time, after the emergence into North America by the different clans from South America and so forth, they met up with different clans that were already residing here in North America. Those resident clans were the people we call the *Motisinom*, the "first people." And then the ones coming from the south are the *Nùutungkwisinom*, the "last people."[1] Today, Hopi society is comprised of two cultures, the North and South American cultures. Part of the North American culture that we talk about today is the emergence into this current way of life, and the southern clans now having to learn how to live in this desert, because the South American clans came from tropical rainforests, so they had to learn how to survive here. The *Motisinom* who were already here taught us to learn how to survive. Of course, the gift of corn, by our spiritual leader *Màasaw*, enabled us to be able to survive here in this semiarid land that is the Southwest today. Part of the history is the big migration traditions of the southern clans. We were told to go in the four directions and establish our footprints out there. And that's the prehistory of the Hopi people.

So over time you can see that the archaeology out in the Southwest is enormous, hundreds of thousands of archaeological sites that have endured time. Because Hopi clans were told specifically to build their homes with rock and also to scatter pottery so that it would endure and preserve the legacy of the Hopi people. And that's what clans did throughout the migration period as they moved from one place to another. Sometimes they collected with other clans who later became phratries,[2] and some independently were still following other groups of Hopi clans. So, the prehistory of the region is enormous and really establishes our principles of life and respect for our history, which became part of our religious teachings today.

So, if you look at the migrations, they lasted for hundreds and hundreds of years. We were told to look for a sign from the heavens, revealed through the appearance of what the Hopis refer to as the "blue star." The blue star was seen during the day too, it was a big phenomenon, that was the sign that Hopis were looking for to enter their final migrations. Scientists say this was the supernova of AD 1054, that was what the Hopis saw, and it ended the migrations of the Hopi clans. A lot of evidence is out there through petroglyphs in particular, especially the spiral, which is the migration symbol of Hopi clans. So that occurred, then we were told that once the migrations ended, clans were to come together at different places and share their respective clan migration histories and present some of their ceremonies to each other.

So, this became part of this era that Mesa Verde is a part of. The Hopis call Mesa Verde Tawtaykya—it means the "Place of the Songs." Spruce Tree House is called Salapa, "Spruce Springs Village." Those are some of the prominent place names that Hopis use to refer to Mesa Verde today.[3] Mesa Verde was then beginning to be inhabited by the first people, the *Motisinom*, and also the people who came from the south. Prominent in terms of some of the early occupation of the Mesa Verde area were *Motisinom* groups such as the Katsina, Badger, Gray Badger, Rabbit, and Tobacco Clans. Those were clans that had lived around that area and were sort of hosts to other clans that were converging into Mesa Verde. I call them the "convergence places"—the places where people were beginning to settle into the villages of Mesa Verde or adjacent areas such as the Ute Mountain Tribal Park.[4] That's where my clan, the Greasewood Clan, lived for a while, right in that Tribal park area. I base it on my observation of petroglyphs and so forth. So that was occurring. Later, other clans began to go over there, including the Flute, Parrot, Greasewood, Bow, and Third Mesa Bamboo Clans. Those are the prominent clans that I know about.

So, Mesa Verde is significant in that it was bringing the clans together after hundreds of years of migration. And the purpose was to share migration experiences, to share their wisdom, share their teaching, share some of the ceremonies that they were carrying. A lot of ceremonies were fully revived in Mesa Verde such as *Powamuy* (the Bean Dance), which began to be the prominent ceremony in Mesa Verde.[5] Of course, other clans performed their own respective ceremonies such as the Flute Ceremony. The other ceremony that was performed was the *Sa'lako* Dance.[6] At least, this was the first time that the ceremony was actually performed publicly. And later, the full ceremony of *Sa'lako* was perfected at Aztec Pueblo and carried into Chaco by the Bow, Greasewood, and Bamboo Clans. So, the *Sa'lako* Dance was also performed up there. It became a habitation period for all these clans to establish themselves and also to leave other evidence, such as what archaeologists call T-shaped doorways that were put into the architecture by Hopi clans. The T-shaped doorway represents the hairdo of our spiritual leader *Màasaw*, with the chin on the bottom and the bangs on each side of head. That's what the Hopis were told to put in there because we were carrying out *Màasaw*'s covenant with us, which was to migrate and put our footprints as evidence out there. That was the way Hopi clans put their insignia in Mesa Verde.

We survived for a period of time until spiritual people, through prayer, were now receiving final instructions as to what the final destination would be. In the interim, the Mesa Verde people interacted with other convergence places such as *Hoo'ovai* (Aztec Pueblo) or even faraway places such as Chaco. The Bears Ears National Monument area was very prominent with a lot of clans up there.[7] Mesa Verde clans interacted with people up in the area we now call Bears Ears. Bear Strap, Snake, Sand, Lizard, Greasewood, Bow, Bamboo, and Flute Clans were up there.[8] Those were the respective clans in Bears Ears that also had their own ceremonies, they say that they shared their ceremonies by invitation with people in Mesa Verde. For example, the Bears Ears people heard about the Bean Dance and asked the Badger and Katsina Clans to come up and perform it during the winter. So that's what happened in one particular instance. Of course, the Flute Clan had the Flute Ceremony up at Bears Ears, and they were invited to come up to Mesa Verde to perform. And they were welcomed in Mesa Verde, and the Flute Clan never went back to Bears Ears. They were asked to stay permanently, because during the ceremony there was a lot of rain, leading to good harvests in Mesa Verde, so Flute was asked to stay permanently until finally instructed to come out to the Hopi Mesas.

Clans at Mesa Verde who were at the top of the hierarchy at those villages were the Katsina and Badger people, they were the ones determining whether clans should perform ceremonies at the villages. Katsina and Badger were very prominent in terms of leadership. As leading clans did later in the Hopi Mesas, they were assigning farming lands, determining the ceremonial calendar to be put into place—things like that were occurring under the leadership of those clans that were the first inhabitants of those villages. The Bow Clan was so powerful that Katsina and Badger didn't allow Bow to perform, because they were a really prominent clan from *Palatkwapi*, and their reputation followed them.[9] So, when Bow and our phratry went to Mesa Verde they weren't allowed to perform their ceremonies, because they were too powerful. So, they never performed up there, but did eventually perform their Two Horn ceremonies at Aztec. They were the ones that built the great kiva and performed *Sa'lako* up there as well. They were really prominent, but perhaps prominent in a way that would distract from the simplicity of the Katsina Dances and Bean Dances. Greasewood people were allowed to perform a medicinal ceremony, the *Yaya't* (Hopi Magician Society), plus four *katsinam* that we call the *Somaykoli*, the four cardinal colors, blue, red, yellow, and white. We were allowed to perform that to bring some healing practices into Mesa Verde.

One thing that's interesting in our Greasewood tradition is the fact that Greasewood went from Bears Ears up to the place called Pamöstukwi (Fog Mountain), a pretty prominent place.[10] I went there to see, and sure enough the mountain had a lot of clouds that settled on the base of the mountain. That's where they migrated to, and then we were on verge of starvation, the Greasewood people, when another group of people came in. Apparently, these were the Ute people, that was their homeland around that area, they were the ones that met up with the Greasewood Clan, brought them bison pelts and bison meat, and that's how the Greasewood people were able to survive out there.[11] It was the Utes who told them there were other clans now in the Mesa Verde region. So, we asked them to lead us there. In our tradition, it was the Utes who led us to the Mesa Verde area. Greasewood settled in Ute Mountain Tribal Park.

Up in the Mesa Verde area, particularly toward Chimney Rock,[12] the Hopi clans who went that far east reported conflict with—I don't know which tribe—but they were the ones that experienced that. I don't know if it's maybe Plains tribes that went west, like the Comanche, or Kiowa or even the Utes. But they experienced that up in the Chimney Rock area. Whereas, in my clan tradition, we had a good strong tradition with Utes, we still call them our brothers and sisters, and vice versa too. So, different types of experiences in the Mesa Verde area.

So, a lot of history, if you get into the specific clan traditions. It was in the Mesa Verde area that Greasewood and Bow and Bamboo, among others, met a culture of pygmies, small people that had a lot of physical prowess, keen eyesight, good runners, good warriors, very territorial. Initially, the pygmies didn't allow some of the Hopi clans to enter into their territory. Eventually, we made a pact with them, and they are now called the Warrior Twins.[13] They originally came from Aztec, New Mexico. They finally entered into a peace pact to protect Hopi clans as they journeyed.

So, all of these things were the dynamics of the villages. For perhaps 100–200 years, these big settlements such as Chaco, Aztec, Salmon, Zuni, Homol'ovi, Wupatki, Tawtaykya, those were the prominent Hopi convergence places. And there was interaction between those villages. At Homol'ovi, the Zunis were there with the Hopis. They went back and forth to share their ceremonies from Zuni to Homol'ovi, for example. So, these were the dynamics of these villages until the ceremonies were fully resurrected and completed and clans were satisfied that, because of their ceremonies, they were now worthy enough to go on their final footsteps which led them to the Hopi Mesas. Today, all of these ceremonies that were developed in those major villages are still practiced here on Hopi as a way to remember their connection to the past.

So, in summary, it's a huge history, that's what we're trying to pass on to the next generation to learn about these clan traditions, so they don't forget. Remember, our ancestral people are still there in those villages. And our evidence is out there to show the future that Hopi clans did indeed make these migrations and establish footprints through the Southwest. So, Mesa Verde is very, very prominent. Right around Mesa Verde are some other big villages, such as Yellow Jacket and other sites that Crow Canyon has mapped and excavated. These are part of the established villages of people who were nearing Mesa Verde and were ready to be called into the convergence places.

So, you see we have so much memory ingrained in ourselves, and we feel good about it, feel good about our connections to these places. How, collectively, clans were able to build the big villages we see in Mesa Verde, contribute as a community to dry farming, rain farming, and were able to produce the additional crops that we still carry on today, particularly corn and some of the bean species, identifying edible wild plants, that was a collective responsibility of people in villages to do so. Gathering of wood was communal too as people pitched in, carried the brush and greasewood out there in the valleys, sometimes even timber—cedar and juniper, pinyon, all collected for the clans to survive the harsh winters up there. Of course, they purposefully built the villages in alcoves facing southwest to get the most out of the moving sun, especially during winter, that was purposeful. They say that habitation rooms were small, just one room, a common room where family lived, and that way they used a minimum of fuelwood to keep the small houses warm during the winter.

Everything was carefully thought out, people began to prepare, and then finally the final messages came in from the spiritual people. They were now going to be led to their final home, the destiny of Hopi clans. That's where the final migrations began to occur from all of these areas I mentioned, to the center of the universe, *Tuuwanasavi*, the center place. That began the settlements of Awat'ovi, Wàlpi, Songòopavi, Musangnuvi, Orayvi. Those were the Mother villages established after the migrations. Early on, when the convergence places started to occur, a lot of the clans began to interact, like Bears Ears to Mesa Verde, Mesa Verde to Aztec, and Aztec to Chaco. So, when the clans did arrive on the Hopi Mesas, eventually they began to get reacquainted with some of the clans they'd interacted with out there a long time ago. That further solidified the Hopi clans' history on migrations. And particularly the first people, the *Motisinom*, who were hosts at these villages, helped to unify people from these same clans that they knew from a long time ago. That's another form of cultural bond and strength of the Hopi people.

So today, when we reminisce about these traditions, it really helps you solidify your passion for understanding the history of Hopi people. You remember events up there in Mesa Verde that help us get a sense of really belonging even today. We don't abandon these sites, we continue to make pilgrimages up there and we prepare our prayer feathers, we get these directional prayer feathers that we place on our shrines, and up to the northeast when we do that, we remember places like Mesa Verde. So, we don't forget these ancient villages, and that way the culture still is bonding, it's a way to have pride in a humble way about our past and rich history as Hopi people.

NOTES

1. For additional information on the Motisinom ("First People") and Nùutungkwisinom ("the later clans"), see Bernardini (2005); Dongoske et al. (1997); and Hopkins et al. (2021). Nùutungkwisinom are also referred to as the "Palatkwapi clans." Palatkwapi was a time/place in Hopi history when Hopi ancestors resided to the south of the Hopi Mesas, potentially including areas ranging from southern Arizona to Mesoamerica (Ferguson and Lomaomvaya 1999, 76–78). According to Yava (1978, 37), Palatkwapi was destroyed after society fell into *koyaanisqatsi* (a life of moral corruption and turmoil). Clans fled north from Palatkwapi, some eventually finding their way to the Hopi Mesas.

2. There is no Hopi word for phratry, but the clans within a phratry do share social and ceremonial responsibilities and practice exogamy within the phratry (see Connelly 1979; Ferguson 2003).

3. For more on Hopi placenames see Hedquist, Koyiyumptewa, Whiteley et al., (2014) and Hedquist, Koyiyumptewa, Bernardini et al. (2015).

4. For more on convergence places, see Bernardini (2005) (where they are termed "staging areas").

5. In contemporary Hopi villages, Powamuy is a ceremony that purifies the earth ahead of the planting season. In the late 1800s and early 1900, Powamuy was controlled by the Badger Clan. This ceremony is described as being "revived" because a version of it was practiced in the south by Nùutungkwisinom, but the ceremony had ceased to be performed after the destruction of Palatkwapi.

6. The Hopi Sa'lako Ceremony is distinct from the more well-known Zuni performance (what Hopis call the Sio Sa'lako). At Orayvi in the late 1800s and early 1900s, Sa'lako was controlled by the Bow Clan.

7. For more on Hopi connections to Bears Ears, see Chuipka (2022).

8. The fact that the same clan is mentioned as being present in multiple locations reflects the complex fissioning and fusing of clans that occurred over the centuries of their migrations (see Bernardini 2005, 2008). Lineages within clans would periodically split off and journey separately from their clan mates, then sometimes reunite in convergence places or in Hopi villages. Anthropologists distinguish between "the members

of a named, exogamic, stipulated descent category spread over several villages, which is not organized" (a clan) and "the organized members of a named, exogamic, stipulated descent group in a particular village" (a subclan) (Aberle 1970, 218).

9. Leigh Kuwanwisiwma explains that part of the reason for the collapse of Palatkwapi society was the abuse of ritual knowledge. It was this history that made the Katsina and Badger Clans wary of accepting Bow Clan members into Mesa Verde villages (Hopkins et al. 2021:20).

10. An unspecified peak in the Abajo Mountains.

11. On a visit to Cliff Palace in the 1890s, Frederick Chapin met a Ute man named Wap, who told Chapin about a Ute tradition that the *"Moquis* [Hopis] are the descendants of the Cliff-dwellers" (Chapin 1890, 205).

12. For information on Hopi connections to Chimney Rock, see Bernardini and Lomayestewa (2015).

13. The Warrior Twins are Pöqangwhoya (the older) and Palöngawhoya (the younger).

REFERENCES

Aberle, David F. 1970. Comments. In *Reconstructing Prehistoric Pueblo Societies*, edited by W. A. Longacre, 215–223. Albuquerque: University of New Mexico Press.

Anyon, Roger. 1999. *Migrations in the North: Hopi Reconnaissance for the Rocky Mountain Expansion Loop Pipeline*. Prepared for SWCA Environmental Consultants, Inc., Salt Lake City, Utah. Tucson, AZ: Heritage Resources Management Consultants, LLC.

Bernardini, Wesley. 2005. *Hopi Oral Tradition and the Archaeology of Identity*. Tucson: University of Arizona Press.

Bernardini, Wesley. 2008. "Identity as History: Hopi Clans and the Curation of Oral Tradition." *Journal of Anthropological Research* 64 (4): 483–509.

Bernardini, Wesley, and Lee Wayne Lomayestewa. 2015. *Hopi Perspectives on Cultural Resources at Chimney Rock National Monument*. Report submitted to the Chimney Rock National Monument, USFS, Chimney Rock, Colorado.

Chapin, Frederick H. 1890. Cliff Dwellings of the Mancos Canyons. *American Antiquarian* 23 (4): 193–210.

Chuipka, Jason. 2022. *Bears Ears Inter-Tribal Coalition: A Collaborative Land Management Plan for the Bears Ears National Monument*. Prepared on behalf of Bears Ears Inter-Tribal Coalition and Resource Legacy Fund. Woods Canyon Archaeological Consultants, Inc., Cortez, CO.

Connelly, John C. 1979. "Hopi Social Organization." In *Handbook of the North American Indians*. Vol. 9, *Southwest*, edited by Alfonso Ortiz, 539–553. Washington, DC: Smithsonian Institution, Government Printing Office.

Dongoske, Kurt E., Michael Yeatts, Roger Anyon, and T. J. Ferguson. 1997. "Archaeological Cultures and Cultural Affiliation: Hopi and Zuni Perspectives in the American Southwest." *American Antiquity* 62 (4): 600–608.

Ellis, Florence Hawley. 1967. "Where Did Pueblo Peoples Come From?" *El Palacio* (Autumn): 35–43.

Ferguson, T. J., ed. 2003. *Yep Hisat Hoopoq'yaqam Yeesiwa (Hopi Ancestors Were Once Here): Hopi-Hohokam Cultural Affiliation Study.* Kykotsmovi, AZ: Hopi Cultural Preservation Office.

Ferguson, T. J., and Micah Lomaomvaya. 1999. *Hoopoq'yaqam niqw Wukoskyavi (Those Who Went to the Northeast and Tonto Basin): Hopi-Salado Cultural Affiliation Study.* Kykotsmovi, AZ: Hopi Cultural Preservation Office, The Hopi Tribe.

Fewkes, J. W. 1924. *The Use of Idols in Hopi Worship.* Washington, DC: US Government Printing Office.

Fewkes, Jesse Walter. 1900. "Tusayan Migration Traditions." In *Nineteenth Annual Report of the Bureau of American Ethnology*, 573–634. Washington, DC: Smithsonian Institution, Government Printing Office.

Fewkes, Jesse Walter. 1911. *Antiquities of the Mesa Verde National Park: Cliff Palace.* Bureau of American Ethnology, Bulletin 51. Washington, DC: Smithsonian Institution.

Hedquist, Saul L., Stewart B. Koyiyumptewa, Peter M. Whiteley, Leigh J. Kuwanwisiwma, Kenneth C. Hill, and T. J. Ferguson. 2014. "Recording Toponyms to Document the Endangered Hopi Language." *American Anthropologist* 116 (2): 1–8.

Hedquist, S. L., S. B. Koyiyumptewa, W. Bernardini, T. J. Ferguson, P. M. Whiteley, and L. J. Kuwanwisiwma, 2015. "Mapping the Hopi Landscape for Cultural Preservation." *International Journal of Applied Geospatial Research* 6 (1): 40–59.

Hopkins, Maren P. 2021. *Ethnographic Overview of the Bears Ears National Monument.* Report contracted by the Hopi Cultural Preservation Office, Kykotsmovi, in preparation.

Hopkins, Maren P., Leigh Kuwanwisiwma, Stewart B. Koyiyumptewa, and Wesley Bernardini. 2021. "Hopi Perspectives on History." In *Becoming Hopi: A History.* Tucson: University of Arizona Press.

Ortman, Scott G. 2012. *Winds from the North: Tewa Origins and Historical Anthropology.* Salt Lake City: University of Utah Press.

Steinbrecher, Barry P., and Maren P. Hopkins. 2019. "Ethnographic Overview of Canyons of the Ancients National Monument. Report submitted to the Canyons of the Ancients National Monument," Tres Rios Field Office, Bureau of Land Management, Dolores, CO.

Stephen, Alexander McGregor. 1936. *Hopi Journal of Alexander M. Stephen*, edited by Elsie Clews Parsons. New York: Columbia University Press.

Voth, H. R. 1905. *The Traditions of the Hopi.* Field Columbian Museum Anthropological Series 8. Chicago: Field Columbian Museum.

Yava, Albert. 1978. *Big Falling Snow: A Tewa-Hopi Indian's Life and Times and the History and Traditions of His People*, edited and annotated by Harold Courlander. New York: Crown Publishers.

6

What the Old Ones Can Teach Us

SCOTT ORTMAN

There are two important trends in US Southwest archaeology today. The first is a recognition, stimulated by passage of the Native American Graves Protection and Repatriation Act, that archaeologists work with the cultural heritage of colonized and marginalized citizens. Archaeology in the US originated in the context of settler colonialism and the simple curiosity of non-Natives about ancestral sites, but in light of critiques by Native people it is now clear that doing archaeology for its own sake—solving mysteries of the past as an intellectual exercise—is not an adequate justification for the field (Atalay 2012; Deloria 1988; Liebmann and Rizvi 2008). As Joseph Suina explains in chapter 7 in this volume, the stakes are higher, in that archaeology carries with it the potential for harm to living descendants of the people who created the archaeological record. Indeed, the entire framing of the archaeological record as nonrenewable cultural resources that are consumed through the archaeological process conflicts with Native values; perhaps more important, Native people often have difficulty seeing themselves in the narratives archaeologists write. These realizations make it clear that for archaeology to transcend its settler colonialist roots,

https://doi.org/10.5876/9781646424597.c006

practitioners need to view their audience as Native as well as professional and public, view it as part of their job to work in partnership with Tribal members as coinvestigators, and bring the science of the archaeological record into dialog with Indigenous knowledge (Bernstein and Ortman 2020; Colwell-Chanthaponh and Ferguson 2008).

The second important trend is an urge to make archaeology more relevant for contemporary issues in society. In the decades since passage of the National Historic Preservation Act, archaeology in the United States has become a multi-billion-dollar industry that documents the archaeological record at a previously unimaginable scale (Altschul 2016; Schlanger et al. 2015), and advances in remote sensing and aerial survey are rapidly expanding our ability to document and measure archaeological remains systematically across broad areas (Canuto et al. 2018; Evans et al. 2007; Friedman et al. 2017; Rassmann et al. 2014). Yet, the field is still struggling to figure out how to take advantage of all these data to benefit society. There are many reasons for this, including inadequate infrastructure for synthesizing the information collected by different projects, shortcomings in the technical skills and training of archaeologists, a devaluing of work with existing collections and data, and the ongoing expense of creating and maintaining cyberinfrastructure (Altschul et al. 2017). But I think the most important reason is an imagination gap between the traditional goals of archaeology and the potential of this rapidly accumulating information base. The archaeological record is the most extensive compendium of human experience there is, but for the most part archaeologists continue to focus on reconstructing the histories of specific groups and regions in ever greater detail and rarely harness archaeological evidence to address more fundamental questions that transcend the past and present (Altschul et al. 2020; Kintigh et al. 2014; Ortman 2019).

One might conclude from the recent literature that these two trends are pulling archaeology in different directions, with Native concerns encouraging archaeologists to focus on the details of lived experience in specific places and the push for contemporary relevance driving them to focus on broad and abstract generalization. In this chapter I argue, on the contrary, that these two trends have the potential to bring the field together and give it a more coherent orientation. The key observation that brings Native interests and contemporary relevance into alignment is that Native people view ancestral sites not as places of the past but as living places that communicate knowledge regarding how to live today. Given this perspective, I suggest the key to an archaeology that resonates with Native people and also plays a larger role in contemporary society is for archaeologists to think about the archaeological record as Native people do. To make this argument, I will first share my experiences and sense of the ways Native people learn from ancestral sites. Then, I will discuss a few ways that a deeper engagement with these views might help the Crow Canyon

Archaeological Center's research in the Mesa Verde region have an even greater impact than it currently enjoys. This chapter is not meant as a critique, as Crow Canyon has been at the forefront of integrating Native voices into archaeological interpretations, educational products, and experimental research for many decades. Rather, I hope it may help guide the Center's mission activities in the next forty years.

NATIVE PERSPECTIVES ON ANCESTRAL SITES

In my career, I have been privileged to spend time visiting, observing, and discussing ancestral sites with many different Native people, initially as a member of the Crow Canyon staff, and today through partnerships with the Pueblos of Pojoaque and Ohkay Owingeh. I would never claim to know the full significance of ancestral sites for Native people, as there is no such thing as a singular or canonical Native perspective on this or any other topic (see Suina, chapter 7 in this volume). Still, I have noticed a few commonalities in the ways Native people think about and interact with ancestral sites that point toward the larger argument I wish to make.

The first commonality is an understanding that ancestral sites are not finished places of the past but are living places in the present. The brochure "Protect Bears Ears" (Bears Ears Coalition n.d.), created by the Bears Ears Intertribal Coalition to advocate for creation of the Bears Ears National Monument, makes this point directly (Bears Ears Coalition n.d., 9):

> For thousands of years, our ancestors lived within the Bears Ears landscape, hunting, foraging, and farming it by hand. They knew every plant and animal, every stream and mountain, every change of season, and every lesson important enough to be passed down through the centuries. We understood this place and cared for it, relating to the earth literally as our mother who provides for us and the plants and animals to which we are related. The Bears Ears landscape is alive in our view and must be nourished and cared for if life is to be sustained.

Many Native people I have worked with further explain that these places are alive, not only in general terms but also in the sense that the people who created them are still there. The spirit of the people who created ancestral sites continues to exist in these locations, just as the physical remains of the site continue to exist, and it is possible for one to communicate with these people, or connect with this spirit, if one's heart, mind, and senses are open to it. So, when Native people approach ancestral sites, they typically announce themselves, give respect to the people who are there, offer some food in the form of cornmeal, and ask permission to enter. In some cases, visitors will even sing traditional songs to the old ones, recognizing that the ancestors may not have heard their language in a very long time. The overall attitude is one of being a guest in someone else's home. Stones and artifacts that have been touched by the ancestors' hands are especially significant in that they provide opportunities for present-day people to make direct contact with the old ones and share breath with them, in the same way living people greet each other traditionally today. Ancestral sites also function like kivas in the sense that both are places of connection with a simultaneous and consubstantial spirit world. Ancestral sites are not "finished" in a very deep way—they continue to have life, can be communicated with, and establish relationships with the people of the present (also see Ferguson and Colwell-Chanthaponh 2006).

The second commonality is that ancestral sites are not just old homes but are places where the entire world and experiences of the old ones are revealed. When non-Native archaeologists visit an ancestral site, they tend look down at the ground for artifacts that yield evidence of its age and of the activities that took place there. Native people, in contrast, typically look up to take in the local environment and the relationships of that location with important landforms and their associated stories and songs. They give equal attention to cultural and natural features of the site, including the plants, the animals, the water sources, the viewsheds, the horizons, and other natural features, perceiving the ancestors' values from the fact that they chose to dwell in locations where these features and relationships occur. They also pay close attention to the ancestors' efforts to care for the local environment and are especially inspired by water control features that still work today, in the sense that they continue to stimulate plant growth, which provides food for the animals, and so forth. In their introduction to *Hopi Katsina Songs*, Emory Sekaquaptewa, Kenneth Hill, and Dorothy Washburn (2015) explain that the ancestral rain spirits come as moisture, causing plant growth, to signal their approval of the people's behaviors and intentions. Water control features at ancestral sites send the same message in that the ancestors who created these features are demonstrating desired behavior—caring for, and sharing with, the plants, the animals, and the people—and its enduring beneficial effects for the world as a whole (Ford and Swentzell 2015; also see Ermigiotti et al., chapter 4 in this volume).

The third commonality is that ancestral sites are memory aids. On a surface level this is apparent in the common association of stories and fables with ancestral sites. Keith Basso (1996) has written eloquently on the ways features of the landscape call to mind specific stories that instruct Western Apache people on proper ways to live. This same phenomenon occurs with ancestral sites, whose features are metonymic reminders of stories that convey important values and lessons. A good example is the Tewa story associated with Old San Juan Pueblo, Áyïbú'oke'ówînge (Harrington 1916, 207–208). The site sits on an eroded bank of the Rio Grande River north of present-day Ohkay Owingeh and is associated with a story of destruction by flood. According to the story, in the old days there were certain ceremonies that required a man to go without food or water for twelve days. One time, a man was shut up in a room to perform this ceremony, with a man and woman appointed to ensure that he neither drank nor ate. On the eleventh day, he broke his fast and ran down to the Rio Grande, drinking so much water that he burst, causing the flood that washed away the Pueblo. The woman fled toward the north and was turned into a stone that can still be seen in the place where she sat down to rest. This story conveys important lessons regarding the consequences of evading responsibility and of the perils of overindulgence, and it is recalled whenever community members visit the traces of the washed-out village or walk along the trail where the stone lies.

This example illustrates the explicit mnemonic qualities of ancestral sites, but there is also a deeper level on which ancestral sites are reservoirs of information that can be brought to consciousness, reremembered perhaps through observation of, and reflection on, the remains. In the "Protect Bears Ears" brochure, Ute Mountain Ute elder Malcolm Lehi elaborates on the way ancestral sites convey such information: "Native People relate to rock art with our hearts. I regularly visit one rock art site that is a holy site. It provides us knowledge of our past and future. We do not view these panels as just art, but almost like a coded message that exists to help us understand. This knowledge informs our life and reality as humans" (Bears Ears Coalition n.d., 9). Statements like this one demonstrate that in addition to serving as memory aids, ancestral sites directly provide information that influence present and future behavior. They also show that the perspectives on ancestral sites that I am discussing are widely shared in Indigenous cultures and are not limited to the Pueblo cultures with which I have the most experience. Over time, Native people learn new things from observation and contemplation of ancestral sites. Again, ancestral sites are not finished places of the past but living places that influence the present and future.

Finally, the fourth commonality I've observed is that ancestral sites are viewed as places that benefit the entire world, not just living descendants. Many traditional activities, which Pueblo people refer to as "doings," take place at ancestral sites (Fowles 2013). Often these focus on blessing features created on the tops of old residences or in other auspicious locations, and the prayers that are uttered are intended not merely for the speaker but for all people, the plants, the animals, and the world at large. Ancestral sites are thus key places from which the living seek to benefit all the world. Diné elder Willie Greyeyes expresses a similar sentiment in the "Protect Bears Ears" brochure: "Protecting Bears Ears is not just about healing for the land and Native people. It's for our adversaries to be healed, too. I truly believe we can all come out dancing together" (Bears Coalition n.d., 13). Statements like these emphasize that, for Native people, the archaeological record has always had contemporary relevance; this relevance is not merely with respect to Tribal heritage but to the information and guidance ancestral sites provide regarding beneficial ways both Native and non-Native people can live today and tomorrow.

WHAT I THINK NATIVE PEOPLE ARE TRYING TO TELL ARCHAEOLOGISTS

My experiences with Native people at ancestral sites suggest that archaeological sites are living places where it is possible to connect with the collected wisdom and experience of past people for the benefit of all. Given this, it is quite ironic that most social scientists, and many archaeologists, do not see similar potential. For example, the role of archaeology in Inter-governmental Panel on Climate Change (IPCC) reports has, for the most part, been limited to the effects of climate change on the archaeological record itself, and, despite an extensive literature on human-environment relationships in archaeology, this work has played little role in discussions of adaptation to climate change (Jackson et al. 2018; Kohler and Rockman 2020; Rockman and Hritz 2020; Simpson et al. 2022).

In addition, archaeology is practically nonexistent in discussions of sustainable development, which typically begin from the twin notions of the *great escape* and the *great acceleration* (Clark and Harley 2020, 333). The former states that the material conditions of life for human beings were invariant and unchanging from earliest times to the onset of the Industrial Revolution but since that time human societies have been fundamentally and qualitatively different; and the latter states that for most of history human impacts on the environment were entirely local but since the industrial revolution these impacts have accelerated and have been driven by new processes. These perceptions lead to the conclusion that archaeological evidence is irrelevant for defining development strategies that meet the needs of the present "without compromising the ability of future generations to meet their own needs" (333).

Archaeological studies demonstrate that these perceptions are inaccurate, in that there is strong evidence for substantial changes in the material conditions of life over time even in preindustrial societies (Jongman et al. 2019; Ober 2010; Ortman and Lobo 2020), there is equally strong evidence for extensive environmental impacts at a variety of scales (Liebmann et al. 2016; Rick and Sandweiss 2020; Stephens et al. 2019), and there is emerging evidence that a wide range of empirical patterns in data for contemporary societies—including demographic, rank-size, gravity, growth, distance-decay, inequality, and scaling relationships—are also found in preindustrial societies of the past (Bettencourt 2021; Kohler and Reese 2014; Kohler et al. 2017). Nevertheless, relatively few archaeologists are comfortable bringing such results to bear on discussions of contemporary issues. This reticence may be a legacy of our training. Most archaeologists of my generation entered graduate school in the era of post-processualism, in which a central argument was that although there is great potential for a science of the archaeological record, archaeologists and the archaeological record itself are so biased that it is inappropriate to use the results of archaeology to inform discussions of the present and future. Another common argument has been that the evolution of human societies is driven by so many interactions among so many different variables that it is foolish to make any sort of predictions regarding what could happen in the future based on things that have happened in the past. On top of this, an aversion to engagement with the present, beyond legitimate concerns regarding cultural heritage and social justice, continues to characterize the perspectives of leading proponents of postprocessualism today. For example, according to Ian Hodder (2018, 43), "Archaeologists have always wanted to be comparative and to seek general trends . . . the construction of an abstract historical and anthropological knowledge from which all can benefit. Important as this generalizing process is, it has proved prone to influence by contemporary concerns. That's a nice way of putting it. A less nice way is that much of archaeology uses the past to play out the contemporary preoccupations of dominant groups and to regurgitate the present in their interests."

While I agree with Hodder that the work archaeologists do is influenced by their subjective experiences and perceptions, this is true for social scientists in every field. And despite this inclination, society still needs social scientists to engage with the world through their various vantage points to help find solutions to present-day problems. Just wanting the world to be better and pointing out all the ways in which we currently fail to make it better are not enough. We also need to collectively learn how to make it better. The whole point of economics is to figure out what causes material prosperity so that societies can encourage more of it; the whole point of sociology is to understand why outcomes vary with respect to various subgroups so that societies can encourage greater inclusiveness and equality of opportunity; the whole point of anthropology is to understand human diversity so that we can incorporate a broader range of ideas and experiences into our ways of doing things; and the whole point of sustainability science is to understand how the human and nonhuman worlds impact each other so that we can do a better job of balancing human needs with those of the earth. The accumulation of human knowledge has always been marred by false starts, errors, failures, and injustice; yet despite all of this, the accumulation of practical knowledge has provided net benefits for humanity (Roser 2020). In this larger context, the reticence of archaeologists to contribute to this process seems puzzling and ultimately self-defeating.

In my experience, Native people encounter the archaeological record from a vantage that seeks to take advantage of the wisdom and experience embedded in the physical remains to chart a positive course into the future. There is no reason why archaeologists cannot do the same, and, in a larger sense, I think

Native people are suggesting this would be a good thing for archaeologists to do. Indeed, I suspect that one of the reasons Native scholars have often objected to the idea of archaeology as a social science (Deloria 1988; Nicholas and Hollowell 2007) is because many archaeologists continue to view their work as a purely intellectual exercise, driven by curiosity and the detective's urge to solve mysteries. In general, archaeologists still shy away from imagining that the knowledge gained through archaeology is relevant for improving the human condition, for Native people or for anyone else. Archaeologists are not wholly to blame for this, but it is important to acknowledge that these are choices that are inconsistent with Native perceptions and values, at least as I understand them.

Based on my experience, then, I believe the goals and interests of archaeologists who seek to use archaeological evidence to address contemporary issues are more closely aligned with the perceptions and interests of Native people, despite the fact that archaeologists and Native people have traditionally used very different approaches to learn from ancestral sites (see Cajete 2000). Regardless of epistemological differences, both groups recognize that ancestral sites embody and summarize human experience and accumulated human knowledge; both recognize that ancestral sites convey new information to observers as their needs and questions change; and both recognize the unity of human societies of the past and present, such that the things we learn from ancestral sites, whether through traditional or scientific means, are relevant for the present and future. Given this alignment, I believe there are great opportunities for archaeologists and Native people to work together to bring the knowledge and wisdom embedded in ancestral sites to bear on discussions of contemporary issues. In this process, archaeologists can contribute methods of systematic observation and analysis of material remains, and Native people can articulate links between behavior, ideas, and values, to investigate questions that are of mutual interest, and answers that benefit everyone (see Ortman 2016 for some initial, tentative steps in this direction).

NATIVE PERSPECTIVES AND CONTEMPORARY RELEVANCE

In the second half of this chapter, I use the discussion above as a jumping-off point for developing a few examples of directions in which Crow Canyon and Native people could work together to expand the contemporary relevance of US Southwest archaeology. I do not mean to suggest that integrating archaeology and traditional knowledge is the only way to enhance contemporary relevance, or that the examples that follow are necessarily the best ways to do it. In fact, I would say that the only essential ingredients of an archaeology with contemporary relevance are a commitment to the idea that human societies possess a fundamental unity—that they are complex networks of elements, processes, and relationships that have nontrivial and somewhat predictable effects—and a willingness to generalize. However, some of these properties, especially those that deal with the realms of culture, ideas, values, and institutions, are more readily apparent in the traditional knowledge systems of descendant communities than they are in the archaeological record. Thus, in keeping with the theme of this chapter, my examples will focus specifically on some areas where it seems to me that deeper integration of archaeology and traditional knowledge can contribute to such discussions.

Material Behavior and Sociopolitical Realities

My first example involves combining archaeology and oral history to deepen understandings of the interrelationships between politics, discourse, and social behavior. In every society there is ongoing conversation, and competition, regarding alternative ways of framing current events. Anyone who follows contemporary politics cannot help but be aware of how differently various factions label, frame, and talk about the issues of the day. Jerome Bruner (1991, 1) has labeled the process through which these distinct sociopolitical realities are created "the narrative construction of reality." It is obvious from recent experience that these constructions play an important role in sociopolitical dynamics. But how exactly?

Archaeologists and Native people can work together to address this question by integrating archaeology and oral history. Traditional approaches to oral history have focused on the question of whether such stories are "true" in the sense that they provide factually based accounts of past events (Lowie 1915; Vansina 1961). However, I think a better way to view oral histories is as politically situated discourses that preserve attempts by past peoples to make sense of important events and make them meaningful in their own terms (Hodges 2011). From this perspective, the interesting question to ask is not whether an oral history is true but what the narrative reveals about the discursive practices of the people who constructed it. In other words, it is in precisely those areas where oral histories and archaeology do not correspond that the greatest potential for interpretation of past sociopolitical processes lies (Schmidt 2006).

A clear opportunity for this sort of integration involves oral histories surrounding the Chaco world. Archaeologists have learned a tremendous amount about the emergence, growth, and decline of the Chaco world, and it is clear from these studies that Chaco represents an ambitious, but also fragile, attempt to forge a regional society that transcended local communities and kin groups (Lekson 2006; Stuart 2014). The regional system centered on Chaco Canyon, in which people of the Mesa Verde region participated (Lipe 2006; Reed 2008), involved an unprecedented scale of ritual integration (Kantner and Vaughn 2012; Sofaer 2007; Van Dyke 2007) but more modest economic integration and substantial levels of inequality (Kennett et al. 2017; Plog and Heitman 2010). Indeed, Chaco Canyon appears to be a place where resources were concentrated (Benson et al. 2003; Guiterman et al. 2016), with subsequent redistribution being limited to prestige goods (Watson et al. 2015; Windes 1992).

Descendant communities maintain rich oral histories surrounding Chaco Canyon. Traditions from several Pueblo communities refer to Chaco as White House, a place where ancestral rain spirits lived with the people in harmony, and all spoke a common language, until the people became greedy and disrespectful, leading to drought, conflict, and migration (Ortiz 1992). The traditions of several Navajo clans, in contrast, discuss Chaco Canyon as a place of many vices, where a person from the distant south known as the Great Gambler enslaved the people and forced them to build the monumental structures before being overthrown by an alliance of the people and their spirit helpers (Begay 2004). These stories, from different descendant communities, discuss Chaco from different social and perhaps also spatial vantage points. There is important information embedded in these differences.

All historical narratives are subjective, post hoc construals of events that enshrine the privileged discourses of the communities from which they emanate. Thus, when one encounters oral histories that offer different interpretations of past events, or which emphasize different details, the right question to ask is not whether they match the archaeological record but what the differences between the stories, and between the stories and the archaeology, reveal about the sociopolitical context in which the narratives were constructed (Ortman 2020). In the process, one can gain insight into the political dynamics of the Chaco World in a way that would otherwise be inaccessible, and one gains the opportunity to learn how discursive practices relate to other aspects of long-term social dynamics that are more readily observable through archaeology. It seems to me that archaeologists and Native people have an opportunity to forge new generalizations concerning how societies come together, and how they come apart, by working to connect the rich corpus of multivocal oral histories surrounding ancestral sites with the rapidly expanding archaeological evidence.

Processes of Institutional Change

A second area of opportunity connects with economics and involves a deeper engagement with the processes of institutional change. I vividly remember Tito Naranjo (Santa Clara Pueblo) commenting during a visit to Lowry Pueblo many years ago that places like Lowry preserve the efforts of the ancestors to build the institutions that govern Pueblo communities today. There is a general awareness that human societies provide for basic human needs to differing degrees and that the provision of these basic needs ultimately derives from such institutions (Acemoglu and Robinson 2012; North et al. 2009; Ostrom 1999). Archaeologists affiliated with Crow Canyon have a long history of investigating the evolution of social institutions under the rubric of community organization (Coffey 2016; Glowacki 2015; Lipe and Hegmon 1989; Varien and Wilshusen 2002), and this work has been successful in charting histories of institutional change (also see Glowacki et al., chapter 12, and Potter et al., chapter 13 in this volume). To carry this work further, a good first step is to recognize that new institutional forms are not created from whole cloth but instead involve rearrangements of existing ideas in new ways, a process that Claude Lévi-Strauss famously labeled *bricolage* (1966). It is also useful to distinguish between invention, which is the appearance of something new, versus innovation, the widespread adoption of this new thing (Schiffer 2011). Is it possible to generalize regarding these processes? Are there patterns in the ways new institutions are invented? What factors govern the spread, or not, of these new ideas? To find out, one needs to not just identify sequences of change but also identify the transformations involved with each invention and consider the innovation process in the context of an ongoing cultural conversation. This is where combining archaeology with historical analyses of present-day Pueblo languages and cultures can really help.

A good example of what is possible using this approach is research on the history of dual organization in ancestral Pueblo communities. Archaeologists associated with Crow Canyon have noted that ancestral Pueblo communities in the Mesa Verde region are often spatially divided into two roughly equal parts, often by a drainage, and have interpreted this as evidence for a form of dual organization (Lipe and Ortman 2000; Kuckelman, chapter 19 in this volume; Ortman and Bradley 2002; Ware 2014) that is especially prominent in Tewa communities today. In historic Tewa culture, these moieties, which are more properly referred to as dual Tribal sodalities (Ware 2014), are part of an alternating pattern of community leadership, where the leader of each group oversees the community during the summer and winter, respectively. These moieties do not regulate marriage, but they do organize life-cycle rituals; and although membership runs through the father's line, people can switch allegiances for a variety of reasons over the course of their lifetimes (Ortiz 1969).

The divided villages of the Mesa Verde region do suggest some sort of dual division, but I think a better argument can be made that they reflect an earlier form of kin-based community organization from which historic Tewa non-kin-based moieties evolved. There are two lines of evidence that support this interpretation. First, Tewa oral histories indicate that Tewa-style moieties derive from village-level institutions, and the archaeological record expresses the stages in this process directly. According to these narratives, the ancestors migrated from their ancestral homeland to northern New Mexico as winter people and summer people, with the winter people coming down first and each group establishing a separate village before the two groups eventually merged into a single village containing both winter people and summer people (Ortiz 1969; Parsons [1926] 1994).

These episodes are physically manifested in the archaeology of at least two ancestral Tewa communities. The first is Cuyamunge, near present-day Pojoaque (Bernstein and Ortman 2020). This community began around AD 1150 as a series of small kin-based residences. During the late AD 1200s these residences coalesced into a small village of about 100 people, and a second village of about 200 people was constructed on an adjacent terrace to the north. The southern village appears to correspond to the winter people, who had deeper ancestry in the area, and the northern village reflects the arrival of a second, larger group corresponding to the summer people. By about AD 1400, these paired villages had coalesced into a single village of about 400 people on the southern terrace, with the summer plaza to the west and the winter plaza to the east. The second community is Tsama, in the Chama River valley (Davis and Ortman 2021). This community initially formed in the middle AD 1200s, when two villages of about 100 people each were established at either end of a terrace above the Rio Chama. The painted pottery of these villages exhibits strong continuities with Mesa Verde Black-on-white. The western, upstream village has an opening in its plaza that faces the midsummer sunrise and thus represents the summer people; and the eastern, downstream village had a strong southeast view toward the midwinter sunrise behind the Truchas Peaks, and thus represents the winter people. By the mid-AD 1400s, these two villages had coalesced into a single village of about 1,000 people around a single, massive plaza at the east end of the terrace, with each moiety maintaining a separate kiva on the western periphery of the new, larger village.

This combined evidence from archaeology and oral history suggests historic Tewa community organization derives from paired village communities that were established as Tewa ancestors entered the northern Rio Grande region. However, the origin narratives also state that Tewa ancestors migrated as winter people and summer people, so it seems possible that the idea of the paired village community was first invented in the ancestral homeland of the migrants. Grant Coffey (2016) has recently found evidence of this in the Sand Canyon locality, where the Sand Canyon and Goodman Point communities were linked by a formalized road as early as the twelfth century AD (also see Schleher et al., chapter 14 in this volume). Coffey's findings raise the possibility Naranjo suggested, that these new governing institutions were first invented in the Mesa Verde homeland of many Tewa people and that they became more widely adopted as part of the migration process.

The second line of evidence, from historical analysis of Tanoan kin terms, suggests the divided villages of the Mesa Verde region reflect a kin-based precursor of paired-village organization. In a recent study, Patrick Cruz and I compiled kin terms across Tanoan languages and used the comparative method to reconstruct the evolution of these terms as the languages diversified over time (Cruz and

Ortman 2021). The analysis revealed several cases where a single kin term in proto-Tanoan has evolved to refer to different relationships in descendant languages: as examples, a term that refers to *mother* in one language is cognate with a term that refers to *mother's sister* in another; and a term that refers to *mother's brother* in one language is cognate with a term for *mother's brother's son* in another. These patterns imply that ancestral Tanoan communities followed an Iroquoian-type kinship system with exogamous matrilineal moieties (Trautman and Whiteley 2012). Basically, each person belonged to the moiety of their mother; father's brother was an additional father and mother's sister an additional mother; parallel cousins (father's brother's children and mother's sister's children) were additional siblings that were off-limits as marriage partners; and cross-cousins (father's sister's children and mother's brother's children) were appropriate as marriage partners. This type of social organization is consistent with both unit pueblos representing matrilineal kin groups and with divided villages representing exogamous matrilineal moieties (Ortman 2018). In addition to adding an additional line of evidence that the Tanoan linguistic homeland was in the San Juan drainage, these findings suggest the idea of the paired village community was abstracted from older, kin-based institutions that regulated marriage.

The point here is that kin-based institutions appear to have played an important role in older, and generally smaller, Mesa Verde region communities but that more inclusive, non-kin-based institutions were typical of the more recent, generally larger, and generally more secure ancestral Tewa communities in the northern Rio Grande (Ortman 2016). To go from one to the other, people had to invent new, non-kin-based institutions; and at least in this case, the new institutions appear to have been abstracted and reformulated from existing institutions. This is just one example of how combining studies of Pueblo languages, cultures, and ancestral sites can lead to new insights regarding processes of institutional change, but it seems to me that additional studies of this process, leading to generalizations regarding the characteristics of successful versus unsuccessful efforts, would be quite valuable as data points to a deeper understanding how societies solve problems effectively, or not.

Native Philosophy and Sustainability Science

My final example is broader and involves investigating the effects of Native values for sustainable development. One of the most important philosophical tenets of Native cultures is that humans and their communities are not separate from nature but are a part of it. Humans do not merely have responsibilities to their families and communities but also to the plants, the animals, and the landscape. As Ute Mountain Ute elder Regina Lopez-Whiteskunk explains, "We are of the land, we don't quite own it but we're here as caretakers" (Bears Ears Coalition n.d., 10). In the Western tradition, in contrast, humans are separate from nature, and this affects everything from concepts of wilderness (the absence of people) to the production of knowledge (humanities, social sciences, and natural sciences) to notions of rationality (costs and benefits for the individual). This basic division leads people to believe that the nonhuman world generally does better in the absence of human action and to relegate the environmental impacts of economic decisions to "externalities" (Kimmerer 2013).

The broad patterns of development in the world today, and the threats to sustainability that have come with it, have occurred largely in the context of Western patterns of thought. New World societies developed independently of this until about five centuries ago and achieved similar scale and complexity to those of the Old World despite technological limitations (metallurgy, wheeled vehicles, sailing ships) and a narrower range of domestic animals for traction, transport, and food (Sachs 2020). Were New World societies more sustainable than their Old World counterparts, relative to their scale? If so, did the distinct conceptualizations of humans and nature play a role in these differences? Would broader adoption of similar views improve the sustainability of human societies today? More fundamentally, how does a conceptualization of humans as a part of nature structure emergent patterns of behavior? Does accounting for this behavior require different models of the human individual? Of human rationality? And how does it change the analytical approaches of archaeologists? Archaeologists affiliated with Crow Canyon have been investigating sustainable development under the rubric of human-environment relationships for decades (Badenhorst et al., chapter 20 in this volume; Bocinsky et al. 2016; Kohler 2012; Kuckelman 2000, 2007; Schollmeyer and Driver 2013, and chapter 21 in this volume; Van West 1994), and studies that consider humans, plants and animals in a single analysis, including studies of food webs (Crabtree et al. 2017), traditional ecological knowledge (Langdon 2007), and convergent behavioral evolution (Barsbai et al. 2021) are beginning to break down the conceptual barrier between humans and nature. Crow Canyon has also contributed to this trend by encouraging specialists in environmental archaeology, architecture, osteology, ceramics, and lithics to integrate their results in synthetic studies (Lipe 1992; Varien and Wilshusen 2002). I have no idea what answers to the questions above will be, but I think the answers will be important for all of us to consider and that partnerships between archaeologists and Native people will be one of the best ways to find them.

Prospect

I hope these examples are sufficient to make my main point, which is that framing the archaeological record the way Native people do and working with Native people as coinvestigators to address questions that all of us care about offer an exciting and productive solution to trends that might otherwise pull archaeology in different directions and create distinct research silos. The fact that

Native people have traditionally learned from ancestral sites in different ways from archaeologists is not a barrier or challenge but a potential strength of an integrated approach that combines systematic observation and analysis of past behavior with a concern for wholeness, unity, spirit, and the future. In my view, scholars have put much more effort into making distinctions between archaeological and Indigenous approaches to ancestral sites than they have in finding connections. I hope this chapter will encourage archaeologists to recognize that if we wish to honor both approaches, a good direction in which to move is toward an archaeology that focuses on what the old ones can teach us. Crow Canyon is in a great position to play a leading role in this over its next forty years.

Acknowledgments. This chapter is dedicated to the Native American Advisory Group at Crow Canyon, and especially the members who inspired me during my years as an employee, including Eric and Jane Polingyouma, Peter and Stella Pino, Herman Agoyo, Ernest Vallo, Rebecca Hammond, Tito Naranjo, Tessie Naranjo, Marie Reyna, Chris Toya, and Harry Walters. I hope this chapter adequately honors them, especially those who have since passed. I also thank the School for Advanced Research, Santa Fe, for fellowship support, and the 2020–2021 resident scholar community there for helpful feedback on the initial draft.

REFERENCES

Acemoglu, Daron, and James A. Robinson. 2012. *Why Nations Fail: The Origins of Power, Prosperity and Poverty.* New York: Crown Business.

Altschul, Jeffrey H. 2016. "The Role of Synthesis in American Archaeology and Cultural Resource Management as Seen through an Arizona Lens." *Journal of Arizona Archaeology* 4 (1): 68–81.

Altschul, Jeffrey H., Keith W. Kintigh, Mark Aldenderfer, Elise Alonzi, Ian Armit, Juan Antonio Barceló, Christopher S. Beekman, Penny Bickle, Douglas W. Bird, Scott E. Ingram, Elena Isayev, Andrew W. Kandel, Rachael Kiddey, Hélène Timpoko Kienon-Kaboré, Franco Niccolucci, Corey S. Ragsdale, Beth K. Scaffidi, and Scott G. Ortman. 2020. "Opinion: To Understand How Migrations Affect Human Securities, Look to the Past." *Proceedings of the National Academy of Sciences* 117 (34): 20342–20345. https://doi.org/10.1073/pnas.2015146117.

Altschul, Jeffrey H., Keith W. Kintigh, Terry H. Klein, William H. Doelle, Kelley A. Hays-Gilpin, Sarah A. Herr, Timothy A. Kohler, Barbara J. Mills, Lindsay M. Montgomery, Margaret C. Nelson, Scott G. Ortman, John N. Parker, Matthew A. Peeples, and Jeremy A. Sabloff. 2017. "Fostering Synthesis in Archaeology to Advance Science and Benefit Society." *Proceedings of the National Academy of Science of the U.S.A.* 114 (42): 10999–11002.

Atalay, Sonya. 2012. *Community-Based Archaeology: Research with, by, and for Indigenous and Local Communities.* Berkeley: University of California Press.

Barsbai, Toman, Dieter Lukas, and Andreas Pondorfer. 2021. "Local Convergence of Behavior across Species." *Science* 371 (6526): 292. https://doi.org/10.1126/science.abb7481.

Basso, Keith. 1996. *Wisdom Sits in Places: Landscape and Language among the Western Apache.* Albuquerque: University of New Mexico Press.

Bears Ears Coalition. n.d. "Protect Bears Ears." Brochure. https://bearsearscoalition.org/wp-content/uploads/2016/03/Bears-Ears-bro.sm_.pdf.

Begay, Richard M. 2004. "Tsé Bíyah 'Anii'áhí: Chaco Canyon and Its Place in Navajo History." In *In Search of Chaco: New Approaches to an Archaeological Enigma*, edited by David Grant Noble, 54–60. Santa Fe, NM: School of American Research Press.

Benson, Larry, Linda Cordell, Kirk Vincent, Howard Taylor, John Stein, G. Lang Farmer, and Kiyoto Futa. 2003. "Ancient Maize from Chacoan Great Houses: Where Was It Grown?" *Proceedings of the National Academy of Science of the U.S.A.* 100 (22): 13111–13115.

Bernstein, Bruce, and Scott G. Ortman. 2020. "From Collaboration to Partnership at Pojoaque, New Mexico." *Advances in Archaeological Practice* 8 (2): 95–110. https://doi.org/10.1017/aap.2020.3.

Bettencourt, Luís M. A. 2021. *Introduction to Urban Science.* Cambridge, MA: MIT Press.

Bocinsky, R. Kyle, Johnathan Rush, Keith W. Kintigh, and Timothy A. Kohler. 2016. "Exploration and Exploitation in the Macrohistory of the Pre-Hispanic Pueblo Southwest." *Science Advances* 2 (4): e1501532. https://doi.org/10.1126/sciadv.1501532.

Bruner, Jerome. 1991. "The Narrative Construction of Reality." *Critical Inquiry* 18 (1): 1–21.

Cajete, Gregory. 2000. *Native Science: Natural Laws of Interdependence.* Santa Fe, NM: Clear Light Publishers.

Canuto, Marcello A., Francisco Estrada-Belli, Thomas G. Garrison, Stephen D. Houston, Mary Jane Acuña, Milan Kováč, Damien Marken, Philippe Nondédéo, Luke Auld-Thomas, Cyril Castanet, David Chatelain, Carlos R. Chiriboga, Tomáš Drápela, Tibor Lieskovský, Alexandre Tokovinine, Antolín Velasquez, Juan C. Fernández-Díaz, and Ramesh Shrestha. 2018. "Ancient Lowland Maya Complexity as Revealed by Air-Borne Laser Scanning of Northern Guatemala." *Science* 361 (6409): eaau0137. https://doi.org/10.1126/science.aau0137.

Clark, William C., and Alicia G. Harley. 2020. "Sustainability Science: Toward a Synthesis." *Annual Review of Environment and Resources* 45 (1): 331–386. https://doi.org/10.1146/annurev-environ-012420-043621.

Coffey, Grant D. 2016. "Creating Symmetry: The Cultural Landscape in the Sand Canyon Locality, Southwestern Colorado." *Kiva* 82 (1): 1–21.

Colwell-Chanthaponh, Chip, and T. J. Ferguson, eds. 2008. *Collaboration in Archaeological Practice: Engaging Descendant Communities.* Lanham, MD: Altamira Press.

Crabtree, Stefani A., Lydia J. S. Vaughn, and Nathan T. Crabtree. 2017. "Reconstructing Ancestral Pueblo Food Webs in the Southwestern United States." *Journal of Archaeological Science* 81 (May): 116–127. https://doi.org/10.1016/j.jas.2017.03.005.

Cruz, Patrick, and Scott G. Ortman. 2021. "The Implications of Kiowa-Tanoan Kin Terms for Pueblo Social Organization." In *Engaged Archaeology in the Southwestern United States and Northwestern Mexico*, edited by K. A. Hays-Gilpin, S. A. Herr, and P. D. Lyons, 141–158. Boulder: University Press of Colorado.

Davis, Kaitlyn E., and Scott G. Ortman. 2021. *The Tewa Community at Tsama Pueblo (LA908): Artifacts from the 1970 Excavations*. Albuquerque: Maxwell Museum Technical Series.

Deloria, Vine. 1988. *Custer Died for Your Sins: An Indian Manifesto*. Norman: University of Oklahoma Press.

Evans, Damian, Christophe Pottier, Roland Fletcher, Scott Hensley, Ian Tapley, Anthony Milne, and Michael Barbetti. 2007. "A Comprehensive Archaeological Map of the World's Largest Preindustrial Settlement Complex at Angkor, Cambodia." *Proceedings of the National Academy of Sciences of the United States of America* 104 (36): 14277–14282.

Ferguson, T. J., and Chip Colwell-Chanthaponh. 2006. *History Is in the Land: Multivocal Tribal Traditions in Arizona's San Pedro Valley*. Tucson: University of Arizona Press.

Ford, Richard I., and Roxanne Swentzell. 2015. "Precontact Agriculture in Northern New Mexico." In *Traditional Arid Lands Agriculture: Understanding the Past for the Future*, edited by Scott E. Ingram and Robert C. Hunt, 330–357. Tucson: University of Arizona Press.

Fowles, Severin M. 2013. *An Archaeology of Doings: Secularism and the Study of Pueblo Religion*. Santa Fe, NM: School for Advanced Research Press.

Friedman, Richard A., Anna Sofaer, and Robert S. Weiner. 2017. "Remote Sensing of Chaco Roads Revisited: Lidar Documentation of the Great North Road, Pueblo Alto Landscape, and Aztec Airport Mesa Road." *Advances in Archaeological Practice* 5 (4): 365–381. https://doi.org/10.1017/aap.2017.25.

Glowacki, Donna M. 2015. *Living and Leaving: A Social History of Regional Depopulation in Thirteenth-Century Mesa Verde*. Tucson: University of Arizona Press.

Guiterman, Christopher H., Thomas W. Swetnam, and Jeffrey S. Dean. 2016. "Eleventh-Century Shift in Timber Procurement Areas for the Great Houses of Chaco Canyon." *Proceedings of the National Academy of Sciences* 113 (5): 1186–1190. https://doi.org/10.1073/pnas.1514272112.

Harrington, John Peabody. 1916. "The Ethnogeography of the Tewa Indians." In *29th Annual Report of the Bureau of American Ethnology*, 29–618. Washington, DC: Government Printing Office.

Hodder, Ian. 2018. "Big History and a Post-truth Archaeology?" *SAA Archaeological Record* 18 (5): 43–45.

Hodges, Adam. 2011. *The "War on Terror" Narrative: Discourse and Intertextuality in the Construction and Contestation of Sociopolitical Reality*. Oxford: Oxford University Press.

Jackson, Rowan C., Andrew J. Dugmore, and Felix Riede. 2018. "Rediscovering Lessons of Adaptation from the Past." *Global Environmental Change* 52 (September): 58–65.

Jongman, Willem M., Jan P. A. M. Jacobs, and Geertje M. Klein Goldewijk. 2019. "Health and Wealth in the Roman Empire." *Economics and Human Biology* 34 (August): 138–150. https://doi.org/10.1016/j.ehb.2019.01.005.

Kantner, John, and Kevin J. Vaughn. 2012. "Pilgrimage as Costly Signal: Religiously Motivated Cooperation in Chaco and Nasca." *Journal of Anthropological Archaeology* 31 (1): 66–82.

Kennett, Douglas J., Stephen Plog, Richard J. George, Brendan J. Culleton, Adam S. Watson, Pontus Skoglund, Nadin Rohland, Swapan Mallick, Kristin Stewardson, Logan Kistler, Steven A. LeBlanc, Peter M. Whiteley, David Reich, and George H. Perry. 2017. "Archaeogenomic Evidence Reveals Prehistoric Matrilineal Dynasty." *Nature Communications* 8 (1): 14115. https://doi.org/10.1038/ncomms14115.

Kimmerer, Robin Wall. 2013. *Braiding Sweetgrass: Indigenous Wisdom, Scientific Knowledge and the Teachings of Plants.* Minneapolis: Milkweed Editions.

Kintigh, Keith W., Jeffrey H. Altshul, Mary C. Beaudry, Robert D. Drennan, Ann P. Kinzig, Timothy A. Kohler, W. Frederick Limp, Herbert D. G. Maschner, William K. Michener, Timothy R. Pauketat, Peter N. Peregrine, Jeremy A. Sabloff, Tony J. Wilkinson, Henry T. Wright, and Melinda A. Zeder. 2014. "Grand Challenges for Archaeology." *American Antiquity* 79 (1): 5–24.

Kohler, Timothy A. 2012. "The Rise and Collapse of Villages in the Central Mesa Verde Region." In *Emergence and Collapse of Early Villages: Models of Central Mesa Verde Archaeology,* edited by Timothy A. Kohler and Mark D. Varien, 247–262. Berkeley: University of California Press.

Kohler, Timothy A., and Kelsey M. Reese. 2014. "Long and Spatially Variable Neolithic Demographic Transition in the North American Southwest." *Proceedings of the National Academy of Science of the U.S.A.* 111 (28): 10101–10106.

Kohler, Timothy A., and Marcy Rockman. 2020. "The IPCC: A Primer for Archaeologists." *American Antiquity* 85 (4): 627–651. https://doi.org/10.1017/aaq.2020.68.

Kohler, Timothy A., Michael E. Smith, Amy Bogaard, Gary M. Feinman, Christina E. Peterson, Aleen Betzenhauser, Matthew C. Pailes, Elizabeth C. Stone, Anna Marie Prentiss, Timothy Dennehy, Laura Ellyson, Linda M. Nicholas, Ronald K. Faulseit, Amy Styring, Jade Whitlam, Mattia Fochesato, Thomas A. Foor, and Samuel Bowles. 2017. "Greater Post-Neolithic Wealth Disparities in Eurasia than in North and Meso-america." *Nature* 551 (November): 619–622.

Kuckelman, Kristin A., ed. 2000. "The Archaeology of Castle Rock Pueblo: A Thirteenth-Century Village in Southwestern Colorado." https://www.crowcanyon.org/resources/the_archaeology_of_castle_rock_pueblo_a_thirteenth_century_village_in_southwestern_colorado/.

Kuckelman, Kristin A., ed. 2007. *The Archaeology of Sand Canyon Pueblo: Intensive Excavations at a Late-Thirteenth-Century Village in Southwestern Colorado.* http://www.crowcanyon.org/sandcanyon.

Langdon, Stephen J. 2007. "Sustaining a Relationship: Inquiry into the Emergence of a Logic of Engagement with Salmon among the Southern Tlingits." In *Native Americans and the Environment: Perspectives on the Ecological Indian*, edited by Michael E. Harkin and David Rich Lewis, 233–273. Lincoln: University of Nebraska Press.

Lekson, Stephen H., ed. 2006. *The Archaeology of Chaco Canyon: An Eleventh-Century Pueblo Regional Center*. Santa Fe, NM: School of American Research Press.

Lévi-Strauss, Claude. 1966. *The Savage Mind*. Chicago: University of Chicago Pres.

Liebmann, Matthew J., Joshua Farella, Christopher I. Roos, Adam Stack, Sarah Martini, and Thomas W. Swetnam. 2016. "Native American Depopulation, Reforestation, and Fire Regimes in the Southwest United States, 1492–1900 CE." *Proceedings of the National Academy of Science of the U.S.A.* 113 (6): e696–e704.

Liebmann, Matthew J., and Uzma Z. Rizvi, eds. 2008. *Archaeology and the Postcolonial Critique*. Lanham, MD: Altamira Press.

Lipe, William D., ed. 1992. *The Sand Canyon Archaeological Project: A Progress Report*. Cortez, CO: Crow Canyon Archaeological Center.

Lipe, William D. 2006. "Notes from the North." In *The Archaeology of Chaco Canyon: An Eleventh-Century Pueblo Regional Center*, edited by Stephen H. Lekson, 261–314. Santa Fe, NM: School of American Research Press.

Lipe, William D., and Michelle Hegmon, eds. 1989. *The Architecture of Social Integration in Prehistoric Pueblos*. Cortez, CO: Crow Canyon Archaeological Center.

Lipe, William D., and Scott G. Ortman. 2000. "Spatial Patterning in Northern San Juan Villages, A.D. 1050–1300." *Kiva* 66 (1): 91–122.

Lowie, Robert H. 1915. "Oral Tradition and History." *American Anthropologist* 17 (July–September): 597–599.

Nicholas, George, and Julie Hollowell. 2007. "Ethical Challenges to a Postcolonial Archaeology: The Legacy of Scientific Colonialism." In *Archaeology and Capitalism: From Ethics to Politics*, edited by Yannis Hamilakis and Philip Duke, 59–82. Walnut Creek, CA: Altamira Press.

North, Douglass C., John Joseph Wallis, and Barry R. Weingast. 2009. *Violence and Social Orders: A Conceptual Framework for Interpreting Recorded Human History*. Cambridge: Cambridge University Press.

Ober, Josiah. 2010. "Wealthy Hellas." *Transactions of the American Philological Association* 140 (2): 241–286.

Ortiz, Alfonso. 1969. *The Tewa World: Space, Time, Being and Becoming in a Pueblo Society*. Chicago: University of Chicago Press.

Ortiz, Simon. 1992. "What We See: A Perspective on Chaco Canyon and Its Ancestry." In *Chaco Canyon: A Center and Its World*, edited by Mary Peck, 65–72. Santa Fe: Museum of New Mexico Press.

Ortman, Scott G. 2016. "Discourse and Human Securities in Tewa Origins." In *The Archaeology of Human Experience*, edited by Michelle Hegmon. In Archeological

Papers of the American Anthropological Association vol. 27, 74–94. Washington, DC: American Anthropological Association.

Ortman, Scott G. 2018. "The Historical Anthropology of Tewa Social Organization." In *Puebloan Societies: Homology and Heterogeneity in Time and Space*, edited by Peter M. Whiteley, 51–74. Santa Fe, NM: School of Advanced Research Press.

Ortman, Scott G. 2019. "A New Kind of Relevance for Archaeology." *Frontiers in Digital Humanities* 6 (16). https://www.frontiersin.org/article/10.3389/fdigh.2019.00016.

Ortman, Scott G. 2020. "Bioarchaeology and the Narrative Construction of Tewa Identity." In *In Identity Revisited: The Bioarchaeology of Identity in the Americas and Beyond*, edited by Christopher M. Stojanowski and Kelly J. Knudson, 56–84. Tallahassee: University of Florida Press.

Ortman, Scott G., and Bruce A. Bradley. 2002. "Sand Canyon Pueblo: The Container in the Center." In *Seeking the Center Place: Archaeology and Ancient Communities in the Mesa Verde Region*, edited by Mark D. Varien and Richard H. Wilshusen, 41–78. Salt Lake City: University of Utah Press.

Ortman, Scott G., and José Lobo. 2020. "Smithian Growth in a Nonindustrial Society." *Science Advances* 6 (25): eaba5694. https://doi.org/10.1126/sciadv.aba5694.

Ostrom, Elinor. 1999. "A General Framework for Analyzing Sustainability of Socio-ecological Systems." *Science* 325 (5939): 419–422.

Parsons, Elsie C. (1926) 1994. *Tewa Tales*. Tucson: University of Arizona Press. Originally published by the American Folklore Society.

Plog, Stephen, and Carrie C. Heitman. 2010. "Hierarchy and Social Inequality in the American Southwest, A.D. 800–1200." *Proceedings of the National Academy of Science of the U.S.A.* 107 (46): 19619–19626.

Rassmann, Knut, René Ohlrau, Robert Hofmann, Carsten Mischka, Nataliia Burdo, Michail Yu Videjko, and Johannes Müller. 2014. "High Precision Tripolye Settlement Plans, Demographic Estimations and Settlement Organization." *Journal of Neolithic Archaeology* 16 (September): 96–134. https://doi.org/10.12766/jna.2014.3.

Reed, Paul F. 2008. *Chaco's Northern Prodigies: Salmon, Aztec, and the Ascendancy of the Middle San Juan Region after A.D. 1100*. Salt Lake City: University of Utah Press.

Rick, Torben C., and Daniel H. Sandweiss. 2020. "Archaeology, Climate, and Global Change in the Age of Humans." *Proceedings of the National Academy of Sciences* 117 (15): 8250. https://doi.org/10.1073/pnas.2003612117.

Rockman, Marcy, and Carrie Hritz. 2020. "Expanding Use of Archaeology in Climate Change Response by Changing Its Social Environment." *Proceedings of the National Academy of Sciences* 117 (15): 8295. https://doi.org/10.1073/pnas.1914213117.

Roser, Max. 2020. *The Short History of Global Living Conditions and Why It Matters That We Know It*. OurWorldInData.org. https://ourworldindata.org/a-history-of-global-living-conditions-in-5-charts.

Sachs, Jeffrey D. 2020. *The Ages of Globalization: Geography, Technology, and Institutions.* New York: Columbia University Press.

Schlanger, Sarah, Richard Wilshusen, and Heidi Roberts. 2015. "From Mining Sites to Mining Data: Archaeology's Future." *KIVA* 81 (1–2): 80–99. https://doi.org/10.1080 /00231940.2015.1118739.

Schmidt, Peter R. 2006. *Historical Archaeology in Africa: Representation, Social Memory, and Oral Traditions.* Lanham, MD: Altamira Press.

Schollmeyer, Karen Gust, and Jonathan C. Driver. 2013. "Settlement Patterns, Source–Sink Dynamics, and Artiodactyl Hunting in the Prehistoric U.S. Southwest." *Journal of Archaeological Method and Theory* 20 (3): 448–478. https://doi.org/10.1007/ s10816-012-9160-5.

Sekaquaptewa, Emory, Kenneth C. Hill, and Dorothy K. Washburn. 2015. *Hopi Katsina Songs.* Lincoln: University of Nebraska Press.

Sofaer, Anna. 2007. "The Primary Architecture of the Chacoan Culture: A Cosmological Expression." In *The Architecture of Chaco Canyon, New Mexico*, edited by Stephen H. Lekson, 225–254. Salt Lake City: University of Utah Press.

Simpson, Nicholas P., Joanne Clarke, Scott Allan Orr, Georgina Cundill, Ben Orlove, Sandra Fatorić, Salma Sabour, Nadia Khalaf, Marcy Rockman, Patricia Pinho, Shobha S. Maharaj, Poonam V. Mascarenhas, Nick Shepherd, Pindai M. Sithole, Grace Wambui Ngaruiya, Debra C. Roberts, and Christopher H. Trisos. 2022. "Decolonizing Climate Change–Heritage Research." *Nature Climate Change* 12 (3): 210–213.

Stephens, Lucas, Dorian Fuller, Nicole Boivin, Torben Rick, Nicolas Gauthier, Andrea Kay, Ben Marwick, Chelsey Geralda Armstrong, C. Michael Barton, Tim Denham, Kristina Douglass, Jonathan Driver, Lisa Janz, Patrick Roberts, J. Daniel Rogers, Heather Thakar, Mark Altaweel, Amber L. Johnson, Maria Marta Sampietro Vattuone, Mark Aldenderfer, Sonia Archila, Gilberto Artioli, Martin T. Bale, Timothy Beach, Ferran Borrell, Todd Braje, Philip I. Buckland, Nayeli Guadalupe Jiménez Cano, José M. Capriles, Agustín Diez Castillo, Çiler Çilingiroğlu, Michelle Negus Cleary, James Conolly, Peter R. Coutros, R. Alan Covey, Mauro Cremaschi, Alison Crowther, Lindsay Der, Savino di Lernia, John F. Doershuk, William E. Doolittle, Kevin J. Edwards, Jon M. Erlandson, Damian Evans, Andrew Fairbairn, Patrick Faulkner, Gary Feinman, Ricardo Fernandes, Scott M. Fitzpatrick, Ralph Fyfe, Elena Garcea, Steve Goldstein, Reed Charles Goodman, Jade Dalpoim Guedes, Jason Herrmann, Peter Hiscock, Peter Hommel, K. Ann Horsburgh, Carrie Hritz, John W. Ives, Aripekka Junno, Jennifer G. Kahn, Brett Kaufman, Catherine Kearns, Tristram R. Kidder, François Lanoë, Dan Lawrence, Gyoung-Ah Lee, Maureece J. Levin, Henrik B. Lindskoug, José Antonio López-Sáez, Scott Macrae, Rob Marchant, John M. Marston, Sarah McClure, Mark D. McCoy, Alicia Ventresca Miller, Michael Morrison, Giedre Motuzaite Matuzeviciute, Johannes Müller, Ayushi Nayak, Sofwan Noerwidi, Tanya M. Peres, Christian E. Peterson, Lucas Proctor, Asa R. Randall, Steve Renette,

Gwen Robbins Schug, Krysta Ryzewski, Rakesh Saini, Vivian Scheinsohn, Peter Schmidt, Pauline Sebillaud, Oula Seitsonen, Ian A. Simpson, Arkadiusz Sołtysiak, Robert J. Speakman, Robert N. Spengler, Martina L. Steffen, Michael J. Storozum, Keir M. Strickland, Jessica Thompson, T. L. Thurston, Sean Ulm, M. Cemre Ustunkaya, Martin H. Welker, Catherine West, Patrick Ryan Williams, David K. Wright, Nathan Wright, Muhammad Zahir, Andrea Zerboni, Ella Beaudoin, Santiago Munevar Garcia, Jeremy Powell, Alexa Thornton, Jed O. Kaplan, Marie-José Gaillard, Kees Klein Goldewijk, and Erle Ellis. 2019. "Archaeological Assessment Reveals Earth's Early Transformation through Land Use." *Science* 365 (6456): 897–902. https://doi.org/10.1126/science.aax1192.

Stuart, David E. 2014. *Anasazi America: Seventeen Centuries on the Road from Center Place.* 2nd ed. Albuquerque: University of New Mexico Press.

Trautman, Thomas R., and Peter M. Whiteley. 2012. "A Classic Problem." In *Crow-Omaha: New Light on a Classic Problem of Kinship Analysis*, edited by Thomas R. Trautman and Peter M. Whiteley, 1–30. Tucson: University of Arizona Press.

Van Dyke, Ruth M. 2007. *The Chaco Experience: Landscape and Ideology at the Center Place.* Santa Fe, NM: School for Advanced Research Press.

Van West, Carla R. 1994. *Modeling Prehistoric Agricultural Productivity in Southwestern Colorado: A GIS Approach.* Department of Anthropology, Washington State University, Pullman, and Crow Canyon Archaeological Center, Cortez, CO.

Vansina, Jan. 1961. *Oral Tradition: A Study in Historical Methodology.* London: Routledge and Kegan Paul.

Varien, Mark D., and Richard H. Wilshusen, eds. 2002. *Seeking the Center Place: Archaeology and Ancient Communities in the Mesa Verde Region.* Salt Lake City: University of Utah Press.

Ware, John A. 2014. *A Pueblo Social History: Kinship, Sodality, and Community in the Northern Southwest.* Santa Fe, NM: School for Advanced Research Press.

Watson, Adam S., Stephen Plog, Brendan J. Culleton, Patricia A. Gilman, Steven A. LeBlanc, Peter M. Whiteley, Santiago Claramunt, and Douglas J. Kennett. 2015. "Early Procurement of Scarlet Macaws and the Emergence of Social Complexity in Chaco Canyon, NM." *Proceedings of the National Academy of Sciences* 112 (27): 8238. https://doi.org/10.1073/pnas.1509825112.

Windes, Thomas C. 1992. "Blue Notes: The Chacoan Turquoise Industry in the San Juan Basin." In *Anasazi Regional Organization and the Chaco System*, edited by David E. Doyel. Anthropological Papers No. 5, 159–168. Albuquerque: Maxwell Museum of Anthropology.

7

The Knowledge Keepers

Protecting Pueblo Culture from the Western World

JOSEPH H. SUINA

THE PUEBLOS

We the Knowledge Keepers are the descendants of the Pueblo ancestors who migrated out of the Four Corners area over 700 years ago. We are referred to as Pueblos, a name given to us by the Spaniards at first European contact. There are twenty-one federally recognized Pueblo tribes in New Mexico, one Pueblo in Texas, Ysleta del Sur, and the Hopi Tribe in Arizona. Each nation refers to itself by its traditional name and language within the Pueblo world. We are independent and separate from one another, with six different languages and dialects. Our traditional social and religious organizations and activities take place in our kivas and on our plazas as handed down to us by our ancestors. We have inherent rights as sovereign nations to govern and make decisions about our people, lands, and resources (Rainie et al. 2017). Using our cultural knowledge without our permission is a direct violation of our sovereign rights.

https://doi.org/10.5876/9781646424597.c007

Western Knowledge

The clash that occurs when certain Pueblo information falls into the hands of outsiders is partly due to differing conceptualizations of knowledge between the Pueblos and Western world. Except for highly classified government and personal information protected by law, just about anything is available to know and share in the dominant world. One only needs time, money, and the desire to acquire it, and it takes less than a minute to Google today's high-speed, fingertip-accessed information. Western knowledge is highly valued, and the monetary rewards and status it brings to academics are substantial. Every field of study has a research component, where the discovery of new information is expected to extend the knowledge base and the careers of those working within it. To deny information is to deny this opportunity, which goes against Western notions of success. Denying information creates suspicion of what people might be hiding or whether this behavior is even lawful and discriminatory toward non-Native enquirers. Herein lies the conflict over information sharing between Pueblos and the Western world.

Pueblo Knowledge

Knowledge is highly valued in the Pueblo world, and there is knowledge that everyone must have to be an effective member of their society. Basic core values and language skills are essential, without limitation on who can and must have it, including children. The sooner children learn core values and language, the better. Thereafter, specialized knowledge is something that not just anyone can access. Internal measures have been thoughtfully put in place to secure this knowledge because, in the wrong hands, it can be devastating. One must earn the right to acquire specific knowledge. Acquisition is based on maturity, gender, and commitment. All members must demonstrate that they are mature enough to learn certain information, make proper use of it, and protect it from "children," referring to those not yet ready for it regardless of numerical age. Keeping religious information from outsiders falls into this category, too.

While men and women are considered equals, certain knowledge is gender based. Both females and males are essential for maintaining a healthy balance between the two energies needed in the world. As with maturity, knowing and applying gender-specific information for the welfare of the Pueblo are important (Martinez and Suina 2005). Knowing what the other gender knows is of little use, so why waste time? However, trust and respect for one another are key to a workable and smooth relationship, particularly between spouses. This matter is addressed with great care when a couple is receiving village prenuptial advice. Neither is to question the other about their knowledge, including when or where he or she is needed for a community obligation. They are reminded that trust is established and maintained by being where you are supposed to be and carrying out your duty. Once the privilege is earned, the mother or the father will take the lead in providing a gender-specific education for their children. They will get the novice up to speed as quickly as possible and make it crystal clear to the student that she or he is now a Knowledge Keeper and must refrain from sharing newly acquired information with anyone not yet prepared. Concealment is not a new concept, and keeping the information within the appropriate group is a responsibility taken seriously.

The highest level of knowledge is earned by agreeing to serve the Pueblo in a unique post of responsibility, a calling that only a small percentage of Pueblo members have. It is one that comes with considerable clout but also with of a lifetime of responsibility. Esoteric knowledge is especially protected, not just from outsiders but from the general Pueblo population, who has no business prying into these matters. To be too curious is said to be inviting something one is not destined for and will ultimately lead to disaster. Keeping this sacred information separate and away from ordinary citizens endows it with spiritual power that is only for the few who earn it through lengthy training and internship. But even this well-hidden domain was not safe from the peering eyes of the outside world. Knowledge and activities were targeted by the Spaniards and, later, the focal point of the cultural genocide campaign undertaken by the US government. Since the 1800s, photographers, scholars, and an assortment of curious outsiders have also caused considerable harm in their attempts to uncover this enticing, hidden information.

In the Pueblo, no one person—no matter how important—will know everything, and that is perfectly okay. Knowing comes with expectations and accountability. If a person fails to hold his or her knowledge responsibly, this violation may be pointed out by those with lesser status. A breach of this unwritten social agreement can lead to banishment from the tribe.

COLONIALISM

Spanish Colonialism

Concealment, as a normal part of Pueblo culture, intensified considerably during the Spanish Colonial Era in Pueblo country. Hand in hand, the military and missionaries sought riches for their majesty and souls for their God. Although the riches never materialized, Pueblo nations were ripe for religious conversion and labor extraction by the Spaniards. Practitioners of Native religions were beaten, and many paid the ultimate price for continued engagement in the forbidden. Pueblos were forced to build huge churches and convert to Catholicism under threat of death. Native religion was at the heart of Pueblo life, and to have it uprooted and replaced with a foreign belief was intolerable. Revolts were attempted without success, that is, not until a unified effort took place in 1680, after eighty-two years of religious suppression.

The iron fist of the military and the watchful eyes of the missionaries kept the Pueblos in line. However, the two could not be everywhere at all times. The Pueblos used this weakness to their advantage and found creative ways to preserve their precious lifeline to the spirit world. By pretending to be devout Catholics—baptizing babies, attending mass, and dancing on saints' days—they avoided scrutiny and detection. They altered their ceremonial calendar ever so slightly to fit the Catholic calendar, which allowed continuation of approved dances and ceremonies. Forbidden rites and beliefs went underground, where they remain today. The result was unwavering as there was community solidarity around this concealment effort—the opposite of what the Spaniards intended.

Mexican Government

Spanish rule gave way to a short-lived Mexican government, which was succeeded by the United States. The 1848 Treaty of Guadalupe Hidalgo gave Mexican citizenship to the Pueblos and the right to sell lands held in common (Sando 1976). While citizenship was a step in the right direction, it took away Mexican government land protections and made them vulnerable to non-Indian squatters. Encroachment on Pueblo lands escalated when the United States took control. Pueblos did not have the same status and protections as did the rest of the tribes in the United States. It was not until 1913, a year after New Mexico's statehood, when Pueblos were lawfully recognized as Indian tribes. Before that, they relied on their own resources to protect their people and property. While outside governments rose and fell, Pueblo governments and traditions continued to thrive under the protective watch of the Knowledge Keepers. However, by the mid-1800s, Pueblos faced renewed attacks on their culture and languages by the latest outside force, the United States government.

United States Government

In 1879, the Carlisle Indian Industrial School was established in Pennsylvania (figure 7.1). Tribal children from across the country, including the Pueblos, were removed from their homes and villages to undergo the Americanization process funded by the federal government (Connell-Szasz 1999).

The solution to the so-called Indian problem that the United States faced was conceived by Captain Richard Henry Pratt, an army officer and Indian fighter. His strategy to "Kill the Indian and save the man" (Adams 1995, 52) meant doing away with Indian cultures and languages and replacing them with that of the whites. Indian agents and the military scoured the lands for Indian children. The goal of federal Indian policy was to assimilate Indians into the dominant world after complete erasure of Tribalism.

Pratt used an old army installation and employed strict military regimentation to transform Indians into whites. Children as young as five were torn from

FIGURE 7.1. *Outdoor group portrait of seventeen unidentified American Indian girls in Native dress, upon arrival at the Carlisle Indian Industrial School. Courtesy of US Army Heritage and Education Center, Carlisle, PA.*

their mothers' arms and shipped off by train to unknown places. Distance and years of no contact with family and tribe were the solution to rub out what whites saw as Indian savagery, laziness, ignorance, and filth, and to prevent further contamination (Adams 1995). By 1901, tens of thousands of Indian students were enrolled in twenty-five boarding schools throughout the United States (figure 7.2). All were focused on obliterating Native culture, replacing it with white culture using military-style education.

Native traditions were major impediments. A sign at one boarding school well into the twentieth century read "Tradition is the Enemy of Progress." Upon returning to their home communities, students "quickly returned to the blanket," or readopted practices that were stripped at school. The government learned that culture is not a suit of clothing one removes and replaces with another; it had underestimated the power of Native communities to reclaim their stolen children.

But not all students returned home. Many died from contagious diseases that swept through overcrowded dorms. It is believed that some of the younger children died from heartache, hungering for the loving arms of their mothers. The graveyards in the back of the school buildings began to grow. Targeted areas of traditional culture in the Pueblo villages went even deeper undercover to prevent further removal of children. Indian animosity and resentment toward the US government deepened.

FIGURE 7.2. *A photo of the students and staff from 1884, Carlisle Indian Industrial School. Courtesy of US Army Heritage and Education Center, Carlisle, PA.*

Religious Crimes Code

To step up the assimilation process, the government imposed the 1883 Religious Crimes Code, which denied Indians their first amendment rights for freedom of religion. It prohibited ceremonial practices that might be contrary to accepted Christian standards and implemented punitive measures against Tribal leaders who encouraged them (Dozier 1970). This law limited when and where Indian dances could occur. Five months out of the year were forbidden to all forms of ceremonial rites. Native people under fifty years of age were not allowed to participate, and public education was carried out on the evils of ceremonialism. The government went great lengths to turn the public against Indian traditions and targeted religious groups, women's clubs, and similar organizations who tried to protect Native people from negative outside forces (including the US government) (James 1974). In 1923, the commissioner of Indian affairs, Charles H. Burke, used the same law to try to stop ceremonies aimed at the Sun Dance of the Plains Indians and the ceremonial activities of the Pueblos.

The Pueblos had no option but to take even greater caution in carrying out their religious obligations, like in the days of Spanish oppression. They kept a close surveillance over their own people. Those who gave information to outsiders were severely punished, and some were put to death. Pressure not to provide information from within, and pressure to do so from the outside, squeezed Pueblo citizens, who were caught in the middle. Hopi leaders, labeled "hostiles," were incarcerated by the federal government for keeping a firm grip on traditions and refusing to send children to boarding schools (James 1974).

Termination Era

In the 1950s, the US government again decided that Indians were better off fully assimilated. In 1953, the official policy was introduced as Public Law 280, which gave the right to states to extend their jurisdiction over some nonterminated tribes (Wilkinson 2005). This policy, referred to as "Indian Termination," stated that Indians could not achieve full American citizenship unless Tribalism was dismantled for all tribes. This meant no more traditional governments, no Indian lands, and the death of Tribal cultures that had been in existence since time immemorial. Termination meant total assimilation for some tribes immediately, and others, considered less prepared, were soon to follow. Apprehension and fear turned into panic in Indian communities throughout the country. This hit home for me personally. "My mom could not conceal her crying at midnight in response to something my dad was relaying. He just came home from a late-night council meeting. What I thought was a family argument, turned out to be about a list that our Pueblo was placed on, 'for doing away with our way of life', as he put it. Her hysterical questions, 'What are we going to do, where are going to go live?' still ring in my mind. As a child, I too became terrified not understanding what the government had in store us" (Suina, personal communication).

Coinciding with this initiative was the Indian Relocation Act of 1956 (also known as Public Law 959 and the Adult Vocational Training Program). It was designed to place Indian families in distant cities and enroll adults in a vocational program to learn a trade. Upon completion, they were provided with job placement assistance and housing in various cities across the US, including Oakland, Chicago, Dallas, Denver, and Phoenix. This program was something my parents never would have thought about doing. The Indian Relocation Act was yet another threat to a way of life that Indians had known since the beginning of time.

As with boarding schools, the training program was a failed experiment. Terminated tribes were soon begging to be reinstated (Wilkinson 2005), and many relocated families discovered they were not cut out for city life. Those who came home could not find jobs or utilize their trade. Those who stayed in urban areas encountered racism and other obstacles. Members from different tribes settled in less-than-desirable parts of cities, where they tried their best to re-create Indian culture.

THE TOURISTS

Visitation by outsiders to Pueblo communities has also contributed to the need to protect knowledge. Their careless, and at times disrespectful, behavior has led Zuni Pueblo to close its well-known Shalako ceremony to outsiders after

FIGURE 7.3. *Highly visible signs remind guests to refrain from recording of any kind. Photo courtesy of author.*

throngs of tourists arrived in Las Vegas casino–style tour buses expecting to be entertained. Their obnoxious sense of entitlement and discarded trash ruined the sacredness of the event. While most outside guests are respectful during open dances, each Pueblo can cite similar experiences. It is for this reason that numerous signs inform outsiders what they cannot do in the Pueblo (figure 7.3).

Scholars and Photographers

Every Pueblo has been the focus of unauthorized publications that have included photographs and sketches never meant to be seen outside the village or out of the proper context of a ceremony. These works are by academics who should know better than most that such exposure is harmful to those for whom the information is sacred. Esoteric knowledge not to be shared with ordinary Pueblo citizens is laid bare for all to see. In some cases, the inside culprit was a trusted, but desperate, Tribal member who took a few dollars to satisfy an addiction. This violation undermines the integrity of the group, who is responsible for the knowledge in the eyes of the community. One elder referring to an incident of this nature stated, "We all have been cheapened" (Suina, personal communication, 2017). This harm remains an open wound for as long as these publications are out in the world.

The Pueblos do not practice knowledge concealment to similar degrees. Information shared comfortably by one Pueblo might be resolutely guarded by another. Usually, the more conservative a Pueblo is, the stricter the security measures and severity of the penalties are for infractions. The physical location of a Pueblo is another factor in determining the degree of security that is required. Eastern Pueblos, especially those along the Rio Grande, guard ceremonies, practitioners, and all restricted information, items, and places with great vigilance. The Spanish colonial presence along the river corridor called for guarded security so that ceremonies could continue unbeknownst to their oppressors (Dozier 1970). Zuni Pueblo in western New Mexico and Hopi in Arizona were further removed from a continual Spanish presence, so constant vigilance was not essential. A major indicator of this difference, as seen in Pueblos today, is that ceremonies open to outsiders in the West are off limits to those in the East. A first-time, eastern Pueblo visitor is shocked at what is on public display during western Pueblo ceremonies, and in the presence of non-Indians nonetheless (Suina 2002).

Artwork with symbols, designs, and images of sacred dancers—that are taboo in the East—are not restricted in the West. Another indicator of Spanish imposition is detected in the surnames of Eastern community members. The mostly Spanish last names were given to people during baptism. The church kept records of newly baptized Indians using the baptismal sponsor's name (who was required to be Spanish) or the name of the priest who provided the sacrament. Common last names include Herrera, Garcia, Trujillo, Chavez, and Quintana among others (Dozier 1970). In addition, many Eastern dances coincide with the church calendar where the Catholicism is practiced in greater numbers. These examples illustrate how Spanish intrusions affected eastern Pueblos differently than western Pueblos, resulting in strict measures taken by the Knowledge Keepers.

Helpless Victim View

Throughout the course of American history, Indian tribes have been perceived as vulnerable to the whims of the government and to outsiders who wanted something from the Indians—be it their land, labor, souls, or their ancestors, remains. While the US recognized tribes as sovereign nations with legitimate governments and engaged in treaties with them, they were made wards of the government through the Indian Non-intercourse Act. Many in America felt that the extinction of Indians was inevitable and required government intervention. Providing government protections legitimized the placement of Indians on reservations and federal laws that severely curtailed Tribal sovereignty. With dislocation, loss of homelands, and loss of subsistence practices, the government "stepped in" with rations, increasing the dependency on Western food and the loss of self-sufficiency, self-protection, and self-respect. The government tried to erase all vestiges of Native culture and language through the painful process of removing children from home communities, disrupting the normal course of intergenerational life during the boarding school era.

The outside world assumed it knew best how to take care of, and deal with, the "Indian problem" and that the Indian was hopelessly caught in the eddy of the powerful current of American civilization with no moorings and sense of control. Yet Indians have successfully responded to the forces of the Western world for centuries in ingenious ways (Wilcox 2009).

Defiance as Defense

Concealment, deception, and adaptability were weapons against the erasure of Pueblo culture by Christianization and assimilation initiatives. Among the Rio Grande Pueblos, deception included shifting the Pueblo ceremonial calendar to coincide with the church calendar. Traditional winter animal dances were moved to Christmas Day and Three Kings Day. Complying with their proselytizers' demands without compromise of their own religion was a motive of the Knowledge Keepers. Regardless of what colonists imposed, eastern Pueblos adapted. The Spanish created offices of the governors, the fiscals (church officers), and sacristans intended to control the Pueblos (positions still held in the church today).

The Spaniards had two views of Pueblo dances and ceremonies. They were out to destroy practices labeled as "pagan" and "devil worship," and yet they approved and encouraged dances and rites for honoring saints, feast days, and memorials of the church. The Spanish assumed that Pueblo spiritual expressions would automatically transfer to Catholicism. Compartmentalization, according to Edward P. Dozier (1970), a Pueblo anthropologist, describes an eastern Pueblo tactic used to privately practice objectionable activities while in the presence of Spanish authorities. For people who did not understand the values and deeper meaning of Christianity, this was an effective tool for addressing behavior that was, to them, just another form of oppression (Dozier 1970). It allowed for the preservation of moiety leaders and involved village-wide activities in traditional rites designed to gain blessings for all people, as was practiced before Spanish contact.

Michael Wilcox (2009, 12) notes social boundaries are set "when a group enacts measures to protect resources, materials, and information from outsiders." These measures create exclusive membership, insulate behaviors from outside influences, and consolidate power. He uses a modern-day plaza dance as an example. The Pueblo establishes a social boundary between the dancers and people of the village watching from the inner circle while the outsiders watch from the outer rim while having to conform to Pueblo rules as guests. Wilcox (2009) continues that on the outside, archaeology, a culture group of its own, enacts its social boundaries through its use of special language and knowledge that many Native people cannot interpret. Barriers, no matter how innocent or friendly, are established between the two.

IMPLICATIONS IN TODAY'S WORLD

Pueblo people have an intimate connection to landscapes and are morally obligated to care for the dwelling places of their ancestors. It is a challenge when an organization like the Crow Canyon Archaeological Center sincerely wishes to establish meaningful relationships with the Pueblos whose ancestors' culture makeup over 95 percent of its subject of study. The social boundary protecting cultural property in the Pueblo is not easily transferred to the outside world. The primary focus of Crow Canyon's work is research and education, meaning creating new information, disseminating it to the public, and upholding the principles of scientific rigor. Western scientific and traditional Native values often clash, although not as violently as in the past. Respect, acceptance, and trust are words often used to describe a successful working relationship between the two stakeholders. How are the words put into action? Occasionally, a research project will come along in which both parties find a deep and shared interest. An example is the Pueblo Farming Project, enjoyed as a great success by both Crow Canyon and the Hopi Tribe (see Ermigiotti et al., chapter 4 in this volume). Working together as equal partners has been the key to establishing trust, along with recognizing and respecting the limits of social boundaries. Equal partnership, a concept unimagined until recently in Native relations with the Western world, is key for Tribal sovereignty, which is so important for Native people today. Inviting Native scholars to teach the public about contemporary Pueblo culture is another example of a respectful relationship. Crow Canyon provides this multivocal approach to education in their Cultural Explorations programs, College Field School, webinars, and camps (see Franklin, chapter 8 in this volume). Multivocal approaches to education benefit students, staff, and board members at Crow Canyon. Learning about the present does teach about the past. Comments made by participants in Crow Canyon's National Endowment for the Humanities K–12 teachers institutes, after witnessing a Santo Domingo feast day dance, include: "Now I understand the many places (ancestral villages) we've visited by seeing modern people exit the kiva and dance in the plaza." It is equally important to the Knowledge Keepers that all who visit their ancestral villages understand that the past continues in the present and that those places are occupied by ancestral spirits.

Modern-day Pueblo interest in the scientific explanation of their ancestors is greater than ever before. Pueblo youth are completing courses in anthropology and archaeology. Almost all Pueblos now have a Tribal Historic Preservation Office, which supports the protection and enhancement of cultural properties of the past and the present. With a boost from the Native American Graves Protection and Repatriation Act, both sides have had to assist one another on mutual concerns such as protecting ancestral sites from oil developers. These delicate and sacred landscapes still have much to tell, and the Knowledge Keepers are still morally obligated to protect them.

Not all Pueblos are ready to engage in a partnership with archaeologists. What works well with the Hopi Tribe may be uncomfortable for the conservative Pueblos in the Rio Grande area. It is important for Crow Canyon and other research institutions to reach out to the Pueblos that they have never been in partnership with and to begin building a trusting relationship that can only come about by sitting together and sharing concerns and dreams.

The hope and goal of these partnerships are to better understand the past to better understand the present and not repeat mistakes. Working together, with different views and perspectives, will force us to see new possibilities for the creation of a more inclusive world for all people.

REFERENCES

Adams, Davis W. 1995. *Education for Extinction: American Indians and the Boarding School Experience 1875–1928*. Lawrence: University of Kansas Press.

Connell-Szasz, Margaret. 1999. *Education and the American Indian: The Road to Self-Determination since 1928*. Albuquerque: University of New Mexico Press.

Dozier, Edward P. 1970. *The Pueblo Indians of North America*. Long Grove, IL: Waveland Press, Inc.

James, Harry C. 1974. *Pages from Hopi History*. Tucson: University of Arizona Press.

Martinez, Julian, and Joseph H. Suina. 2005. "Two Perspectives on the Pajarito Plateau." In *The Peopling of Bandelier: New Insights from the Archaeology of the Pajarito Plateau*, edited by Robert P. Powers, 129–133. Santa Fe, NM: School of American Research.

Rainie, Stephanie C., Desi Rodriguez-Lonebear, and Andrew Martinez. 2017. *Policy Brief: Indigenous Data Sovereignty in the United States*. Tucson, Native Nations Institute, University of Arizona.

Sando, Joe S. 1976. *The Pueblo Indians*. San Francisco: The Indian Historian Press.

Suina, Joseph H. 2002. "The Persistence of the Corn Mothers." In *Archaeologies of the Pueblo Revolt: Identity, Meaning, and Renewal in the Pueblo World*, edited by Robert W. Preucel, 212–216. Albuquerque: University of New Mexico Press.

Wilcox, Michael V. 2009. *The Pueblo Revolt and the Mythology of Conquest: An Indigenous Archaeology of Contact*. Berkeley: University of California Press.

Wilkinson, Charles. 2005. *Blood Struggle: The Rise of Modern Indian Nations*. New York: W.W. Norton and Company.

Archaeology and Public Education

8

Conceptualizing the Past

The Thoughtful Engagement of Hearts and Minds

M. ELAINE FRANKLIN

Since its founding in 1983, public engagement has been a fundamental aspect of the Crow Canyon Archaeological Center's mission. This chapter presents a synthesis of the Center's education work and contextualizes it within the constructs of cognitive theory and social semiotics. Included in this discussion are essential aspects of educational practice that have characterized Crow Canyon's public education programs for four decades; among these are experiential education and inquiry pedagogy, situated learning, multivocality, and the inclusion of descendant communities.

When novelist L. P. Hartley (1953, 17) said, "The past is a foreign country, they do things differently there," he summarized the challenges of understanding other times, cultures, and places from our situated position in the present. I begin with this quote because it lays bare the task that heritage professionals face—whether they be historians, archaeologists, educators, or museum specialists—when they work to help others conceptualize the past, or even to conceptualize it for themselves. To successfully work in one of these fields, it is necessary to not only understand the complexities of conveying accurate

https://doi.org/10.5876/9781646424597.c008

information about the past but also to recognize the equally complex realm of how people learn, how we construct knowledge, and how we make sense of our world. Crow Canyon has deep roots in bringing these domains of archaeological research and education together through an integrated mission that places value on intellectual engagement, rigorous research, and inclusion.

Each word in the title for this chapter is essential to a discussion of the educational work Crow Canyon has conducted over the last forty years, with engagement perhaps being key. Outreach and engagement are not the same. The two terms are often used interchangeably; however, they differ in some significant ways. In the most basic sense, outreach is done *for* others and engagement is done *with* others. Outreach generally occurs in one direction, with the organization offering educational information, whereas engagement is a collaborative, relational process. Both are equally important, but regarding public impact, outreach and engagement are qualitatively and quantitatively different. While Crow Canyon does conduct some outreach activities, it is, to its core, a publicly engaged institution.

As the title reflects, I look at the work the Center conducts in heritage education through both a cognitive and affective lens. From a cognitive perspective, I discuss the characteristics of educational practices that are informed by our knowledge of how people learn. Through the affective lens, I focus on the social, emotional, and cultural facets of the human past. These aspects can evoke the kind of caring that leads to conservation and preservation, but they can also lead to conflict and pain in the present. History—the human past—is sometimes passionate, often contested, too often political, and, undeniably, can be a source of present-day trauma and division. Effective public engagement and responsible heritage work require a commitment to acknowledging this complexity and to encouraging critical thought among learners of all ages as they grapple with making meaning of the past. In this chapter, I depict the work that Crow Canyon has undertaken over the last four decades to achieve this goal.

THINKING OUR WAY INTO THE PAST

Constructing Knowledge

Archaeologists study dinosaurs; "Indians" live in teepees; and societies continually progress toward greater complexity and sophistication. These are obvious and, perhaps, not so obvious misconceptions about archaeology, society, and culture. As Crow Canyon educators have long noted, these ideas are often expressed by children, but they are not exclusive to children. Some of us go on believing naive and inaccurate information as adults because we have not been confronted with information powerful enough to shatter and destroy these erroneous mental constructs. A significant body of research has explored and explained why this happens, why we form these misconceptions, and why they appear to be so intractable (Guzzetti and Hynd 1998).

To gain insight and consider the pedagogical approaches that might be most useful for moving past such misconceptions, it is necessary to look at some basic understandings about how people learn. To begin, it is important to recognize that we all possess conceptual maps that have been forming from our lived experiences since the day we were born—the proverbial "blank slate" does not exist. We carry our past with us, and we are generally not conscious of how our past affects our present-day concepts of reality, or how it impacts the way we process new information (Berger and Luckman 1967; Bowers 1987). The literature on this cognitive theory, generally known as constructivism, is far too vast to properly summarize in this chapter; however, it is useful to recognize two fundamental positions—cognitive and social constructivism.

Cognitive constructivism is often associated with the Swiss psychologist, Jean Piaget (Scheurman 1998). Key to his theory of learning is the notion that knowledge is acquired as a result of the individual's attempt to maintain intellectual equilibrium. According to Piaget, new information is assimilated within a paradigm of what we already know and understand about the world. When we confront new information that is incompatible with our prior understanding, which he referred to as perturbations, we are left in a state of disequilibrium. In order to restore equilibrium, we are forced to recast our mental models (Guzzetti and Hynd 1998; Scheurman 1998).

The undoing or disruption of deeply ingrained prior beliefs, such as stereotypes, generally requires new information of such a powerful nature that it can often make the learner feel uncomfortable or *perturbed*. This is the disequilibrium to which Piaget referred (Montangero and Maurice-Naville 1997). When the new information is incorporated into the learner's conceptual understanding, they experience a paradigm shift and equilibrium is again achieved. When new information lacks power or credibility for one reason or another, the learner simply holds onto their prior understanding.

The social constructivist perspective is generally associated with the Russian psychologist Lev Vygotsky (Scheurman 1998). He accepted Piaget's views of how individuals build private understandings, but he moved beyond the individual to say that knowledge is co-constructed in social contexts, resulting in public understandings of objects and events. From this perspective, knowledge is not objective but is a product of the interactions and agreements of society. To understand this, one might think of humor and the way it is socially and culturally situated. Humor generally involves a great deal of insider knowledge and, if absent, we simply do not *get it*. While all the members of a cultural group are not likely to agree on what is funny, they will generally understand why something is *supposed* to be funny. Researchers who have focused specifically on the teaching and learning of history have documented the challenges that our social and cultural lenses can impose on our ability to learn about the human past.

Educational psychologist Sam Wineburg (2001) says that historical thinking is an unnatural act because of our desire to make the past familiar rather than become amazed at its strangeness. In interviews with both high school students and adults, he found that their natural inclination was to explain historical events in terms of existing beliefs or according to the rules of their culturally bound logic. Numerous instructional strategies have been informed or influenced by constructivist learning theory, focusing particularly on the importance of prior knowledge and the need to have the learner confront their misconceptions (NSTA 2021). The work of American philosopher, psychologist, and educator John Dewey, a contemporary of Piaget's and Vygotsky's, is perhaps the most notable and influential. Dewey recognized the crucial place held by experience in the learning process (1938). He argued that in order for education to be most effective, the student must be an active participant and that content must be presented in a way that allows the student to relate the information to prior experiences. Dewey's ideas laid the foundation for experiential education and informed the modern theory of experiential learning, as well as other approaches such as inquiry and Problem or Project Based Learning (PBL), in which experience and reflection are also at the center. The coupling of reflection with experience was, according to Dewey, critical. He said we do not learn from experience; we learn from reflecting on an experience (1938). Throughout the experiential learning process, the learner should be actively engaged in posing questions, investigating, experimenting, being curious, solving problems, assuming responsibility, being creative, and constructing meaning (Association of Experiential Education 2021).

Caring about the Past: Everyone's History Matters

Conceptualizing or *thinking our way into the past* is both an intellectual endeavor and an affective one. "Current scholarship on cognition recognizes the inseparable relationship of thought and feeling in cognitive development" (Barton and Levstik 2004, 236). Historians and archaeologists are careful to point out the danger of letting feelings enter our understanding of the past—the stories we tell need to be fully grounded in evidence obtained through rigorous scholarly inquiry. However, an empirical understanding of past events does not demand the exclusion of feelings or of a caring frame of mind. "Care is the motivating force behind nearly all historical research, and it shapes our interest in its products: we attend to books, articles, documentaries, museums and historic sites only because we care about what we find there" (Barton and Levstik 2004, 228).

Studies conducted with the general public have documented a high level of interest in the human past. This connection holds true as long as the studies are describing experiences out of school. When referring to history in school, adjectives such as "dry," "irrelevant," and "boring" are common (Rosenzweig and

Thelen 1998). The approach to history in school experienced by many of these respondents was generally of the survey variety, with a fact-filled march through time, from war-to-war and king-to-king. They simply could not find a way to connect—a reason to care. Emotion has often been seen as a threat to objectivity, and passion does pose a threat to historical understanding, especially when the forces of emotion cause us to hold on to deeply held beliefs in the face of evidence to the contrary. Yet it would be difficult to imagine a serious historical work in which emotion played no role (Wineburg 2001).

In the early 2000s, educators at the Crow Canyon Archaeological Center made explicit a fundamental belief that characterizes the Center's values: *Everyone's History Matters*. This is true for groups of people, just as it is for individuals. This phrase acknowledges that what we have been, where we have been, and what we have experienced are all factors in carving our path to the present. How we care—or do not care—about the past informs actions and reactions in the present. *Everyone's History Matters* also recognizes that caring about the past is integral to how we go about studying it in the present and how we thoughtfully engage others in that study.

Throughout this section, I have highlighted some essential aspects of sound educational practices and how they relate to studies of the human past. In the following section I use these lenses to look at the work of Crow Canyon's public education programs from 1983 to the present.

ROOTS

In the 1960s, classroom teacher Dr. Edward F. Berger frustrated with the restrictions he felt existed in the traditional curriculum, began creating supplemental education programs for his Denver-area students (Berger 2000; Lightfoot and Lipe, chapter 2 in this volume). Experiential curricula that engaged students in authentic community-based projects was central to the programs he designed. After a time, these supplemental programs grew into more intensive service learning, and by 1968 his local history project evolved into a summer program in southwestern Colorado (Berger 2000). Archaeology and the study of past cultures became the core of these programs as he felt these studies can give us unique insights into our own lives and culture (2000). In 1972, Berger founded a nonprofit organization called the Interdisciplinary Supplemental Education Program (I-SEP) to formalize this work, and in 1974 he purchased eighty acres of land in Crow Canyon, near Cortez, Colorado, to give that program a home (see Lightfoot and Lipe, chapter 2 in this volume). Although originally named the I-SEP school, according to Berger, locals began calling it the Crow Canyon School (2000).

The curricula were thoughtfully constructed, with attention to both hands-on experiences and reflection on those experiences. He saw that a student needed to be able to make associations between what they were learning and what they already knew and understood. The Crow Canyon School provided, in Berger's words, "concentrated, thematic, experiential immersion programs" (Berger 2000, xii). By 1983, the Crow Canyon School merged with Northwestern University's Center for American Archaeology and became known as the Crow Canyon Archaeological Center. The merger lasted for two years, and Crow Canyon emerged from it as an independent nonprofit organization (see Lightfoot and Lipe, chapter 2 in this volume). In 1986, the Bergers left the Center feeling that the educational mission and programs of the institution were well established (Berger 2000).

This account is but a brief overview of Crow Canyon's roots. My purpose in including it is twofold: to shine a light on the educational nature of Crow Canyon's genesis and to illuminate the quality and character of that work. The fact that the earliest programs were designed and conducted by educators who were committed to experience-based, immersive programs that truly engage learners has had a lasting impact on the Center's mission and has helped shape it for the last forty years. In the following sections, I look closely at key strategies that grew out of, and beyond, these roots to actively involve learners of all ages in conceptualizing the past.

CITIZEN SCIENCE AND INQUIRY LEARNING

Since 1983, Crow Canyon has unarguably been a national forerunner in the practice of citizen science. As defined by the National Geographic Society, "Citizen science is the practice of public participation and collaboration in scientific research to increase scientific knowledge. Through citizen science, people share and contribute to data monitoring and collection programs" (National Geographic 2021). This definition well reflects the research partnership that Crow Canyon holds with members of the public. Tens of thousands of individuals, from middle-school-age students to senior citizens, have contributed to the Center's ongoing research into the ancestral Pueblo history of the Mesa Verde region. They have contributed through participation in excavation and survey, as well as through artifact analysis and classification. Lessons learned in these authentic research experiences are vast, some simple and others more complex. Distinguishing between a piece of sandstone and a pottery sherd is surely one of the more basic lessons, but embedded in it is knowledge about the construction of pottery (temper, firing, slip), geology (local and nonlocal clays and minerals), and even some simple geometry and awareness of spatial relationships (curvature, arcs, and relation of parts to the whole).

Lessons about the nature of archaeology and the nature of science in general are woven throughout Crow Canyon's programs. Participants are made aware of research questions and design, and why a particular approach was selected, and are informed about technologies involved in the research process. Preconceptions about archaeology abound, some exciting, some not, and many

FIGURE 8.1. *Students collecting data from the field, Haynie site. Courtesy of the Crow Canyon Archaeological Center.*

inaccurate. After spending a few hours methodically scraping dirt, taking measurements, and recording findings, any delusions of glamour fall away (figure 8.1). Confronted with powerful data of a contradictory nature, learners find that it becomes impossible to hold on to old ideas, and their concepts of what archaeology is and what archaeologists do are revised.

Some of the more sophisticated lessons learned are of the big picture variety and may be as informed by setting as by the activity. Many of Crow Canyon's citizen science participants are from places that are far less arid than the Mesa Verde region. As they spend time in this environment and learn about village population sizes and subsistence patterns, their curiosity about things such as how ancestral Pueblo people survived, and even thrived, is reflected in the growing complexity of their questions. As is the goal in inquiry instruction, learners become intrinsically motivated to pursue further study. For a significant number of participants, the desire is strong enough to bring them back to Crow Canyon again and again, some as alumni, some as interns, and sometimes as staff members.

IMMERSIVE ENVIRONMENTS

In 1985, the first replica structure was built on the Crow Canyon campus. This was the Basketmaker III period (AD 500–750) Pithouse Learning Center, a partially underground building constructed of adobe, wooden posts, and brush or twigs. The pithouse has gone through numerous rebuilds over the decades, often with newer strategies for extending the life of the building but always with a commitment to stay true to the authentic look and feel of a seventh-century AD household. This structure has served as a classroom to thousands of students who have visited the campus over the last thirty to forty years. Their time spent in and around it involves learning about the lifestyles of people who would have lived in such houses, including subsistence, clothing, and technologies appropriate to the era. The educator guiding them through this exploration helps them develop their conceptual understanding through a series of thoughtful questions such as, "How would you build this house?" "What would you do first, second . . . ?" The educator would also respond to the numerous student questions that are inevitably inspired by the pithouse itself: "What's the floor made of?" "How did it get so hard?" On colder days, the students might comment on how much warmer it is inside than out. Other observations might refer to textures and smells.

Since its inception, the pithouse has been an important instructional tool for student groups, along with a simulated excavation, a visit to Mesa Verde National Park, and "Windows into the Past" (an inquiry lesson with replica artifact assemblages). This series of lessons is designed to build understanding around the cultural history and chronology of the region, as well as about archaeological research methods. In 1998, when I served as director of education at the Center, we designed a research plan to investigate if, and to what extent, fourth and fifth grade students were meeting these learning objectives. We suspected that some time periods might be more firmly established in the students' minds than others, which was what we indeed found, but not in the way we expected. Results of the study pointed clearly to the fact that students were remembering far more

FIGURE 8.2. *Students engaging with Crow Canyon educator Rebecca Hammond at the Pueblo Learning Center. Courtesy of the Crow Canyon Archaeological Center.*

about the Basketmaker time period than any other. We had anticipated that knowledge of the Pueblo III period (AD 1150–1300) might be most prominent because of the students' visit to Mesa Verde National Park and the impressive structures they saw there. Instead, their illustrated timelines were much richer with details from the Basketmaker period. When they could not remember the kind of house associated with a time period, they simply drew a pithouse. After a close analysis of the activities included in the curriculum, the explanation became readily apparent; the pithouse was their only immersive experience, and the weight of it skewed their understanding. Given that knowledge of ancestral Pueblo cultural continuity and change is a cornerstone of the Center's education curriculum, a case could be made for expanding the campus's immersive learning environments. Thus, in 2003 the Pueblo Learning Center (PLC) was constructed. The PLC was based on a twelfth-century AD site in Mesa Verde National Park and, like the Basketmaker Pithouse Learning Center, was constructed with a commitment to the authentic look and feel of structures from the era. After the integration of the PLC into the curriculum, we conducted a follow-up study in 2004 that indicated a far more balanced understanding of the time periods and of changes across time (figure 8.2).

Immersive environments are powerful teaching tools because of their ability to make multisensory impressions, which is one of the reasons that Crow

Canyon places so much emphasis on authenticity. The more information that can be embedded in a particular source, the greater its power to shape conceptual understanding. In this sense, one picture truly is worth a thousand words. If that picture is incorrect or carries confusing information, faulty ideas can be formed that may be difficult to undo. In a larger sense, the natural setting itself can be seen as an immersive learning environment. This could be said for all variety of programs at Crow Canyon or any location where the past is studied in the place where it happened. The arid climate, the brilliant blue of the sky, the aroma of juniper and sage, and the color and texture of the sandstone are as much a part of the present as they were of the past and contribute to what learners think and feel about the history they are studying.

Experience is integral to all programs at the Center, but, as Dewey noted, we do not learn from experience, but rather we learn from reflection on experience (1938), which is the way educators end the lessons held in the Basketmaker Pithouse and Pueblo Learning Centers: "Many of the students' comments reveal that they are in the process of comparing their own daily lives to those of the ancient people they are learning about and are on the verge of changing the way they conceptualize life in other cultures and earlier times. Watching students change their attitudes toward people different than themselves is always a powerful and rewarding experience" (Parks 2000, 36).

MULTIVOCALITY AND INCLUSION

If everyone's history matters, then the inclusion of members of descendant communities in the telling of those histories and in the research process itself is essential. For Crow Canyon, this has meant developing relationships with Indigenous peoples of the region including Diné, Ute, and especially the Pueblos of New Mexico and Arizona. In the 1990s the Center formalized these connections through the establishment of an advisory group comprised of individuals who share expert knowledge and insights on research and education issues, as well as serve as scholars on various programs, both on and off campus.

The consultations and collaborations that have grown out of these relationships have served to dramatically enrich Crow Canyon's work in countless ways, but the conversations haven't always been easy. Complications come from several directions. Archaeological and Indigenous approaches to understanding the past differ; the border between the sacred and the secular is often less defined in some Indigenous cultures than in Western societies, and, perhaps most important, great diversity exists among the Indigenous people of the Southwest, even among the groups collectively referred to as Pueblo (see Suina, chapter 7 and Kuwanwisiwma and Bernardini, chapter 5 in this volume). Today there are thirty-two Pueblo communities in New Mexico and Arizona, representing five different language groups. Cultural traditions vary between the Pueblos, just as they must have 800 years ago, and knowledge of traditional practices within a Pueblo may be gendered.

There are numerous examples of how traditional Pueblo knowledge has informed the work of Crow Canyon, but two are particularly notable in the way they shaped education programs at the Center. The first involves the grinding of corn. For many years, students who visited the Center would have an opportunity to experience corn grinding with stone manos and metates when they visited the Pithouse Learning Center. This was deemed a valuable experience by Crow Canyon staff since it helped students develop an appreciation for the work that went into processing a major source of ancestral Pueblo food. After the formation of the Native American Advisory Group in 1995 and increased consultation, educators at the Center became aware that some of the Pueblo advisors considered this an inappropriate activity, particularly for males. In many of the Pueblos, corn grinding is still very much a part of traditional ceremonies and is only performed by females. As a result of numerous discussions, both internally and with Pueblo advisors, the decision was made to continue including the manos and metates in the two learning centers but to cease the act of corn grinding. The grinding stones themselves provide an opportunity to not only talk about the importance of corn and how it was processed traditionally but also to talk about why the Center does not include corn grinding in the lifestyle activities.

The other example involved the construction of the Pueblo Learning Center, which was modeled after a Pueblo III period site on Mesa Verde proper that included a roomblock, tower, and kiva. In the interest of authenticity and conveying accurate details about Pueblo houses and communities in the eleventh and twelfth centuries AD, Crow Canyon designed a plan to incorporate all of the architectural components, including the kiva. This was problematic from the perspective of the Pueblo advisors, as kivas continue to serve ceremonial functions today and should only be built by certain people and may only be entered by people who are initiated into a particular group. The difficult conversations that transpired eventually led to the decision that a kiva would not be built but that its absence would inspire a teachable moment. This takes the form of reflective discussions that engage students in thinking about what is missing from the household layout and requires them to make inferences about why there is no kiva. The lessons taught through the omission of the kiva might well be more profound than any that could be conveyed with its inclusion.

The impact that collaboration with the Native American Advisory Group and other American Indian partners has had on Crow Canyon's educational programming is immeasurable. Their advice on educational content has helped shaped the Center's curricula for all age groups and for both on- and off-campus programs. Perhaps, even more significant than their advice has been their actual presence as coinstructors in numerous programs across the years, from High

FIGURE 8.3. *Crow Canyon educator Dan Simplicio teaching students about kiva architecture. Courtesy of the Crow Canyon Archaeological Center.*

School Field Schools, to College Field Schools, to Cultural Explorations, to National Endowment for the Humanities Summer Institutes and Workshops for K–12 teachers (figure 8.3). This multivocal approach adds diversity and dimension to the stories of the past and encourages learners to engage in critical thought about culture, history, and what it means to be human across space and time.

CONCLUDING THOUGHTS

Delivering a true synthesis of Crow Canyon's educational work over the last forty years is a daunting task, and what I have presented here is in no way comprehensive. My primary goal has not been to show that the Center's educational work is sound but to show *why* it is sound. In this chapter, I hope to have provided an educational frame for viewing some of the Center's approaches to teaching about archaeology and the ancestral Puebloan history of the region. These programs have prioritized depth of understanding, authentic engagement, and an ethic of respect over methods that might have been simpler or more expedient. A deep appreciation for the challenges presented in conceptualizing the past and a dedication to engaging the hearts and minds of learners are rooted in Crow Canyon's past and will undoubtedly guide it forward as it embraces new ways to make the human past accessible and relevant.

REFERENCES

Association of Experiential Education. n.d. "What Is Experiential Education?" Accessed January 18, 2021. https://www.aee.org/what-is-ee.

Barton, Keith, and Linda Levstik. 2004. *Teaching History for the Common Good.* London: Lawrence Erlbaum Associates.

Berger, Edward. 2000. "Forward." In *Windows into the Past: Crow Canyon Archaeological Center's Guide for Teachers,* edited by M. Elaine Davis and Marjorie R. Connolly, xi–xiii. Dubuque, IA: Kendall/Hunt Publishing.

Berger, Peter, and Thomas Luckman. 1967. *The Social Construction of Reality: A Treatise in the Sociology of Knowledge.* New York: Anchor Books.

Bowers, Chet. 1987. *The Promise of Theory: Education and the Politics of Cultural Change.* New York: Teachers College Press.

Dewey, John. 1938. *Experience and Education.* New York: Touchstone.

Guzzetti, Barbara, and Cynthia Hynd. 1998. *Perspectives on Conceptual Change.* London: Lawrence Erlbaum Associates.

Hartley, L. P. 1953. *The Go Between.* New York: New York Review of Books.

Montangero, Jacques, and Danielle Maurice-Naville. 1997. *Piaget or the Advance of Knowledge.* London: Lawrence Erlbaum Associates.

National Geographic Resource Library Encyclopedic Entry. n.d. "Citizen Science." Accessed January 18, 2021. https://www.nationalgeographic.org/encyclopedia/citizen-science/.

National Science Teachers Association (NSTA). n.d. "Constructivism—A Paradigm for Teaching Collection." Accessed March 1, 2021. https://my.nsta.org/collection/71mZj57fcVQ_E.

Parks, Andrea. 2000. "Exploring Ancient Lifestyles." In *Windows into the Past: Crow Canyon Archaeological Center's Guide for Teachers,* edited by M. Elaine Davis and Marjorie R. Connolly, 33–37. Dubuque, IA: Kendall/Hunt Publishing.

Rosenzweig, Roy, and David Thelen. 1998. *The Presence of the Past: Popular Uses of History in American Life.* New York: Columbia University Press.

Scheurman, Geoffrey. 1998. "From Behaviorist to Constructivist Teaching." In *Social Education* 62 (1): 6–9. Washington, DC: National Council for the Social Studies.

Wineburg, Sam. 2001. *Historical Thinking and Other Unnatural Acts: Charting the Future of Teaching the Past.* Philadelphia: Temple University Press.

9

Making a Place for Archaeology in K–12 Education

WINONA J. PATTERSON, M. ELAINE FRANKLIN,
AND REBECCA HAMMOND

THE BENEFITS AND IMPORTANCE OF
ARCHAEOLOGICAL EDUCATION

Crow Canyon Archaeological Center was founded on philosophies of experiential and hands-on learning opportunities for students in need of a nontraditional classroom (Lightfoot and Lipe, chapter 2, also Franklin, chapter 8 in this volume). In providing these educational opportunities, Crow Canyon has spent the last forty years exemplifying the benefits and importance of archaeological education for K–12 students in public and private schools. Archaeological content adds a well-rounded or "big picture" understanding of the world and how the people within that world work (Popson and Selig 2019). Crow Canyon has always attempted to evolve with the ever-changing face of education and is now working to create curriculum opportunities that keep in the same vein of teaching and learning that makes Crow Canyon unique but also add elements that are of high priority in the world of education, such as science, technology, engineering, and math (STEM).

There sometimes seems to be a fundamental need within certain fields of science to obscure or ignore the human side of scientific study, or at least a failure

https://doi.org/10.5876/9781646424597.c009

to acknowledge human connections. Yet, to a great extent, scientific knowledge is a product of the human experience, and many areas of science are dedicated to studying all aspects of humanness. Others focus on how humans have impacted the earth and how to mitigate the harmful effects. Still, others exist to advance knowledge in fields like technology and medicine. To approach science as purely data-driven and erase humanity from the picture diminishes scientific endeavors and serves to alienate many young people who might otherwise choose to pursue a career in science. As noted by Franklin (chapter 8 in this volume), "an empirical understanding of past events does not demand the exclusion of feelings or of a caring frame of mind."

Archaeology is generally considered to be among the social sciences, which, unfortunately, are typically separated from the *hard* sciences, such as biology, chemistry, and physics. This classification can be problematic for young people who are interested in studying the human past but cannot see how their interests might articulate with other scientific fields. Recognizing archaeology for what it is—a multidisciplinary field of study—helps resolve this dilemma for students. Archaeology combines *hard* sciences with social sciences, making it ideally situated to bridge K–12 subject matter (Mullins 2019). This multidisciplinary approach allows students who are introduced to the field during their studies an opportunity to experience science in all of its dimensions and, in the process, gain insight into the shared humanity of our past, present, and future.

This positioning of archaeology as an integrative discipline is an important message for Crow Canyon to be able to convey to the larger educational community. High-stakes testing and demand for rigid adherence to discipline-specific curriculum standards have made it increasingly difficult for teachers to justify student field trips to study topics not explicitly listed in their standard course of study.

In this chapter, we *unpack* the discipline of archaeology to demonstrate how STEM and other K–12 subjects are embedded in archaeological research and to show how important archaeology is to advancing knowledge of the human past for young learners. In our discussion, we suggest new curricula that Crow Canyon might develop to better build the Center's brand as a place where K–12 students experience authentic STEM, history, and social studies education.

SOCIAL STUDY, SOCIAL SCIENCE, SCIENCE?

Most opportunities available for teaching archaeology to students in K–12 classrooms are grounded in archaeology's connection to social studies, including elements of history, culture, and geography. The field of archaeology, however, also reaches into many interconnected, STEM-based areas (Mullins 2019), resulting in enormous, missed opportunities for introducing archaeology in K–12 curricula. We argue that these scientific elements can and should serve as an important bridge for helping precollege students learn about the discipline.

The classification of archaeology as a social science or *soft science* prevents its inclusion in the standard course of study for K–12 education in the United States. There is no doubt that archaeology is social, but within the field there is little doubt that it is a scientific practice based in data-driven analyses and research-based theory. This chapter does not aim to diminish the importance of archaeology as a social science but instead aims to elucidate the scientific aspects of archaeology to show how it can be used to broaden opportunities for students, allowing them to explore a greater array of subjects throughout their academic careers.

Archaeology utilizes method and theory from many different fields of science, including chemistry, geology, botany, biology, zoology, mathematics, and others with the goal of gaining insight into the beliefs, behaviors, and practices of past cultures and societies. Through a heavy reliance on data, statistics, and analyses, archaeologists can gain insights into elements of the human past, create foundations of knowledge to share broadly, expand understanding of past peoples, and make connections to the present.

INQUIRY-BASED LEARNING

Instruction in American K–12 schools has traditionally involved a considerable amount of didactic instruction with an emphasis on rote learning. In the last two decades, the pendulum has gradually swung away from this style to instruction that is more student centered and inquiry based. In this paradigm, students have greater agency for what and how they learn, with teachers taking on the role of facilitators. This model is well suited to science and history education, since inquiry forms the basis of all scientific and historical research and is inherent to the work of archaeologists. STEM-focused lessons can also provide opportunities for student-centered, inquiry-based learning. The development of critical thought requires that students be active participants in their education; rote learning or traditional didactic instruction is not the most effective way to engage student interest, enhance concept development, or activate long-term memory.

In archaeology, the need to posit questions and seek answers to those questions is a never-ending process. Creating lessons in which students are given the opportunity to develop research questions and design methods for exploring them promotes student-centered, inquiry-based learning opportunities. A prime example of this type of lesson is the simulated excavation module presented at Crow Canyon. In this module, students participate in a mock excavation in which they are asked to create a research question and hypothesize their findings before they begin collecting relevant data from their excavation units. This approach reinforces two key ideas: first, archaeologists only excavate to gain an understanding and knowledge of the past, and second, the incorporation of inquiry allows students to experience the constant flow of thought and questioning that takes place throughout the archaeological process. In addition to their research questions, students also work to identify the period in which the site was occupied through the analyses of several diagnostic artifacts, furthering the process of inquiry throughout the activity.

Students need stimulating, hands-on, multimodal activities that allow them to think, conceptualize, research, and analyze. In the following sections, we present the challenges of bringing this type of inquiry into the classroom through archaeology and discuss approaches that may be utilized to break through some of those barriers.

OPPORTUNITIES AND APPLICATION

There are many opportunities for creating K–12 STEM-based lessons that are contextualized in the discipline of archaeology. Investigations into soil samples, pottery composition, and animal science will help students understand *big picture* anthropological concepts such as subsistence and foodways, giving greater relevance to their studies. Additionally, archaeology is a wonderful way to integrate studies of human geography with environmental science, exploring ways past peoples interacted with their world, the impact that interaction has had on the earth, and the implications for the present.

Through classroom visits, archaeologists can offer lessons on topics such as the analysis of plant materials, chemical analysis, stratigraphy, and laws of superposition (Kelly and Thomas 2010, 88, 103). Lessons created on these topics can work as tie-ins with existing course material but with the added benefit of archaeological context. Since the implementation of these elements would be built into the existing curriculum, this would allow teachers to include the lessons as extensions, problems of practice, career exploration (Mullins 2019), or simply as another lesson or unit within general instruction. By including archaeology in this way, students can be given archaeological content in small chunks, allowing them to see what is possible within the field.

Whether students come to the archaeologist, or the archaeologist comes to the students, this type of collaboration provides educators with opportunities to present STEM lessons in a context that makes the concepts and skills more interesting and relevant. Interactions with archaeologists also provide students with insight into career possibilities they may never have considered. While it is ideal to be able to interact with students who are physically in the classroom, it is also possible to work with them via online video-conferencing platforms where lessons utilizing Pear Deck—an interactive extension for Google Slides presentations—would be ideal. Companies such as Nepris coordinate classroom visits for scientists and other professionals with students around the globe.

CREATING AND ADAPTING STEM-BASED
ARCHAEOLOGICAL CURRICULA

Archaeologists who seek to offer educational opportunities to younger students have found themselves thoroughly rutted in an educational niche that prevents them from finding a legitimized place in K–12 schools. Those who are working to provide educational opportunities for students to learn about archaeology find themselves in a labyrinth of seemingly insurmountable obstacles except, perhaps, those in postsecondary settings. The maze of red tape, standards, and mandated curricula can be effective deterrents for those who seek to introduce younger students to archaeology (Davis 2000 and 2003). The current emphasis on narrowly defined STEM content further complicates efforts to find a fit for interdisciplinary fields in formal public education.

When archaeology educators provide teachers with lessons that are aligned to curriculum standards and are STEM focused, it can help alleviate some of these obstacles. Having a portfolio of lessons that are designed with these parameters in mind can facilitate the inclusion of archaeology in public education, whether working for an archaeological project, presenting in a classroom or on a field trip, or simply providing resources to colleagues who teach archaeology. The following discussion provides an overview of lessons currently available at Crow Canyon that are STEM based, those that can be adapted within STEM curricula, and opportunities for broadening an understanding of the interdisciplinary nature of archaeology for teachers and other members of the public.

STEM Lessons

Spoonful of Dirt is a one-hour lesson developed by Crow Canyon educators and archaeologists that helps students understand what can be discovered by analyzing sediment found on archaeological sites. Student groups are presented with four soil samples from different areas of the site. They are then asked to complete several tests on the soil that allow them to explore visual analysis, chemical analysis, palynology, and microartifacts of their soil samples. Students are asked to use data to determine what part of a site their sample came from and record and share their findings.

Another STEM-based lesson developed at Crow Canyon, titled Introduction to Dendrochronology, presents students with the basic methods for tree-ring dating and teaches them how archaeologists date samples of wood to determine when a site was occupied. This lesson lends itself to digitization, allowing students to move the samples around on screen and interact with the materials in a new way. It also provides educators with a means to create additional materials for lesson extensions in their own classrooms. Lesson extensions and add-on materials present students with options for further exploration of a specific concept or topic of interest. For example, students who have been given a basic lesson on the study of archaeology could be provided with an extension in which they complete a more authentic hands-on activity, like a simulated excavation, to clarify information and bring the lesson to life.

One of Crow Canyon's most recently developed STEM-based lessons aims to teach students about remote sensing. The focus of the lesson is to introduce students to geophysical survey methods, specifically electrical resistivity survey, how it works, and how data can indicate site layout and density without the need for excavation. This lesson allows students to analyze data collected during a recent survey, interpret the data, and report their findings. While the lesson has been developed for in-person learning, it may be adapted for online delivery.

Although not currently available from Crow Canyon, survey-focused lesson plans could be developed that range in difficulty and depth, based on available resources. An e-learning module focused on archaeological survey methods would engage students in the virtual survey of an area by placing digital pin flags where material culture is identified. Students would be able to explore the digital terrain by looking for architecture and other features. For a more hands-on survey project, students could physically walk a survey grid with replica or simulated artifacts and features that represent a given time period. To integrate elements of technology into the lesson, the survey project could include the utilization of a handheld Global Positioning Systems (GPS) device or a smartphone that georeferences data points.

Another type of survey lesson could be focused on mapping a portion of a school, a classroom, or specific area of the landscape using a compass and tape. If school grounds are unavailable, or if conducted in a virtual environment, students alternatively may create sketch maps of their homes and discuss their discoveries with the class. For a high-tech approach to mapping, electronic distance meters, a Trimble or other technology could be used for mapping if available.

The goals of K–12 survey and mapping lessons are to emphasize the mathematical elements of the archaeological process, as well as the importance of collecting, recording, and analyzing data. Survey and mapping can also teach students about the geographic features of an area, including its topography and natural resources. Gaining an understanding of an area through surveying and mapping will help students understand why people built their houses and communities where they did, how people utilized the resources available in a given area, and how people in the past survived in a place that may seem uninhabitable.

Another lesson developed by Crow Canyon educators and archaeologists is called Cactus Ruin, which is a simulated paper excavation. The Cactus Ruin lesson can be found on the Crow Canyon website, https://www.crowcanyon .org/educationproducts/CactusRuin/IntroPage.asp. This lesson could easily be adapted to a digital format and enhanced with images of the site and excavation units. The general concepts taught through the digital version would be the same as for the paper excavation: students would create a research question and hypothesis for their excavation, choose units to excavate that provide the best data for testing their hypothesis, analyze data from their selected units, and report their findings; but their level of understanding and engagement would still be greatly enhanced. The digital conversion would provide a fillable PDF where students record their work. Teachers could further enhance the lesson with a presentation using Pear Deck, a presentation add-on program that allows students to interact in real time. Additionally, the lesson could be completely revamped as a *webquest*, which is an assignment or project that requires students to use the internet to research a question or problem of study. Students could work collaboratively in groups or independently, reporting their findings to the group at the end of the lesson. This would give them an opportunity to practice their presentation skills and summarize their findings like a professional archaeologist (Hölscher 2020).

Integration of archaeology lessons can also move beyond science and social studies and be fitted in an English Language Arts (ELA) class or even a music lesson. At Crow Canyon, students were invited to attend an evening program featuring David Nighteagle playing the flute. In this lesson, he not only played music for the students but also taught the parts of the flute and how it works in terms of physics; in doing so, he created a great cross-curricular example for students to connect physics to musical instruments and see the science in music.

Rich Resources for Future Curriculum Development

In addition to the lessons referenced so far, the Crow Canyon website offers additional resources such as timelines showing the cultural chronology of the region, research papers, and site reports that can be utilized in the classroom. Crow Canyon offers weekly webinars about various topics in archaeology that are recorded and available to view on the Center's YouTube channel. These talks can be presented in classrooms as topics for discussion, used as lesson extensions, or linked to STEM education lessons. In addition to recordings of the weekly webinars, the YouTube channel offers various videos on other topics, including regional geography, Ute history, agriculture, Native American perspectives in archaeology, and other topics related to STEM, history, and social studies content.

Crow Canyon also offers content on its website that can help bridge and create cross-curricular connections. A few of these connections are presented in the Village Ecodynamics Project (VEP), the Pueblo Farming Project (https://pfp .crowcanyon.org), and several other data-driven projects completed throughout the last forty years. The VEP (https://crowcanyon.github.io/veparchaeology/) provides content and connections between multiple fields of study, including geology, geography, computer science, economics, and others. The project was designed to reconstruct the past through computer simulation and analysis of all known archaeological sites in a portion of southwestern Colorado and northern New Mexico. There are numerous sets of data available as a result of this project, such as climate, soil, and sources of lithic material.

Other resources available through the Center's website, such as the Pueblo Farming Project (PFP), presents research data that can inform curriculum development for K–12 classrooms. The PFP includes agricultural content and provides data from ongoing agricultural farming plots on the Crow Canyon campus. This project looks at dry farming techniques used by Pueblo farmers in the past and in Pueblo communities today. Through this study, farmers who work in drought-ridden areas, or those who have a general lack of rainfall, can create a plan for farming with the little water available and still have crops that flourish. Students could work to create their own experimental archaeology project within these confines to determine if they can find success in utilizing dry farming techniques.

IMPLEMENTATION, COLLABORATION, AND ETHICAL CONSIDERATIONS OF ARCHAEOLOGICAL CURRICULA

Implementation of archaeological lessons in K–12 settings requires consideration of the context in which learning takes place. Lessons are often presented through an extracurricular activity, field trip, or camp. In this context, students may be given significantly less time to study archaeology than if it were being presented in a more formal education context. Educators in these more informal settings will need very specific plans for the scope and pacing of their lessons to ensure that they are able to address the essential understandings they are hoping to convey. Even when archaeology education takes place in the context of formal schooling, there are often still challenges related to time, space, and restrictions on materials. Chunking portions of a lesson into multiple shorter periods may be necessary due to time constraints, and alternative teaching spaces such as gyms or outdoor areas may be required, depending on the activity.

In addition to the concerns just mentioned, a number of ethical points should also be considered when implementing an archaeological curriculum. Archaeologists often study a people's history and culture that is different from their own. For Crow Canyon, this is the history and culture of the Pueblo people. However, the ancestral Pueblo landscape is also home to the Diné (Navajo), Ute, Paiute, Apache, and Anglos. To teach about archaeological research in ethical and respectful ways requires inclusion and collaboration at many levels (Davis and Connolly 2000). The following is a discussion of how Crow Canyon educators approach curriculum implementation with ethical considerations in mind.

Native Voices

Native American perspectives and contributions have not always been present in the field of archaeology. This exclusion is now recognized as a disservice to the discipline and to building trusting relationships between descendant community members and archaeologists. Native American voices need to have a prominent place in the shaping of research designs and in the telling of their own histories, not just in theory or consultation, but in practice. This has been accomplished, in part, through Indigenous archaeology. Indigenous archaeology attempts to add Native voices to archaeological study and to normalize the inclusion of Native American archaeologists in the field. Additionally, and perhaps to a greater degree, Indigenous archaeology attempts to push archaeological research topics and questioning to better align with the wants and needs of Native American groups and to bring about the end of, or at least lessen, the Eurocentric viewpoint that has been present in western archaeology for hundreds of years (Watkins 2000, 19). By including Native voices, archaeologists are welcoming partnerships and building relationships with Native people, which should have been a focus from the start of archaeological research on Indigenous lands (Mullins 2019).

At Crow Canyon, opportunities to work and build relationships with Native communities and partners are of great importance (see Suina, chapter 7, and Ortman, chapter 6 in this volume). This work is practiced by including Native scholars in program delivery to provide a multivocal approach to understanding the past, developing and maintaining partnerships with various tribes, incorporating the Native American Advisory Group in mission-related activities and projects, and the awarding of scholarships for Native American K–12 and college students.

Cultural Sensitivities

Many Native groups have sensitivities to material culture remains, and every effort should be made when creating lessons to present information in a culturally sensitive manner. For example, Crow Canyon provides programs to Native students on a regular basis and has found several ways to ensure students are able to participate in programming while also respecting their cultural taboos (Davis 2001). Some Native students are not able to work with authentic artifacts or faunal remains due to traditional cultural beliefs; thus Crow Canyon provides replica artifacts for them to examine. Crow Canyon also asks every student group about cultural sensitivities to make sure that they are providing the best experience for Native and other students. These are examples of modifications that can be made for students, but instructors will need to allow for feedback throughout the lesson to make sure that students' needs are met.

Conservation Archaeology

Over the last several decades, archaeological research in the academic and research setting has shifted away from the complete excavation of sites to limited excavation. This practice, commonly referred to as *conservation archaeology* (Lipe 1974), allows for research to be conducted while also leaving as much of the site intact as possible (Kelly and Thomas 2010, 393). This shift is also more fitting with Native beliefs that sites should not be disturbed, that they should be left as they are, and that by excavating sites, we are disturbing the resting place of their ancestors (Suina, chapter 7 in this volume).

Conservation archaeology involves a shift from excavation and focuses instead on the preservation and stabilization of sites (Lipe 1974; Pedeli and Stefano 2014). This is accomplished through remote-sensing techniques and a reliance on data that have already been collected and published or curated for use by other archaeologists. Is conservation archaeology always ideal? Not necessarily—every site is different and holds its own story—but by excavating only a small portion of the site, archaeologists are able to advance their understanding of the people who lived there and also preserve the site. Conservation archaeology better aligns with Indigenous viewpoints on excavation, which most tribes agree should not happen (Suina, chapter 7 in this volume). It is important to introduce this concept when teaching students about archaeology and to explain that there is more to archaeology than excavation. Of key importance is pointing out that excavation is a destructive process that destroys the site being studied. By implementing conservation archaeology, archaeologists ensure greater safety and preservation of the site, as well as provide opportunities for future research, using previously collected data and other portions of the site.

Why Archaeology? Creating Responsible Citizens

In creating archaeological curricula, we must be aware of the messaging that we send to students. The importance of archaeology and its purpose must be explicit. Students should come away from the lesson, unit, or course knowing that archaeology is not about digging up artifacts but about uncovering the human past, particularly the unwritten past. Without archaeology, the only historical narrative that is legitimized and perpetuated is that which was written down, eliminating the majority of human narratives by excluding the voices of those without access to the tools of literacy or power. When archaeology reveals unwritten histories, it becomes a powerful tool for social justice, as those who feel they have no voice often feel they have no power in the present. Archaeology can illuminate steps we need to take in the present to build a better future.

Crow Canyon Archaeological Center has spent the last forty years exemplifying the benefits and importance of teaching archaeology to K–12 public and private school students. In creating an environment where students can experience learning through hands-on, experiential methods, Crow Canyon has opened up the world of archaeology to students around the US and beyond. Through access to online content and the creation of STEM-based lessons, Crow Canyon has set the standard for what archaeological education can be for K–12 students in public and private schools.

Archaeology provides an opportunity for different, yet interconnected, viewpoints in scientific fields such as biology, environmental science, geology, geography, botany, and many others (Mullins 2019). Despite the lack of archaeological curricula in K–12 settings, there are numerous ways in which archaeology can be integrated or introduced to students as an opportunity for cultural, career, and STEM-based exploration (2019). This chapter highlighted a few of the possibilities available at Crow Canyon as well as the potential for additional STEM-based lessons in the field of archaeology. Lessons ranging from hands-on, inquiry-based explorations, to fully online lessons, are suggested. Implementation of archaeology lessons should take into consideration voices of descendant communities, cultural sensitivities, and preservation concepts, such as conservation archaeology. These key ideas act as a guide in the lesson-planning process to ensure the responsible teaching of archaeology as a field of study, emphasizing its importance in expanding knowledge of the human past, and inspiring future archaeologists.

Archaeology education presents a plethora of opportunities for students to engage in inquiry-based learning experiences. These experiences provide opportunities that challenge students to think critically and learn about the world. It can shape the way in which students learn about the past so that they will be able to make better, more informed decisions as they move into their future.

REFERENCES

Davis, M. Elaine. 2000. "Archaeology Education and the Political Landscape of American Schools." In *Antiquity* 74 (283): 194–198. Durham, UK: Durham University.

Davis, M. E. 2001. "Knowing Others and Other Ways of Knowing: Cultural Issues in the Teaching of Science." In *Professional Development in Science Teaching and Learning*, edited by J. Rhoton and P. Bowers, 113–124. Arlington, VA: NSTA Press.

Davis, M. Elaine. 2003. "Governmental Education Standards and K–12 Archaeology Education Programs." In *The Archaeology Education Handbook: Sharing the Past with Kids*, edited by C. Smardz and S. Smith, 54–71. Walnut Creek, CA: Altamira Press.

Davis, M. Elaine, and Marjorie R. Connolly. 2000. *Windows into the Past*. Dubuque, IA: Kendall/Hunt Publishing.

Hölscher, David Frederik. 2020. "Mobile Technology and Science Outreach in Archaeology: Integrating Didactics." In *Communicating the Past in the Digital Age: Proceedings of the International Conference on Digital Methods in Teaching and Learning in Archaeology (12–13 October 2018)*, edited by Sebastian Hageneur, 156–166. London: Ubiquity Press.

Kelly, Robert L., and Thomas, David Hurst. 2010. *Archaeology*. 5th ed. Belmont, CA: Wadsworth Cengage Learning.

Lipe, William D. 1974. "A Conservation Model for American Archaeology." *Kiva* 39, no. 3/4 (Spring–Summer): 213–245.

Mullins, Cailey D. 2019. "Archaeology for the People: Community-Based Research, Hands-On Education, and Their Place in Archaeology." MA thesis, Chapel Hill.

Pedeli, Corrado, and Stefano Pulga. 2014. *Conservation Practices on Archaeological Excavations: Principles and Methods*. Los Angeles: Getty Trust Publications.

Popson, Colleen P., and R. Selig. 2019. "Putting Archaeology and Anthropology into Schools: A 2019 Update." *Journal of Archaeology and Education* 3, no. 3 (March): 1–26. https://digitalcommons.library.umaine.edu/jae/vol3/iss3/1/.

Watkins, Joe. *Indigenous Archaeology: American Indian Values and Scientific Practice*. Walnut Creek, CA: Alta Mira Press, 2000.

Community and Regional Studies

10

Community Development and Practice in the Basketmaker III Period

A Case Study from Southwestern Colorado

KARI SCHLEHER, SHANNA DIEDERICHS,
KATE HUGHES, AND ROBIN LYLE

With this chapter, we begin the volume's examples of archaeological research, conducted in dialogue with American Indian partners and in conjunction with public educational programing, as discussed by Franklin (chapter 8 in this volume). The Basketmaker Communities Project (BCP) was the first Crow Canyon multiyear research project to focus primarily on the earliest permanent Pueblo occupation in the Mesa Verde region—the Basketmaker III period (AD 500–750). Before the BCP, much of Crow Canyon's research focus had been on the Pueblo III period (AD 1150–1300), and we had little knowledge of the Basketmaker III period in the region (Lightfoot and Lipe, chapter 2 in this volume). The BCP interpretive report and companion database are together the most recent publication on Crow Canyon's website, a tradition that Kohler et al. (chapter 3 in this volume) discuss, starting with the reporting of the Dolores Archaeological Program (DAP) and continuing with Crow Canyon's multiyear research projects through today. Crow Canyon's Native American Advisory Group was involved in the development of the research questions addressed through the BCP (Ortman et al. 2011), and discussions with advisory

https://doi.org/10.5876/9781646424597.c010

group members contributed to interpretations of Pueblo history viewed through the archaeological evidence collected.

INTRODUCTION

From 2011 to 2017 the Crow Canyon Archaeological Center conducted the Basketmaker Communities Project (BCP), a multifaceted investigation of Basketmaker III period (AD 500–750) sites on Indian Camp Ranch (ICR), a 1,200-acre, or 4.85 km², private, residential development in southwest Colorado (Diederichs 2020a). Indian Camp Ranch represents one of the densest and best-preserved Basketmaker III period settlement clusters in the central Mesa Verde region, which was developed for farming during this period (Ortman et al. 2011). The ranch was successfully nominated to the Colorado State Register of Historic Properties and the National Register of Historic Places as the Indian Camp Ranch Archaeological District, the only archaeological district in the northern Southwest that highlights the Basketmaker III period (Varien and Diederichs 2011).

In this chapter, we explore how the social structure of the ICR community shifted over time, transitioning from a small, clustered settlement of diverse immigrants focused on integrative ritual with an even economy to a dispersed, but cohesive, community dominated by a few long-standing prosperous lineages. We believe this transition resulted from concerted emphasis on social integration in this rapidly growing settlement and that this integration resulted in cohesive communities of practice, as we discuss in the following sections (Diederichs 2020a; Schleher and Hughes 2020).

Communities are a major theme throughout this volume, and volume authors identify communities in slightly different ways (Adler and Hegmon, chapter 16, Glowacki et al., chapter 12, Potter et al., chapter 13, Schleher et al., chapter 14, Throgmorton et al., chapter 11 in this volume). Later communities are often centered on densely occupied community centers, with extensive domestic and public architecture and multicentury occupations (Glowacki et al., chapter 12, Potter et al., chapter 13 in this volume). Pueblo I period (AD 750–950) (see Throgmorton et al., chapter 11 in this volume) through Pueblo III (AD 1150–1300) period (see Schleher et al., chapter 14 in this volume; Varien, Lipe et al. 1996; Varien, Van West et al. 2000) communities centers in the Mesa Verde region are typically defined as dominating a 2 km resource procurement radius, or approximately 12 square km, more than double the ICR study area. We argue that the community at ICR differs from later communities, in that its population was purposefully dispersed, extending far beyond the boundaries of ICR and the 2 km community center radius but nonetheless focused on a central public structure—the great kiva at the Dillard site. As highlighted by R. J. Sinensky et al. (2022), this settlement pattern is enigmatic of Basketmaker III period colonization practices after a severe sixth-century cold period disrupted earlier demographic and social traditions.

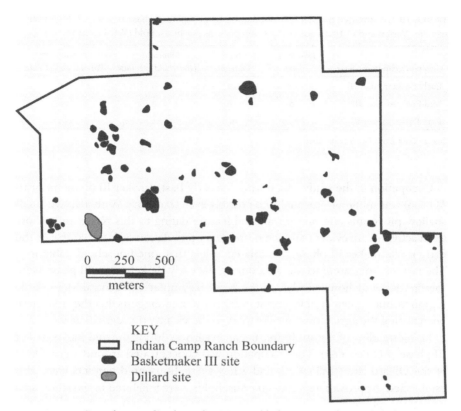

KEY
☐ Indian Camp Ranch Boundary
● Basketmaker III site
● Dillard site

FIGURE 10.1. *Distribution of Basketmaker III period habitations and an early habitation cluster with a great kiva (Dillard site) on the 1,200-acre Indian Camp Ranch in southwest Colorado. Courtesy of Crow Canyon Archaeological Center.*

These widely shared practices were a fundamental step toward the development of ancestral Pueblo community centers.

To reconstruct the demographic history in the ICR study area during the Basketmaker III period, we determined the number of households that "seeded" the 1,200-acre ICR study area, the speed and nature of population growth, and how settlement shifted across the landscape over the course of three consecutive phases (Diederichs 2020c). Following Ortman and colleagues (2016), we used pit-houses as an indicator of households, the location and occupation duration (of which were determined using surface survey), geophysical imaging, and exca-vation data collected over the course of the BCP (figure 10.1). These methods generated an estimated total of 110 Basketmaker III period households in the study area occupied across the early, middle, and late phases of the settlement (Diederichs 2020c).

TABLE 10.1. Estimated momentary population by occupation phase based on fifteen-year use-life (Varien and Ortman 2005) and seven persons per household (Wilshusen 1999, 214).

General Occupation Phase	Length of Phase	Total Households	Momentary Household Estimate	Momentary Population Estimate
Early Basketmaker III	180	0	0	0
Mid-Basketmaker III	60	16	4	28
Late Basketmaker III	65	94	22	153

Source: Data from Diederichs (2020c).

Occupation in the study area during the early Basketmaker III phase (prior to AD 600) was minimal, seasonal, and possibly even transitory. With just two small, shallow pit rooms and one extramural feature dating to this phase, only short-term activities are evident and the momentary population over the course of the early Basketmaker III phase is estimated at less than one household (table 10.1). The farmers migrating to this area during the early Basketmaker III phase were the first wave of homesteaders in the previously unfarmed central Mesa Verde region frontier. Their light footprint in the study area suggests that they may have been testing the agricultural productivity in the vicinity (Diederichs 2020c).

Homesteading of the study area began in earnest during the mid-Basketmaker III phase (AD 600–660). This occupation was concentrated around a great kiva at the Dillard site (5MT10647), and a few single-household hamlets were also established. Approximately sixteen households were inhabited in the study area during this phase with a momentary population of five households, or 25 to 30 people (Diederichs 2020c).

The population rose exponentially during the late Basketmaker III phase (AD 660–725) to an estimated 94 households over the entire phase and a momentary population of 22 households, or approximately 110 to 154 people, at any given time. These estimates indicate that the population roughly quadrupled between the middle and late Basketmaker III phases with an implied growth rate of about 8 percent per year (Diederichs 2020c).

COMMUNITY INTEGRATION

The presence of a great kiva at the Dillard site is the most compelling evidence that the Indian Camp Ranch Basketmaker III population conceived of itself as a community (figure 10.2). The construction of the 11 m diameter, semisubterranean structure—covered by a wood, rock, and adobe superstructure weighing over a ton—required the cooperation and labor of many households to build and maintain (Diederichs 2020b). Great kivas appear during the Basketmaker III period and persist until the Pueblo III period in the Mesa Verde region, but they are uncommon in the Basketmaker III period (Ryan 2013; Wilshusen et al. 2012).

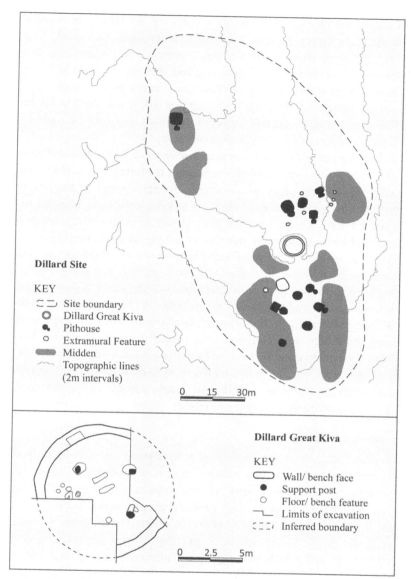

FIGURE 10.2. *Map of the Dillard site and Dillard great kiva (5MT10647). Courtesy of Crow Canyon Archaeological Center.*

When the ICR great kiva was first constructed in the mid-Basketmaker III phase, it had the capacity to hold the entire population of the ICR community. Periodic remodeling kept the structure in use for ritualized group activities for the next 105 years, from AD 620 to 725. Toward the end of its use-life, only about one-third of the ICR population would have been able to enter it at the same time. Despite outgrowing the great kiva, segments of the community population would have continued regular ritual gatherings inside the structure. There is evidence that the settlement held community-scale feasts in, and around, the great kiva during remodeling events and the structure's final closure (Diederichs 2020b). The collective energy invested in the great kiva indicates that it was the focal point of the Indian Camp Ranch community and functioned as a rare example of Basketmaker III public architecture (Diederichs 2020b).

Public architecture refers to structures accessible to at least some individuals from across an entire community for gathering in suprahousehold groups (Hegmon 1989, 7; Ryan 2013, 2015a, 91). Group rituals help to create and maintain integration when strong political institutions are lacking, and public architecture provides a space for these rituals to take place (Ryan 2015a, 91). The form and size of public architecture affect the number of people who can participate in group activities, as well as the kinds of activities that can occur (Hegmon 1989, 7). Notably, for the great kiva at the Dillard site, public architecture allows for the persistence and repetition of integrative activities by tying them to a particular location and, thus, providing a context for symbolically charged actions (Ryan 2015a, 91). Public architecture, in this way, validates social rules that perpetuate social identity and integration (Hegmon 1989, 2002; Ryan 2013, 2015a, 91). The long use-life of the Dillard great kiva created a persistent place amid a landscape characterized by relatively frequent household moves, as indicated by short use-life of most residential pithouses (Diederichs 2020b, 2020c). This persistence contributes to the community's long-term stability.

DIVERSE POPULATIONS

We argue that initially, the Indian Camp Ranch settlement was a multicultural community and that variation in various elements of material culture and architecture reflects the diverse origins of the residents. One way of viewing variation in social networks is through practice theory, which allows us to differentiate the actions of people embedded in different networks of social interaction (Joyce 2012). A community of practice reflects the learning network of a group of individuals making a particular class of materials, be it pottery (e.g., Cordell and Habicht-Mauche 2012; Schleher 2017) or architecture (Miller 2015; Ryan 2013).

Archaeologically, communities of practice are visible in the manufacturing process, from material selection, to production method, to design style. The residents of the ICR community exhibit diversity in architectural style, pottery production, and lithic material procurement, which indicates different communities of practice within the larger community. We also note that the diversity we see in communities of practice for pottery, architecture, and stone tool materials is also reflected in the settlement's textile production, subsistence practices, and culinary styles (Adams 2020; Diederichs 2020b, 2020d; Smith 2020). A variety of traditions, and even distinct ethnicities, are represented in this milieu, including Colorado Plateau late Archaic, Eastern Basketmaker II, Western Basketmaker II, late Pithouse period Mogollon, Pioneer period Hohokam, Chuska region Basketmaker III, central Mesa Verde region Basketmaker III, and western Mesa Verde region Basketmaker III (Diederichs 2020e).

Diversity in Pithouse Architectural Communities of Practice

Variation in Basketmaker III pithouse construction style has been identified as learned techniques rooted in specific communities of practice (Miller 2015). Several pithouse construction styles were detected during the BCP, and these styles can be traced to specific regional communities of practice to the south and west (Diederichs 2020b). Bench-supported, leaner-post construction was the most common roof support system identified during the project and demonstrates that the ICR community was part of shared Mesa Verde and north Chuska Mountain architectural traditions (Kearns 1995, 2012; Miller 2015; Murrell and Vierra 2014; Shelley 1990, 1991). However, a few structures at the Dillard site were built in a vertical jacal style, which developed to the west in southeastern Utah and northeastern Arizona (Allison et al. 2012; Chenault and Motsinger 2000; Chenault et al. 2003; Miller 2015, 185; Neily 1982).

Diversity in Lithic Procurement Practices

Lithic assemblages from the BCP indicates the ICR community had ties to a variety of lithic procurement areas. The strongest of these connections is with southeastern Utah and northern New Mexico but also includes northeastern Arizona, as seen in the amount and variety of nonlocal lithic material from these locations (table 10.2). These patterns and connections continue for nonlocal lithic materials through the Pueblo III period in the region (Arakawa et al., chapter 15 in this volume). Knowledge of these sources and their consistency in the assemblage suggest that portions of the ICR population migrated from, or had connections with, specific regions of Utah, Arizona, and New Mexico.

The presence of nonlocal lithic materials suggests that migrants to the ICR settlement came from, or were in contact with, dispersed source populations across the Southwest. The various types of obsidian found across the study area are an example of this source diversity. The majority of obsidian originated from the Jemez Mountains and Mount Taylor sources in New Mexico. Two pieces of obsidian source to more distant locations—one from Government Mountain near Flagstaff, Arizona, and one from Wild Horse Canyon in western Utah (Shackley 2013, 2015, 2017). Other nonlocal lithic materials include red jasper, likely originating from southeast Utah, and Narbona Pass chert, from

TABLE 10.2. Counts of nonlocal lithic artifacts by material type by Basketmaker III temporal phase, BCP.

Occupational Phase	Nonlocal Lithic Material Types								Total
	Nonlocal chert / Siltstone		Obsidian		Red Jasper		Narbona Pass Chert		
	Formal Tools	Debitage	Formal Tools	Debitage	Formal Tools	Debitage	Formal Tools	Debitage	
Early Basketmaker III									0
Mid-Basketmaker III		3	4	5		12	4	13	41
Late Basketmaker III	2	2	1	8	2	10	1	6	32
All Phases Basketmaker III	4		2	3	1	13		29	5
Total	6	5	7	16	3	35	5	48	125

Source: Data from Schleher and Hughes (2020).

northwest New Mexico. While the small amounts of nonlocal lithic materials do not conclusively point to migration from these source areas, they illustrate the breadth and variety of the settler's connections with geographically distant communities of practice in lithic material procurement.

Interestingly, there is evidence that the ICR settlers identified not only with geographically distant communities but also with their distant past. Several Archaic projectile points were recovered during the BCP. These earlier dart points include one Bajada, a few Northern and Sudden Side-Notched, and a few San Pedro points (Schleher and Hughes 2020). These older projectile points stylistically date from the Archaic (6000 BC–1000 BC) to the dawn of the Basketmaker III period. Many of these points were reused as knives. It is possible that the local Basketmaker III populations harvested the older points from the landscape as useful tools or their presence could indicate a deeper connection and continuity with the Archaic and Basketmaker II groups that produced these points, suggesting diverse cultural identities of the founding population of the ICR community.

Increasing Efficiency and Conformity in Pottery Production and Design

As population grew and settlement density increased, ceramic production practices became more efficient and systematic by the late Basketmaker III phase. Much like other Basketmaker III period sites across the Colorado Plateau (e.g., Toll and Wilson 1999; Wilshusen 1999), the pottery assemblage from the ICR settlement is dominated by plain gray ware ceramics, with smaller amounts of white ware and brown ware. Most of the formal types in the assemblage are Chapin Gray, Chapin Black-on-white, and Twin Trees Utility—the most dominant brown/gray wares in the assemblage (Schleher and Hughes 2020).

Regarding pottery production, a community of practice is the social group in which potters learn to make vessels. Variations in the pottery assemblage reflects a variety of activities, including changes in the composition of the potting group, and/or a broadening, or restricting, of the learning network associated with pottery production (e.g., Crown 2007; Schleher 2017). Here, we highlight the increasing consistency and efficiency of the pottery production process as detected in material selection, the processing of temper, and decorative design choice, thus reflecting changes in ICR communities of practice through time.

Through both binocular and petrographic analyses of all rim sherds in the pottery assemblage, we identified two primary types of temper added to clay by the communities' potters: mixed lithic sand and crushed igneous rock, both of which are available locally (Schleher and Hughes 2020). Initially, our interpretation of these data was that there were different communities of practice present in the community; however, if we analyze temper data by phase, a different interpretation develops. If we examine gray ware and white ware pottery temper through time, there is a shift in practice from the use of primarily sand-tempered pottery to primarily crushed igneous rock tempered pottery (table 10.3). This shift is similar to those documented in other areas of the broader northern Southwest, including the La Plata Valley and the Southern Chuska Valley (Reed 1998; Trowbridge 2014, 336). Late Basketmaker III phase sites located nearer to the BCP area also show the use of primarily igneous rock temper, including at a single pithouse habitation site near Pleasant View, Colorado (Fetterman and Honeycutt 1995, 7–41), and at Casa Coyote on White Mesa, Utah (Hurst 2004). This trend continued as potters increasingly utilized crushed igneous rock temper in Pueblo I and Pueblo II period sites in the central Mesa Verde region (e.g., Errickson 1998).

Pottery designs reflect highly visible elements of the pottery production process compared to less-visible technological elements. Because designs can be copied from pots themselves, they do not necessarily only reflect communities of practice within one community but may also reflect a broader, shared identity. Linda Honeycutt (2015) identified nine design motifs utilized during the Basketmaker III period throughout the San Juan region based on a sample of approximately 1,500 black-on-white bowls and bowls sherds from seventy-six sites. We build on Honeycutt's research by analyzing designs found on BCP pottery. Of the 1,145 painted sherds from the project, 418 of them (37 percent) are painted with at least one of Honeycutt's identified design motifs, whereas most other painted sherds have a simple line along the rim. If we look at the

TABLE 10.3. Pottery temper by Basketmaker III temporal phase.

Temper	Early Basketmaker III N	% of N	Mid-Basketmaker III N	% of N	Late Basketmaker III N	% of N	All Phases Basketmaker III N	% of N	Total N	% of N
Plain gray ware										
Igneous rock	2	25.00	126	52.72	213	71.72	253	57.24	594	60.24
Mixed lithic or quartz sand / sandstone	5	62.50	99	41.42	73	24.58	160	36.20	337	34.18
Clay pellets / shale	1	12.50	8	3.35	9	3.03	22	4.98	40	4.06
Black, tabular/ oval shiny inclusions			4	1.67			4	0.90	8	0.81
Self-tempered, no added temper			2	0.84			2	0.45	4	0.41
Sherd					2	0.67	1	0.23	3	0.30
Total plain gray ware	8	100.00	239	100.00	297	100.00	442	100.00	986	100.00
White ware										
Igneous rock	1	33.33	50	81.97	76	82.61	96	76.80	223	79.36
Mixed lithic or quartz sand / sandstone	2	66.67	9	14.75	11	11.96	17	13.60	39	13.88
Clay pellets/ shale			2	3.28	5	5.43	11	8.80	18	6.41
Black, tabular/ oval shiny inclusions							1	0.80	1	0.36
Total white ware	3	100.00	61	100.00	92	100.00	125	100.00	281	100.00

Source: Schleher and Hughes (2020, table 24.15).

distribution of these design motifs across the community, most sites have all, or the majority of, motifs present in their pottery assemblages, indicating that potters at all sites in the community interacted enough to share production practices and common designs (Schleher and Hughes 2020).

These designs were used during the entire occupation of the community. Table 10.4 shows the range of design motifs in the early, mid-, and late Basketmaker III phases. Only two sherds were identified in the early phase with design motifs; thus early phase designs are not considered further. All motifs are present in both the mid- and late phases, indicating that, in the study area, there are no temporal trends in the use of the design motifs. Design motifs in the BCP study area reflect a single community of practice for design execution. This single community of practice suggests close connections between residents of the communities' different households. Both the design data, with no change over time, and the temper data, with a change from sand to crushed igneous rock over time, suggest that the pottery production communities of practice are fully integrated by the end of the Basketmaker III period. In addition, the similarity in designs seen in the study area connects the ICR community with a pan-regional Basketmaker III identity. This association parallels the communities' dedication to great kiva rituals, which were also part of the pan Basketmaker III regional tradition.

INTEGRATION TO MANAGEMENT

Social integration, as promoted through great kiva gatherings, would have been an essential practice to mitigate any small-scale conflict in the diverse and growing ICR community. We believe the focus on social integration likely led to the development of social and political power wielded by long-standing lineages.

The great kiva at the Dillard site was a continuous focal point for community ritual and gatherings, however by the late seventh century AD, architectural and artifact data indicate that the Dillard site was depopulated (Diederichs 2020c). A residential buffer formed around this ritually charged public structure. Despite this retraction, households on the ridgetops east and west of the Dillard site, each with a view of the great kiva, rose in social and economic status. During the late Basketmaker III phase families built oversized pithouses over earlier habitations dating to the mid–Basketmaker III phase (Diederichs 2020b). This superpositioning likely emphasized an unbroken occupation of hereditary lineages for many generations.

Oversized pithouses are large, up to eight times the size of a standard-sized pithouse, and, like the great kiva, likely required suprahousehold labor to construct. Unlike great kivas, these structures had a domestic function inferred from their construction style, floor features, and material assemblages. The wealth of these households is evident in higher proportions of trade goods, large cooking

TABLE 10.4. Honeycutt (2015) Design Motifs by Basketmaker III temporal phase, BCP (Schleher and Hughes 2020, table 24.22).

Motif Number	Early Basketmaker III		Mid-Basketmaker III		Late Basketmaker III		All Phases Basketmaker III		Total	
	N	% N	N	% N	N	% N	N	% N	N	% N
Motif 1			3	4.41	2	1.48	4	3.74	9	2.88
Motif 2			3	4.41	6	4.44	7	6.54	16	5.13
Motif 3	1	50.00	9	13.24	15	11.11	9	8.41	34	10.90
Motif 4			6	8.82	10	7.41	10	9.35	26	8.33
Motif 5			31	45.59	31	22.96	38	35.51	100	32.10
Motif 6			3	4.41	20	14.81	3	2.80	26	8.33
Motif 7			5	7.35	12	8.89	17	15.89	34	10.90
Motif 8			3	4.41	25	18.52	13	12.15	41	13.10
Motif 9	1	50.00	5	7.35	14	10.37	6	5.61	26	8.33
Total	2	100.00	68	100.00	135	100.00	107	100.00	312	100.00

vessels, weaving materials, and ritual fauna, along with extensive surface room-blocks that could store many times the amount of corn and other resources needed to feed an extended family (Diederichs 2020d). Like the Dillard site great kiva, these oversized pithouses could have been used to host suprahousehold events, such as feasts or other distinct ritual gatherings that differed from great kiva rituals. Lineages used suprahousehold events at the oversized pithouses and at the Dillard great kiva to solidify their higher status in the community.

The rise of prestigious lineages on the ridgetops east and west of the Dillard site is likely the result of social integration within the ICR community. As early settlers, founding families settled agriculturally productive locals and accumulated local knowledge and status for generations. The founding families would have participated in, and carried on, traditions of communal gatherings in the Dillard great kiva, and perhaps in their domestic, oversized pithouses. When the Dillard site was converted into a public rather than a domestic space, the occupants of the adjacent ridgetops inherited the oversite of the great kiva and likely the prestige and authority associated with this responsibility.

The community "standing" these lineages gained through their association with the institutions of social integration likely translated to authority in other aspects of community management. The biggest challenge to a new and growing community, such as the ICR settlement, would be mitigating individual household risk and intrahousehold competition. Out of this problem would arise the need for management of resource distribution, production efficiency, and economic intensification.

For instance, long-standing and prestigious lineages may have exercised authority over land tenure to manage intrahousehold competition and maximize agricultural production across the settlement. There is evidence that—beyond the Dillard site and the high-status households on the adjacent ridgetops—most habitations were small hamlets organized in a gridded settlement pattern (statistically evenly dispersed) across productive farming soils (Diederichs 2016; Schwindt et al. 2016). The ability to distribute settlements in such a pattern and adhere to this practice across multiple generations is evidence of land tenure mores operating in the ICR community and social institutions, such as managerial lineages, with authority to enforce those mores.

CONCLUSION

The central Mesa Verde region was a new frontier for farmers in the seventh and eight centuries AD. Ancestral Pueblo farmers who established settlements in the Indian Camp Ranch study area integrated culturally diverse immigrants into a cohesive and stable community. These settlers brought with them production practices from various traditions across the Southwest.

For the ICR settlement to overcome individual household-risk and intrahousehold competition in a newly colonized frontier, social integration was imperative. Public gatherings at the Dillard site great kiva served this purpose for over a century. As the community grew, descendants of the original settlers found themselves with managerial control of the great kiva and, in extension, many production practices across the community. This development appears to have contributed to the community's economic viability and stability despite contributing to increasing wealth disparities between older and more recent immigrants.

The invention of new integrative and managerial institutions during the Basketmaker III period is an important development in ancestral Pueblo history. As Crow Canyon has detected on other projects, great kivas become iconic, integrative spaces for ancestral Pueblo people; the management of these spaces and of the communities they create often falls to a deeply invested, and possibly related, segment of the population. The Crow Canyon Archaeological Center's focus on communities for the last forty years has emphasized Pueblo II period (e.g., Ryan 2015b; Ryan 2015c) and Pueblo III period (e.g., Coffey 2018; Kuckelman 2007, 2017) community centers and social organization. The BCP expands the temporal story of the Mesa Verde region, with exploration of community development and social organization going back to the first farmers who initially settled the region at AD 500.

REFERENCES

Adams, Karen R. 2020. "Archaeobotanical Remains." In *The Basketmaker Communities Project*, edited by Shanna R. Diederichs, 586–644. Accessed January 18, 2021. https://www.crowcanyon.org/ResearchReports/BasketmakerCommunities/basketmaker_communities_project_final.pdf.

Allison, James R., Winston B. Hurst, Jonathan D. Till, and Donald C. Irwin. 2012. "Meanwhile in the West: Early Pueblo Communities in Southeastern Utah." In *Crucible of Pueblos: The Early Pueblo Period in the Northern Southwest*, edited by Richard H. Wilshusen, Gregson Schachner, and James R. Allison, 35–52. Los Angeles: Cotsen Institute of Archaeology Press.

Chenault, Mark L., and Thomas N. Motsinger. 2000. "Colonization, Warfare, and Regional Competition: Recent Research into the Basketmaker III Period in the Mesa Verde Region." In *Foundations of Anasazi Culture: The Basketmaker-Pueblo Transition*, edited by Paul F. Reed, 45–68. Salt Lake City: University of Utah Press.

Chenault, Mark L., Thomas N. Motsinger, and Kevin P. Gilmore. 2003. "The Basketmaker III Period in the Mesa Verde Region." In *Archaeological Investigations along the Towaoc Lateral and Lone Pine Lateral Components of the Dolores River Reclamation Project, Montezuma County, Colorado*. Vol. 1, *Project Background and Synthesis*. Prepared for the U.S. Bureau of Reclamation Western Colorado Area Office, Contract No.1425-3-CS-40-12590. Durango, CO: U.S. Bureau of Reclamation Western Colorado Area Office.

Coffey, Grant D., ed. 2018. *The Goodman Point Archaeological Project: Goodman Point Community Testing*. Accessed January 1, 2021. (tDAR id: 447957), https://doi.org 10.6067 /XCV8447957.

Cordell, Linda, and Judith Habicht-Mauche. 2012. "Practice Theory and Social Dynamics among Prehispanic and Colonial Communities in the American Southwest." In *Potters and Communities of Practice: Glaze Paint and Polychrome Pottery in the American Southwest, AD 1250 to 1700*, edited by Linda Cordell and Judith Habicht-Mauche, 1–7. No. 75 of *Anthropological Papers of the University of Arizona*. Tucson: University of Arizona Press.

Crown, Patricia L. 2007. "Learning about Learning." In *Archaeological Anthropology: Perspectives on Method and Theory*, edited by James Skibo, Michael W. Graves, and Marian Stark, 198–217. Tucson: University of Arizona Press.

Diederichs, Shanna R. 2016. "Basketmaker III Colonization and the San Juan Frontier." MA thesis, Department of Anthropology, Northern Arizona University, Flagstaff.

Diederichs, Shanna R., ed. 2020a. *The Basketmaker Communities Project*. Accessed January 18, 2021. https://www.crowcanyon.org/ResearchReports/BasketmakerCommunities/basketmaker_communities_project_final.pdf.

Diederichs, Shanna R. 2020b. "Architecture of the Basketmaker III Period." In *The Basketmaker Communities Project*, edited by Shanna R. Diederichs, 426–474.

Accessed January 18, 2021. https://www.crowcanyon.org/ResearchReports/
BasketmakerCommunities/basketmaker_communities_project_final.pdf.

Diederichs, Shanna R. 2020c. "Chronology and Occupational History." In *The Bas-
ketmaker Communities Project*, edited by Shanna R. Diederichs, 475–512. Accessed
January 18, 2021. https://www.crowcanyon.org/ResearchReports/Basketmaker
Communities/basketmaker_communities_project_final.pdf.

Diederichs, Shanna R. 2020d. "The Ridgeline Site (5MT10711)." In *The Basketmaker Communities Project*, edited by Shanna R. Diederichs, 263–294. Accessed January 18, 2021.
https://www.crowcanyon.org/ResearchReports/BasketmakerCommunities
/basketmaker_communities_project_final.pdf.

Diederichs, Shanna R. 2020e. "Basketmaker Communities Project Synthesis." In *The
Basketmaker Communities Project*, edited by Shanna R. Diederichs, 862–894. Accessed
January 18, 2021. https://www.crowcanyon.org/ResearchReports/Basketmaker
Communities/basketmaker_communities_project_final.pdf.

Errickson, Mary. 1998. "Ceramic Material Culture." In *The Puebloan Occupation of the Ute
Mountain Piedmont. Volume 6: Material Culture Studies*, edited by Brian R. Billman, 2.1–
2.105. Vol. 22, No. 6 of *Soil Systems Publications in Archaeology*. Cortez, CO: Soil Systems.

Fetterman, Jerry, and Linda Honeycutt. 1995. *Excavations at Northwest Pipeline Cor-
poration's Pleasant View Compressor Station, Southwestern Colorado*. Prepared for
Northwest Pipeline Corporation. Yellow Jacket, CO: Woods Canyon Archaeological
Consultants.

Hegmon, Michelle. 1989. "Social Integration and Architecture." In *The Architecture
of Social Integration in Prehistoric Pueblos*, edited by William D. Lipe and Michelle
Hegmon, 5–14. Occasional Papers, no. 1. Cortez, CO: Crow Canyon Archaeological
Center.

Hegmon, Michelle. 2002. "Concepts of Community in Archaeological Research." In
Seeking the Center Place: Archaeology and Ancient Communities in the Mesa Verde Region,
edited by Mark D. Varien and Richard H. Wilshusen, 263–279. Salt Lake City: University of Utah Press.

Honeycutt, Linda. 2015. "Motifs 1–7: An Overview; Part of a Study of Basketmaker III
Black-on-white Bowl Motifs in the Four Corners Region." *Pottery Southwest* 31 (1):
2–24.

Hurst, Winston. 2004. "Ceramic Artifacts from 42SA3775." In *Archaeological Data Recovery at Casa Coyote (42SA3775), A Basketmaker III Pit House Hamlet on White Mesa, San
Juan County, Utah*, edited by William E. Davis, 269–312. Bluff, UT: Abajo Archaeology.

Joyce, Rosemary A. 2012. "Thinking about Pottery Production as Community Practice."
In *Potters and Communities of Practice: Glaze Paint and Polychrome Pottery in the American Southwest, AD 1250 to 1700*, edited by Linda Cordell and Judith Habicht-Mauche,
149–154. No. 75 of *Anthropological Papers of the University of Arizona*. Tucson: University of Arizona Press.

Kearns, Timothy, ed. 1995. *Project Overview, Background, and Implementation: Pipeline Archaeology 1990–1993. The El Paso Natural Gas North System Expansion Project, New Mexico and Arizona.* Vol. 1 of *Cultural Resource Management Report No. WCRM(F)074.* Farmington, NM: Cultural Resource Management.

Kearns, Timothy, ed. 2012. *Pipeline Archaeology 1990–1993: The El Paso Natural Gas North System Expansion Project, New Mexico and Arizona.* 13 vols. Farmington, NM: Western Cultural Resource Management.

Kuckelman, Kristin A., ed. 2007 *The Archaeology of Sand Canyon Pueblo: Intensive Excavations at a Late-Thirteenth-Century Village in Southwestern Colorado.* http://www.crowcanyon.org/sandcanyon.

Kuckelman, Kristin A., ed. 2017. *The Goodman Point Archaeological Project: Goodman Point Pueblo Excavations.* Accessed January 1, 2021. (tDAR id: 446779), https://doi.org/10.6067/XCV8PC359D.

Miller, Kye. 2015. "Basketmaker III and Pueblo I Communities of Architectural Practice in the Chuska Valley, New Mexico." MA thesis, Department of Anthropology, Northern Arizona University, Flagstaff. (tDAR id: 398690), https://doi.org/10.6067/XCV86M384V.

Murrell, Monica L., and Bradley J. Vierra. 2014. *Bridging the Basin: Land Use and Social History in the Southern Chuska Valley.* Vol. 4, *Synthesis.* Technical Report 14–20. Albuquerque: Statistical Research.

Neily, Robert B. 1982. *Basketmaker Settlement and Subsistence along the San Juan River, Utah: The US 163 Archaeological Project.* Prepared for Utah Department of Transportation. Salt Lake City: Antiquities Section, Division of State History.

Ortman, Scott G., Shanna R. Diederichs, and Kristin A. Kuckelman. 2011. "A Proposal to Conduct Archaeological Testing at Indian Camp Ranch, Montezuma County, Colorado." Proposal submitted to the Colorado State Historic Preservation Office, Denver. Cortez, CO: Crow Canyon Archaeological Center.

Ortman, Scott G., Shanna Diederichs, Kari Schleher, Jerry Fetterman, Marcus Espinosa, and Caitlin Sommer. 2016. "Demographic and Social Dimensions of the Neolithic Revolution in Southwest Colorado." *Kiva* 82 (3): 232–258.

Reed, Lori Stephens. 1998. "Basketmaker III to Pueblo III Ceramic Trends in the Southern Chuska Valley." In *Exploring Ceramic Production, Distribution, and Exchange in the Southern Chuska Valley: Analytical Results from the El Paso Natural Gas North System Expansion Project,* edited by Lori Stephens Reed, Joell Goff, and Kathy Niles Hensler, 7-1-7-40. Vol. 11, Book 1 of *Pipeline Archaeology 1990–1993: The El Paso Natural Gas North System Expansion Project, New Mexico and Arizona.* Farmington, NM: Western Cultural Resource Management.

Ryan, Susan C. 2013. "Architectural Communities of Practice: Ancestral Pueblo Kiva Production during the Chaco and Post-Chaco Periods in the Northern Southwest." PhD diss., School of Anthropology, University of Arizona, Tucson.

Ryan, Susan C. 2015a. "Architecture." In *The Archaeology of Albert Porter Pueblo (Site 5MT123): Excavations at a Great House Community Center in Southwestern Colorado*, edited by Susan C. Ryan. Accessed January 10, 2021. https://www.crowcanyon.org /ResearchReports/AlbertPorter/Albert_Porter_Pueblo_Final.pdf.

Ryan, Susan C. ed. 2015b. "The Archaeology of Albert Porter Pueblo (Site 5MT123): Excavations at a Great House Community Center in Southwestern Colorado [PDF Title]." Accessed January 10, 2021. https://www.crowcanyon.org/ResearchReports /AlbertPorter/Albert_Porter_Pueblo_Final.pdf.

Ryan, Susan C. ed. 2015c. "The Archaeology of Shield Pueblo (Site 5MT3807): Excavations at a Mesa-Top Community Center in Southwestern Colorado [PDF Title]." http://www.crowcanyon.org/shieldspueblo.

Schleher, Kari L. 2017. "Learning and Production: The Northern Rio Grande Glaze Ware Community of Practice at San Marcos Pueblo during the Protohistoric Period." In *The Archaeology and History of Pueblo San Marcos: Change and Stability*, edited by Ann F. Ramenofsky and Kari L. Schleher, 107–128. Albuquerque: University of New Mexico Press.

Schleher, Kari L., and Kate Hughes. 2020. "Artifacts." In *The Basketmaker Communities Project*, edited by Shanna R. Diederichs, 711–861. Accessed January 18, 2021. https:// www.crowcanyon.org/ResearchReports/BasketmakerCommunities/basketmaker _communities_project_final.pdf.

Schwindt, Dylan M., R. Kyle Bocinsky, Scott G. Ortman, Donna M. Glowacki, Mark D. Varien, and Timothy A. Kohler. 2016. "The Social Consequences of Climate Change in the Central Mesa Verde Region." *American Antiquity* 81 (1): 74–96.

Shackley, M. Steven. 2013. *An Energy-Dispersive X-Ray Fluorescence Analysis of Obsidian Artifacts from the Dillard Site (5MT10647), Southwestern Colorado*. Report prepared for Crow Canyon Archaeological Center, Cortez, CO. Albuquerque: Geoarchaeological X-Ray Fluorescence Spectrometry Laboratory.

Shackley, M. Steven. 2015. *An Energy-Dispersive X-Ray Fluorescence Analysis of Obsidian Artifacts from 5MT10647 and 5MT2032, Southwestern Colorado*. Report prepared for Crow Canyon Archaeological Center, Cortez, CO. Albuquerque: Geoarchaeological X-Ray Fluorescence Spectrometry Laboratory.

Shackley, M. Steven. 2017. *An Energy-Dispersive X-Ray Fluorescence Analysis of Obsidian Artifacts from Various Sites in the Basketmaker Communities Project, Southwestern Colorado*. Report prepared for Crow Canyon Archaeological Center, Cortez, CO. Albuquerque: Geoarchaeological X-Ray Fluorescence Spectrometry Laboratory.

Shelley, Steven D. 1990. "Basketmaker III Social Organization: An Evaluation of Population, Aggregation, and Site Structure." Paper presented at the 55th Annual Meeting of the Society for American Archaeology, Las Vegas.

Shelley, Steven D. 1991. "The Potential for Distinct Populations during Basketmaker III on the Colorado Plateau." Paper presented at the 56th Annual Meeting of the Society for American Archaeology, New Orleans.

Sinensky, R. J., Gregson Schachner, Richard H. Wilshusen, and Brian N. Damiata. 2022. "Volcanic Climate Forcing, Extreme Cold and the Neolithic Transition in the Northern US Southwest." *Antiquity* 96 (385): 123–141.

Smith, Susan J. 2020. "Pollen Analysis." In *The Basketmaker Communities Project*, edited by Shanna R. Diederichs, 643–677. Accessed January 18, 2021. https://www.crowcanyon .org/ResearchReports/BasketmakerCommunities/basketmaker_communities _project_final.pdf.

Toll, H. Wolcott, and C. Dean Wilson. 1999. "Locational, Architectural, and Ceramic Trends in the Basketmaker III Occupation of the La Plata Valley, New Mexico." In *Foundations of Anasazi Culture: The Basketmaker-Pueblo Transition*, edited by Paul F. Reed, 19–43. Salt Lake City: University of Utah Press.

Trowbridge, Meaghan A. 2014. "Ceramic Analysis." In *Bridging the Basin: Land Use and Social History in the Southern Chuska Valley*. Vol. 3, *Analysis*, edited by Monica L. Murrell and Bradley J. Vierra, 259–342. Technical Report 14-08. Albuquerque: Statistical Research.

Varien, Mark D., and Scott G. Ortman. 2005. "Accumulations Research in the Southwest United States: Middle-Range Theory for Big-Picture Problems." *World Archaeology* 37 (1): 132–155.

Varien, Mark D., and Shanna R. Diederichs. 2011. *Nomination of the Indian Camp Ranch Archaeological District, Site 5MT19927, to the National Register of Historic Places*. Nomination submitted to the US Department of the Interior, National Park Service, National Register of Historic Places, Washington, DC. Manuscript on file, Crow Canyon Archaeological Center, Cortez, CO.

Varien, M. D., W. D. Lipe, M. A. Adler, I. M. Thompson, and B. A. Bradley. 1996. "Southwestern Colorado and Southeastern Utah Settlement Patterns: A.D. 1100 to 1300." In *The Prehistoric Pueblo World, A.D. 1150–1350*, edited by M. A. Adler, 86–113. Tucson: University of Arizona Press.

Varien, M. D., C. R. Van West, and G. S. Patterson. 2000. "Competition, Cooperation and Conflict: Agricultural Production and Community Catchments in the Central Mesa Verde Region." *Kiva* 66 (1): 45–65.

Wilshusen, Richard H. 1999. "Basketmaker III (A.D. 500–750)." In *Colorado Prehistory: A Context for the Southern Colorado River Basin*, edited by W. D. Lipe, M. D. Varien, and R. H. Wilshusen, 166–194. Denver: Colorado Council of Professional Archaeologists.

Wilshusen, Richard H., Scott G. Ortman, and Ann Phillips. 2012. "Processions, Leaders, and Gathering Places: Changes in Early Community Organization as Seen in Architecture, Rock Art, and Language." In *Crucible of Pueblos: The Early Pueblo Period in the Northern Southwest*, edited by Richard H. Wilshusen, Gregson Schachner, and Jim R. Allison, 198–218. Los Angeles: Cotsen Institute of Archaeology Press, University of California.

11

Bridging the Long Tenth Century

From Villages to Great Houses in the Central Mesa Verde Region

KELLAM THROGMORTON, RICHARD WILSHUSEN, AND GRANT D. COFFEY

Over the past forty years, the Crow Canyon Archaeological Center's long-term, place-based research agenda has brought clarity to many periods of Pueblo history and, by contrast, has made the murkier ones increasingly evident. The most notable knowledge gap in the central Mesa Verde region is a period we call the Long Tenth Century (LTC; AD 890–1030).[1] This 140-year period serves as coda to the formation and collapse of early aggregated villages in the Mesa Verde region (Wilshusen et al. 2012) and prelude to the classic Chaco period (AD 1080–1130), when great houses served as community centers and Chaco society expanded its influence beyond the confines of the San Juan Basin (Lekson 2006; Van Dyke 2007). To chart the transformation of villages into great house communities, we must examine and bridge the Long Tenth Century.

In Europe, historians use the term Long Tenth Century to refer to the late ninth through mid-eleventh centuries, when empires broke down and the first feudal societies emerged (West 2013). As in Europe, the Southwest LTC involved social dissolution and realignment and a shift in population centers and political spheres. Unlike Europe, where the LTC marked the development of

https://doi.org/10.5876/9781646424597.c011

decentralized and shifting political alliances, in the Southwest it laid the groundwork for the centralization of Chacoan power.

LOCATING THE LONG TENTH CENTURY IN THE PAST AND THE PRESENT

Pueblo society during the Long Tenth Century was a response to the dramatic social changes and historical events of the preceding early Pueblo period (AD 600–890). The Dolores Archaeological Program (see Kohler et al., chapter 3 in this volume, for a discussion of the DAP) shaped archaeologists' perception of the early Pueblo period. The DAP demonstrated that the development of aggregated villages—dense settlements of ten or more households, frequently within the same structure—marked a significant innovation in Pueblo architecture and social organization (Wilshusen et al. 2012). Not long after the DAP, Crow Canyon initiated several projects that produced the regional Village Ecodynamics Project (VEP) site database critical for charting long-term demographic trends (Kohler and Varien 2012; see Kohler et al., chapter 3, and Glowacki et al., chapter 12 in this volume). The VEP established the empirical patterns and methods to create detailed reconstructions of population growth and decline in the region, identifying the LTC as a major trough in regional population.

The depopulation of the central Mesa Verde region was likely a consequence of several factors. Dry and cold conditions produced challenges to productive agriculture, and Pueblo people responded with movement to destinations both near and far (Petersen 1987; Schlanger 1988; Schlanger and Wilshusen 1993). The ecological issues, concatenated with the social problems inherent in many nascent village societies, created political crises (Wilshusen et al. 2012). The resulting turmoil led to a decline in population from perhaps 11,500 to 4,000 between AD 880 and 940 (Schwindt et al. 2016).

At some villages, like McPhee Pueblo, depopulation coincided with the violent death and burial of male and female pairs on the floors of pit structures with ritual features. The pit structure roofs were dismantled and collapsed upon the paired individuals, perhaps even as they lay dying. Other pit structures with ritual features were burned, as were nearby oversized community pit structures (Wilshusen 1986). In other villages, like Grass Mesa, depopulation was less dramatic. People built temporary structures while departure was planned and executed, followed by the ritual burning of the village months or years after depopulation (Wilshusen and Ortman 1999). At some small settlements, like the Duckfoot hamlet investigated by Crow Canyon, depopulation may have been marked by famine or disease, with many members of the household simultaneously buried in pit structures that were immediately burned (Lightfoot 1994). These examples paint a picture of the end of the ninth century AD and the beginning of the tenth: food insecurity, population decline, and a loss of faith in the social and ritual practices that had sustained communities for over a hundred years.

If the beginning of the LTC in the Mesa Verde region is found in the terminal histories of villages and hamlets throughout the region, its end lies in the development of great house communities during the eleventh century AD. Numerous projects during the 1990s and 2000s considered the development of Chaco-style communities north of the San Juan River, including the central Mesa Verde region (Cameron 2009; Lekson, chapter 17 in this volume; Ryan 2015). However, most of these projects investigated great houses from the early twelfth century that did not have significant LTC components.

Throughout the 2000s and 2010s, projects on Tribal and private lands identified sites that connected early Pueblo period villages with later Chaco-era great house communities (Bradley 2010; Dove 2006; Potter 2015; Smith 2009; Throgmorton 2019). Other projects identified smaller settlements from the LTC (Coffey 2004, 2006; Shanks 2010). Together, these projects demonstrated that the LTC was much more than a decline or a gap; rather, it was a period with variation in settlement patterns and community structure and a period of significant social and political transformation.

One outcome of research over the past forty years is realization that the AD 880–890 depopulation resulted in a much smaller population in a much more open landscape. Many Pueblo oral histories and ceremonial songs describe how people explored the potential relationships in new landscapes, including landscapes transformed by violence, social upheaval, and environmental change. The revelations inspired by new landscapes shaped the history of a clan or people (see Kuwanwisiwma and Bernardini, chapter 5 in this volume). Research on the LTC also disrupts how archaeologists characterize Chacoan influence north of the San Juan River. Archaeologists debate whether Chaco-style great house communities beyond the walls of Chaco Canyon represent either the emulation or the export of Chacoan architecture, ceremony, and political structure. As we suggest in the section "The Late LTC (AD 975–1030): Reemergence of Great Houses and a Landscape Redefined," there is evidence for great houses much before the presumed post-AD 1075 introduction of Chaco-style architecture north of the San Juan River.

Crow Canyon's unanticipated discovery of a tenth-century AD community center at the Haynie site—sitting above an aggregated village and beneath two Chaco-style great houses—offers an excellent opportunity to chart the changing configurations of place and people over the *longue durée* and the development of Chaco-style communities (Fladd et al. 2018; Ryan 2013; Simon et al. 2017; Throgmorton et al. 2019). The Haynie site completes a Crow Canyon legacy of archaeological research on the AD 600–1300 interval in southwest Colorado.

The LTC component at the Haynie site is a bridge between early Pueblo villages, great house communities, and their late-twelfth- and thirteenth-century successors.

In the following sections, we expand upon this literature review and give a summary of what is currently known about the LTC. We end with a discussion of the critical questions in LTC research and their relationship to other themes in the archaeology of the central Mesa Verde region.

CLIMATE AND THE LONG TENTH CENTURY

The paleoclimate reconstructions for the LTC illustrate a period of great climate variability but with few episodes of dramatic environmental change. Palmer Drought Severity Indices suggest dry conditions were common throughout the first third of the LTC (AD 890–925). These conditions ameliorated somewhat during the middle third (AD 925–975) and returned during the last third (AD 975–1030) (Van West and Dean 2000). The beginning of the LTC (up until about AD 915) was marked by below-average temperatures, with the potential for at least two additional periods of shortened growing season around AD 980–1000 and 1015–1030 (Salzer 2000). Throughout the LTC, streambeds across the region were aggrading (after a period of arroyo cutting in the late ninth century AD) and the water table consequently rising. From AD 890 to 990 the dryland farming belt was relatively high and narrow (limited by temperature on the upper elevation and moisture on the lower), but it expanded downward during the last third of the period, after AD 990 or 1000. These data indicate dry farming during the early and late LTC was tenuous over a broad swath of the northern Southwest and was limited by adequate growing seasons and available water. Upland locations outside of cold air drainages, as well as warmer areas to the south, where runoff events or other supplemental water could be harnessed, provided attractive options to farmers adapting to those difficult agricultural times.

SETTLEMENT PATTERNS AND ARCHITECTURE, AD 890–1030

We divide the LTC into three subperiods based on distinct environmental regimes, settlement patterns, and architectural trends. The early LTC (AD 890–925) is characterized by communities that relocated to more favorable, nearby locales amidst the crises of the late ninth century AD. During the middle LTC (AD 925–975), people reinhabited several ninth-century AD villages and established new settlements in lowland locales. During the late LTC (AD 975–1030) the settlement patterns, architecture, and cultural landscape changed dramatically, initiating a shift from aggregated to dispersed settlements that was a prelude to the period of great house communities of the mid- to late eleventh century AD.

The Early LTC (AD 890–925)

Many people left the central Mesa Verde region altogether during the depopulation of Dolores Valley villages (Wilshusen et al. 2012), but a few communities either persisted or relocated locally during the first interval of the LTC. Tree-ring dates from the Mitchell Springs Ruin Group (Smith 2009) and the Far View Group at Mesa Verde National Park (Robinson and Harrill 1974) indicate some people remained in those communities, whereas dates from a residential site near Dove Creek indicate others established themselves in a relatively unpopulated area (Coffey 2004). Based on pottery data, the Champagne Springs site was first established around this time as was a cluster of villages near the head of Cross Canyon east of Dove Creek (Dove 2006). Probabilistic analyses of pottery recorded during surveys reveals scattered settlements throughout the Great Sage Plain, the Montezuma Valley, and beyond (Kohler and Varien 2012; Potter 2015). However, our knowledge of ceramic technological and stylistic change during this period is limited, and more work may be necessary to refine our estimates of the number of sites likely inhabited during the early LTC. Similarly, there are early LTC tree-ring cutting dates or near-cutting dates from around the region from sites with limited documentation. While population declined, some groups of people persisted and maintained continuity with the preceding decades.

For instance, the layout of the villages east of Dove Creek, referred to here as the Upper Cross Canyon cluster, bear a striking resemblance to the long, contiguous roomblocks found on the east side of the Dolores River, and one of them (the Gillota-Johnson site) had a great kiva (Coffey 2006). The layouts of other early LTC communities are not as easy to characterize, as they are overlain by later components or have been damaged by mechanical excavation. Regardless of their exact layout, all these settlements are aggregated, with limited evidence for a sparser hinterland.

The Middle LTC (AD 925–975)

Pottery evidence indicates that the Mitchell Springs Ruin Group, Champagne Springs, and sites at Mesa Verde National Park persisted into the middle and late LTC but that the Upper Cross Canyon cluster was on the decline (Coffey 2006). Excavation and remote-sensing activities at Champagne Springs identified at least fifty pit structures and multiple roomblocks spanning the entire tenth century AD, as well as a great kiva that was probably constructed around AD 940–960 (Dove 2006). The settlement is split between north and south complexes. Middle LTC pit structures at Champagne Springs were more complex than those from the early LTC, and many exhibited nondomestic floor features and elaborate closing rituals (Dove 2012). People lived at Mitchell Springs throughout the tenth century and into the early eleventh century AD (Dove 2021; Smith 2009), and much of the early and middle LTC architecture is obscured by later construction.

After a two-generation hiatus, people returned to select late ninth-century villages depopulated around AD 880–890. These villages tended to be those that were located near the confluence of midsized watercourses that may have been suitable for channeling runoff water. The exact timing of this return is not well established by dendrochronology, but archaeomagnetic and pottery dates from McPhee Pueblo (5MT4475) and Masa Negra (5MT4477) indicate that people refurbished and reinhabited several ninth-century structures sometime between AD 910 and 980, with the evidence best supporting a post-AD 930 occupation (Brisbin et al. 1988; Kuckelman 1988). The Stix and Leaves Pueblo (5MT11555) is very well dated, with date clusters suggesting construction events between AD 949 and 974 (Bradley 2010). Site 5MT2350, located in Mancos Canyon, has several cutting dates between AD 945 and 973, indicating construction activity at almost the same time (Farmer 1975).

In each case, a large, arcing masonry roomblock was constructed directly atop the floor plan of an earlier ninth-century AD structure (figure 11.1). The room suite pattern established between AD 760 and 890 continued, with large front habitation rooms and paired back rooms exhibiting fewer floor features. Pit structure morphology changed as square pit structures became rounder in their overall shape, benches were needed, and roof support posts were incorporated into benches, with early examples of masonry and wood pilasters appearing near the end of the period (Wilshusen 1988, 627). While these are undoubtedly aggregated habitations lived in by multiple households, they are smaller in scale than the villages of the preceding century, and usually only one or two large roomblocks within an earlier village were reinhabited.

We know of other large settlements dating to the AD 925–975 interval from surface survey. Morris 40, south of Mancos Canyon, was a ninth-century village remodeled during the tenth century AD (Throgmorton 2019). It is unclear if there was an early LTC hiatus at Morris 40. The village at Barker Arroyo may have been established in the early LTC but was certainly inhabited by the middle tenth century AD (Potter 2015). Both Barker Arroyo and Morris 40 have great kivas dated to the middle LTC by associated pottery samples. And as noted earlier, probability estimates indicate that there are likely more small settlements than we currently can document with our very limited excavation data for this period (Dykeman 1986).

Continuity and Change, AD 890–975

The first eighty-five years of the LTC exhibited both change and continuity with the past. Small, dispersed settlements of one to three households were common in the eighth and ninth centuries and continued to exist in the LTC. Notably, aggregated villages remained an important settlement form, albeit

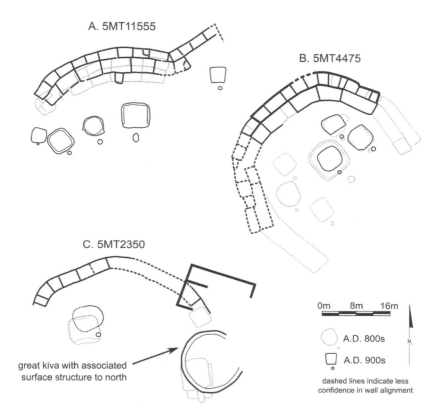

A. 5MT11555

B. 5MT4475

C. 5MT2350

0m   8m   16m

○ A.D. 800s

☐ A.D. 900s

dashed lines indicate less
confidence in wall alignment

great kiva with associated
surface structure to north

FIGURE 11.1. *Plan maps of mid-tenth-century AD components atop earlier ninth-century roomblocks. Tenth-century AD components in black, ninth-century components in gray. (A) Stix and Leaves Pueblo (5MT11555) (adapted from Bradley 2010, fig. 6.1); (B) McPhee Pueblo (5MT4475) (adapted from Brisbin et al. 1988, figs. 2.9 and 2.93); (C) 5MT2350 (adapted from Farmer 1975, fig. 2).*

of a smaller scale than the previous century. The existence of aggregated sites during a period of low regional population density is contrary to the expectations of prior models. The layout and construction techniques of some villages, such as the Upper Cross Canyon cluster, resembled ninth-century AD predecessors, and the mid-tenth-century reoccupations of several late ninth-century villages adhered closely to the original floor plans and room suites. However, settlement patterns changed dramatically. With few exceptions, much of the Dolores and Montezuma Valleys witnessed a notable loss of population between AD 890 and 925. As population slowly began to increase, it is tempting to imagine elders leading community members back to villages they knew as children some forty to fifty years before, and it begs the question—where had these people spent the last two generations and what did they learn and experience there? Communities in the upper San Juan and Fruitland areas (Chuipka et al. 2010; Wilshusen and Wilson 1995) or even the San Juan Basin are possibilities.

Southeast Utah is also a likely population reservoir during the early LTC. The Upper Cross Canyon sites (including Champagne Springs) may be the eastern extent of a settlement cluster that developed in the early LTC as people rapidly repopulated southeastern Utah, which had been thinly inhabited between AD 850 and 880 (Allison 2004; Allison et al. 2012). Based on available evidence, these settlements do not resemble either of the two village styles that dominated the late ninth-century AD central Mesa Verde region (Wilshusen and Ortman 1999), perhaps reflecting an effort to establish new social practices in the aftermath of the Dolores Valley depopulation.

A commonality among sites securely dated to AD 890–925 is a concern with water availability, though two different strategies are evident. People on Mesa Verde and in Upper Cross Canyon relied on higher-elevation mesa top locales, balancing greater precipitation (and soil moisture retention) against shorter seasons (see Ermigiotti et al., chapter 4 in this volume). Others, like those at Mitchell Springs, settled near the confluences of midsized watercourses in lowland settings, perhaps balancing increased runoff potential against the potential for cold air drainage. The potential importance of floodwater farming complicates models of social change that focus primarily on the maize dry farming niche, and the differences between these two techniques and associated landscapes require further inquiry (Ermigiotti et al., chapter 4 in this volume).

Great kivas had ceased to be an important part of community ceremonialism at most aggregated villages in the latter half of the ninth century AD (Schachner 2001, 182), but they were increasingly constructed during the AD 890–975 period, especially after 940. The reappearance of great kivas could be perceived as a revitalization of ceremonies that emphasized community solidarity as opposed to the achievements of specific households. Nonetheless, variation in floor features suggests that a hierarchy of ritual practices—including decommissioning practices (Dove 2012; Lipe et al. 2016)—likely occurred within non–great kiva pit structures, not unlike the late ninth century AD. The question of social inequality and ritual hierarchy needs more thorough examination, but it is telling that there are no obvious great house–like structures dating to AD 890–975 in the central (or western) Mesa Verde region, despite their presence at several late ninth-century AD villages a generation or two before (Wilshusen et al. 2012, 28) and their prevalence in the San Juan Basin during the LTC.

THE LATE LTC (AD 975–1030): REEMERGENCE OF
GREAT HOUSES AND A LANDSCAPE REDEFINED

Various villages—such as the Upper Cross Canyon cluster, Stix and Leaves Pueblo, and Mitchell Springs—were evident across the LTC landscape, but from AD 975 to 1030 an increasing percentage of the population resided in habitation compounds, typically occupied by one or two households. These compounds consisted of post-and-adobe architecture that enclosed an earthen-lined pit structure (figures 11.2A, 11.2B). The central rooms of the compound were often constructed of rough masonry, with copious adobe mortar, and had upright slab foundations.

Post-and-adobe compounds were a striking departure in construction technology and domestic use of space from the aggregated masonry room-blocks of the middle LTC, and people built them in a wide range of mesa top locations, such as in the Goodman Point community (Coffey 2014; Kent 1991; Shanks 2010), near Pleasant View (Kuckelman and Morris 1988; Martin 1938; Morris 1991); and Mesa Verde National Park (Lancaster and Pinkley 1954). The appearance of this habitation style corresponds to a period when the dryland farming belt also expanded into lower elevation mesa top settings. Post-and-adobe architecture shares the closest resemblance with settlements found in northeastern Arizona and southeastern Utah, raising the question whether these are a local approach to moving onto long-fallowed mesa top areas, or a reflection of population movement from other regions. Nonetheless, there are hints that similar "compounds" appeared at existing LTC settlements, such as Morris 40 (Throgmorton 2019).

In the last decade or two of the LTC, early great houses emerged that were distinguished from other contemporary architecture by having six to twelve large, equally sized masonry rooms with scabbled, tabular, single-wythe masonry construction. Examples of these structures include Pueblo B at Mitchell Springs (figure 11.3A; Dove, personal communication, 2021); the east core of the Haynie west great house (Throgmorton et al. 2021), Phase I at at Wallace Ruin (figure 11.3B; B. Bradley and C. Bradley 2020; B. Bradley, personal communication, 2022); and Site 875 (Lister 1965) in the Far View community (figure 11.3C). Some had higher-than-average ceilings (Pueblo B, Mitchell Springs), and at least one (Wallace Ruin) was multistoried. Some were accompanied by large, circular pit structures with comparable tabular masonry lining their subterranean walls (Dove, personal communication, 2021). Site 875 included a crypt room containing numerous secondary interments associated with Cortez and Mancos Black-on-white pottery. Other possible examples that employed a blockier masonry style and that may date slightly later include the north half of Pipe Shrine House in the Far View community (admittedly a tenuous example) and the AD 1050 component of Pueblo A at Mitchell Springs (Dove 2021). Based on this sample, cardinally paired great houses were common in the early AD 1000s—the Haynie

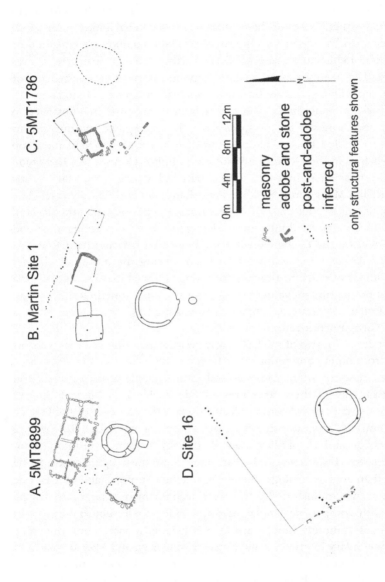

FIGURE 11.2. *Examples of vernacular residential structures dating ca. AD 975–1030. (A) 5MT8899 (adapted from Hammack et al. 2000, fig. 2.18); (B) Martin Site 1 (1937 Season) (adapted from Martin 1938, map. 6); (C) Gnatsville (5MT1786) (adapted from Kent 1991, figs. 2 and 3); (D) Site 16, Mesa Verde National Park (adapted from Lancaster and Pinkley 1954, pl. 20).*

A. Pueblo "B" Mitchell Springs   B. Haynie West Great House   C. Site 875, Far View Community

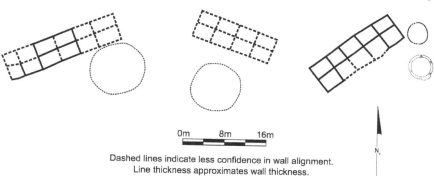

0m   8m   16m

Dashed lines indicate less confidence in wall alignment.
Line thickness approximates wall thickness.

N

FIGURE 11.3. *Possible early great houses at Mitchell Springs, the Haynie site, and the Far View community, ca. AD 1020–1050. (A) Pueblo "B" Mitchell Springs adapted from Dove (n.d.); (B) east half of the west great house at the Haynie site (5MT1905), reconstruction based on Claudia Haynie's unpublished 1983–1985 excavation notes (Throgmorton et al. 2021); (C) Site 875 adapted from Lister (1965, fig.4).*

west great house and Wallace Ruin (north-south), Pueblos A and B at Mitchell Springs (north-south), Site 875 and Pipe Shrine House at the Far View community (east-west). Unfortunately, there are few, if any, tree-ring dates associated with these structures, which have been dated to the early eleventh century AD based on masonry style, or in some cases roughly equal proportions of Mancos and Cortez Black-on-white, and Mancos Corrugated utility ware accompanied by small amounts of Mancos Gray.

TOWARD A MORE DYNAMIC LTC NARRATIVE

Early eleventh-century great houses in the central Mesa Verde region were dramatically different than the post-and-adobe architecture and earthen-lined pit structures found at most residential sites, and their careful masonry construction and ceiling height distinguished them from other masonry houses. Their presence complicates the research questions surrounding great houses in the central Mesa Verde region. Not only must we consider how early twelfth-century AD great houses related to Chaco and Aztec, but also we must consider how the early eleventh-century ones related to a very different-looking Chaco world. Evidence from the LTC suggests that the emulation-versus-export debate is not a matter of *which*, but of *when*. Great houses are not a phenomenon confined to the Chaco world, so it is also imperative to consider the internal dynamics of LTC communities. What was the relationship of early eleventh-century AD great house residents to one another and to non–great house residents? Several of the best early great house examples are not located near known clusters of post-and-adobe style structures (e.g., Pleasant View, Goodman Point). Did the trend toward settlement dispersal, especially into landscapes uninhabited for a hundred years, encourage the development of early great houses, or was it a consequence of their development?

Along these lines, our review indicates that during most of the LTC people in the central Mesa Verde region rejected the U-shaped proto–great houses that had characterized many late ninth-century AD villages (e.g., McPhee Pueblo) and instead revitalized a tradition of great kiva construction. Do great kivas and great houses represent contrasting forms of sociopolitical organization in the central Mesa Verde region, as they may have in the San Juan Basin to the south (Van Dyke 2007, 90)? If so, what can this pattern tell us about changes in political organization throughout the LTC and after?

Environmental fluctuation clearly played a role in creating conditions of possibility for inhabitants of the central Mesa Verde region. We have built our conceptual models of the human-environment relationship around dryland farming, yet our developing understanding of the LTC points to floodwater farming playing a more important role in the development of some early great houses. We think it is important to investigate the variables involved in floodwater farming and consider how this style of agriculture might alter our perception of human-environment relationships in the Pueblo past. What differences exist between mesa top LTC sites, a location where dryland farming occurred, and lowland LTC sites, where floodwater was possible?

Study areas are drawn to reflect the realities of working in the contemporary world—permit systems, data repositories, and land statuses affect how we conduct our research. We know these boundaries did not exist in the Pueblo past, yet it is difficult to avoid them in our research agendas. We set out to investigate the central Mesa Verde region during the LTC. However, if the centers of population shifted westward, eastward, and southward, then an investigation of the LTC in the central Mesa Verde may, in fact, be investigating the edges of strong patterns that developed in adjacent regions because of demographic and social upheaval circa AD 880–890. To evaluate the significance of the early LTC cluster in Upper Cross Canyon, the reoccupation of some villages in the middle LTC, and the appearance of post-and-adobe compounds during the late LTC, it will be necessary to consider social and historical conditions outside the confines of the central Mesa Verde region.

It is possible that a unifying theme for all these questions is to be found in landscapes. In southwestern Colorado, we have usually focused our energies at three geographic scales—the regional database, localities, and individual sites. Each scale has been deployed in making arguments about both general social processes and specific local histories, such as the chapters in this volume by

Schleher et al., chapter 10, on Basketmaker III period community development and chapter 14, on Pueblo II and III period communities at Goodman Point and Sand Canyon. Yet it can be difficult to navigate between these different scales of inquiry, and this has, at times, obfuscated the social and historical connections that shaped the lives of Pueblo people in the past. Landscapes are the qualitative topography wherein individuals experience and influence the environmental and sociopolitical conditions that directly affect their lives. They are relational spaces, centered on connections at a variety of scales.

Unlike the short-lived and densely clustered villages of the early Pueblo period, people in LTC communities had the time and space to develop expansive, complex cultural landscapes that became intimately entangled with ceremonies, historical narratives, and perhaps language (Throgmorton 2019). The scalar flexibility of landscape offers a useful analytical tool to make sense of the shift from the loosely demarcated landscapes of villages and hamlets to the well-inscribed landscapes of great house communities. Consultations with elders and Tribal leaders regularly remind us that these landscapes still hold significance and have much to teach us (Ortman, chapter 6 in this volume).

When we consider the trajectory that led from villages to great houses during the LTC, we see potentially meaningful shifts in how the very definition of a cultural landscape was conceived as well as where community centers were located. Early great houses can be found at the confluence of midsized drainages with watersheds linking highland and lowland, encompassing a much larger territory than any ninth-century AD village. Early great houses may occur in cardinally oriented pairs, an expression of dualism and an increasingly structured built environment. By making sense of the variety of landscapes characteristic of the LTC and how they take shape as an emerging local cultural canon, it may be possible to discern local developments from those influenced by Chaco participants. This analysis may help guide our understanding of how far and fast the Chaco polity unfolded better than identifying local or nonlocal construction techniques in great house architecture and site design.

The bridge we are building for the LTC allows us to connect two seemingly different worlds. In the same way that it would have been difficult to predict the emergence of great house landscapes out of what came before, few could have imagined forty years ago the many connections we now see between Crow Canyon's archaeological research, public education, and American Indian communities. Building bridges that connect our histories and our communities may be what Crow Canyon does best.

NOTE

1. For this study, the central Mesa Verde region is an area roughly coterminous with the VEP II study area (Schwindt et al. 2016), with extensions to the south and north. Our

dates are derived from Bocinsky et al. (2016), who identified a notable inflection in the tree-ring cutting date frequency distribution between AD 890 and 1030.

REFERENCES

Allison, James R. 2004. "Surface Archaeology of the Red Knobs Site: A Southeastern Utah Great House." *Kiva* 69 (4): 339–360.

Allison, James R., Winston B. Hurst, Jonathan D. Till, and Donald C. Irwin. 2012. "Meanwhile, in the West: Early Pueblo Communities in Southeastern Utah." In *Crucible of Pueblos: The Early Pueblo Period in the Northern Southwest*, edited by Richard H. Wilshusen, Gregson Schachner, and James R. Allison, 35–52. Los Angeles: Cotsen Institute of Archaeology, University of California.

Bocinsky, R. Kyle, Johnathan Rush, Keith Kintigh, and Timothy A. Kohler. 2016. "Exploration and Exploitation in the Macrohistory of the Pre-Hispanic Pueblo Southwest." *Science Advances* 2 (4): e1501532.

Bradley, Bruce. 2010. *Report of Archaeological Research Conducted at Stix and Leaves Pueblo (5MT11555), Montezuma County, Colorado*. Primitive Tech Enterprises, Inc., Cortez, CO. Report on file at Crow Canyon Archaeological Center. Cortez, CO: Primitive Tech Enterprises.

Bradley, Bruce, and Cynthia Bradley. 2020. *Annual Report on Excavations at the Wallace Great House (5MT6970) 2020*. Primitive Tech Enterprises, Inc. Cortez, CO. Report on file at Crow Canyon Archaeological Center. Cortez, CO: Primitive Tech Enterprises.

Brisbin, Joel M., Allen E. Kane, and James N. Morris. 1988. "Excavations at McPhee Pueblo (Site 5MT4475): A Pueblo I and early Pueblo II Multicomponent Village." In *Dolores Archaeological Program: Anasazi Communities at Dolores: McPhee Village*, edited by Allen E. Kane and Christine K. Robinson, 63–406. Denver: US Department of the Interior.

Cameron, Catherine M. 2009. *Chaco and After in the Northern San Juan: Excavations at the Bluff Great House*. Tucson: University of Arizona Press.

Chuipka, Jason, Richard Wilshusen, and Jerry Fetterman. 2010. *The Northern San Juan Settlement Pattern Survey of the Animas, Upper San Juan, and Piedra Drainages in Archuleta and La Plata Counties, Colorado: Prehistoric Context and Research Design*. Yellow Jacket, CO: Woods Canyon Archaeological Consultants.

Coffey, Grant. 2004. "Regional Migration and Local Adaptation: A Study of Late Pueblo I and Early Pueblo II Sites in the East Dove Creek Area." MA thesis, Northern Arizona University, Flagstaff.

Coffey, Grant. 2006. "Reevaluating Regional Migration in the Northern San Juan during the Late Pueblo I Period: A Reconnaissance Survey of the East Dove Creek Area." *Kiva* 72 (1): 55–70.

Coffey, Grant. 2014. "The Harlan Great Kiva Site: Civic Architecture and Community Persistence in the Goodman Point Area of Southwestern Colorado." *Kiva* 79 (4): 380–404.

Dove, David M. n.d. "Mitchell Springs." Accessed January 30, 2023. https://web.archive
.org/web/20210419032018/http://fourcornersresearch.com/Mitchell-Springs.html.

Dove, David M. 2006. *Topographical Mapping, Geophysical Studies and Archaeological
Testing of an Early Pueblo II Village near Dove Creek, Colorado. Report to the Colorado Historical Society.* Report on file at History Colorado, Denver, CO.

Dove, David M. 2012. "Multiple Animal Offerings in an Early Kiva." *Southwestern Lore* 78
(2): 1–17.

Dove, David M. 2021. "Greathouse Formation: Agricultural Intensification, Balanced
Duality, and Communal Enterprise at Mitchell Springs." *Southwestern Lore* 87 (1): 5–49.

Dykeman, Douglas D. 1986. *Excavations at 5MT8371, an Isolated Pueblo II Pit Structure in
Montezuma County, Colorado.* Studies in Archaeology No. 2. Division of Conservation
Archaeology, San Juan County Museum Association, Farmington, NM.

Farmer, Travis R. 1975. "Salvage Excavations in Mancos Canyon, Colorado, 1975." MA
thesis, University of Colorado, Boulder.

Fladd, Samantha, Rebecca L. Simon, Susan C. Ryan, Shanna R. Diederichs, Kari L.
Schleher, Caitlin A. Sommer, Steven R. Copeland, and Grant D. Coffey. 2018. *The
Northern Chaco Outliers Project Annual Report, 2018 Field Season.* Cortez, CO: Crow
Canyon Archaeological Center.

Hammack, Nancy S., Jack B. Bertram, and Mark Hovezak. 2000. "Site 5MT8899:
Towaoc Canal Reach I Project." In *Towaoc Canal Reach I*, compiled by Nancy S. Hammack, 17–70. CASA 92–73. Cortez, CO: Complete Archaeological Service Associates.

Kent, Susan. 1991. "Excavations at a Small Mesa Verde Pueblo II Anasazi Site in Southwestern Colorado." *Kiva* 57:55–75.

Kohler, Timothy A., and Mark D. Varien. 2012. *Emergence and Collapse of Early Villages:
Models of Central Mesa Verde Archaeology.* Berkeley: University of California Press.

Kuckelman, Kristin A. 1988. "Excavations at Masa Negra Pueblo (Site 5MT4477): Pueblo
I/Pueblo II Habitation." In *Dolores Archaeological Program: Anasazi Communities at
Dolores: McPhee Village*, edited by Allen E. Kane and Christine K. Robinson, 407–558.
Denver: US Department of the Interior.

Kuckelman, Kristin A., and James N. Morris. 1988. *Archaeological Investigations on South
Canal.* Four Corners Archaeological Report No. 11. Complete Archaeological Service
Associates, Cortez, CO.

Lancaster, James A., and Jean M. Pinkley. 1954. "Excavation at Site 16 of Three Pueblo
II Mesa-Top Ruins." In *Archeological Excavations in Mesa Verde National Park, Colorado,
1950, by James A. Lancaster, Jean M. Pinkley, Philip F. Van Cleave, and Don Watson,
23–86. Archeological Research Series, No. 2. Washington, DC: National Park Service.

Lekson, Stephen H. 2006. *The Archaeology of Chaco Canyon: An Eleventh Century Pueblo
Regional Center.* Santa Fe, NM: School of American Research Press.

Lightfoot, Ricky R. 1994. *The Duckfoot Site.* Vol. 2, *Archaeology of the House and Household.*
Occasional Papers, no.4. Cortez, CO: Crow Canyon Archaeological Center.

Lipe, William D., R. Kyle Bocinsky, Brian S. Chisholm, Robin Lyle, David M. Dove, R. G. Matson, Elizabeth Jarvis, Kathleen Judd, and Brian M. Kemp. 2016. "Cultural and Genetic Contexts for Early Turkey Domestication in the Northern Southwest." *American Antiquity* 81 (1): 97–113.

Lister, Robert H. 1965. *Contributions to Mesa Verde Archaeology: II, Site 875, Mesa Verde National Park, Colorado*. University of Colorado Studies Series in Anthropology, No. 11. Boulder: University Press of Colorado.

Martin, Paul S. 1938. *Archaeological Work in the Ackmen-Lowry Area, Southwestern Colorado, 1937*. Anthropological Series 23 (3). Field Museum of Natural History, Chicago.

Morris, James N. 1991. *Archaeological Investigations on the Hovenweep Laterals, Montezuma County, Colorado*. Four Corners Archaeological Report No. 16. Complete Archaeological Service Associates, Cortez, CO.

Petersen, K. L. 1987. "Summer Warmth: A Critical Factor for the Dolores Anasazi." In *Dolores Archaeological Program: Settlement and Environment*, compiled by K. L. Petersen and J. D. Orcutt, 61–71. Denver: US Department of the Interior.

Potter, James M. 2015. *Wetis Orapugat Navachukwak ("Reconnecting Our Past"): Barker Arroyo Archaeological Project (Phase III)*. Technical Report No.15-65. Farmington, NM: PaleoWest Archaeology.

Robinson, William J, and B. G. Harrill. 1974. *Tree-Ring Dates from Colorado V Mesa Verde Area*. Laboratory of Tree-Ring Research. Tucson: University of Arizona.

Ryan, Susan. 2013. "Architectural Communities of Practice: Ancestral Pueblo Kiva Production during the Chaco and Post-Chaco Periods in the Northern Southwest." PhD diss., Department of Anthropology, University of Arizona, Tucson.

Ryan, Susan, ed. 2015. *The Archaeology of Albert Porter Pueblo (Site 5MT123): Excavations at a Great House Community Center in Southwestern Colorado*. Cortez, CO: Crow Canyon Archaeological Center.

Salzer, Matthew W. 2000. "Temperature Variability and the Northern Anasazi: Possible Implications for Regional Abandonment." *Kiva* 64 (4): 295–318.

Schachner, Gregson. 2001. "Ritual Control and Transformation in Middle Range Societies: An Example from the American Southwest." *Journal of Anthropological Archaeology* 20:168–194.

Schlanger, Sarah H. 1988. "Patterns of Population Movement and Long-Term Population Growth in Southwestern Colorado." *American Antiquity* 53 (4): 773–793.

Schlanger, Sarah, and Richard H. Wilshusen. 1993. "Local Abandonments and Regional Conditions in the North American Southwest." In *The Abandonment of Settlements and Regions: Ethnoarchaeological and Archaeological Approaches*, edited by Catherine Cameron and Steve Tomka, 85–98. Cambridge: Cambridge University Press.

Schwindt, Dylan M., R. Kyle Bocinsky, Scott G. Ortman, Donna M. Glowacki, Mark D. Varien, and Timothy A. Kohler. 2016. "Social Consequences of Climate Change in the Northern Southwest." *American Antiquity* 81 (1): 74–96.

Shanks, Bryan D. 2010. *Kinder Morgan Goodman Point CO2 Compressor Facility and Flow-lines: Survey, Excavation, and Monitoring.* Cortez, CO: Woods Canyon Archaeological Consultants.

Simon, Rebecca L., Susan C. Ryan, Shanna R. Diederichs, Kari L. Schleher, Caitlin A. Sommer, Steven R. Copeland, and Grant D. Coffey. 2017. *The Northern Chaco Outli-ers Annual Report, 2017 Field Season.* Cortez, CO: The Crow Canyon Archaeological Center.

Smith, R. Linda Wheeler, comp. 2009. *The Mitchell Springs Ruin Group: Further Investiga-tions of a Large Community in the Middle Montezuma Valley.* Accessed January 19, 2021. http://www.fourcornersresearch.com/Mitchell_Springs_Report_1998-2004.pdf.

Throgmorton, Kellam. 2019. "Peoplehood and the Political Power of Landscape Change: Chaco Interventions in the Northern San Juan Region." PhD diss., Bing-hamton University, Binghamton, NY.

Throgmorton, Kellam, Susan C. Ryan, Benjamin A. Bellorado, Steven R. Copeland, and Timothy D. Wilcox. 2021. *Excavation at the Haynie Site (5MT1905) by the Crow Canyon Archaeological Center, Annual Report 2020.* Cortez, CO: Crow Canyon Archaeological Center.

Throgmorton, Kellam, Kari L. Schleher, Susan C. Ryan, Samantha G. Fladd, Rebecca Simon, Steven R. Copeland, Timothy D. Wilcox, Laurie D. Webster, Cynthia M. Fadem, and Grant D. Coffey. 2019. *The Northern Chaco Outliers Project Annual, 2019 Field Season.* Cortez, CO: Crow Canyon Archaeological Center.

Van Dyke, Ruth M. 2007. *The Chaco Experience: Landscape and Ideology at the Center Place.* Santa Fe, NM: School for Advanced Research Press.

Van West, Carla, and Jeffrey Dean. 2000. "Environmental Characteristics of the AD 900–1300 Period in the Central Mesa Verde Region." *Kiva* 66 (1): 19–44.

West, Charles. 2013. "The Long Tenth Century, c.880 to c.1030." Part 2 of *Reframing the Feudal Revolution: Political and Social Transformation between Marne and Moselle, c.800–c.1100.* Cambridge: Cambridge University Press.

Wilshusen, Richard H. 1986. "The Relationship between Abandonment Mode and Rit-ual Use in Pueblo I Anasazi Protokivas." *Journal of Field Archaeology* 13 (2): 245–254.

Wilshusen, Richard H. 1988. "Architectural Trends in Prehistoric Anasazi Sites During A.D. 600 to 1200." In *The Dolores Archaeological Program: Supporting Studies: Additive and Reductive Technologies*, compiled by Eric Blinman, Carl J. Phagan, and Richard H. Wilshusen, 599–634. Denver: United States Department of the Interior, Bureau of Reclamation.

Wilshusen, Richard H., and Scott G. Ortman. 1999. "Rethinking the Pueblo I Period in the San Juan Drainage: Aggregation, Mitigation, and Cultural Diversity." *Kiva* 64 (3): 369–399.

Wilshusen, Richard H., Gregson Schachner, and James R. Allison, eds. 2012. *Crucible of Pueblos: The Early Pueblo Period in the Northern Southwest.* Los Angeles: Cotsen Institute of Archaeology, University of California.

Wilshusen, Richard H., and C. Dean Wilson. 1995. "Reformatting the Social Landscape in the Late Pueblo I–Early Pueblo II Period: The Cedar Hill Data in Regional Context." In *The Cedar Hill Special Treatment Project: Late Pueblo I, Early Navajo, and Historic Occupations in Northwestern New Mexico*, compiled by Richard H. Wilshusen, 43–80, La Plata Archaeological Consultants Research Papers No. 1. Dolores, CO: La Plata Archaeological Consultants.

12

Community Centers

Forty Years of Sustained Research in the Central Mesa Verde Region

DONNA M. GLOWACKI, GRANT D. COFFEY,
AND MARK D. VARIEN

An essential aspect of Stuart Struever's vision for Crow Canyon was creating an institution that could support long-term research by teams of specialists (Struever 1968; see also Kohler et al., chapter 3, and Lightfoot and Lipe, chapter 2 in this volume). Perhaps nothing illustrates this vision and the value of long-term collaborative research more than Crow Canyon's sustained documentation of central Mesa Verde region community centers. Begun in 1983, Crow Canyon's research into the largest sites in the region (i.e., community centers or what some call large, central villages) continues to this day. Many chapters in this volume discuss community centers, including chapters by Adler and Hegmon, chapter 16, Kuckelman, Potter et al., chapter 13, and Schleher et al., chapter 14.

Over the last forty years, Crow Canyon's community center research integrated many different projects and involved numerous Crow Canyon staff and collaborators (table 12.1). These collaborators include several Crow Canyon research associates, regional archaeologists, and many institutions: Washington State University, University of Notre Dame, PaleoWest LLC, the Ute Mountain Ute Tribal Historic Preservation Office (THPO), Mesa Verde National Park,

https://doi.org/10.5876/9781646424597.c012

TABLE 12.1. Community center research history.

Project Name	Study Area	Project Dates	Time Period of Study AD	Centers Studied	Publications
Community Center Mapping and Excavations	Central Mesa Verde Region	1983–present	600–1300	10	Publications for each site: https://www.crowcanyon.org/index.php/access-our-research/site-reports-databases
Pueblo Cultures in Transition Conference / Pueblo III Volume	Northern San Juan Region	1989–1990	1100–1300	109	Adler and Varien (1994); Kenzle (1997); Varien et al. (1996)
Village Mapping Project	Central Mesa Verde Region	1993–1995	1050–1300	30	Lipe and Ortman (2000)
Varien PhD	Central Mesa Verde Region	1994–1997	950–1300	135	Varien (1999); Varien (2002)
Glowacki PhD	Northern San Juan Region	2004–2013	1150–1300	253	Glowacki (2015)
VEP I	Central Mesa Verde Region, southwestern Colorado: 1,817 km²	2003–2006	600–1300	106	Glowacki and Ortman (2012); Varien et al. (2007)
Mesa Verde Village Assessment Project	Mesa Verde National Park	2007–2008	725–1300	55	Glowacki (2007)
VEP II	Central Mesa Verde Region, southwestern Colorado: 4,600 km²	2009–2014	725–1300	13	Schwindt et al. (2016); Reese et al. (2019)
Ute Mountain Ute Lands Community Center Studies	Ute Mountain Ute Nation Lands	2012–2020	800–1300	9	Potter et al., chapter 13 in this volume
Community Center Reassessment Project	Central Mesa Verde Region, southwestern Colorado	2016–2021	600–1300	13	Glowacki et al. (2017)

Hovenweep National Monument (National Park Service), Canyons of the Ancients National Monument (Bureau of Land Management), and the US Forest Service. Collaborators also include many generous private landowners who gave us permission to study sites on their property. Finally, the National Science Foundation, National Geographic Society, History Colorado State Historical Fund, Institute for Scholarship in the Liberal Arts (Notre Dame), and Crow Canyon provided funding for community center research. Table 12.1 summarizes the projects that contributed to the community center database.

Crow Canyon defines a community center as containing at least one of the following: fifty or more structures; nine or more pit structures (kivas); and/or public or civic-ceremonial architecture (Adler and Varien 1994; Glowacki and Ortman 2012, 220–221; Varien 1999). A threshold of nine pit structures suggests a minimum population of about 45–50 people residing at these sites. However, sites with seven or eight pit structures, or even fewer, can qualify if they have either public architecture or high numbers of associated rooms. According to a database recently compiled from Colorado and Utah state records, archaeologists have recorded about 21,000 Puebloan residential sites in the central Mesa Verde region of southwestern Colorado and southeastern Utah (database on file, Crow Canyon Archaeological Center). Only 263 of these meet the criteria for community centers. Thus, only 1 percent of known settlements grew large enough to become centers. When compared to the tens of thousands of smaller residential sites in the region, their size, longevity, and the presence of public architecture indicate community centers played a particularly important role in structuring social, economic, and political activities in communities and in the larger regional settlement system. The community centers served as focal sites for larger communities comprised of smaller residential sites and as important nodes in the larger regional social landscape.

In this chapter, we discuss the forty-year history of community center research at Crow Canyon, describe the current state of our community center database, and discuss large-scale patterns and variation in community centers across space and through time (AD 600–1290) in an area slightly larger than the central Mesa Verde region (figure 12.1). We close by evaluating the impact of Crow Canyon's long-term community center research, discussing our ongoing initiatives, and laying out our plans for future studies.

A BRIEF HISTORY OF COMMUNITY CENTER RESEARCH

Community center research emerged as a central focus for the institution in the 1980s, when community organization was becoming an important concept across the Southwest (e.g., Kane 1983; Marshall et al. 1979; Rohn 1977; Wills and Leonard 1994). It coincided with the inception of Crow Canyon, when E. Charles Adams, Bruce Bradley, and Michael Adler mapped Sand Canyon Pueblo in 1983 (Kohler

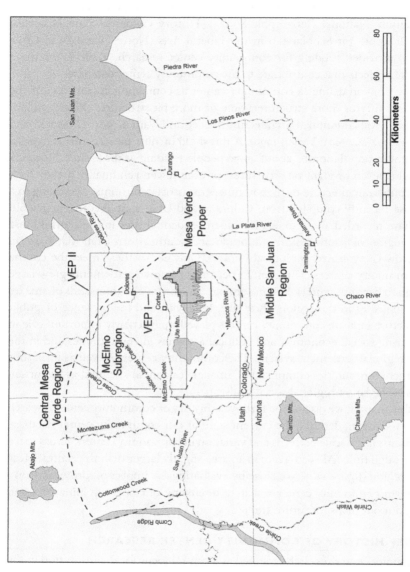

FIGURE 12.1. *Map showing central Mesa Verde region, McElmo subregion, Mesa Verde proper, middle San Juan region, and locations of VEP I and II study areas. Courtesy of the Crow Canyon Archaeological Center.*

et al., chapter 3, and Lightfoot and Lipe, chapter 2 in this volume). Although Crow Canyon's excavations at Sand Canyon Pueblo (1984–1993) and nine community centers thereafter were not specifically designed as part of the community center research project, these excavations provided invaluable calibration for the interpretation of centers known only from surface remains. For these data and detailed reports, see Crow Canyon's online research database (https://www .crowcanyon.org/index.php/access-our-research/site-reports-databases).

The first community center inventory was begun for the Wenner-Gren–funded Pueblo Cultures in Transition Conference in 1990 that focused on characterizing the distribution of large sites throughout most of the greater Southwest between AD 1150 and 1350 (Adler 1996). As discussed by Kohler and others in this volume (see chapter 3), this conference represents an important milestone in Crow Canyon's history where the Center, for the first time, took on regional and macroregional research. A team of Crow Canyon archaeologists, led by William Lipe and Mark Varien, compiled this initial list of centers in southwestern Colorado and southeastern Utah (table 12.1). They obtained site forms for recorded sites; however, a formal database was not constructed. Collectively, team members informally visited roughly 75 percent of these sites ($n = 80$). They used tree-ring dated (excavated) sites to characterize how pottery, architecture, and site layout changed through time, and then used these characterizations to qualitatively assess sites without tree-ring dates and assign them to fifty-year time periods (Varien et al. 1996).

The Village Mapping Project (Lipe and Ortman 2000) subsequently used this community center inventory to identify thirty centers for further study. Directed by William Lipe, Richard Wilshusen, and Scott Ortman, this project took stereo-pair aerial photographs of thirty centers, mapped fifty centers using photogrammetry and a Topcon GTS-303 total station, conducted in-field pottery and lithics analyses, and nominated six of these newly documented centers to the National Register of Historic Places. Crow Canyon then excavated small portions of three of these centers—Woods Canyon (Churchill 2002), Yellow Jacket (Kuckelman 2003), and Hedley (Ortman et al. 2000) Pueblos—as part of the Village Testing Project (Varien and Wilshusen 2002, 11–12).

Two PhD dissertations also focused on community centers, adding new ones to the inventory, and conducting new analyses. Mark Varien's (1999) research focused on 135 centers dating between AD 950 and 1300 in a 14,022 km² area of the central Mesa Verde region. He conducted a catchment analysis that illustrated how successive centers formed the nucleus of persistent communities that occupied specific localities for at least three centuries. Donna Glowacki's (2015) study included the entire northern San Juan region and specifically focused on centers dating between AD 1150 and 1280, nearly doubling the number of centers considered by previous studies ($n = 253$). She analyzed intraregional variation in community center distribution, size, population, and organization (public architecture) and conducted a regional compositional analysis to reconstruct pottery production and interaction. Her findings show strong differences in the histories of intraregional organization and interaction between, and among, eastern and western Mesa Verde centers that shaped how migration and regional depopulation unfolded throughout the mid- to late 1200s.

The Village Ecodynamics Project (VEP) represents a long-term, multi-institutional, and multidisciplinary research program (2002–2016) focused on understanding the relationship between ancestral Pueblo people and their environment from AD 600 to 1760 (Kohler and Varien 2012; Kohler et al., chapter 3 in this volume). Funded primarily (but not exclusively) by two large National Science Foundation grants (numbers 0119981 and 0816400), the two successive phases of the project (VEP I and VEP II) expanded the geographic focus in central Mesa Verde region by increasing the southwestern Colorado study area from 1,817 km^2 (VEP I) to 4,600 km^2 (VEP II) and shifting the temporal scope to include an earlier period (AD 600–1280).

An important component of the VEP included a community center survey to systematically expand and upgrade the community center database. The VEP project created a database of all recorded sites in the expanded study area, over 18,000 sites. Using this database, the community center survey cross-checked the existing database of centers to identify additional centers not in the inventory. This expanded list of community centers was further assessed to identify those with inadequate documentation. The VEP community center survey revisited as many of these sites as possible to make new maps and conduct in-field pottery analysis (Glowacki and Ortman 2012). Over the course of both VEP projects, researchers conducted fieldwork at seventy-one centers. We also systematically compiled existing data for centers in the VEP study area, resulting in a new database with information on 172 centers. Finally, the VEP team developed new quantitative methods to determine the periods of occupation for each center and to estimate the number of people living at each center during each period of occupation (Ortman et al. 2007; Schwindt et al. 2016; Varien et al. 2007).

The VEP II community center survey focused on documenting centers in Mesa Verde National Park (MVNP). Survey practices at MVNP recorded individual roomblocks—regardless of how close they were to each other—as separate sites; therefore, we had to identify the sites that needed to be consolidated into distinct community centers. This assessment began with the Mesa Verde Village Assessment Project (MVVAP), which was tasked with identifying the status of site data across the park to evaluate needs for the VEP analyses (Glowacki 2007). The MVVAP synthesized information on the major communities throughout the park and laid the groundwork for the VEP II community center fieldwork at MVNP.

Between 2012 and 2020, Crow Canyon assisted the Ute Mountain Ute THPO and PaleoWest, LLC, to create preservation plans for nine community centers on Ute Mountain Ute lands (Potter et al. 2020). This effort involved fieldwork that included creating new maps, assessing architecture, and conducting in-field surface pottery analysis. This fieldwork is only a small part of the more ambitious preservation plans developed by the THPO and PaleoWest for these sites, yet it dramatically improved our understanding of these centers (Potter et al., chapter 13 in this volume). In some cases, these efforts provided the first official documentation of these centers.

From 2016 to the present, our research into community centers continued through the Community Center Reassessment Project. We first critically reexamined the VEP II–generated demographic estimates for each community center (Schwindt et al. 2016), comparing the occupation period results with the archaeological record for each site. This process of critical assessment made it clear that some community centers needed additional research efforts to improve the data underlying large-scale demographic reconstructions. To address some of these site-specific issues, we conducted new fieldwork. In 2017, three community centers in Mesa Verde National Park (MVNP) were reevaluated (Glowacki et al. 2017), and nine centers, or potential centers, in the broader study area (outside the park boundaries) were revisited. This reevaluation included completing pottery tallies at sites with insufficient pottery data and remapping selected sites for which only sketch maps, or other less-detailed maps, existed. These analyses resulted in over 3,800 sherds from thirty-four pottery tallies to be incorporated into our regional analyses. On a more limited basis, site-specific reevaluations elsewhere in our study area have taken place as opportunities arise. One such study was the recent (2019) collections-based reevaluation of pottery obtained by Fort Lewis College during excavations at Morris 25 (Firor and Riches 1988). We are also reviewing site forms and reports to cross-check or add center data in other cases to further augment the database.

Our critical review process also identified discrepancies in some of the occupation spans generated by the demographic profiles estimated via VEP II Bayesian analyses (Schwindt et al. 2016) versus what researchers know from the extant archaeological data. These discrepancies are largely related to the difficulties presented by these large multicomponent community centers; their complex and long histories present an interesting challenge for our analytical methods that estimate population size for each period of occupation. Therefore, the reassessment also includes a critical evaluation of these VEP methods as applied to community centers, a process that is ongoing.

The community center surveys and subsequent research have benefited greatly from the assistance of many archaeologists who were not directly involved in the project. Their expertise and knowledge helped us immensely with identifying centers and adding key historical and archaeological information. We remain grateful for all their assistance and generosity over the years. The community centers database has also been used by other researchers and was incorporated into other important research initiatives, including CyberSW (http://cyberSW .org) and the Chaco Research Archive (http://chacoarchive.org).

THE COMMUNITY CENTER DATABASE

The current community center database consists of all centers identified by the projects listed in table 12.1 (n = 325; figure 12.2). As centers from each new project were added to the inventory, we removed duplicate entries and corrected, or updated, records as needed. When new fieldwork was conducted, we used the methods developed at the inception of the VEP (Glowacki 2012; Glowacki and Ortman 2012). Crow Canyon excavations provide data for ten of these community centers, and centers have been excavated by other researchers and institutions (e.g., chapters in this volume by Kuckelman, Potter et al. [chapter 13] and Schleher et al. [chapter 14] discuss partially excavated community centers, and chapters by Arakawa et al. [chapter 15], Oas and Adams [chapter 22], and Schollmeyer and Driver [chapter 21], and Badenhorst et al. [chapter 20] examine the lithics, botanical remains, and faunal remains from excavated centers). However, the majority of data on centers comes from the analysis of surface remains. Because of VEP projects and Crow Canyon's research focus, the most intensively studied community centers are located in southwestern Colorado—with our understanding of centers in southeastern Utah and some just across the Colorado–New Mexico border coming from other projects listed in table 12.1. The total number of existing, or potential, centers within the area shown in figure 12.2 (i.e., central Mesa Verde region) is 263. An additional sixty-two centers come from Glowacki's (2015) regional analysis of Pueblo III period centers located in the middle San Juan region, but these are not the focus of this chapter.

COMMUNITY CENTERS: DISTRIBUTION
AND BROAD TRENDS OVER TIME

The distribution of all the community centers in the database (figure 12.2) illustrates how highly concentrated the centers were in the Mesa Verde core (i.e., the McElmo and Mesa Verde proper subregions; figure 12.1). In part, this high concentration occurs due to the many research projects conducted in this area, but it likely also occurs because the Mesa Verde core contains many favorable environmental and ecological characteristics, including abundant, high-quality arable land, more precipitation, and longer growing seasons on the Mesa Verde cuesta. Note that early centers in southeastern Utah are likely underrepresented for the AD 600–900 period, as they have not been the focus of projects contributing to the community center database to date. Thus, the concentration of community

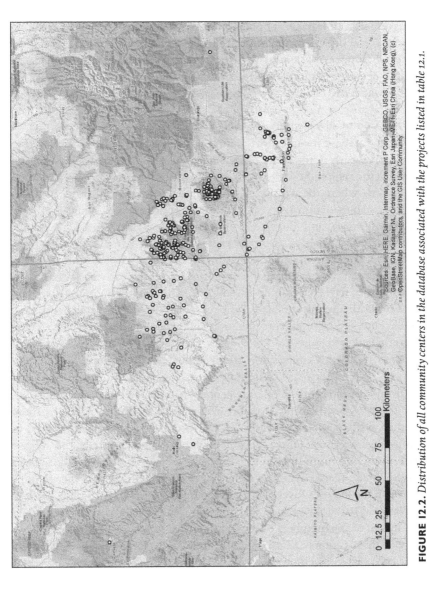

FIGURE 12.2. *Distribution of all community centers in the database associated with the projects listed in table 12.1. Courtesy of the Crow Canyon Archaeological Center.*

centers in the Mesa Verde core is best evidenced with the most comparable data by the distribution of the late period centers (see section "Late Cycle Community Centers [AD 900–1280]"). Glowacki (2015) has described the high density of late community centers in this area as being part of the McElmo Intensification (AD 1225–1260), a time when population levels and aggregation increased and a dramatic social organizational shift occurred. To further examine our current database, we focus on the central Mesa Verde region specifically and consider the differences between community centers during the early and late aggregation cycles (Glowacki and Ortman 2012; Varien et al. 2007; Wilshusen 2002).

Early Cycle Community Centers (AD 600–900)

The current database includes forty-nine early centers, which are displayed in figure 12.3. The early community centers are generally dispersed across the central Mesa Verde region; however, there are two subregions—Dolores and Mesa Verde proper—where the density of early centers is higher (figure 12.1). Again, archaeological biases contribute to this pattern as both areas had the largest projects (Breternitz 1993) and longest research attention (Nordenskiöld [1893] 1990) when compared to other parts of the central Mesa Verde region. Likely, there are also cultural and environmental reasons for how and why these areas exhibit higher population densities and larger villages during the early cycle. For example, both locales have geographic advantages, including the Dolores River and its access to both agricultural land and large game (Kohler and Reed 2011), and the arable land and favorable precipitation and growing season on Mesa Verde (Adams and Petersen 1999).

Not all of these early centers have room counts, but the majority do have estimates ($n = 32$), and for these centers the average number of rooms is 103 and ranges from 8 to 486 rooms. For early centers, roomblock count and length are more often recorded than pit structure count because surface rubble is more visible than pit structure depressions. Thus, roomblock count is often used as a measure of center size. Of the 44 centers with roomblock counts, the average number is 10 with a range from 1 to 37. Examples of large centers include villages such as McPhee Village (Kane and Robinson 1988) and Grass Mesa Village (Lipe et al. 1988) in the Dolores River valley and the Badger House community in Mesa Verde National Park (Hayes and Lancaster 1975). At some of these large centers, most if not all of the members of the community lived in the center itself.

Many of these centers are associated with public architecture, generally great kivas or other mass assembly structures ($n = 17$). Four early centers have two great kivas recorded, suggesting either extended use of these sites with great kiva construction over a longer span or intensified use of public architecture at some sites. That only roughly one-third of the centers have well-defined public architecture suggests that the social and natural conditions of centers varied, and

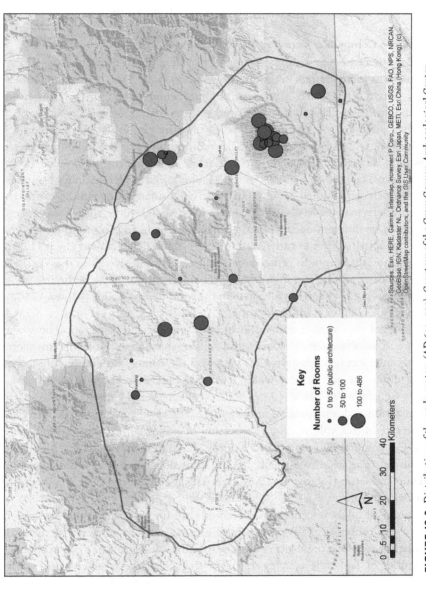

FIGURE 12.3. *Distribution of the early centers (AD 600–900). Courtesy of the Crow Canyon Archaeological Center.*

Key

Number of Rooms

· 0 to 50 (public architecture)

● 50 to 100

● 100 to 486

0 5 10   20   30   40
Kilometers

N

communal gatherings were facilitated via different means (Glowacki and Ortman 2012, 238–239, table 14.3; Wilshusen et al. 2012). The conditions promoting aggregation were not widely shared, and different models of community integration or identity construction were present across the study area during this period.

Late Cycle Community Centers (AD 900–1280)

The 230 late centers in the database are displayed in figure 12.4. There are nearly five times as many centers in the late aggregation cycle. This increase in number is due, in part, to the focus of many community center projects on this late period and the inclusion of late centers in southeastern Utah ($n = 53$) (Glowacki 2015); however, an increase in population levels during this period also plays a role.

The location and distribution of late community centers in southwestern Colorado differ from the early cycle. Notable high-concentration areas are at the head of, and along, canyons in the McElmo area, which includes Canyons of the Ancients National Monument, and two distinct groups in the northern and southern parts of MVNP. In the case of the MVNP centers, the two concentrations have different occupational histories, as the northern group of centers were depopulated by the early AD 1200s (e.g., Morefield Canyon Great House Village), and the southern centers are dominated by cliff dwellings that reached their peak size during the mid- to late AD 1200s. Also, of note is the relatively regular spacing between large centers in the Montezuma Valley (Glowacki 2015; Potter et al., chapter 13 in this volume).

There are also distinct differences in both number and distribution between centers in southwestern Colorado and southeastern Utah. Not only are there fewer centers in southeastern Utah, but also the centers predominantly occur along drainages and exhibit wider spacing. These differences in distribution across Central Mesa Verde (CMV) point to intraregional variation in the social organization and relationships among these largest villages (see Schleher et al., chapter 14 in this volume, for a discussion of potential relationships between Sand Canyon and Goodman Point Pueblos). Additionally, situating settlements on canyon rims, at canyon heads, and on talus slopes becomes more common than upland settings across the CMV in the late aggregation cycle (e.g., Glowacki and Ortman 2012).

Among all of these centers, room counts are the most consistent means of identifying center size; 146 centers have estimated room counts. The average number of rooms at these late centers is 95, with a range from 3 to 700. Although a number of late-cycle centers are larger than the largest center in the early period, there are also many that minimally meet the fifty-room threshold for center status. An important development in the AD 1200s is the change in village layout from what had been a conventional San Juan pattern linear roomblock arrangement to a more aggregated and inwardly focused village configuration

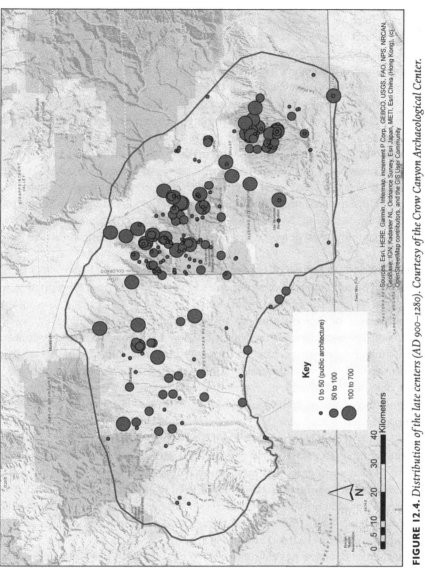

FIGURE 12.4. *Distribution of the late centers (AD 900–1280). Courtesy of the Crow Canyon Archaeological Center.*

(Glowacki 2015, 167–171; Lipe 2006; Lipe and Ortman 2000). The mix of village types in the AD 1200s suggests there were different types of social and religious organizations that were emerging as people were aggregating into increasingly larger villages (Glowacki 2015).

These changing and intensifying social dynamics are also evident in the frequency, distribution, and diversity of public architecture, including great houses, great kivas, plazas, and bi-wall or tri-wall structures. Forty-one centers have at least one great house, 65 centers have at least one great kiva; 77 centers have plazas; and 22 centers have either D-shaped, bi-wall, or tri-wall structures (see Lekson, chapter 17 in this volume, for a discussion of tri-wall structures). The type of public architecture present varies through time and corresponds to broader cultural developments in the study area: most great houses occur between AD 1075 and 1140; most D-shaped, bi-wall, or tri-wall structures occur from AD 1225 to 1280, and great kivas occur throughout the period but were common from AD 1000 to 1225. Plazas become larger and better defined at aggregated villages dating after AD 1225. The expanded use of public architecture shows that significant cultural changes were occurring that increasingly emphasized communal gatherings and indicate that there were different ideas about social and ceremonial practices.

Terminal Period Community Centers (AD 1250–1280)

Community centers played different roles in the final decades of occupation in the central Mesa Verde region. In particular, the largest villages were among the last locations to be depopulated, especially in the McElmo subregion (Glowacki 2015, 2020; Lipe 1995), suggesting that there may have been some sense of security or sunk-cost investment afforded by centers as social and climatic conditions deteriorated. To examine the distribution of terminal late community centers in the database, we examine centers that date between AD 1250 and the final depopulation of the region. Using the VEP analysis allows for a narrower focus on those centers with a post-AD 1260s occupation; this analysis has not yet been applied to centers in southeastern Utah, so we begin this period at AD 1250 to facilitate comparison across the entire central Mesa Verde region. Additionally, current evidence suggests that emigration from southeastern Utah was occurring earlier than in southwestern Colorado (Glowacki 2015; Matson et al. 2015; see also Bellorado and Windes, chapter 18 in this volume, on the depopulation of Cedar Mesa). Thus, the terminal period of occupation likely varies east to west across the central Mesa Verde region.

The current database has eighty-one terminal Pueblo III period centers; these are displayed in figure 12.5. Most of the terminal centers had lower population levels than were present at their peak occupation, and these centers were most often located in canyon settings, including canyon rims, canyon heads, and cliff dwellings. In general, there were somewhat fewer terminal community centers

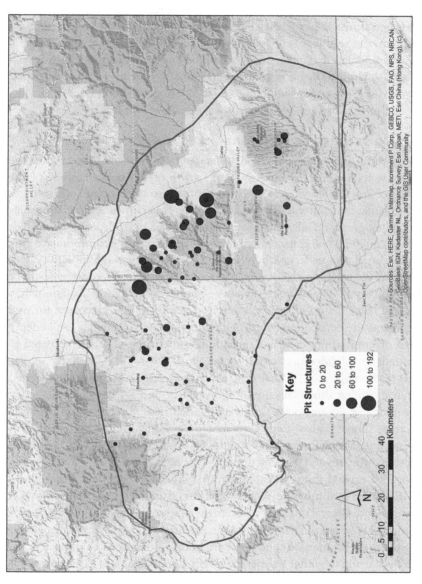

FIGURE 12.5. *Distribution of the terminal late centers (AD 1250–1280). Courtesy of the Crow Canyon Archaeological Center.*

in southeastern Utah, and they are markedly smaller than those in southwestern Colorado. In southwestern Colorado, Yellow Jacket and Goodman Point Pueblos are the largest, followed by Hampton Ruin, Sand Canyon Pueblo, and Yucca House. Located near the Colorado-Utah border, the Hedley Main Ruin, which is part of the larger Hedley Site Complex, represents the largest terminal period center in southeastern Utah. Hedley Main Ruin has eighty-five pit structures, which makes it slightly smaller than the largest centers in southwestern Colorado. Additionally, the next largest terminal center in southeastern Utah, the 10-Acre Site, is roughly one-third the size of Goodman Point Pueblo, and less than one-fourth the overall size of Yellow Jacket Pueblo at its peak.

ONGOING STUDIES AND FUTURE DIRECTIONS

The long-term research coordinated and supported by Crow Canyon over the last forty years has enabled the continual growth of our understanding of the largest ancestral Pueblo villages. We now know more about population changes, social organization, interaction, and changing trajectories and relationships at larger geographic scales than would have been possible otherwise. This important ongoing commitment to institutional support for community center research also allows us to continue to plan for future research initiatives. Our community center research continues to locate new centers and to cross-check, update, and revise data using recent survey and documentation. Additionally, a systematic reevaluation of VEP's Bayesian methods to better account for multicomponent site occupation contexts is underway. Once complete, an in-depth analysis of community center organization and change will be conducted to better understand differences among subregions.

New technologies are also being applied to ongoing community center research including drone-based photogrammetry and LiDAR (light detection and ranging) for site mapping (Coffey and Varien 2022; Potter et al. 2020; Varien et al. 2021). These highly accurate technologies allow for the compilation of more accurate site maps and, in conjunction with ground-truthing, ultimately better size estimates and feature counts.

Efforts to expand the regional study area are also underway. Although PII and PIII centers in southeastern Utah have been studied at regional scales (e.g., Cameron 2009; Glowacki 2015), a systematic assessment of the Pueblo occupation from AD 600 to 1290 has not yet been undertaken. A new initiative seeking to expand the VEP methods and apply them to southeastern Utah centers has begun by starting to gather site data in a centralized database. This project will eventually allow comparison between the social and settlement dynamics in the eastern and western parts of the central Mesa Verde region and show differences in timing of occupation. This effort will likely identify more early centers in the west and will collect new data to better define late cycle centers in southeastern

Utah. Beyond this effort, eastern centers (e.g., Sacred Ridge, Blue Mesa), particularly the early centers, have not yet been included in the CMV community center database; we plan to incorporate these into our future research.

Compilation of the community center database has stimulated a great deal of research on these large sites, and much has been learned about the largest ancestral Pueblo villages in the central Mesa Verde region and the important social, religious, economic, and political roles they played in Pueblo life and history in the region. This research includes studies that have focused on sociopolitical organization and social power, demographic scaling, stone tool procurement, and exchange networks (e.g., Arakawa 2012; Coffey 2016; Coffey and Ryan 2017; Crabtree et al. 2017; Lipe 2002; Glowacki 2015; Kohler and Varien 2010; Ortman and Coffey 2017). We look forward to future work that will continue to build on this long and productive trajectory of research initiated by the Crow Canyon Archaeological Center.

REFERENCES

Adams, Karen R., and Kenneth L. Petersen. 1999. Environment. In *Colorado Prehistory: A Context for the Southern Colorado River Basin*, edited by William D. Lipe, Mark D. Varien, and Richard H. Wilshusen, 14–50. Denver: Colorado Council of Professional Archaeologists.

Adler, Michael A., ed. 1996. *The Prehistoric Pueblo World, A.D. 1150–1350*. Tucson: University of Arizona Press.

Adler, Michael A., and Mark D. Varien. 1994. The Changing Face of the Community in the Mesa Verde Region A.D. 1000–1300. In *Proceedings of the Anasazi Symposium, 1991*, compiled by A. Hutchinson and J. E. Smith, 83–97. Mesa Verde, CO: Mesa Verde Museum Association.

Arakawa, Fumiyasu. 2012. "Tool-Stone Procurement in the Mesa Verde Core Region through Time." In *Emergence and Collapse of Early Villages: Models of Central Mesa Verde Archaeology*, edited by Timothy A. Kohler and Mark D. Varien, 175–196. Berkeley: University of California Press.

Breternitz, David A. 1993. "The Dolores Archaeological Program: In Memoriam." *American Antiquity* 58 (1): 118–125.

Cameron, Catherine M. 2009. *Chaco and After in the Northern San Juan: Excavations at the Bluff Great House*. Tucson: University of Arizona Press.

Churchill, Melissa J., ed. 2002. "The Archaeology of Woods Canyon Pueblo: A Canyon-Rim Village in Southwestern Colorado." https://www.crowcanyon.org/resources /the_archaeology_of_woods_canyon_pueblo_a_canyon_rim_village_in_south western_colorado/.

Coffey, Grant. 2016. "Creating Symmetry: The Cultural Landscape in the Sand Canyon Locality, Southwestern Colorado." *KIVA: The Journal of Southwestern Anthropology and History* 82 (1): 1–21.

Coffey, Grant D., and Susan C. Ryan. 2017. "A Spatial Analysis of Civic-Ceremonial Architecture in the central Mesa Verde Region, United States." *Journal of Anthropological Archaeology* 47 (September): 12–32.

Coffey, Grant D., and Mark D. Varien. 2022. "Chaco Great Houses in the Great Sage Plain of Southwestern Colorado." Paper presented at the 87th Annual Meeting of the Society for American Archaeology, Chicago.

Crabtree, Stefani, R. Kyle Bocinsky, Paul L. Hooper, Susan C. Ryan, and Timothy A. Kohler. 2017. "How to Make a Polity (in the Central Mesa Verde Region)." *American Antiquity* 82 (1): 71–95.

Firor, James, and Susan Riches. 1988. *Surface Recordation and Test Excavations of the Huntington Site, 5LP2164.* Unpublished report on file at Fort Lewis College, Department of Anthropology, Durango, CO.

Glowacki, Donna M. 2007. "Mesa Verde Village Assessment Project." Manuscript on file at Crow Canyon Archaeological Center, Cortez, CO.

Glowacki, Donna M. 2012. "The Mesa Verde Community Center Survey Documenting Large Pueblo Villages in Mesa Verde National Park with contributions by R.K. Bocinsky, E. Alonzi, and K. Reese." Manuscript on file with NSF, Mesa Verde National Park, Crow Canyon Archaeological Center, Cortez, CO, and Washington State University, Pullman.

Glowacki, Donna M. 2015. *Living and Leaving: A Social History of Regional Depopulation in Thirteenth-Century Mesa Verde.* Tucson: University of Arizona Press.

Glowacki, Donna M. 2020. "The Leaving's the Thing: The Contexts of Mesa Verde Emigration." In *Detachment from Place: Beyond an Archaeology of Settlement Abandonment,* edited by M. Lamoureux-St-Hilaire and S. A. Macrae, 23–44. Louisville: University Press of Colorado.

Glowacki, Donna M., R. Kyle Bocinsky, Kelsey M. Reese, and Katherine A. Portman. 2017. *The Mesa Verde Community Center Survey Summer 2017.* Manuscript on file with Mesa Verde National Park, Mesa Verde, CO, and Crow Canyon Archaeological Center, Cortez, CO.

Glowacki, Donna M., and Scott G. Ortman. 2012. "Characterizing Community Center (Village) Formation in the VEP Study Area, A.D. 600–1280." In *Emergence and Collapse of Early Villages: Models of Central Mesa Verde Archaeology,* edited by Timothy A. Kohler and Mark D. Varien, 219–246. Berkeley: University of California Press.

Hayes, Alden C., and James A. Lancaster. 1975. *Badger House Community, Mesa Verde National Park.* Washington, DC: US Department of the Interior, National Park Service.

Kane, Alan E. 1983. "An Introduction to Field Investigation and Analysis." In *Dolores Archaeological Program: Field Investigations and Analysis—1978.* Prepared under the supervision of D. A. Breternitz, 1–37. Denver: Bureau of Reclamation, Engineering and Research Center.

Kane, Alan E., and C. K. Robinson. 1988. *Dolores Archaeological Program: Anasazi Communities at Dolores: McPhee Village*. Denver: USDI Bureau of Reclamation, Engineering and Research Center; https://doi.org/10.6067/XCV8HX1C0.G.

Kenzle, Susan C. 1997. "Enclosing Walls in the Northern San Juan: Sociophysical Boundaries and Defensive Fortifications in the American Southwest." *Journal of Field Archaeology* 24 (2): 195–210.

Kohler, Timothy A., and Charles Reed. 2011. "Explaining the Structure and Timing of Formation of Pueblo I Villages." In *Sustainable Lifeways: Cultural Persistence in an Ever-Changing Environment*, edited by Naomi F. Miller, Katherine M. Moore, and Kathleen Ryan, 150–179. Philadelphia: University of Pennsylvania Museum of Archaeology and Anthropology.

Kohler, Timothy A., and Mark D. Varien. 2010. "A Scale Model of Seven Hundred Years of Farming Settlements in Southwestern Colorado." In *Becoming Early Villagers: Comparing Early Village Societies*, edited by Matthew S. Bandy and Jake R. Fox, 37–61. Tucson: University of Arizona Press.

Kohler, Timothy A., and Mark D. Varien. 2012. *Emergence and Collapse of Early Villages: Models of Central Mesa Verde Archaeology*. Berkeley: University of California Press.

Kuckelman, Kristin A., ed. 2003. *The Archaeology of Yellow Jacket Pueblo (Site 5MT5): Excavations at a Large Community Center in Southwestern Colorado*. https://www.crowcanyon.org/resources/the_archaeology_of_yellow_jacket_pueblo_excavations_at_a_large_community_center_in_southwestern_colorado/.

Lipe, William D. 2002. "Social Power in the Central Mesa Verde Region, A.D. 1150–1300." In *Seeking the Center Place: Archaeology and Ancient Communities in the Mesa Verde Region*, edited by Mark D. Varien and Richard H. Wilshusen, 203–232. Salt Lake City: University of Utah Press.

Lipe, William D. 2006. "Notes from the North." In *The Archaeology of Chaco Canyon: An Eleventh Century Pueblo Regional Center*, edited by Stephen Lekson, 261–313. Santa Fe, NM: School of American Research Press.

Lipe, William D., James N. Morris, and Timothy A. Kohler. 1988. *Dolores Archaeological Program: Anasazi Communities at Dolores: Grass Mesa Village*. Denver: USDI Bureau of Reclamation, Engineering and Research Center. https://doi.org/10.6067/XCV8CR5SPT.

Lipe, William D., and Scott G. Ortman. 2000. "Spatial Patterning in Northern San Juan Villages, A. D. 1050–1300." *KIVA: The Journal of Southwestern Anthropology and History* 66 (1): 91–122.

Marshall, Michael P., John R. Stein, Richard W. Loose, and Judith Novotny. 1979. *Anasazi Communities of the San Juan Basin*. Albuquerque: Public Service Company of New Mexico, and Santa Fe: New Mexico Historic Preservation Bureau.

Matson, R. G., William D. Lipe, and Diane Curewitz. 2015. "Dynamics of the Thirteenth-Century Depopulation of the Northern San Juan: the View from Cedar Mesa." *KIVA: The Journal of Southwestern Anthropology and History* 80 (3–4): 324–349.

Nordenskiöld, Gustav. [1893] 1990. *The Cliff Dwellers of the Mesa Verde. Reprint, Mesa Verde, CO: Mesa Verde Museum Association*. Originally published Royal Printing Office, Stockholm.

Ortman, Scott G., and Grant D. Coffey. 2017. "Settlement Scaling in Middle Range Societies." *American Antiquity* 82 (4): 662–682.

Ortman, Scott G., Donna M. Glowacki, Kristin A. Kuckelman, and Melissa J. Churchill. 2000. "Pattern and Variation in Northern San Juan Village Histories." *KIVA: The Journal of Southwestern Anthropology and History* 66 (1): 123–146.

Ortman, Scott G., Mark D. Varien, and T. Lee Gripp. 2007. "Empirical Bayesian Methods for Archaeological Survey Data: An Application from the Mesa Verde Region." *American Antiquity* 72 (2): 241.

Potter, James M., Mike Mirro, Grant Coffey, and Mark D. Varien. 2020. *Large-Site Mapping and Photogrammetry in the Ute Tribal Park, Southwest Colorado*. PaleoWest Technical Report No. 20-699. On file, PaleoWest, Monrovia, CA.

Reese, Kelsey M., Donna M. Glowacki, and Timothy A. Kohler. 2019. "Dynamic Communities on the Mesa Verde Cuesta." *American Antiquity* 84 (4): 728–747.

Rohn, Arthur H. 1977. *Cultural Change and Continuity on Chapin Mesa*. Lawrence: The Regents Press of Kansas.

Schwindt, Dylan M., R. Kyle Bocinsky, Scott G. Ortman, Donna M. Glowacki, Mark D. Varien, and Timothy A. Kohler. 2016. "The Social Consequences of Climate Change in the Central Mesa Verde Region." *American Antiquity* 81 (1): 74–96.

Struever, Stewart. 1968. "Problems, Methods, and Organization: A Disparity in the Growth of Archeology." In *Anthropological Archeology in the Americas*, edited by Betty J. Meggers, 131–151. Washington, DC: Anthropological Society of Washington.

Varien, Mark D. 1999. *Sedentism and Mobility in a Social Landscape: Mesa Verde and Beyond*. Tucson: University of Arizona Press.

Varien, Mark D. 2002. "Persistent Communities and Mobile Households: Population Movement in the Central Mesa Verde Region, A.D. 950–1290." In *Seeking the Center Place: Archaeology and Ancient Communities in the Mesa Verde Region*, edited by Mark D. Varien and Richard H. Wilshusen, 163–184. Salt Lake City: University of Utah Press.

Varien, Mark D., Grant D. Coffey, Gert Riemersma, Vincent MacMillan, and Steve McCormack. 2021. "LiDAR Mapping Sand Canyon Pueblo: Technical Collaboration for Site Visualization and Reassessment." Poster presented at the 86th Annual Meeting of the Society for American Archeology Meeting, online. https://www.routescene.com/wp-content/uploads/2019/08/SAA-Sand-Canyon-Poster.pdf.

Varien, Mark D., William D. Lipe, Michael A. Adler, Ian M. Thompson, and Bruce A. Bradley. 1996. "Southwestern Colorado and Southeastern Utah Settlement Patterns: A.D. 1100 to 1300." In *The Prehistoric Pueblo World, A.D. 1150–1350*, edited by Michael A. Adler, 86–113. Tucson: University of Arizona Press.

Varien, Mark D., Scott G. Ortman, Timothy A. Kohler, Donna M. Glowacki, and C. David Johnson. 2007. "Historical Ecology in the Mesa Verde Region: Results from the Village EcoDynamics Project." *American Antiquity* 72 (2): 273–300. https://doi .org/10.2307/40035814.

Varien, Mark D., and Richard H. Wilshusen. 2002. "A Partnership for Understanding the Past: Crow Canyon Research in the Central Mesa Verde Region." In *Seeking the Center Place: Archaeology and Ancient Communities in the Mesa Verde Region*, edited by Mark D. Varien and Richard H. Wilshusen, 3–23. Salt Lake City: University of Utah Press.

Wills, W. H., and Robert D. Leonard. 1994. *The Ancient Southwestern Community: Models and Methods for the Study of Prehistoric Social Organization*. Albuquerque: University of New Mexico Press.

Wilshusen, Richard H. 2002. *Estimating Population in the Central Mesa Verde Region*, edited by Mark D. Varien and Richard H. Wilshusen, 101–120. Salt Lake City: University of Utah Press.

Wilshusen, R., Scott G. Ortman, and Ann Phillips. 2012. "Processions, Leaders, and Gathering Places: Changes in Early Pueblo Community Organization as Seen in Architecture, Rock Art, and Language." In *Crucible of Pueblos: The Early Pueblo Period in the Northern Southwest*, edited by R. Wilshusen, G. Schachner, and J. Allison, 198–218. Los Angeles: Cotsen Institute of Archaeology Press, UCLA.

13

Community Organization on the Edge of the Mesa Verde Region

Recent Investigations at Cowboy Wash Pueblo,
Moqui Springs Pueblo, and Yucca House

JAMES M. POTTER, MARK D. VARIEN,
GRANT D. COFFEY, AND R. KYLE BOCINSKY

This chapter examines the formation of three large villages, also called community centers, on the piedmont of Ute Mountain: Yucca House, Moqui Springs Pueblo, and Cowboy Wash Pueblo (figure 13.1). Two villages, Moqui Springs and Cowboy Wash, occupy the southernmost edge of central Mesa Verde region and as such represent borderland or frontier communities. Yucca House sits on the eastern Ute Piedmont, and while it too lies near the edge of the distribution of community centers in the central Mesa Verde region, it is located closer to the concentration of central Mesa Verde villages that lie to the north (see Glowacki et al., chapter 12 in this volume, for the distribution of community centers). The occupation of each village dates to the final decades of ancestral Pueblo occupation in the central Mesa Verde region and therefore inform on how communities on these borderlands were organized just prior to, and during, the depopulation of the region. Our examination of these Ute Piedmont villages complements many chapters in this volume that discuss late Pueblo III period community centers, including the chapters by Adler and Hegmon (chapter 16), Glowacki et al. (chapter 12), Kuckelman (chapter 19), and

https://doi.org/10.5876/9781646424597.c013

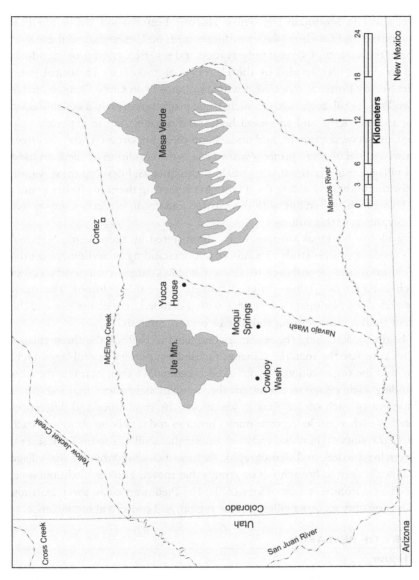

FIGURE 13.1. *Location of key sites discussed in text. Courtesy of the Crow Canyon Archaeological Center.*

Schleher et al. (chapter 14), in this volume, on Sand Canyon and Goodman Point Pueblos.

The research discussed here presents years of collaborative work by the Crow Canyon Archaeological Center (CCAC), PaleoWest, LLC, the National Park Service, and Ute Mountain Ute Tribal Historic Preservation Office (THPO). Moqui Springs and Cowboy Wash Pueblo are both on Ute lands, and these sites have been the subject of several preservation and research grant projects administered by the THPO, funded by the History Colorado State Historical Fund, and directed by Potter at PaleoWest with assistance from Crow Canyon archaeologists (Potter et al. 2013, 2015). As such, these projects represent a collaboration among archaeologists and an established Tribal organization to explicitly help manage, preserve, document, and understand these important Tribal resources. The primary goal of these projects was to assess the condition of these archaeological villages using nondestructive field techniques and develop preservation plans for them, thereby aiding the THPO in preserving them for future generations. This goal is well in line with the mission and vision of Crow Canyon (see Perry, chapter 23 in this volume)

Yucca House National Monument is administered by Mesa Verde National Park. This comparative study expands our understanding of settlement on the Ute Piedmont and contributes to Crow Canyon's larger community center research initiative (see Glowacki et al., chapter 12 in this volume). The study also provided the National Park Service with a detailed map of the site and the results of both remote sensing and surface pottery analysis.

We begin by describing the research conducted at each of the three villages. Next, we compare the material remains, focusing on pottery assemblages, architecture, and the organizational layout at each center. We then examine the sites surrounding each village to document the occupational history that led to the development of each center. Finally, we discuss the similarities and differences exhibited by each, considering community histories and ritual organization at each village. Our results suggest that variation among these villages stems from several social, environmental, and demographic factors, including whether the village housed locally derived households or groups that moved into the piedmont area; the specific environmental conditions of the Ute Piedmont areas; social isolation from, or proximity to, other villages in the region; and concern about violence.

HISTORY OF RESEARCH

Yucca House

Located on the east piedmont of Ute Mountain, Yucca House represents one of the first documented villages in the Mesa Verde region when W. H. Holmes published a map and discussed the site, which he called Aztec Springs, in 1878. Fewkes also published on the site and facilitated it becoming a National

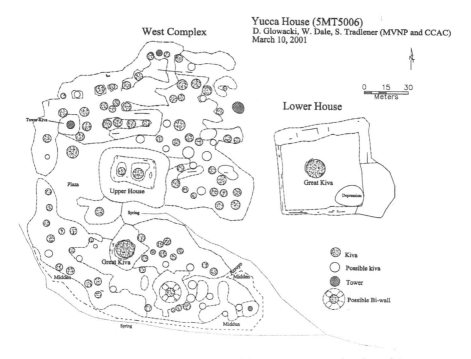

FIGURE 13.2. *Map of Yucca House. Courtesy of the Crow Canyon Archaeological Center.*

Monument in 1919. Fewkes renamed the site Yucca House based on the Tewa name for Ute Mountain, Papin, which translates as Yucca Mountain. National Park Service archaeologists collected tree-ring samples from the site in 1953, and then conducted limited testing and stabilization in 1964.

Crow Canyon and Mesa Verde National Park conducted the Yucca House Mapping Project in 2000 (figure 13.2). A crew led by Donna Glowacki mapped the site with a total station, conducted remote sensing, and analyzed a sample of surface pottery along with a smaller sample from the site curated at the park. Our discussion of Yucca House relies on data reported from this project (Glowacki 2001).

Archaeologists have conducted limited, but important, surveys in the area surrounding Yucca House, and several sites have been excavated. This includes the 1894 excavations by Richard Wetherill at Snider's Well, a mass inhumation inside a kiva located on a ridge south of Yucca House (Glowacki 2001, appendix A). Under the direction of Ralph Luebben, Grinnell College conducted excavations (1974–1983) at four Pueblo III period unit pueblos (Luebben 1982, 1983; Luebben and Nickens 1982), and three additional sites were excavated to clear a right of way (Fuller 1988). A survey of 160 acres recently added to Yucca House National

Monument documented many sites, including seven isolated kiva depressions on a ridge immediately south of Yucca House (McBride and McBride 2014). These surveys and excavations provide important context for our interpretations of Yucca House.

Moqui Springs Pueblo

Located on the southeastern piedmont of Ute Mountain, Moqui Springs Pueblo was originally recorded in 1976 by the University of Colorado for the Mobil Oil Corporation and referred to as Tribal site number 5MTUMR2803 (Traylor and Breternitz 1976). The site was described as a "D-shaped" pueblo with more than sixty rooms. In 1984, Complete Archaeological Service Associates (CASA) included a description of the site in their Aneth Road Corridor report and, for the first time, referred to it as Moqui Springs (Fuller 1984). CASA described the site as a large, Mesa Verde phase (PIII) pueblo, but they further noted that prior to the Mesa Verde phase, the nucleated site may have served as a community center for unit pueblos surrounding the village.

In 1986, La Plata Archaeology Consultants recorded the site as part of the Petty Ray Geophysical 8507 Project. It was described as a PII/PIII period habitation dating from AD 900–1300. In 1988, as part of the Ute Irrigated Lands Survey, CASA remapped the site, simplifying its shape and constituents (Fuller 1988).

In 2015, PaleoWest and Crow Canyon remapped the site in greater detail, documenting eighty-eight features in four loci (Potter et al. 2015) (figure 13.3). They also mapped the main pueblo with a drone (Locus A) and conducted analysis of over 4000 surface pottery sherds in Loci A and B.

Cowboy Wash Pueblo

Cowboy Wash Pueblo (5MT7740) lies on the southern piedmont of Ute Mountain near the Four Corners and was first recorded in 1983 by Michael Marshall and Steve Fuller with CASA as part of the Aneth Road Cultural Resources Survey. They produced the only previous map of the site, describing it as a large, late Pueblo habitation containing at least ten kivas, one round, bi-wall structure, and over thirty rooms (Marshall and Fuller 1983).

In 2003, this general area was the subject of extensive archaeological work as part of the Ute Mountain Ute Irrigated Lands Archaeology Project (UMUILAP), during which excavations were conducted to mitigate the impact of more than 7,000 acres of irrigated farm fields developed by the Ute Mountain Ute Tribe. In July 2012, archaeologists from PaleoWest and Crow Canyon conducted mapping, in-field artifact analysis, and an intensive nondestructive investigation of the portions of the sites exposed in the arroyo (figure 13.4). Four contributions resulted from this work: (1) it increased the number of kivas evident on the surface of the site from nine to thirteen; (2) it dramatically altered the plan configuration and

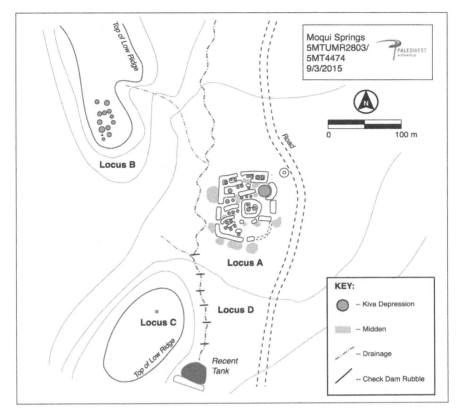

FIGURE 13.3. *Map of Moqui Springs Pueblo. Courtesy of PaleoWest.*

shape of the site compared to the previous map; (3) it identified midden areas, looted areas, and areas that are actively eroding, especially in the Cowboy Wash arroyo; and (4) it identified a possible D-shaped structure in the center of the site (Potter et al. 2013).

In 2016, PaleoWest and the University of Colorado, Boulder, conducted a two-week field school that focused on excavating the rooms exposed by erosion in the Cowboy Wash arroyo. This fieldwork also confirmed the D-shape layout of the central building and sampled the midden areas. The report for this work is in progress; the ceramic analysis results are included here in this chapter (Reeder et al. 2017).

RESULTS

Table 13.1 summarizes the architectural and pottery characteristics of each village; we discuss each center in the sections that follow.

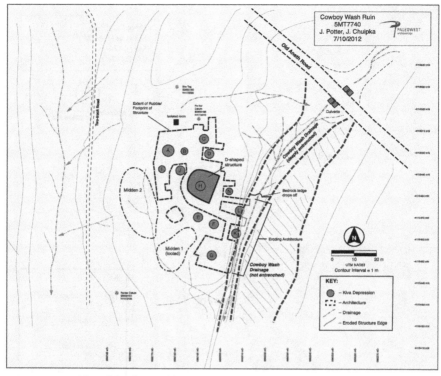

FIGURE 13.4. *Map of Cowboy Wash Pueblo. Courtesy of PaleoWest.*

TABLE 13.1. Characteristics of each village.

Characteristic	Cowboy Wash	Moqui Springs	Yucca House
Number of kivas	13	41	81
Public architecture	D-shaped bi-wall building	Plaza Great Kiva Great House Bi-wall Tower Isolated Kivas	Great House (2?) Great Kiva (2) Reservoir Tower Kiva Plaza (2) Circular bi-wall structure
Pottery	Mesa Verde Black-on-white; Many bowls with exterior paint; Late Pueblo III (AD 1225–1285)	Mesa Verde Black-on-white; Many bowls with exterior paint; Late Pueblo III (AD 1225–1285)	Mesa Verde Black-on-white; Many bowls with exterior paint; Late Pueblo III (AD 1225–1285)

Source: Table created by authors.

Cowboy Wash Pueblo

Cowboy Wash Pueblo is the smallest community center in our study and contains the least amount of public architecture—a single D-shaped bi-wall. Based on its height, this centrally situated mound was a two-story building. The western two-thirds of this mound are circular, but the east wall, which faces Cowboy Wash, appears to be straight. D-shaped bi-wall structures have been recorded at other sites in the Mesa Verde region, including examples at Sand Canyon and Goodman Point Pueblos that have been partially excavated (Kuckelman 2007, 2017; Lekson, chapter 17 in this volume; Ortman and Bradley 2002, 55–62; Schleher et al., chapter 14 in this volume).

Interestingly, this site contains no great kiva, very few surface artifacts, very sparse middens, and no large, enclosed plaza, and unlike other late Pueblo III period villages in the Mesa Verde region, it does not enclose, nor is proximate to, a spring. It does, however, occupy the edge of a relatively large drainage (hence the erosional issues with the site), which is a common trait of late Pueblo III period villages.

The decorated pottery assemblage recovered from Cowboy Wash Pueblo contained predominantly Mesa Verde Black-on-white sherds, a presence that signifies a late Pueblo III period occupation. The high percentage of exterior bowl designs (44 percent), on Mesa Verde Black-on-white bowls, lends further support to a post AD 1250 occupation (Reeder et al. 2017). This frequency is at the high end of those found at late Pueblo III period sites and is higher than excavated pueblos to the north such as Castle Rock, Sand Canyon, Goodman Point, and Woods Canyon Pueblos. Additionally, based on corrugated jar accumulation rates, Kelsey Reeder et al. (2017) conclude that it was a short-lived occupation that likely lasted no longer than a generation.

Moqui Springs

Moqui Springs Pueblo comprises four separate loci (see figure 13.3). Locus A is the main village (figure 13.5). It contains twenty-eight kivas (or kiva depressions), and, in contrast to Cowboy Wash Pueblo (see figure 13.4), it also has numerous public architectural elements, including a great kiva, a bi-wall tower, an enclosed plaza, and a large, central building with three blocked-in kivas (possibly a post-Chaco great house or a D-shaped structure). This site is interesting for its enclosed, inward-focused configuration. Moqui Springs Pueblo also contains numerous large and deep midden areas, six of which are situated on the exterior of the village.

Locus B occupies a knoll on the other side of the drainage (see figure 13.3). This locus contains twelve kiva depressions, no surface architecture, and a sparse artifact scatter. Locus C consists of a single kiva depression (with no surface architecture) on top of a low ridge to the south of the main village (figure 13.3). Locus D comprises six breached check dams in the arroyo on the west

FIGURE 13.5. *Moqui Springs Pueblo, Locus A. Courtesy of PaleoWest. Courtesy of PaleoWest.*

side of Locus A (see figure 13.3); their spatial association with the main pueblo, construction techniques, and the materials used suggests they were part of the Pueblo III period landscape and support the interpretation of the importance of floodwater farming in the southern piedmont communities (Huckleberry and Billman 1998).

The results of our Moqui Springs pottery analysis indicate that occupation began sometime between AD 1225 and 1260 and continued until the region was depopulated at about AD 1280. The demographic reconstruction, based on the method developed by Ortman and others (Ortman et al. 2007), estimates the population at twenty-one households (approximately 105 people) from AD 1225–1280 and twenty (approximately 100 people) in the AD 1260–1280 period. The planned layout suggests the shape and size of the pueblo (Locus A) were established at the outset of its occupation and that population growth, and decline, by accretion was limited. Ratios of McElmo to Mesa Verde Black-on-white are consistent across the site and are not statistically different between interior and exterior units, suggesting a single occupation date range for Locus A.

Loci B and C appear to be late, dating to the decades just before regional depopulation. Pottery data also indicate that the primary activity associated with the kivas in Locus B involved the use of decorated bowls. Several factors suggest that Loci B and C were not used for daily residential activities: the absence of surface roomblocks; the absence of concentrated middens; the low numbers of sherds from corrugated gray ware cooking jars and white ware storage jars; and low artifact diversity, including the near absence of flaked-stone and ground-stone tools. The activities in Loci B and C that involved the use of serving bowls likely were more specialized and focused on ritual feasting (Potter and Ortman 2004).

Yucca House

Two main areas characterize the architectural layout of Yucca House—the West Complex, which contains a massive building known as the "Upper House" and a separate unit known as the "Lower House" (see figure 13.2). Intensive mapping activities recorded eighty-one kiva depressions; it contains an additional twenty-three "possible" kiva depressions (Glowacki 2001). These features make Yucca House one of the five largest late Pueblo III period villages in the entire central Mesa Verde region. It also contains numerous and diverse public architectural elements, including two great house–like structures (Upper and Lower House), a tower kiva, two great kivas (upper and lower), and two plazas (upper and lower). Additionally, the West Complex architecture wraps around a drainage and encloses a spring. The outer walls around the periphery of the West complex likely form an enclosing wall. The Upper House, the largest building in the West Complex, faces the drainage and the spring, similar to the position of large, D-shaped bi-wall structures at Sand Canyon, Goodman Point, and Cowboy Wash Pueblos.

The absence of small kivas and refuse middens indicates that the Lower House was not a domestic structure. Donna Glowacki (2001, 43) identifies a possible analogue for this building in the far Kayenta region, and Ortman (Ortman 2010, 242–244) argues the building shows ties to the northern Rio Grande region.

Pottery and tree-ring dates indicate that, like Cowboy Wash Pueblo and Moqui Springs, the site dates to the mid-to-late AD 1200s, with most occupation likely after AD 1250. Tree-ring dates from the Upper House include an AD 1263vv date. Pottery includes high frequencies of Mesa Verde Black-on-white, including many bowls with painting on both the interior and exterior of the vessels, which indicates post AD 1250 occupation (Glowacki 2001; Hegmon 1991; Ortman 2000).

A ridge just south of Yucca House includes six sites defined by seven isolated kiva depressions dating to the late Pueblo III period (McBride and McBride 2014);

this ridge bears a similarity to the isolated kivas in Locus B on the ridge west of Moqui Springs Pueblo. A possible shrine (5MT20921) that represents a feature for observing astronomical events is present on the south end of this ridge (Bell 2020).

Yucca House exhibits many of the characteristics that William Lipe and Scott Ortman (2000) attribute to late Pueblo III period central Mesa Verde region villages: the architecture in the West Complex encloses a spring; main architectural units are separated by a shallow drainage; the buildings on the perimeter of the West Complex likely form an enclosing wall; and the village includes multiple examples of public architecture, much of which cluster in one part of the village. These traits are notably absent from both Cowboy Wash and Moqui Springs Pueblos.

RECONSTRUCTING THE COMMUNITY

Each of these villages developed in the context of historic settlement in the surrounding locality, and they exhibit characteristics that suggest they were community centers for larger, dispersed populations, including their relatively large size and public architecture (Glowacki et al., chapter 12 in this volume). Employing the method developed by Ortman, Mark Varien, and T. Lee Gripp (2007) for the Village Ecodynamics Project (VEP) (see Kohler et al., chapter 3 in this volume, for a discussion of the VEP), several interesting patterns emerge.

At Cowboy Wash Pueblo, when a 7 km radius around the center is analyzed using the VEP method, a more continuous settlement pattern between AD 1020 and 1225 is detected than as evidenced by the UMUILAP excavations—which document repeated settlement and depopulation of the wash during this interval (figure 13.6). A similar pattern is apparent for the final periods; only a portion of the community occupied the village. Most people in the Cowboy Wash Pueblo community lived in small hamlets, even in the late thirteenth century AD (figure 13.7).

At Moqui Springs Pueblo, a different pattern emerges during the final period. A larger proportion of the community lived in the main pueblo. Similar to Cowboy Wash, Pueblo occupation was short lived. Interestingly, the number of small-site households within 7 km of the main village did not decrease substantially during the later period, suggesting that the groups who built and occupied Moqui Springs immigrated into the area rather than deriving from local small-site occupants, a process that likely occurred in the Cowboy Wash community.

At Yucca House, an even starker pattern is evident. During the final decades, most people lived in the large village. It also appears, given the large number of households present in the later period, that there was a large population influx, not simply an aggregation of the local population. This contrasts with the history of occupation of the Cowboy Wash, which again appears to have been the result of the aggregation of the local population rather than population immigration and nucleation.

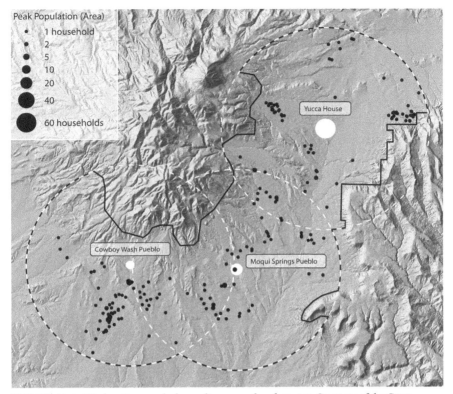

FIGURE 13.6. *Site locations and 7 km radius around each center. Courtesy of the Crow Canyon Archaeological Center.*

The differences noted thus far among these three community centers are significant in terms of size, organization, landscape position, associated communal architecture, and occupation history. The only comparable attributes among them are their overlap in occupation (AD 1250–1280), their relatively short occupation span (one or two generations), and the fact that they are the largest sites in their respective areas. Variables that likely contributed to these differences include not only the provenance of the occupants (local or nonlocal) but also local environmental factors such as rainfall and soil fertility and the proximity to other central Mesa Verde communities.

The Cowboy Wash community, for example, appears to have been built and occupied by locals. This community was also the most isolated community in the study in that they were located the farthest from other communities in the central Mesa Verde region. One indication of the economic and social isolation of this community is the raw materials used for lithic production, which are different from the raw materials from sites located elsewhere in the central

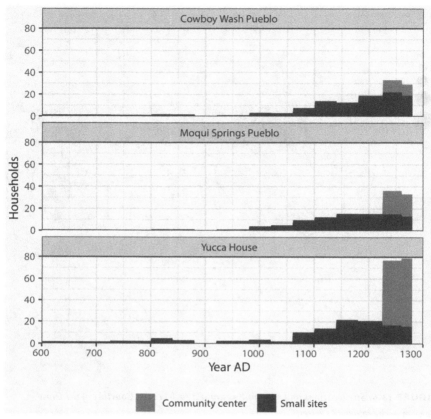

FIGURE 13.7. *Momentary population estimates based on number of households for the three community centers and surrounding small sites, 7 km radius. Courtesy of the Crow Canyon Archaeological Center.*

Mesa Verde region, especially the relatively high proportion of igneous minette at Cowboy Wash (Arakawa 2006; Arakawa and Gerhardt 2007; Arakawa et al., chapter 15 in this volume; Potter et al. 2013, 11).

Moreover, of the three communities analyzed here, this community was associated with the harshest landscape that was the most tenuous for farming (Huckleberry and Billman 1998). As Ermigiotti et al. note in chapter 4 in this volume, during droughts, including the late AD 1200s when ancestral Pueblo people migrated from the region, better lands in the Four Corners would have produced sufficient yields even during years when environmental conditions were significantly below average. By contrast, as demonstrated by Crow Canyon's campus gardens, only negligible yields are attained in poorer areas (like Cowboy Wash). It is perhaps not surprising then that this community was the smallest and its members built and occupied the smallest central village with the least amount of communal architecture.

Moqui Springs Pueblo likely represents immigration of groups to the toe of the Ute Mountain who established a new organizational format for a village—the plaza-oriented, inward-focused village. This format is rare in the Mesa Verde area and is more akin to the organizational format of villages in the northern Rio Grande (Ortman 2012). Another uncommon trait of this village is the cluster of kivas ($n = 12$) on an adjacent ridge that lacks evidence of habitation (e.g., dense middens or aboveground architecture). Moqui Springs appears to represent a new form of social organization and a new way of living and conducting rituals on the edge of the Mesa Verde region just prior to depopulation.

Yucca House, the largest of the three villages, even more clearly represents immigration into the local area. This community, rather than experimenting with new organizational and ritual forms, resembles other terminal Pueblo III period villages in the region (Lipe and Ortman 2000). The exception to this is the Lower House, which has no analogues in the region. Yucca House also appears to be the village most tied into other communities within the central Mesa Verde region, as reflected in its organizational layout.

Each community dealt with the challenges of environmental stress and social isolation that came with occupying the Ute Piedmont in different ways. Another difficulty that each community had to contend with was violence. Settlement in the dispersed communities that predate Cowboy Wash, Moqui Springs, and Yucca House Pueblos includes small sites with abundant evidence of conflict and violence, most of which dates to about AD 1150. The evidence for violence includes disarticulated human bones that were broken and reduced, along with the presence of burning, cut marks, and skull fractures. These remains come from four sites near Cowboy Wash Pueblo, one site near Moqui Springs Pueblo, and one near Yucca House. Altogether, the remains include a minimum of twenty-four people, with both sexes and ages from newborns to elderly represented (Billman 2003, 6.21–6.28).

The violence occurred immediately before depopulation at most sites at around 1150, and Brian Billman (2003, 8.5) argues that the entire Cowboy Wash community was extinguished at this time, leaving the southern piedmont temporarily depopulated. The Grinnell site near Yucca House differs because the disarticulated remains of seven people were gathered from elsewhere and buried in a cist on the floor of a kiva at the site, with the site remaining occupied after this interment.

Evidence for conflict and violence also exists for the mid-to-late thirteenth century AD, when each of the community centers discussed here were occupied. Billman (2003, 8.5) reports on a site in Cowboy Wash where a kiva was burned and at least one woman and three juveniles were killed sometime after

AD 1248. Near Yucca House, Richard Wetherill excavated a kiva at the Snider's Well site that contained mass inhumation of individuals that appear to have died as the result of conflict. Archaeologists have relocated Snider's Well and argue it dates to mid-to-late AD 1200s based on surface pottery. The aggregated villages that formed on the Ute Piedmont clearly developed in an area whose history included an episode of severe violence, and violence likely continued during the time when these centers were constructed and occupied (see Kuckelman, chapter 19 in this volume, for additional examples).

CONCLUSIONS

These contemporaneous, late Pueblo III period communities clearly organized themselves differently on the Ute Piedmont landscape. We have made the argument that this variation is due to several social, environmental, and demographic factors, including the provenance of households, local environmental vagaries, the degree of social and economic isolation of a village, and the choices made regarding the types of communal architecture adopted, or experimented with, and the rituals they facilitated. One factor that seems consistent, though, is the persistent threat and presence of violence throughout the history of all of these communities (see Kohler et al., chapter 3 in this volume).

Contrary to findings at large villages in the heart of the Mesa Verde region, such as Sand Canyon Pueblo and Castle Rock Pueblo, one of the more interesting patterns we detect regarding violence is that on the Ute Piedmont, it occurred predominantly in small sites rather than the large centers. This concentration may be due to more excavation occurring at small sites. Regardless, the recurrence of these events at small sites likely encouraged the eventual aggregation of households into larger (and therefore "safer") villages, a process proposed by Richard Wilshusen and James Potter (2010) for village formation in the Pueblo I period (AD 700–900). Notably, much of the Cowboy Wash community chose to remain living in small sites during the Pueblo III period; they also did not invest in communal architecture—and by extension the rituals they housed—to the extent that other communities did. The Moqui Springs and Yucca House communities, by contrast, appear to have committed more to the idea of the central village and to performing novel and diverse rituals within them, strategies perhaps aimed at mitigating both environmental and social stress wrought by living on the edge of the central Mesa Verde region in the late thirteenth century AD.

Acknowledgments. We would like to thank and acknowledge the Ute Mountain Ute Tribal Historic Preservation Officer, Mr. Terry Knight, for allowing us to conduct investigations at Cowboy Wash Pueblo and Moqui Springs Pueblo and for allowing us to discuss and publish the results of these investigations in this chapter. We would also like to acknowledge History Colorado for supporting the fieldwork through grants awarded to the THPO. Donna Glowacki and Kelsey Reeder conducted ceramic analyses on the excavated materials from Cowboy Wash Pueblo, and Fumi Arakawa conducted lithic analysis on both the survey data (in-field analysis) and on the excavated materials. Thanks to Scott Ortman who co-led the field school at Cowboy Wash. Jim Potter's work at Cowboy Wash Pueblo was supported by the PaleoWest Foundation. We are grateful to Larry Nordby, who was chief archaeologist at Mesa Verde National Park, for approaching Crow Canyon to collaborate on the Yucca House Mapping Project and to Donna Glowacki, who directed that project while working for Crow Canyon.

REFERENCES

Arakawa, Fumiyasu. 2006. "Lithic Raw Material Procurement and the Social Landscape in the Central Mesa Verde Region, A.D. 600–1300." PhD diss., Washington State University, Pullman.

Arakawa, Fumiyasu, and Kimberlee Gerhardt. 2007. "Toolstone Procurement Patterns on the Wetherill Mesa from A.D. 600 to 1280." *Kiva* 73:69–87.

Bell, Bernard W. Jr. 2020. "Easy Accurate Site Horizon Calibration: Tewa Days of the Sun at Yucca House National Monument." In *Before Borders: Revealing the Greater Southwest's Ancestral Cultural Landscape*. Occasional Papers on Cultural Astronomy No. 1, edited by Gregory E. Munson, Ray A. Williamson, and Bryan C. Bates, 3–21. SCCAS Multimedia Publications, Dolores, Colorado.

Billman, Brian R. 2003. "The Puebloan Occupation of the Ute Mountain Piedmont. Volume 7: Synthesis and Conclusions." *Soil Systems Publications in Archaeology* vol. (7) (Phoenix).

Fuller, Steven L. 1984. "Cultural Resources Inventory of the Aneth Road Corridor, BIA Route UMU 201, Ute Mountain Ute Indian Reservation, Montezuma County, Colorado, Volume I." Complete Archaeological Service Associates, Cortez, CO.

Fuller, Steven L. 1988. "Cultural Resources Inventories for the Dolores Project: The Ute Irrigated Lands Survey. Four Corners Archaeological Project Report Number 13." Complete Archaeological Service Associates, Cortez, CO.

Glowacki, Donna M. 2001. "Yucca House (5MT5006) Mapping Project Report." Unpublished report on file, Crow Canyon Archaeological Center and Mesa Verde National Park, CO.

Hegmon, Michelle. 1991. "Six Easy Steps to Dating Pueblo III Ceramic Assemblages." Manuscript on file, Crow Canyon Archaeological Center, Cortez, CO.

Huckleberry, Gary A., and Brian R. Billman. 1998. "Floodwater Farming, Discontinuous Ephemeral Streams, and Puebloan Abandonment in Southwestern Colorado." *American Antiquity* 63:595–516.

Kuckelman, Kristin A. 2007. "The Archaeology of Sand Canyon Pueblo: Intensive Excavations at a Late-Thirteenth-Century Village in Southwestern Colorado." Crow Canyon Archaeological Center, Cortez, CO.

Kuckelman, Kristin A., ed. 2017. "The Goodman Point Archaeological Project: Goodman Point Pueblo Excavations." Accessed January 18, 2021. www.crowcanyon.org
/ResearchReports/GoodmanPointPueblo/Goodman_Point_Pueblo.pdf.

Lipe, William and Scott Ortman. 2000. "Spatial Patterning in Northern San Juan Villages, A.D. 1050–1300." *Kiva* 66:91–122.

Luebben, R. A. 1982. "Two Pueblo III Kiva Complexes Associated with Subterranean
Rooms, Southwestern Colorado." *Kiva* 48:63–81.

Luebben, R. A. 1983. "The Grinnell Site: A Small Ceremonial Center Near Yucca House,
Colorado." *Journal of Intermountain Archaeology* 2:1–26.

Luebben, R. A., and P. R. Nickens. 1982. "A Mass Interment in an Early Pueblo III Kiva
in Southwestern Colorado." *Journal of Intermountain Archeology* 1:66–79.

Marshall, Michael, and Steven Fuller. 1983. "Cowboy Wash Pueblo: 5MT7740. Colorado
Cultural Resource Survey Inventory Record." Preservation Office, Denver.

McBride, Robert. C., and Diane E. McBride. 2014. "Cultural Resource Survey of the
Bernard and Nancy Karwick Property Montezuma County, Colorado: A Study of
the Greater Yucca House Community." Manuscript on file, Crow Canyon Archaeological Center, Cortez, CO.

Ortman, Scott. 2000. "Conceptual Metaphor in the Archaeological Record: Methods
and an Example from the American Southwest." *American Antiquity* 65 (4): 613–645.

Ortman, Scott. 2010. "Evidence of a Mesa Verde Homeland for the Tewa Pueblos." In
Leaving Mesa Verde: Peril and Change in the Thirteenth Century Southwest, edited by
T. Kohler, M. Varien, and A. Wright, 222–261. Tucson: Amerind Foundation and Uni-
versity of Arizona Press.

Ortman, Scott. 2012. *Winds from the North: Tewa Origins and Historical Anthropology*. Salt
Lake City: University of Utah Press.

Ortman, Scott G., and Bruce A. Bradley. 2002. "Sand Canyon Pueblo: The Container
in the Center." In *Seeking the Center Place: Archaeology and Ancient Communities in the
Mesa Verde Region*, edited by M. D. Varien and R. H. Wilshusen, 41–78. Salt Lake City:
University of Utah Press.

Ortman, Scott G., Mark D. Varien, and T. Lee Gripp. 2007. "Empirical Bayesian Methods for Archaeological Survey Data: An Application from the Mesa Verde Region."
American Antiquity 72:241–272.

Potter, James M., and Scott Ortman. 2004. "Community and Cuisine in the Prehispanic
Southwest." In *Identity, Feasting, and the Archaeology of the Greater Southwest*, edited by
Barbara J. Mills, 173–191. Boulder: University Press of Colorado.

Potter, James, Mark Varien, and Jason Chuipka. 2013. "The Cowboy Wash Mapping
Project: Report of Findings and Preservation Plan for Site 5MT7740, Montezuma
County, Colorado. Historical Fund (SHF) Grant #2011-AS-003." PaleoWest Technical
Report No. 13-55. Farmington, NM.

Potter, James, Mark Varien, and Jason Chuipka. 2015. "Moqui Springs Mapping and Preservation Project: Report of Findings and Preservation Plan for Site 5MT4474, Montezuma County, Colorado. SHF Grant # 2014-M1002." PaleoWest Technical Report 15-120. Farmington, NM.

Reeder, Kelsey M., Molly Iott, Katherine Portman, Donna M. Glowacki, James Potter, and Scott G. Ortman. 2017. "Preliminary Pottery Analysis at Cowboy Wash Pueblo: A Central Village on the Ute Piedmont Frontier." SAA poster.

Traylor, Robert S., and David Breternitz. 1976. "Report of Cultural Resource Evaluation, Mobil Oil Corporation Uranium Exploration, Ute Mountain Ute Reservation." Bureau of Anthropological Research, Department of Anthropology, University of Boulder, CO.

Wilshusen, Richard H., and James M. Potter. 2010. "The Emergence of Early Villages in the American Southwest: Cultural Issues and Historical Perspectives." In *Becoming Villagers: Comparing Early Village Societies*, edited by Matthew S. Bandy and Jake R. Fox, 165–183. Tucson: University of Arizona Press.

14

Formation and Composition of Communities

Material Culture and Demographics in the
Goodman Point and Sand Canyon Communities

KARI SCHLEHER, SAMANTHA LINFORD, GRANT D. COFFEY,
KRISTIN KUCKELMAN, SCOTT ORTMAN, JONATHAN TILL,
MARK D. VARIEN, AND JAMIE MEREWETHER

Building on the history of community center studies discussed in this volume (e.g., Adler and Hegmon, chapter 16, Glowacki et al., chapter 12, Potter et al., chapter 13 in this volume), this chapter examines fine-grained patterns in material culture to better understand social dynamics in the closely connected Goodman Point and Sand Canyon communities (figure 14.1) during the Pueblo II (AD 900–1150) and Pueblo III (AD 1150–1280) periods. Specifically, we explore materials and designs used in the manufacture of pottery in these two communities. Material preferences allow us to better understand choices people made about pottery technology and production, as well as the social elements those choices represented for the communities and the broader region. We demonstrate greater continuity in the materials used for pottery production, particularly temper, in the Goodman Point community as compared to the Sand Canyon community. Artifact data for the Goodman Point community suggest a more conservative approach to technological change than the approach that was present in the Sand Canyon community—as well as many other communities across the region—suggesting greater stability within pottery production groups in

https://doi.org/10.5876/9781646424597.c014

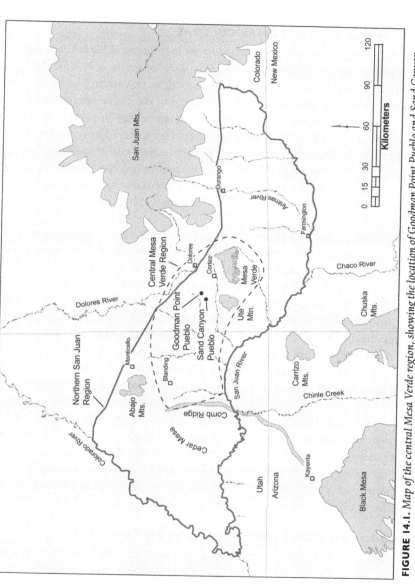

FIGURE 14.1. *Map of the central Mesa Verde region, showing the location of Goodman Point Pueblo and Sand Canyon Pueblo. Courtesy of the Crow Canyon Archaeological Center.*

the Goodman Point community. We also see significant difference in pottery designs in the Goodman Point versus Sand Canyon communities, which further supports our theory of differences in the respective communities of practice.

COMMUNITIES AND MATERIAL CULTURE

Community studies have enjoyed a long history in the central Mesa Verde region (Adler 1996; Hurst 2011; Jalbert 1999; Jalbert and Cameron 2000; Kolb and Snead 1997; Lipe et al. 1999; Mahoney 2000; Ortman et al. 2007; Varien, Lipe et al. 1996; Varien, Van West et al. 2000) and are a major focus of the archaeological research presented in this volume (Adler and Hegmon, chapter 16, Glowacki et al., chapter 12, Potter et al., chapter 13, Schleher et al., chapter 10, and Throgmorton et al., chapter 11 in this volume). Here, we use the term *community* to indicate a group of people who live close together and interact regularly (Lipe 1992, 3; Murdock 1949). Many archaeologists infer that clusters of contemporary, or roughly contemporary, habitation sites represent communities (Coffey and Kuckelman 2014; Varien 1999a).

Communities exist on a landscape, and, thus, residents of a specific community will have similar access to local materials. Differences in materials chosen for material culture production across the community reflect changes in the production group (or groups) or social boundaries (Arakawa et al., chapter 15; Schleher et al., chapter 10 in this volume) in the community. Choices of materials by the production group reflect learning traditions tied to a particular location on the landscape. These choices reflect a community of practice in the production, distribution, and use of pottery, reflecting social networks at various scales (e.g., Cordell and Habicht-Mauche 2012). The range of variation in the pottery assemblage reflects a variety of factors, including changes in the composition of the potting group or a broadening, or restricting, of the learning network (e.g., Crown 2007; Schleher 2017a). Here we explore communities of practice as reflected in raw materials used to make pottery vessels and designs chosen to decorate them. Variation in these communities of practice reflect changes in the production group that can include the movement of people into the community (immigration) or the adoption of technologies or design ideas from external production groups.

THE GOODMAN POINT AND SAND CANYON COMMUNITIES

The Goodman Point community lies near the head of Goodman Canyon and includes both mesa top and canyon settings. Numerous sites and features are located within the Goodman Point Unit of Hovenweep National Monument (figure 14.2), located approximately 9.5 miles northwest of present-day Cortez, Colorado (Coffey 2018a; Connolly 1992; Kuckelman et al. 2009; Kuckelman 2017a). The Goodman Point community was the focus of a field project carried

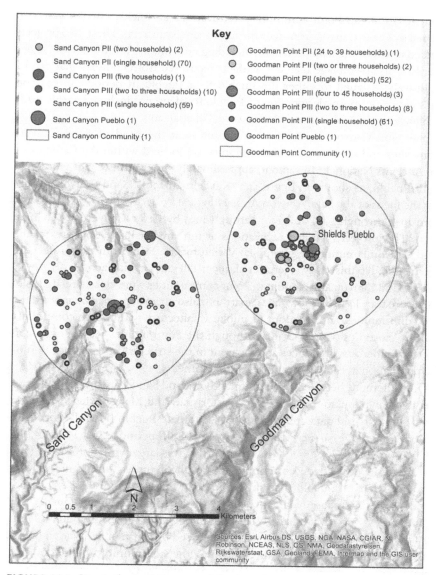

Key

◎	Sand Canyon PII (two households) (2)	◎	Goodman Point PII (24 to 39 households) (1)
○	Sand Canyon PII (single household) (70)	○	Goodman Point PII (two or three households) (2)
⬤	Sand Canyon PIII (five households) (1)	○	Goodman Point PII (single household) (52)
⬤	Sand Canyon PIII (two to three households) (10)	◎	Goodman Point PIII (four to 45 households) (3)
●	Sand Canyon PIII (single household) (59)	◉	Goodman Point PIII (two to three households) (8)
⬤	Sand Canyon Pueblo (1)	●	Goodman Point PIII (single household) (61)
▢	Sand Canyon Community (1)	⬤	Goodman Point Pueblo (1)
		▢	Goodman Point Community (1)

Shields Pueblo

Sand Canyon

Goodman Canyon

0 0.5 1 2 3 4
Kilometers

Sources: Esri, Airbus DS, USGS, NGA, NASA, CGIAR, N Robinson, NCEAS, NLS, OS, NMA, Geodatastyrelsen, Rijkswaterstaat, GSA, Geoland, FEMA, Intermap and the GIS user community

FIGURE 14.2. *Sites in the Sand Canyon and Goodman Point communities, as identified in the Village Ecodynamics Project database. Courtesy of the Crow Canyon Archaeological Center.*

out from 2005 through 2011 by the Crow Canyon Archaeological Center (Crow Canyon). The project included archaeological testing of fifteen habitations sites, including Goodman Point Pueblo. Shields Pueblo, located just outside of the Goodman Point Unit of Hovenweep National Monument, was also part of the ancient Goodman Point community. Excavations at Shields Pueblo were conducted by Crow Canyon from 1997 through 2000 (Ryan 2015). These two projects yielded much of the data used here, including information for more than 150,000 sherds. This assemblage includes artifacts recovered from contexts that can be exclusively assigned to either the Pueblo II or Pueblo III periods; mixed contexts with a temporal designation of Pueblo II/III are not included in this study (Schleher 2017b; Schleher and Coffey 2018; Till et al. 2015).

The Sand Canyon community is located near the head of Sand Canyon; many sites and features of this community are located within the Canyons of the Ancients National Monument, approximately 3 mi. southwest of Goodman Point Pueblo, as shown in figure 14.2 (Kuckelman 2007). Sand Canyon Pueblo was the focus of the Sand Canyon Archaeological Project, which was conducted from 1984 through 1989 and 1991 through 1993 by Crow Canyon (Kuckelman 2007). This project included excavations at ten smaller habitation sites in the Sand Canyon community (Lipe 1992; Varien 1999b). Data from this project are also included in this study (Pierce et al. 1999; Till and Ortman 2007).

The Sand Canyon and Goodman Point communities were closely related. Not only were they located a few miles apart, but also an ancient road connected the two communities, and locations of public architecture within each community indicate close ties (Coffey 2016). Although the communities were closely connected, numerous differences are apparent in the structure and composition of the population in each community through time.

One difference between the Goodman Point and Sand Canyon communities was in their population histories. Scott Ortman and Mark Varien (2007) analyzed survey-based data and suggest that from late Pueblo II / early Pueblo III period times (AD 1150–1225) to late in the Pueblo III period (AD 1225–1280), the population of the Goodman Point community was larger and more stable than that of the Sand Canyon community—a result of more immigrants moving into Sand Canyon Pueblo than into Goodman Point Pueblo. However, more recent, excavation-based data presented by Kristin Kuckelman (2017b) and Grant Coffey (2015, 2018b) suggest that the population of the Goodman Point community was less stable than as characterized by Ortman and Varien (2007), with additional households migrating into the community after Goodman Point Pueblo was founded about AD 1260. Specifically, Coffey argues that there were approximately 85 households at sites in the Goodman Point Unit and at Shields Pueblo before Goodman Point Pueblo was founded (Coffey 2018b, 551), and Kuckelman documents approximately 114 households at Goodman Point Pueblo during the final decades of the community (Kuckelman et al. 2009). These data suggest that both Sand Canyon and Goodman Point communities incorporated immigrants but that more immigrants joined Sand Canyon Pueblo than Goodman Point Pueblo.

A second difference between the Goodman Point and Sand Canyon communities is the degree of population nucleation through time. As shown in figure 14.2, the Goodman Point community was more tightly nucleated, or residentially clustered, around Shields Pueblo and the Goodman Point Pueblo from the Pueblo II period through late Pueblo III period than the Sand Canyon community was clustered around Sand Canyon Pueblo during that same time. That is, during that same time, the Sand Canyon community was more dispersed and less centered on the canyon rim where Sand Canyon Pueblo was built. These demographic and spatial differences—immigration and nucleation—play a role in explanations of the patterns discussed in this chapter for the pottery communities of practice in the Sand Canyon and Goodman Point communities.

POTTERY IN THE GOODMAN POINT AND SAND CANYON COMMUNITIES: TEMPER AND DESIGN

We explore two attributes of painted white ware pottery in the sample: temper and design. We then compare these data to patterns recognized across the broader central Mesa Verde region to shed light on stability and variation in pottery production in the Goodman Point and Sand Canyon communities through time.

The pottery manufactured in both communities primarily consists of corrugated gray ware and white ware vessels, with little change in the percentage of each in the total assemblage for the Pueblo II period versus the Pueblo III period (Pierce et al. 1999; Schleher 2017b; Schleher and Coffey 2018; Till and Ortman 2007). Nonlocal pottery (defined as having a provenance outside of the central Mesa Verde region) composes less than 1 percent of the pottery assemblage for all sites in both communities and for both time periods, including the large, late PIII villages of Goodman Point Pueblo (Schleher 2017b; Schleher and Coffey 2018) and Sand Canyon Pueblo (Pierce et al. 1999; Till and Ortman 2007). This pattern is true for the broader region; few pots were imported from outside the northern San Juan region late in the Pueblo III period, even though intraregional trade was common during this time (Glowacki 2006).

Pottery Temper

In the central Mesa Verde region, the most common temper materials added to clay by potters were crushed igneous rock, sherd, or crushed sandstone/sand (Breternitz et al. 1974; Ortman 2006). Crow Canyon temper analysis follows methods presented in Ortman and colleagues (2005). Potters in the Goodman Point and Sand Canyon communities used mostly igneous rock and sherd tempers. Limited outcrops of igneous rock occur in the region, with Sleeping Ute Mountain and alluvial terraces of McElmo creek being the closest sources to both communities (Pierce et al. 2002, 195). Potters in these two communities tempered gray ware pottery almost exclusively with crushed igneous rock

TABLE 14.1. Dominant temper types for white ware bowl rims by temporal period, Goodman Point community.

	Pueblo II		Pueblo III	
Temper Material	N	% of count	N	% of count
Igneous rock	145	57.09	1,085	50.16
Sherd	89	35.04	847	39.16
Other (sandstone/sand/ shale/indeterminate)	20	7.87	231	10.68
Total	254	100.00	2,163	100.00

Source: Data from Schleher (2017b, table 5.13); Schleher and Coffey (2018, table 23.14); Till et al. (2015, table 10.38).

Note: $\chi_2 = 4.86$, df $= 2$, $p = 0.088037$.

during both the Pueblo II and the Pueblo III periods (Pierce et al. 1999; Schleher 2017b; Schleher and Coffey 2018; Till et al. 2015; Till and Ortman 2007). Temper used to make white ware bowls was more variable, with finely crushed igneous rock and sherd temper utilized most. From the Pueblo II period to the Pueblo III period in the Goodman Point community, there were no statistically significant changes in temper materials for white ware bowls, with only a slight decrease in the amount of crushed igneous rock temper and a slight increase in the amount of crushed sherd temper used (table 14.1). Assemblages from a few of the smaller sites in the Goodman Point community that date from the Pueblo II period, such as the Harlan Great Kiva and Lupine Ridge sites, contain slightly higher percentages of sherds with more igneous rock temper than the average (Schleher and Coffey 2018). Temper percentages are relatively consistent across architectural blocks at Goodman Point Pueblo, although greater amounts of white ware bowl sherds containing sherd temper were found in one block, which we discuss later in the chapter (Schleher 2017b).

The slight change in the percentages of white ware bowl sherds that contain igneous rock temper versus sherd temper in the Goodman Point community differs significantly from temper materials used during the Pueblo II and Pueblo III periods in many other communities across the central Mesa Verde region. In the Sand Canyon community, preference in pottery temper changed significantly from the Pueblo II period to the Pueblo III, with a dramatic shift from primarily igneous rock temper to almost exclusively crushed sherd temper (Till and Ortman 2007), as shown in table 14.2. Similarly, in the Woods Canyon community, also investigated by Crow Canyon (Churchill 2002; Ortman 2002), white ware bowl temper preference also shifted significantly through time; use of sherd temper increased, whereas use of crushed rock temper declined (table 14.3). Even the temper used in white ware vessels at the Ute Piedmont sites near Sleeping Ute Mountain, the source of igneous rock, changed from the Pueblo II

TABLE 14.2. Dominant temper types for white ware bowl rims by temporal period, Sand Canyon community.

| | PII Pottery Types* | | Sand Canyon Pueblo (PIII) | |
Temper Material	N	% of count	N	% of count
Igneous	12	40.00	25	8.31
Sherd	10	33.33	235	78.07
Sandstone/sand	8	26.67	41	13.62
Total	30	100.00	301	100.00

* PII pottery types from sites other than SCP

Source: From Till and Ortman (2007).

Note: χ2 = 35.030, df = 2, p = 0.0000.

TABLE 14.3. Dominant temper types for white ware bowl rims by temporal period, Woods Canyon Community.

| | Pueblo II | | Pueblo III | |
Temper Material	N	% of Count	N	% of Count
Igneous rock	48	17.91	137	9.11
Sherd	99	36.94	829	55.12
Other (quartz / shale / metamorphic rock / indeterminate)	2	0.75	8	0.53
Sandstone/sand	119	44.40	530	35.24
Total	268	100.00	1,504	100.00

Source: Data from Ortman (2002, table 26).

Note: χ2 = 36.633, df = 3, p = 0.0000.

TABLE 14.4. Temper types for white ware bowl rims by temporal period, Ute Piedmont sites.

| | Pueblo II | | Pueblo III | |
Temper Material	N	% of Count	N	% of Count
Igneous	376	30.27	57	8.28
Sherd	725	58.37	495	71.95
Other (sandstone/sand/mixed)	141	11.35	136	19.77
Total	1,242	100.00	688	100.00

Source: From Errickson (1998).

Note: χ2 = 130.166, df = 2, p = 0.0000.

period to the Pueblo III; sherd temper replaced crushed igneous rock as the most common temper type used in Pueblo III period white ware vessels (Errickson 1998), as shown in table 14.4. Although this pattern of changing white ware temper occurs at many communities across the region, some villages located extremely close to the source of igneous rock, such as Castle Rock Pueblo and the Cowboy Wash site, do use crushed igneous rock as temper in white ware vessels in the Pueblo III period (Ortman 2000a, table 21; Pierce et al. 2002, 194).

Pottery Design

Pottery designs reflect different elements of the pottery production process. When materials, such as temper, used to manufacture a vessel are not visible to the observer, designs may be studied to infer production practices (e.g., Carr 1995). Next, we discuss design variation on Pueblo III period vessels from Sand Canyon and Goodman Point Pueblos to explore similarities and differences in designs used by communities of practice in each location.

Following methods used in Ortman (2000b), Samantha Jo Linford (2018) explored design variation in a sample of 898 rim sherds from McElmo Black-on-white and Mesa Verde Black-on-white pottery vessels from Sand Canyon and Goodman Point Pueblos. Table 14.5 and figure 14.3 summarize the differences in frequencies of design attributes for the sites. At 24 percent, coiled basketry texture patterns (framing-line bands) are twice as frequent in the Goodman Point Pueblo sample as in the Sand Canyon Pueblo sample. Twill-tapestry band design (diagonal bands) and twill-tapestry all-over designs (angled bands) are more common in the Sand Canyon Pueblo sample. Twill-tapestry band designs compose 28 percent of the designs in the Sand Canyon Pueblo sample but only 13 percent of the designs in the Goodman Point Pueblo sample. Twill-tapestry all-over designs compose about 2 percent of the designs in the Sand Canyon sample versus 0.22 percent in the sample from Goodman Point Pueblo. Coiled basketry color pattern (white background) and twill-plaiting color pattern (solid all-over line pattern) are also more common in the Sand Canyon Pueblo sample. In summary, four design attributes are more common in the Sand Canyon Pueblo sample, and two design attributes are more frequent in the sample from Goodman Point Pueblo. The greater prevalence of twill-tapestry designs for Sand Canyon Pueblo suggests connections with Cedar Mesa in Utah, where cotton textile designs are common on pottery (Bellorado and Windes, chapter 18 in this volume; Bellorado 2020; Crabtree and Bellorado 2016). With greater numbers of immigrants settling at Sand Canyon Pueblo than at Goodman Point Pueblo (Coffey 2018b; Kuckelman 2007; Ortman and Varien 2007), the use of these textile or tapestry designs on pottery suggest that some of the immigrants who settled at Sand Canyon Pueblo originated from Cedar Mesa.

Because designs reflect more visible elements of the pottery production process than raw material, the differences in designs from Sand Canyon versus Goodman Point Pueblo suggest that potters used designs to intentionally signal their membership in a specific group at each pueblo, reflecting different communities of practice.

TABLE 14.5. Percentage of designs present at Sand Canyon Pueblo (5MT765) and Goodman Point Pueblo (5MT604).

Design layout	Code	Source industry	Cases at Sand Canyon	Cases at Goodman Point	Percent in Sand Canyon	Percent in Goodman Point	Difference in percentage	P-Value
Coiled basketry color pattern	solbkgd (solid background)	Coiled basketry	450	448	5.91	2.64	3.27	0.01
Coiled basketry texture pattern	frambnd (framing line band)	Coiled basketry	450	448	12.38	24.55	−12.17	<0.0001
Non–loom band design	sectbnd (sectioned band)	Nonloom weaving	450	448	1.11	3.79	−2.68	0.01
Simple plaiting	checkbd (checkerboard)	Plaited basketry	450	448	1.56	0.89	0.67	0.37
Twill-plaiting texture pattern	hatchline (all-over hatched line pattern)	Plaited basketry	450	448	1.78	1.79	−0.01	0.99
Twill-plaiting color pattern	solidline (all-over solid line pattern)	Plaited basketry	450	448	6.89	1.79	5.10	0.0002
Plain-tapestry band design	contbnd (continuous rectangular band)	Loom-woven cotton cloth	450	448	7.78	5.80	1.98	0.24
Twill-tapestry texture	bkdhatch (background hatchure)	Loom-woven cotton cloth	450	448	14.22	11.16	3.06	0.17
Twill-tapestry band design	diagbnd (continuous diagonal band)	Loom-woven cotton cloth	450	448	28.00	12.95	15.05	<0.0001
Twill-tapestry all-over design	angbnd (angled bands)	Loom-woven cotton cloth	450	448	2.22	0.22	2.00	0.007
Nontextile design	otherdes (other design)	Other, nontextile pattern	450	448	3.24	5.58	−2.34	0.08

Source: From Linford (2018, table 5.1).

Note: Statistically significant results at the 0.05 level are highlighted.

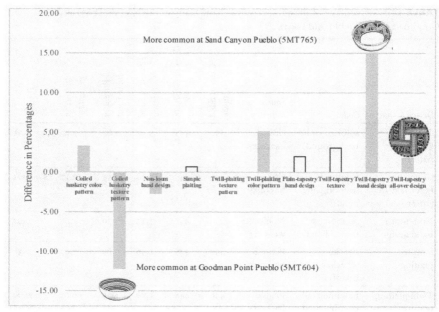

FIGURE 14.3. *Designs present on sherds at Sand Canyon and Goodman Point Pueblos. Figure modified from Linford (2018, fig. 5.1). Statistically significant bars are highlighted (p < 0.05). Courtesy of Samantha Linford.*

DISCUSSION

The temporal and spatial patterning in pottery materials and design differ for the Goodman Point and Sand Canyon communities, reflecting differences in the communities of practice for potters living in these distinct, yet closely connected, communities. We see differences in the designs used to decorate vessels, a highly visible production attribute. Potters at Sand Canyon Pueblo and Goodman Point Pueblo intentionally used different designs to signal their participation in the social life of their community. These may reflect different clans (Kuwanwisiwma and Bernardini, chapter 5 in this volume), moieties (Linford 2018), or other kinds of social groups. Temper selection reflects social learning frameworks occurring within a community of practice (e.g., Cordell and Habicht-Mauche 2012). Temper materials used in the Goodman Point community are remarkably consistent, especially compared to the variation and change through time in materials used by residents of many other communities in the central Mesa Verde region, including that of Sand Canyon. We argue that these different patterns of design and temper reflect differences in the social identities of those living in each community and that consistency in the use of pottery production materials in the Goodman Point community results from the relative stability of population in that community through time.

Earlier research suggests that the population of the Goodman Point community was larger and more stable than the Sand Canyon community from late Pueblo II / early Pueblo III period times to late Pueblo III period times (Coffey 2018b; Kuckelman 2017b; Ortman and Varien 2007). The greater stability of the population in the Goodman Point community, in terms of fewer immigrants and greater nucleation earlier in time, compared to the Sand Canyon community, suggests that residents of Goodman Point Pueblo had less need to signal identity than did residents of Sand Canyon Pueblo (e.g., Ortman and Varien 2007).

Because pottery production was more stable in the Goodman Point community than in the Sand Canyon community—and both communities incorporated immigrants—it is likely that social differences resulted in the observed patterns in pottery manufacture. Perhaps resident potters at Goodman Point Pueblo required immigrants to conform to the traditional pottery-making techniques of the village, which is indicative of a closed-learning framework (Crown 2007; Wallaert 2012). In other words, the community of practice was more stable in the Goodman Point community because existing social groups applied pressure on newcomers to conform. Another possibility is that if the overall population of the Goodman Point community was comparatively more stable than that of the Sand Canyon community, this could have resulted in greater continuity in pottery production methods through time. That is, the resident potting families of the Goodman Point community did not change dramatically and thus they continued to use traditional methods of producing pottery that had been utilized since the founding of the community (Schleher and Coffey 2018).

We argue that the general pattern of consistency in materials utilized in the manufacture of pottery and pottery designs reflects differences between the Sand Canyon and Goodman Point communities. The greater stability in communities of practice in the Goodman Point community correlates with more stability in population than that seen in other communities across the central Mesa Verde region, including the Sand Canyon community. Residents of the Goodman Point community, even after aggregating into the community center of Goodman Point Pueblo late in the Pueblo III period, continued making pottery using the same materials used during the Pueblo II period. Sherd-tempered white ware pottery did not become the most common white ware at Goodman Point Pueblo as it did across much of the Mesa Verde region during the Pueblo III period (Errickson 1998; Glowacki 2001; Ortman 2002; Till and Ortman 2007). Although potters produced a larger variety of white ware vessel forms (Schleher et al. 2014), the temper constituency of white ware bowls seems to have changed little through time. At Goodman Point Pueblo, pottery from one architectural block is more similar to the broader regional pattern of greater proportions of white ware sherds containing sherd temper than igneous rock temper. The temper in white ware bowl sherds from Architectural Block 200, one of the northernmost blocks at Goodman Point Pueblo, is 63 percent sherd and only 32 percent igneous (Schleher 2017b, table 5.14). The greater use of sherd temper is suggestive of a different production group residing in this area of the village, and Kuckelman (2017b) demonstrates that there were some immigrants at Goodman Point Pueblo. Pottery data thus support the inference of immigrants at Goodman Point Pueblo, with Architectural Block 200 as a likely residence of immigrants who resided in their own area of the village and brought different pottery-making traditions.

In conclusion, stability in the selection of materials used for pottery production through time within the Goodman Point community suggests that specific technological changes were not uniformly adopted across the central Mesa Verde region. Different decisions regarding the use of tempering materials hint at different production groups with diverse histories, and different choices in designs reflect social differences across the region. Patterns in pottery material and design help highlight differences between two of the largest and most closely connected villages in the central Mesa Verde region and illustrate the significance of differences and similarities between residents of these important places on the landscape. This chapter presents a nuanced view of social dynamics within two large communities in the central Mesa Verde region, research that was made possible through many of the large, multiyear research projects conducted since 1983 by Crow Canyon (Lightfoot and Lipe, chapter 2 in this volume; Kohler et al., chapter 3 in this volume).

REFERENCES

Adler, Michael. 1996. "Fathoming the Scale of Anasazi Communities." In *Interpreting Southwestern Diversity: Underlying Principles and Overarching Patterns*, edited by Paul R. Fish and J. Jefferson Reid, 97–106. Anthropological Research Papers, no. 48. Tempe: Arizona State University.

Bellorado, Benjamin A. 2020. "Leaving Footprints in the Ancient Southwest: Visible Indicators of Group Affiliation and Social Position in the Chaco and Post-Chaco Eras (A.D. 850–1300)." PhD diss., University of Arizona, Tucson.

Breternitz, David A., Arthur H. Rohn Jr., and Elizabeth A. Morris. 1974. *Prehistoric Ceramics of the Mesa Verde Region*. Flagstaff: Museum of Northern Arizona Ceramic Series No. 5.

Carr, Christopher. 1995. "A Unified Middle-Range Theory of Artifact Design." In *Style, Society, and Person: Archaeological and Ethnological Perspectives*, edited by Christopher Car and Jill E. Neitzel, 171–258. New York: Plenum Press.

Churchill, Melissa J. ed. 2002. *The Archaeology of Woods Canyon Pueblo: A Canyon-Rim Village in Southwestern Colorado*. Accessed January 1, 2021. https://www.crowcanyon .org/ResearchReports/WoodsCanyon/Text/wcpw_introduction.asp.

Coffey, Grant D. 2015. "The Harlan Great Kiva Site: Civic Architecture and Community Persistence in the Goodman Point Area of Southwest Colorado." *Kiva* 79 (4): 380–404.

Coffey, Grant D. 2016. "Creating Symmetry: The Cultural Landscapes in the Sand Canyon Locality, Southwestern Colorado." *Kiva* 82 (1): 1–21.

Coffey, Grant D., ed. 2018a. *The Goodman Point Archaeological Project: Goodman Point Community Testing*. (tDAR id: 447957), https://doi.org/10.6067/XCV8447957.

Coffey, Grant D. 2018b. "Summary and Conclusions." In *The Goodman Point Archaeological Project: Goodman Point Community Testing*, edited by Grant D. Coffey. (tDAR id: 447957), https://doi.org/10.6067/XCV8447957.

Coffey, Grant D., and Kristin A. Kuckelman. 2014. "Public Architecture of the Goodman Point Community, Southwestern Colorado, A.D. 1000 to 1280." Paper presented at the Society for American Archaeology Annual Meeting, Austin.

Connolly, Marjorie R. 1992. "The Goodman Point Historic Land-Use Study." In *The Sand Canyon Archaeological Project: A Progress Report*, edited by W. D. Lipe, 33–44. Occasional Papers, no. 2. Cortez, CO: Crow Canyon Archaeological Center.

Cordell, Linda, and Judith Habicht-Mauche. 2012. "Practice Theory and Social Dynamics among Prehispanic and Colonial Communities in the American Southwest." In *Potters and Communities of Practice: Glaze Paint and Polychrome Pottery in the American Southwest, AD 1250 to 1700*, edited by Linda Cordell and Judith Habicht-Mauche, 1–7. Anthropological Papers of the University of Arizona, Number 75. Tucson: The University of Arizona Press.

Crown, Patricia L. 2007. "Learning about Learning." In *Archaeological Anthropology: Perspectives on Method and Theory*, edited by James Skibo, Michael W. Graves, and Marian Stark, 198–217. Tucson: University of Arizona Press.

Crabtree, Stefani A., and Benjamin A. Bellorado. 2016. "Using Cross-Media Approaches to Understand an Invisible Industry: How Cotton Production Influenced Pottery Designs and Kiva Murals in Cedar Mesa." *Kiva* 82 (2): 174–200.

Errickson, Mary. 1998. "Ceramic Material Culture." In *The Puebloan Occupation of the Ute Mountain Piedmont*. Vol. 6, *Material Culture Studies*, edited by Brian R. Billman, 2.1–2.105. Vol. 22, No. 6 of *Soil Systems Publications in Archaeology*. Cortez, CO: Soil Systems.

Glowacki, Donna M. 2001. "2001 Yucca House (5MT5006) Mapping Project Report." Report on file at the Crow Canyon Archaeological Center, Cortez, CO.

Glowacki, Donna M. 2006. "The Social Landscape of Depopulation: The Northern San Juan Region, A.D. 1150–1300." PhD diss., Arizona State University, Tempe.

Hurst, Winston B. 2011. "A Tale of Two Villages: Basketmaker III Communities in San Juan County, Utah." *Blue Mountain Shadows* 44:7–18.

Jalbert, Joseph P. 1999. "Northern San Juan Region Great House Communities: Assessing Chacoan versus Regional Influences." MA thesis, Department of Anthropology, University of Colorado, Boulder.

Jalbert, Joseph Peter, and Catherine Cameron. 2000. "Chacoan and Local Influences in Three Great House Communities in the Northern San Juan Region." In *Great House Communities across the Chacoan Landscape*, edited by John Kantner and Nancy M. Mahoney, 79–90. Anthropological Papers of the University of Arizona, No. 64. Tucson: University of Arizona Press.

Kolb, Michael J., James E. Snead. 1997. "It's a Small World After All: Comparative Analyses of Community Organization in Archaeology." *American Antiquity* 62 (4): 609–628.

Kuckelman, Kristin A., ed. 2007. *The Archaeology of Sand Canyon Pueblo: Intensive Excavations at a Late-Thirteenth-Century Village in Southwestern Colorado.* http://www.crowcanyon.org/sandcanyon.

Kuckelman, Kristin A., ed. 2017a. *The Goodman Point Archaeological Project: Goodman Point Pueblo Excavations.* (tDAR id: 446779), https://doi.org/10.6067/XCV8PC359D.

Kuckelman, Kristin A. 2017b. "Population." In *The Goodman Point Archaeological Project: Goodman Point Pueblo Excavations*, edited by Kristin A. Kuckelman. (tDAR id: 446779), https://doi.org/10.6067/XCV8PC359D.

Kuckelman, Kristin A., Grant D. Coffey, and Steven R. Copeland. 2009. *Interim Descriptive Report of Research at Goodman Point Pueblo (Site 5MT604), Montezuma County, Colorado, 2005–2008.* https://www.crowcanyon.org/ResearchReports/Goodman Point/interim_reports/2005_2008/GPP_interim_report_2005_2008.pdf.

Linford, Samantha Jo. 2018. "Moieties in the Northern Rio Grande: Ceramic Design Analysis and Social Identity in Southwest Colorado and Northern New Mexico." MA thesis, Department of Anthropology, University of Colorado, Boulder.

Lipe, William D., ed. 1992. *The Sand Canyon Archaeological Project: A Progress Report.* Occasional Papers, no. 2. Cortez, CO: Crow Canyon Archaeological Center.

Lipe, William D., Mark D. Varien, and Richard H. Wilshusen, ed. 1999 *Colorado Prehistory: A Context for the Southern Colorado River Basin.* Denver: Colorado Council of Professional Archaeologists.

Mahoney, Nancy M. 2000. "Redefining the Scale of Chacoan Communities." In *Great House Communities across the Chacoan Landscape*, edited by John Kantner and Nancy M. Mahoney, 19–27. Anthropological Papers of the University of Arizona, no. 64. Tucson: University of Arizona Press,

Murdock, George P. 1949. *Social Structure.* New York: Macmillan.

Ortman, Scott G. 2000a. "Artifacts." In *The Archaeology of Castle Rock Pueblo: A Thirteenth-Century Village in Southwestern Colorado*, edited by Kristin A. Kuckelman. Accessed January 20, 2021. https://www.crowcanyon.org/ResearchReports/CastleRock/Text/crpw_contentsvolume.asp.

Ortman, Scott G. 2000b. "Conceptual Metaphor in the Archaeological Record: Methods and an Example from the American Southwest." *American Antiquity* 65 (4): 613–645.

Ortman, Scott G. 2002. "Artifacts." In *The Archaeology of Woods Canyon Pueblo: A Canyon-Rim Village in Southwestern Colorado*, edited by Melissa J. Churchill. http://www.crowcanyon.org/woodscanyon.

Ortman, Scott G. 2006. "Ancient Pottery of the Mesa Verde Country: How Ancestral Pueblo People Made It, Used It, and Thought about it." In *The Mesa Verde World*, edited by David Grant Noble, 101–109. Santa Fe, NM: School of American Research Press.

Ortman, Scott G., Erin L. Baxter, Carole L. Graham, G. Robin Lyle, Lew W. Matis, Jamie A. Merewether, R. David Satterwhite, and Jonathan D. Till. 2005. *The Crow Canyon Archaeological Center Laboratory Manual, Version 1.* Accessed February 8, 2017. https://www.crowcanyon.org/resources/laboratory_manual_version_1/.

Ortman, Scott G., and Mark D. Varien. 2007. "Settlement Patterns in the McElmo Dome Study Area." In *The Archaeology of Sand Canyon Pueblo: Intensive Excavations at a Late-Thirteenth-Century Village in Southwestern Colorado*, edited by Kristin A. Kuckelman. http://www.crowcanyon.org/sandcanyon.

Ortman, Scott G., Mark D. Varien, and T. Lee Gripp. 2007. "Empirical Bayesian Methods for Archaeological Survey Data: An Application from the Mesa Verde Region." *American Antiquity* 72 (2): 241–272.

Pierce, Christopher, Donna M. Glowacki, and Margaret M. Thurs. 2002. "Measuring Community Interaction: Pueblo III Pottery Production and Distribution in the Central Mesa Verde Region." In *Seeking the Center Place: Archaeology and Ancient Communities in the Mesa Verde Region*, edited by Mark D. Varien and Richard H. Wilshusen, 185–202. Salt Lake City: The University of Utah Press.

Pierce, Christopher, Mark D. Varien, Jonathan C. Driver, G. Timothy Gross, and Joseph W. Keleher. 1999. "Artifacts." In *The Sand Canyon Archaeological Project: Site Testing*, edited by Mark D. Varien, chapter 15. https://www.crowcanyon.org/Research Reports/SiteTesting/Text/Report.asp.

Ryan, Susan C. ed. 2015. "The Archaeology of Shield Pueblo (Site 5MT3807): Excavations at a Mesa-Top Community Center in Southwestern Colorado." http://www.crowcanyon.org/shieldspueblo.

Schleher, Kari L. 2017a. "Learning and Production: The Northern Rio Grande Glaze Ware Community of Practice at San Marcos Pueblo during the Protohistoric Period." In *The Archaeology and History of Pueblo San Marcos: Change and Stability*, edited by Ann F. Ramenofsky and Kari L. Schleher, 107–128. Albuquerque: University of New Mexico Press.

Schleher, Kari L. 2017b. "Artifacts." In *The Goodman Point Archaeological Project: Goodman Point Pueblo Excavations*, edited by Kristin A. Kuckelman. (tDAR id: 446779), https://doi.org/10.6067/XCV8PC359D.

Schleher, Kari L., and Grant D. Coffey. 2018. "Artifacts." In *The Goodman Point Archaeological Project: Goodman Point Community Testing*, edited by Grant D. Coffey. (tDAR id: 447957), https://doi.org 10.6067/XCV8447957.

Schleher, Kari L., Jamie Merewether, Cherise Bunn, and Megan Smith. 2014. "Material Culture of Public and Private Spaces in the Mesa Verde Region." Paper presented at the 79th Annual Society of American Archaeology Conference, Austin.

Till, Jonathan, Jamie Merewether, Robin Lyle, and Scott Ortman. 2015. "Pottery." In *The Archaeology of Shields Pueblo (Site 5MT3807): Excavations at a Mesa-Top Community Center in Southwestern Colorado*, edited by Susan C. Ryan. http://www.crowcanyon.org /shieldspueblo.

Till, Jonathan D., and Scott G. Ortman. 2007. "Artifacts." In *The Archaeology of Sand Canyon Pueblo: Intensive Excavations at a Late-Thirteenth-Century Village in Southwestern Colorado* [HTML Title], edited by Kristin A. Kuckelman. Accessed http://www .crowcanyon.org/sandcanyon.

Wallaert, Hélène. 2012. "Apprenticeship and the Confirmation of Social Boundaries." In *Archaeology and Apprenticeship: Body Knowledge, Identity, and Communities of Practice*, edited by Willeke Wendrich, 20–42. Tucson: University of Arizona Press.

Varien, Mark D. 1999a. *Sedentism and Mobility in a Social Landscape: Mesa Verde and Beyond*. Tucson: University of Arizona Press.

Varien, Mark D. ed. 1999b. *The Sand Canyon Archaeological Project: Site Testing*. Accessed January 1, 2021. https://www.crowcanyon.org/ResearchReports/SiteTesting/start .asp.

Varien, Mark D., William D. Lipe, Michael A. Adler, Ian M. Thompson, and Bruce A. Bradley. 1996. "Southwestern Colorado and Southeastern Utah Settlement Patterns: A.D. 1100 to 1300." In *The Prehistoric Pueblo World, A.D. 1150–1350*, edited by Michael A. Adler, 86–113. Tucson: University of Arizona Press.

Varien, Mark D., Carla R. Van West, and G. Stuart Patterson. 2000. "Competition, Cooperation and Conflict: Agricultural Production and Community Catchments in the Central Mesa Verde Region." *Kiva* 66 (1): 45–65.

15

Lithic Analyses and Sociopolitical Organization

Mobility, Territoriality, and Trade in the Central Mesa Verde Region

FUMI ARAKAWA, JAMIE MEREWETHER, AND KATE HUGHES

This chapter demonstrates how Crow Canyon Archaeological Center (CCAC) has effectively developed and implemented lithic analyses over the past forty years. Most lithic assemblages recovered from CCAC's excavations originated from agricultural, sedentary villages dating from the Basketmaker III period to the Pueblo III (AD 500–1300) period. Unlike lithic studies in hunting and gathering societies, lithic assemblages derived from agricultural societies in the American Southwest have been neglected (Whittaker 1987). In this chapter, we contend that lithic studies offer a great deal of knowledge pertaining to sociopolitical organization in ancestral Pueblo society, including mobility, territoriality, and trade. To successfully address these themes, CCAC researchers have carried out sourcing studies and developed standardized raw material classification (Ortman et al. 2005). By developing a repeatable and replicable lithological and sourcing methodology, CCAC researchers can successfully address the topic of sociopolitical organization through time.

Archaeologists in the American Southwest have long investigated changes in community organization (see Schleher et al., chapter 14, Glowacki et al., chapter

https://doi.org/10.5876/9781646424597.c015

12, and Potter et al., chapter 13 in this volume). In the central Mesa Verde region, settlement analyses indicate that the cultural trajectory of agricultural societies went through two major cycles of dispersion and aggregation, the first beginning during the Basketmaker III (AD 500–750) period and ending with the Pueblo I period (AD 750–900) period, and the second from the Pueblo II (AD 900–1050) period to the Pueblo III (AD 1050–1300) period (Arakawa 2012a; Kohler and Ellyson 2019). During the first cycle in the Basketmaker III (BMIII) period, ancestral Pueblo people lived in relatively dispersed settlement clusters (Wilshusen 1999). Although the BMIII settlements were mostly dispersed in the central Mesa Verde region, there is one example where these households occur in conjunction with public architecture, a great kiva at the Dillard site (see Schleher et al., chapter 10 in this volume). The Basketmaker Communities Project, a multifaceted research and public education initiative conducted by Crow Canyon from 2011 to 2017, examined the Dillard site and the surrounding settlements, and it represents one of the best examples of a Basketmaker III period community center in the region (Diederichs 2020).

From the late AD 700s to 900s, there was a major transition in settlement organization in the central Mesa Verde region. Site 13 on Alkali Ridge is one of the largest villages in the western portion of the central Mesa Verde region (Brew 1946). The layout of Site 13 contrasts with Sacred Ridge, another large village in the Animas River drainage (Potter and Chupuka 2007; Potter et al. 2012) located in the eastern portion of the central Mesa Verde region. Villages in the Dolores River valley, located in the middle of the central Mesa Verde region, are interpreted as having characteristics of both the eastern and western Mesa Verde region (Wilshusen and Ortman 1999). By the early AD 900s, the first cycle of aggregation ended in the region.

During the tenth and early eleventh centuries AD (see Throgmorton et al., chapter 11 in this volume), population density declined in the Village Ecodynamics Project (VEP) I study area (see Glowacki et al., chapter 12 in this volume; Kohler et al., chapter 3 in this volume; Varien et al. 2007, 284), which encompasses approximately 1,800 km². The population decline corresponds with the earliest construction of great houses in Chaco Canyon (Plog and Heitman 2010; Powers et al. 1983; Wilshusen and Van Dyke 2006; Windes 2003), and several authors have speculated that ancestral Pueblo people moved out of the central Mesa Verde region and migrated south, contributing to the demographic buildup that triggered coalescence in Chaco Canyon (Wilshusen 1995; Wilshusen and Van Dyke 2006). From AD 1020 to 1140, Chaco great houses were constructed in the central Mesa Verde region, such as the Haynie site, Wallace Ruin, and Escalante Ruin. Based on lithic data, there was more interregional interaction and trade between the people in the central Mesa Verde region and Chaco Canyon (Cameron 2001; Ward 2004) during that time.

Ancestral Pueblo people in the central Mesa Verde region experienced dramatic cultural change during the post-Chaco era, or the Pueblo III period. This change includes an increase in population (Varien et al. 2007), an increase in conflict, and warfare (Kohler et al., chapter 3 in this volume; Kuckelman 2010; Kuckelman et al. 2000; Kuckelman, chapter 19 in this volume), a shift in settlement location from the tops of mesas to canyon settings (Varien 1999), the development of the largest aggregated villages (Lipe and Ortman 1998) in the region, and finally, the depopulation of the region at the end of the thirteenth century AD (Adler and Hegmon, chapter 16, Schleher et al., chapter 14 in this volume). During the AD 1200s, large, aggregated villages and politically complex social organization were apparent in the region, as evidenced by sites investigated by Crow Canyon such as Sand Canyon Pueblo, Goodman Point Pueblo, Yellow Jacket Pueblo, and Woods Canyon Pueblo (Arakawa 2012a; Churchill 2002; Kuckelman 2003, 2007; Kuckelman et al. 2009). Populations increased in the region between AD 1140 and 1280; however, long-distance trade declined based on the low frequency of nonlocal pottery and lithic raw materials in site assemblages from that period (Arakawa 2006; Arakawa and Duff 2002; Glowacki 2015; Lipe 2006; Neily 1983).[1]

In addition, faunal remains (Driver 2002) and the frequency of projectile points compared to other artifact classes (Arakawa et al. 2013) recovered from the central area (McElmo–Yellow Jacket District and the western area, Cedar Mesa and Canyonlands Districts) indicate that residents did not often participate in large game hunting. Rather, they relied on small animals (e.g., lagomorphs) and domesticated turkey to acquire protein (Schollmeyer and Driver, chapter 21 in this volume). There is also no evidence that they obtained large game through exchange with other regions during the AD 1200s (Driver 2002). Localized, intraregional exchange may have intensified during the AD 1200s (Arakawa and Gerhardt 2007; Glowacki 2006, 2015). The decline of items obtained from long-distance exchange and intensified intraregional exchange suggest that the central Mesa Verde region was politically autonomous during the thirteenth century AD. The lack of long-distance exchange during this time differs from earlier time periods, when more long-distance exchange of materials occurred.

THE DEVELOPMENT OF CROW CANYON LITHIC STUDIES

In this chapter, we evaluate whether ancestral Pueblo people in the study area exhibited political autonomy during the AD 1200s, by analyzing chipped-stone data. To achieve this goal, we begin by discussing how CCAC researchers developed a lithic analysis methodology. Then, we address the application of these methods used in this study. Finally, we shed light on the sociopolitical organization (i.e., mobility, territoriality, and trade) and the development of political autonomy.

Lithic studies started at Crow Canyon, when Crow Canyon researchers began archaeological research at the Duckfoot site from 1983 to 1991 (Kohler et al., chapter 3 in this volume; Lightfoot and Etzkorn 1993). Crow Canyon researchers, interns, and participants excavated entire structures and middens and recovered tens of thousands of artifacts dating to the Pueblo I period (AD 750–900). During lithic analysis, Crow Canyon researchers analyzed formal tools, such as projectile points, bifaces, and drills, and informal tools, such as peckingstones, modified flakes, and utilized flakes. They analyzed lithic debitage and classified these artifacts by local and nonlocal material type. They designated local as those raw materials that could be procured within a 25 km radius of the site and nonlocal raw materials as materials that could be procured beyond a 25 km radius (Lightfoot and Etzkorn 1993, 158). Notably, they linked the type of stone with geological formations when classifying raw material types. For example, "Morrison" claystone, mudstone, siltstone, and chert were identified as rocks that were derived from the Morrison Formation from the Jurassic period. "Dakota" quartzite (orthoquartzite) was named for the Dakota Formation in the Cretaceous period from which they came. Nonlocal rocks were also identified, such as obsidian, Narbona Pass chert (formerly called Washington Pass chert), and red jasper. The presence of these materials suggested that they were procured by long-distance trade. For debitage, Crow Canyon researchers recorded general morphological categories, including flakes with platforms, flakes without platforms, edge-damaged flakes, and others (Lightfoot and Etzkorn 1993, 180).

After completing the Duckfoot site assemblage, Crow Canyon researchers continued to follow similar formal tool analysis methods (with the exception of debitage) for the Sand Canyon, Yellow Jacket Pueblo, and Woods Canyon Pueblo assemblages. However, when they began working at Shields Pueblo in 1998, Crow Canyon researchers introduced a new way of analyzing debitage, which was called "mass analysis," originally proposed by Ahler (1989). This method focuses on identifying material type, size grading into four categories (1 in., 0.5 in., 0.25 in., and smaller than 0.25 in.), identifying the presence or absence of cortex, and recording the count and weight. Of importance, mass analysis allows researchers to analyze large debitage assemblages efficiently and easily. Crow Canyon researchers adopted this method of analysis in the late 1990s, and it is still used in lithic artifact analyses today (Ortman et al. 2005).

With assistance from Crow Canyon researchers, Arakawa (2000) analyzed the Yellow Jacket Pueblo (5MT5) chipped-stone assemblage for his thesis research. One goal of his research was to define which local, semilocal, and nonlocal raw materials were used at Yellow Jacket Pueblo. To achieve the goal, he conducted a reconnaissance of local lithic sources and quarries around Yellow Jacket Canyon and redefined local raw material types, including rocks from the Morrison, Burro Canyon, and Dakota Formations (Arakawa 2000, 2013; Arakawa and Nicholson 2020).

Arakawa, in collaboration with Kimberly Gerhardt, a local geologist, continued to define and classify raw material types for the broader central Mesa Verde region. They visited several quarry sites and geological outcrops in the early 2000s (Arakawa 2006, 2012b; Arakawa and Gerhardt 2007, 2009). Using the local and regional lithological sourcing data, Crow Canyon researchers also began using the new material type system for tool analysis (Ortman et al. 2005).

For forty years, Crow Canyon has devoted time and energy to developing its own chipped-stone analyses. These analyses are innovative because Crow Canyon researchers delved into sourcing studies and associated raw material types with local and regional lithologies. Data derived from sourcing studies allow researchers to explore several topics regarding sociopolitical organization in pre-Hispanic society (Arakawa 2006, 2012b; Arakawa et al. 2013; Arakawa et al. 2011; Arakawa and Nicholson 2020). In the following section, we demonstrate how chipped-stone studies based on these raw material classifications can address questions of sociopolitical organization, especially the development of political autonomy from AD 600 to AD 1300 in the McElmo–Yellow Jacket District of the central Mesa Verde region.

METHODOLOGY

We compiled chipped-stone data from twelve sites and fifteen chronological components from the McElmo–Yellow Jacket district (table 15.1) (Varien 1999, 86). Most of these sites are classified as community centers in the Pueblo II and Pueblo III periods. Community centers are large sites that have long occupation spans and often contain public architecture (see Glowacki et al., chapter 12 in this volume). The Basketmaker III and Pueblo I period sites are from small habitations (figure 15.1). We use counts, not weights, to collect data on both tools and debitage. We also investigate tools (cores, peckingstones, projectile points, bifaces, and drills) and debitage using five raw material categories: local high-quality material, local low-quality material, semilocal material, nonlocal material, and other stone material types. We are interested in broad patterns of tool-stone procurement patterns through time, so we have aggregated these data into the Basketmaker III, Pueblo I, Pueblo II, or Pueblo III periods.[2] We used only contexts that could be confidently assigned to one of these time periods.[3]

Among the five raw material categories, local materials are classified as either high or low-quality materials. High-quality local materials include highly silicified agate/chalcedony (ACH), Cretaceous Dakota / Burro Canyon quartzite (KDB), and Cretaceous Burro Canyon chert (KBC). These types are commonly used in formal tool production, such as projectile points and bifacial tools (knives) (Arakawa 2006; Arakawa and Gerhardt 2007), and their quarries are well

TABLE 15.1. Lithic assemblages used for this study, showing the temporal period and the count of chipped-stone materials.

Time Period	Site Number	Site Name	Core	Peckingstone	Projectile Point	Biface	Drill	Debitage
BMIII	5MT10647	Dillard Pueblo	34	25	11	15	7	6,885
BMIII	5MT10711	Ridgeline Site	7	4	2	1	3	593
BMIII	5MT2032	Switchback	3				1	806
BMIII	5MT10631	Mueller Little House	7			2	1	701
PI	5MT3868	Duckfoot		381	50	23	9	507
PI	5MT3807	Shields Pueblo	2					389
PII	5MT123	Albert Porter Site	79	42	26	11	4	181,048
PII	5MT3807	Shields Pueblo	145	228	67	38	15	1,421,400
PII	5MT5	Yellow Jacket Pueblo	9	5		2	1	10,921
PIII	5MT3807	Shields Pueblo	114	127	24	15	5	511,246
PIII	5MT5	Yellow Jacket Pueblo	56	42	24	25	5	135,708
PIII	5MT604	Goodman Point Pueblo	101	113	41	32	7	272,232
PIII	5MT1825	Castle Rock Pueblo	33	43	19	2	4	282
PIII	5MT765	Sand Canyon Pueblo	203	188	41	29	22	5,612
PIII	5MT11842	Woods Canyon Pueblo	33	10	4	4		13,457
Total			826	1,208	309	199	84	2,561,787

Source: Table by authors.

known, recorded, and relatively ubiquitous in this study area (except for ACH) (Arakawa 2006; Arakawa and Nicholson 2020). These quarries fall within 18 km of most villages in the study area (Arakawa 2006; Varien 1999). For instance, Shields Pueblo is approximately 3 km from the nearest KDB quarry, whereas Yellow Jacket Pueblo is 12 km from the nearest KDB quarry (Arakawa 2006).

Low-quality (less silicified sedimentary rocks) local materials include Morrison Formation rocks (e.g., siltstone, mudstone, chert, and silicified sandstone). Of

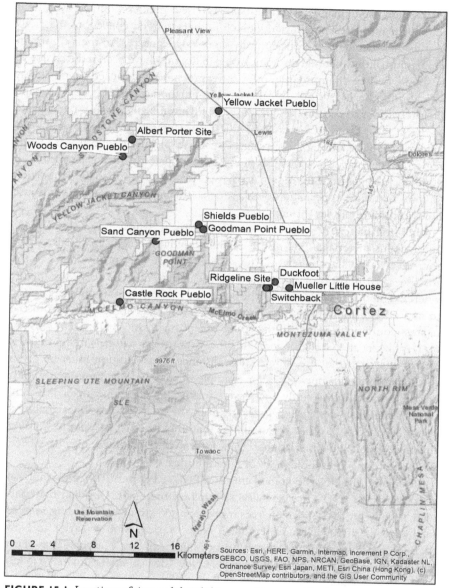

FIGURE 15.1. *Locations of sites and their lithic assemblages used in this study. Courtesy of the Crow Canyon Archaeological Center.*

interest, Robert Neily (1983), Arakawa and Kimberlee Gerhardt (2007), and Arakawa and Andrew Duff (2002) recognized that the central Mesa Verde residents used a larger proportion of these local, low-quality materials during the Pueblo II and III periods. As population increased and communities became increasingly aggregated, communities exercised greater control over their immediate resources, making it difficult for others to freely collect raw materials. As a result, Pueblo people came to rely on resources nearest to their communities, limiting lithic material diversity. Accessibility may have been reduced due to hostilities between communities or by other pressures that caused people to stay away from other territories. In general, as populations increase, people expand their territories to procure new resources. However, Neily (1983), Arakawa and Gerhardt (2007), and Arakawa and Duff (2002) suggest that this phenomenon did not take place among the ancestral Pueblo people in the central Mesa Verde region. To determine whether this premise is supported by data generated from lithic assemblages from the region, we pay particular attention to the proportion of local materials, especially Morrison rocks, that were recovered from households and communities through time.

Semilocal materials consist of Jurassic Morrison Brushy Basin chert (JMC) and igneous materials (OIG). Both of these medium-quality materials can be sourced (Arakawa 2006, 2012b). The sources of JMC are mostly found in the southwestern portion of the study area (near the Four Corners Monument), whereas igneous materials are in the southern portions of the study area close to and on Ute Mountain. Both sources are more than 18 km away from the nearest community center in the study, except for Castle Rock Pueblo (figure 15.1) (Arakawa and Gerhardt 2007). If lithic data reveals patterns in the frequencies of materials that are unrelated to distance, consideration must be given to supracommunity networks. For example, it may be that some households or communities in the study area have a relatively high frequency of JMC and igneous materials despite being distant from the quarries, possibly signaling a strong alliance with other communities that are closer to the quarries. Using this assumption and based on these data, we can infer that there may have been alliances among households and/or communities.

Obsidian (OBS), Narbona Pass chert (WPC), red jasper (RJS), and nonlocal chert/silt stone (NCS) are classified as nonlocal materials. Obsidian materials were usually procured from sources more than 300 km away, including sources in the northern Rio Grande region in New Mexico, Mount Taylor in New Mexico, and sources near Flagstaff, in northern Arizona. Narbona Pass chert can be traced to the Chuska Mountains in New Mexico, approximately 140 km away (Lightfoot and Etzkorn 1993, 158). Red jasper materials are most likely procured from areas near Cedar Mesa in southeastern Utah, about 100 km away. The nonlocal chert/siltstone category is used for raw material types not found in local or semilocal areas and often includes fairly high-quality materials used for making projectile points and bifaces.

Finally, other stone material types include conglomerate, gypsum/calcite/barite, metamorphic rocks, petrified wood, quartz, slate/shale, unknown chert/

siltstone, unknown silicified sandstone, and unknown stone. These materials would have been presumably procured and used for chipped-stone tools, ground-stone tools, and materials for jewelry making or other decoration. It is important for researchers to identify these raw material types as either local, semilocal, or nonlocal materials, especially petrified wood and unknown raw materials that were most likely used for chipped-stone tools.

RESULTS

Figure 15.2 illustrates the general trend for tools recovered from sites dating to the Basketmaker III period through Pueblo III period. Most cores and pecking-stones consist of low-quality materials, with only a few examples from local high-quality materials. For the formal tools, including projectile points, bifaces, and drills, local high-quality material types were most frequently used, although local low-quality and nonlocal materials were also used.

These results illustrate three patterns. First, the percentage of cores and peckingstones made of local low-quality materials (i.e., Morrison rocks) gradually increased from the Pueblo II period to the Pueblo III period.[4] Second, during the Pueblo II and III periods, formal tools (projectile points, bifaces, and drills) represent a high proportion of the local high-quality materials. Finally, the high proportion of nonlocal material types for projectile points, bifaces, and drills during the Basketmaker III period indicates these materials were preferred for formal tools.

Figure 15.3 shows the overall result of debitage analysis from sites during the Basketmaker III–Pueblo III periods. The majority of debitage materials consist of local low-quality material types, followed by local high-quality materials. The proportion of semilocal, nonlocal, and other raw material types is low. To better understand the broad pattern of each raw material type, we created figure 15.4. This result reveals interesting patterns. First, although the percentage of local high-quality material types does not change much in the Basketmaker III, Pueblo II and Pueblo III periods, the highest amount of local high-quality materials was used during the Pueblo I period. In addition, figure 15.4 shows a slight increase of these materials from the Pueblo II period to the Pueblo III.[5] Second, the ancestral Pueblo people of the Basketmaker III period used the most local low-quality materials of all time periods. Third, semilocal material types, especially Brushy Basin chert (107,924 pieces total; 922 igneous pieces total), were most commonly used during the Pueblo II period. Finally, the ancestral Pueblo people acquired nonlocal material types more commonly during the Pueblo I period, and there was a slight increase of these materials from the Pueblo II period to the Pueblo III. These results show that the Pueblo III period had the highest use of nonlocal material types.

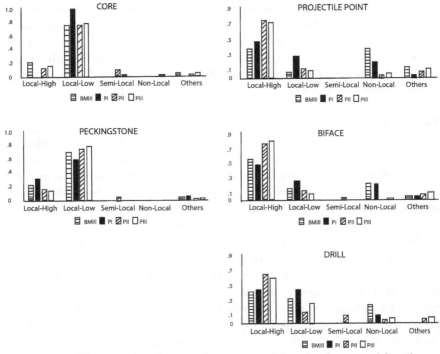

FIGURE 15.2. *The proportion of cores, peckingstones, and formal tools recovered from the CCAC excavated sites based on five different raw material types. Courtesy of the Crow Canyon Archaeological Center.*

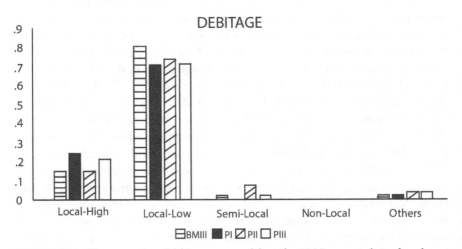

FIGURE 15.3. *The proportion of debitage recovered from the CCAC excavated sites based on five different raw material types. Courtesy of the Crow Canyon Archaeological Center.*

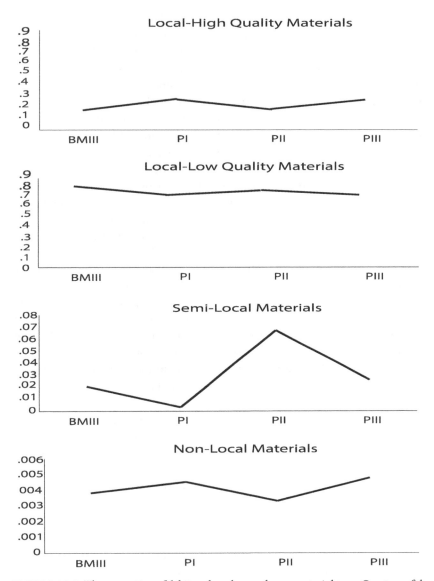

FIGURE 15.4. *The proportion of debitage based on each raw material type. Courtesy of the Crow Canyon Archaeological Center.*

INTERPRETATIONS

This research demonstrates several aspects of lithic procurement and, indirectly, sociopolitical organization in the study area from AD 600 to 1300. First, the study of raw material types, when associated with their lithological and geological formations, helps reconstruct where and how ancestral Pueblo people procured their lithic raw materials. Since Crow Canyon researchers have accurately developed a detailed analysis of lithology in the study area, studies focused on mobility, territoriality, and resource acquisition are possible. For example, the increasing proportion of Brushy Basin chert (semilocal material) during the Pueblo II period reveals that ancestral Pueblo people procured and used this raw material type for special purposes, such as ritual use. Although the quality of this material is equivalent to other local high-quality materials (e.g., ACH, KBC, and KDB), they preferred to acquire Brushy Basin chert despite being located more than 18 km away from the nearest community center (apart from Castle Rock Pueblo). Notably, Brushy Basin chert materials were typically used for tchamahia production; these tools may have been used for ceremonial purposes as noted by Parsons in her study of the Hopi (Parsons 1936). In addition, the high proportion of Brushy Basin chert utilized during the Pueblo II period suggests frequent mobility and/or interaction between those in the study area and the inhabitants in or near the Brushy Basin quarries of the Four Corners area. In fact, similar tool-stone procurement patterns are demonstrated for the Wetherill Mesa lithic assemblages in Mesa Verde National Park (Arakawa and Gerhardt 2007). Based on these results, we find that the proportion of Brushy Basin chert exponentially increased during the late Pueblo II period. This suggests that intraregional integration and/or trade increased in the Pueblo II period between people in the Mesa Verde National Park area and the McElmo–Yellow Jacket district. These data strengthen support for this premise.[6]

The results of debitage analyses based on raw material types indicate that tool-stone procurement of local high-quality materials increased from the Pueblo II period to the Pueblo III, while the proportion of semilocal materials decreased. This might indicate that ancestral Pueblo people relied heavily on chipped-stone raw materials close to their habitation areas and preferred not to travel or encroach on the territories of other groups. The reduction and/or restriction of territories might suggest that during the Pueblo III period, there is evidence for political autonomy in tandem with intraregional interaction, mobility, and/or migration. However, the proportion of nonlocal materials (obsidian, red jasper, Narbona Pass chert, and nonlocal chert/siltstone) increases slightly from the Pueblo II period to the Pueblo III. This indicates that although people experienced political autonomy and increased intraregional interactions within the study area, they also developed alliances and social networks, signaling a strong cooperation with communities in areas to the south, such as the northern Rio Grande region in New Mexico (Arakawa et al. 2011). The slight increase in the proportion of nonlocal material types is also seen in formal tools.

DISCUSSION AND CONCLUSION

This study demonstrates that lithic studies can provide reliable and essential data for understanding and reconstructing sociopolitical organization in agricultural societies. These data are attainable because Crow Canyon researchers have developed a reliable and repeatable lithic raw material classification system over the last forty years. In addition, Crow Canyon has developed a large and valuable lithic database (https://www.crowcanyon.org/site-reports-database-list/).

Although Crow Canyon's lithic database is rich, only a few researchers have utilized it for research. Lithic studies are informative because we can pinpoint potential sourcing areas at the local and regional scales. As this study demonstrates, researchers can use the proportion of tools and debitage assemblages to illuminate tool-stone procurement patterns. By doing so, these data also help us reconstruct sociopolitical organization—such as mobility, territoriality, and trade—and the development of political autonomy in agricultural societies through time.

NOTES

1. Arakawa et al. (2011) argued that the frequency of obsidian increased prior to the depopulation of the region around the late AD 1200s. This suggests that ancestral Pueblo people in the central Mesa Verde region connected and affiliated with people in the northern Rio Grande region, the location where immigrants settled as part of the migration process (see also the contention of the hypothesis by Moore et al. 2020).

2. The Duckfoot site and Castle Rock Pueblo lithic assemblages were originally analyzed by Arakawa (2006) as part of his dissertation research; others were analyzed by CCAC researchers. For the Duckfoot site and Castle Rock Pueblo lithic assemblages, when there were more than 300 pieces of debitage materials, Arakawa selected subsamples by using Randomtos Random Number Generator software. For example, when there were more than 300 pieces of Dakota/Burro Canyon silicified sandstone, he first segregated them by the four different size grades. If size 1 had 50 pieces, he selected subsamples of 25 (50 percent) from each size grade and the other size grades to obtain a total sample of about 150.

3. The majority of debitage recovered from these sites came from nonstructures (middens and cultural fills), but the BMIII, PII, and PIII assemblages also contained debitage recovered from structures. When we looked at the material type of the debitage recovered from nonstructure and structure contexts, we found they produced similar results, so we combined the datasets for this study.

4. Both the Duckfoot site and the Pueblo I assemblage at Shields Pueblo contained only two cores; both are made of JMS. This may be due to the small sample size from Pueblo I period contexts at these sites.

5. It is important that although Arakawa (2006) investigated more than ninety local quarries in the central Mesa Verde region, it is possible that high-quality materials have yet to be sourced to all the local high-quarry sites in existence.

6. It might be possible to argue that a "middle person" (or trader) brought Brushy Basin chert to these communities, since the material type had a significant meaning or had a commodity value for ancestral Pueblo people. If this indeed took place, it might be difficult to argue for an increased social network, because the middle person from other areas would have brough them to sites in Mesa Verde National Park and others in the central Mesa Verde region. However, we argue that Brushy Basin chert is deposited in many areas in the Four Corners area; thus ancestral Pueblo people who resided near the quarries could have easily procured and moved them to other communities. Therefore, we insist that a direct relationship existed between ancestral Pueblo people in Mesa Verde National Park and those in the Four Corners area.

REFERENCES

Ahler, Stanley A. 1989. "Mass Analysis of Flaking Debris: Studying the Forest Rather than the Tree." In *Alternative Approaches to Lithic Analysis*, Archeological Papers No. 1, edited by D. Henry and G. Odell, 85–118. Arlington, VA: American Anthropological Association.

Arakawa, Fumiyasu. 2000. "Lithic Analysis of Yellow Jacket Pueblo as a Tool for Understanding and Visualizing Women's Roles in Procuring, Utilizing, and Making Stone Tools." MA thesis, University of Idaho, Moscow.

Arakawa, Fumiyasu. 2006. "Lithic Raw Material Procurement and the Social Landscape in the Central Mesa Verde Region, AD 600–1300." PhD diss., Washington State University, Pullman.

Arakawa, Fumiyasu. 2012a. "Cyclical Cultural Trajectories: A Case Study from the Mesa Verde Region." *Journal of Anthropological Research* 68.1 (March): 35–69.

Arakawa, Fumiyasu. 2012b. "Toolstone Procurement Patterns in the Central Mesa Verde Region through Time." In *Emergence and Collapse of Early Villages: Models of Central Mesa Verde Archaeology*, edited by Timothy Kohler and Mark Varien, 175–196. Berkley: University of California.

Arakawa, Fumiyasu. 2013. "Gendered Analysis of Lithics from the Central Mesa Verde Region." *Kiva* 78 (3): 279–312.

Arakawa, Fumiyasu, and Andrew I. Duff. 2002. *Transitions in Mesa Verde Region Communities and Lithic Procurement Strategies.* Denver: Society for American Archaeology.

Arakawa, Fumiyasu, and Kimberlee M. Gerhardt. 2007. "Toolstone Procurement Patterns on the Wetherill Mesa from A.D. 600 to 1280." *Kiva* 73 (1): 69–87.

Arakawa, Fumiyasu, and Kimberlee M. Gerhardt. 2009. "Geoarchaeology Investigation of Lithic Resources in the Central Mesa Verde Region, Colorado, USA." *Geoarchaeology* 24 (2): 204–223.

Arakawa, Fumiyasu, and Christopher Nicholson. 2020. "Identifying New Quarries as a Method for Expanding Research: A GIS Case Study from the Mesa Verde Region in the American Southwest." *Journal of Archaeological Science: Report* 33 (October): 1–9.

Arakawa, Fumiyasu, Christopher Nicholson, and Jeff Rasic. 2013. "The Consequences of Social Processes: Aggregate Populations, Projectile Point Accumulation, and Subsistence Patterns in the American Southwest." *American Antiquity* 78 (1): 147–164.

Arakawa, Fumiyasu, Scott Ortman, M. Steve Shackley, and Andrew Duff. 2011. "Obsidian Toolstone Procurement in the Central Mesa Verde." *American Antiquity* 76.4 (October): 773–795.

Brew, John O. 1946. *Archaeology of Alkali Ridge, Southeastern Utah*. Vol. 21, Papers of the Peabody Museum of American Archaeology and Ethnology, Harvard University. Cambridge, MA: Harvard University Press.

Cameron, Catherine M. 2001. "Pink Chert, Projectile Points, and the Chacoan Regional System." *American Antiquity* 66.1 (January): 79–101.

Churchill, Melissa J., ed. 2002. *The Archaeology of Woods Canyon Pueblo: A Canyon-Rim Village in Southwestern Colorado*. https://www.crowcanyon.org/ResearchReports/WoodsCanyon/Text/wcpw_contentsvolume.asp.

Diederichs, Shanna R., ed. 2020. "The Basketmaker Communities Project." https://www.crowcanyon.org/ResearchReports/BasketmakerCommunities/basketmaker_communities_project_final.pdf.

Driver, Jonathan C. 2002. "Faunal Variation and Change in the Northern San Juan Region." In *Seeking the Center Place: Archaeology and Ancient Communities in the Mesa Verde Region*, edited by Mark D. Varien and Richard H. Wilshusen, 143–162. Salt Lake City: University of Utah Press.

Glowacki, Donna M. 2006. "The Social Landscape of Depopulation: The Northern San Juan, A.D. 1150–1300." PhD diss., Arizona State University, Tempe.

Glowacki, Donna M. 2015. *Living and Leaving: A Social History of Regional Depopulation in Thirteenth-Century Mesa Verde*. Tucson: University of Arizona Press.

Kohler, Timothy A., and Laura Ellyson. 2019. "In and Out of Chains? The Changing Social Contract in the Pueblo Southwest, AD 600–1300." In *Ten Thousand Years of Inequality: The Archaeology of Wealth Differences*, edited by Timothy A. Kohler and Michael E. Smith, 130–154. Tucson: University of Arizona Press.

Kuckelman, Kristin A., ed. 2003. "The Archaeology of Yellow Jacket Pueblo (Site 5MT5): Excavations at a Large Community Center in Southwestern Colorado." http://www.crowcanyon.org/yellowjacket.

Kuckelman, Kristin A. 2007. "The Archaeology of Sand Canyon Pueblo: Intensive Excavations at a Late-Thirteenth-Century Village in Southwestern Colorado." http://www.crowcanyon.org/sandcanyon. Accessed May 9, 2021.

Kuckelman, Kristin A. 2010. "The Depopulation of Sand Canyon Pueblo: A Large Ancestral Pueblo Village in Southwestern Colorado." *American Antiquity* 75.3 (July): 497–526.

Kuckelman, Kristin A., Grant D. Coffey, and Steve R. Copeland. 2009. "Interim Descriptive Report of Research at Goodman Point Pueblo (5MT604). Montezuma County,

Colorado. 2005–2008." https://www.crowcanyon.org/ResearchReports/Goodman Point/interim_reports/2005_2008/GPP_interim_report_2005_2008.pdf.

Kuckelman, Kristin A., Ricky Lightfoot, and Debra L. Martin. 2000. "Changing Patterns of Violence in the Northern San Juan Region." *Kiva* 66.1 (July): 147–166.

Lightfoot, Ricky R., and Mary C. Etzkorn, eds. 1993. *The Duckfoot Site, Volume 1: Descriptive Archaeology.* Occasional Papers, no. 3. Cortez, CO: Crow Canyon Archaeological Center.

Lipe, William D. 2006. "Notes from the North." In *The Archaeology of Chaco Canyon: An Eleventh-Century Pueblo Regional Center,* edited by Stephen H. Lekson. 261–313. Santa Fe, NM: School of American Research Press.

Lipe, William D., and Scott G. Ortman. 1998. "Spatial Patterning in Northern San Juan Villages, A.D. 1050–1300." *Kiva* 66 (1): 91–122.

Moore, James L., Eric Blinman, and M. Steven Shackley. 2020. "Temporal Variation in Obsidian Procurement in the Northern Rio Grande and Its Implications for Obsidian Movement into the San Juan Area." *American Antiquity* 85 (1): 152–170.

Neily, Robert B. 1983. "The Prehistoric Community on the Colorado Plateau: An Approach to the Study of Change and Survival in the Northern San Juan Area of the American Southwest." PhD diss., Southern Illinois University, Carbondale.

Ortman, Scott G., Erin L. Baxter, Carole L. Graham, G. Robin Lyle, Lew W. Matis, Jamie A. Merewether, R. David Satterwhite, and Jonathan D. Till. 2005. "The Crow Canyon Archaeological Center Laboratory Manual, Version 1." https://www.crowcanyon.org/ResearchReports/LabManual/LaboratoryManual.pdf.

Parsons, Elsie Clews. 1936. "Early Relations between Hopi and Keres." *American Anthropologist* 38:554–560.

Plog, Stephen, and Carrie Heitmann. 2010. "Hierarchy and Long-Term Social Inequality in the American Southwest, A.D. 800–1200: Microcosm and Macrocosm." *Proceedings of the National Academy of Science (USA)* 107.46 (October): 19619–19626.

Potter, James M., and Jason P. Chupuka. 2007. "Early Pueblo Communities and Cultural Diversity in the Durango Area." *Kiva* 72 (4): 407–429.

Potter, James M., Jason P. Chupuka, and Jerry Fetterman. 2012. "The Eastern Mesa Verde Region: Migrants, Cultural Diversity, and Violence in the East." In *Crucible of Pueblos: The Early Pueblo Period in the Northern Southwest,* edited by Richard H. Wilshusen, Gregson Schachner, and James R. Allison, 53–71. Los Angeles: Cotsen Institute of Archaeology Press.

Powers, Robert P., William B. Gillespie, and Steven H. Lekson. 1983. *The Outlier Survey: A Regional View of Settlement in the San Juan Basin.* Reports of the Chaco Center no. 3. Albuquerque: Division of Cultural Research, National Park Service.

Varien, Mark D. 1999. *Sedentism and Mobility in a Social Landscape: Mesa Verde and Beyond.* Tucson: University of Arizona Press.

Varien, Mark D., Scott G. Ortman, Timothy A. Kohler, Donna M. Glowacki, and C. David Johnson. 2007. "Historical Ecology in the Mesa Verde Region: Results from the Village Project." *American Antiquity* 72.2 (April): 273–299.

Ward, Christine G. 2004. "Exploring Meanings of Chacoan Community Great Houses through Chipped Stone: A Biographical Approach." PhD diss., Department of Anthropology, University of Colorado, Boulder.

Wilshusen, Richard H. 1995. *The Cedar Hill Special Treatment Project: Late Pueblo I, Early Navajo, and Historic Occupations in Northwestern New Mexico*. Research Paper 1. Dolores, CO: La Plata Archaeological Consultants.

Wilshusen, Richard H. 1999. "Basketmaker III (A.D. 500–750)." In *Colorado Prehistory: A Context for the Southern Colorado River Basin*, edited by William D. Lipe, Mark D. Varien, and Richard H. Wilshusen, 166–194. Cortez: Colorado Council of Professional Archaeologists.

Wilshusen, Richard H., and Scott G. Ortman. 1999. "Rethinking the Pueblo I Period in the San Juan Drainage: Aggregation, Migration, and Cultural Diversity." *Kiva* 64 (3): 369–399.

Wilshusen, Richard H., and Ruth M. Van Dyke. 2006. "Chaco's Beginnings." In *The Archaeology of Chaco Canyon: An Eleventh-Century Pueblo Regional Center*, edited by Stephen H. Lekson, 211–260. Santa Fe, NM: School of American Research Press.

Windes, Thomas C. 2003. "This Old House: Construction and Abandonment at Pueblo Bonito." In *Pueblo Bonito: Center of the Chacoan World*, edited by Jill E. Neitzel, 14–32. Washington, DC: Smithsonian Press.

Whittaker, John C. 1987. "Making Arrowpoints in the Prehistoric Pueblo." *Lithic Technology* 16 (1): 1–12.

16

Leaving Town

Similarities and Differences in Ancestral Pueblo Community
Dissolution Practices in the Mesa Verde and Northern Rio Grande Regions

MICHAEL ADLER AND MICHELLE HEGMON

Both authors of this chapter are privileged to have been part of Crow Canyon's early years. Adler began work at Crow Canyon in 1983, and Hegmon began in 1986. Crow Canyon's early focus on Sand Canyon Pueblo strongly influenced both of our subsequent research interests and is the primary reason we chose to contrast Sand Canyon Pueblo's occupation with Pot Creek Pueblo, a roughly contemporaneous experiment in village life in the northern Rio Grande region.

Ancestral Pueblo communities in the Southwest have unique histories of occupation, settlement growth, and, in many cases, the departure of community members to other settlements both near and far. These unique trajectories, when compared across time and space, often display important parallels in the processes through which individuals and groups coalesced and subsequently moved. These similarities provide important avenues to broadening our understandings of how villagers contended with conflict, negotiated periods of resource scarcity, and experimented with social strategies and beliefs foundational to descendant Pueblo communities living in the Southwest today.

https://doi.org/10.5876/9781646424597.c016

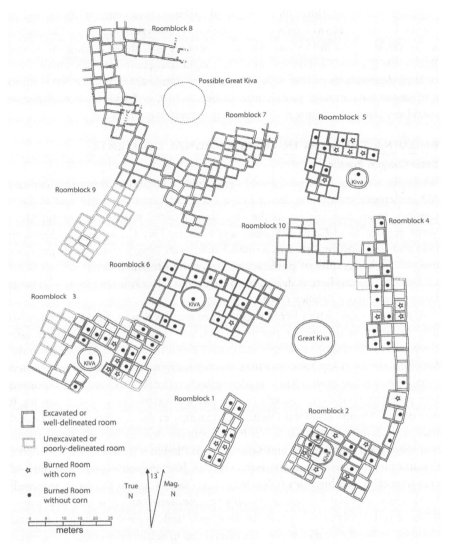

FIGURE 16.1. *Plan map, Pot Creek Pueblo. Map adapted by Adler.*

To that end we compare two large, relatively brief village occupations in the northern Southwest: Sand Canyon Pueblo and Pot Creek Pueblo (figure 16.1). Our comparison is guided by several basic questions: Where did the people come from before they aggregated and formed each village? How many people lived there, and for how long? What can we say about their social organization? Finally, what were the circumstances that brought each occupation to an end, and how did people leaving the settlements prepare various village spaces as part of their departure decision? Although the regional aftermath associated with the end of Sand Canyon Pueblo saw tens of thousands of Pueblo people leaving the central Mesa Verde region in the late thirteenth century AD, those leaving Pot Creek Pueblo likely moved a short distance into neighboring communities where some of their descendants still live today. Despite this significant difference, we want to emphasize the common foundations of how, when, and why these community members came together and subsequently moved to new places.

BUILDING THE SITES IN THEIR REGIONAL CONTEXTS

Sand Canyon Pueblo

We begin with Sand Canyon Pueblo (5MT765), a large, late thirteenth-century AD settlement situated on the rim of a small canyon at the north end of Sand Canyon, in an area known as the "McElmo Dome" within the central Mesa Verde region. Sand Canyon Pueblo was excavated by Crow Canyon between 1984 and 1993 and reported in Kristin Kuckelman (2007); that report provides links to a bibliography of publications about the site and a detailed map. Most of what we discuss here is drawn from that report, Kuckelman (2010), and Scott Ortman and Bruce Bradley (2002).

Across the larger Mesa Verde region, sites such as Sand Canyon Pueblo with fifty or more structures or public architecture are community centers (see Glowacki et al., chapter 12 in this volume). Fifteen of these are known from the McElmo Dome study area, and they are regularly spaced (Ortman and Varien 2007). Overall, the central Mesa Verde region is estimated to have had a momentary population of 25,000 people by the mid-thirteenth century AD, making it one of the densest ancestral Pueblo occupations in the northern Southwest at that time. Some central Mesa Verde community centers include several sites that were used sequentially, and Sand Canyon Pueblo is part of such a complex. Community centers across the northern San Juan region display a variety of characteristics and histories (Glowacki 2015). Sand Canyon Pueblo is one well-known example, but it is not necessarily representative of the region as a whole. While it is unlikely that any one site be considered "typical," William Lipe and Ortman (2000) document some commonalities in settlement layout for central Mesa Verde community centers.

Prior to about AD 1250, many central Mesa Verde community centers served dispersed communities with habitations scattered across the landscape, a community dynamic stretching back as far as the Basketmaker III period in this area (Schleher et al., chapter 10 in this volume). After that time, however, this dispersed settlement configuration was largely replaced with a highly aggregated settlement strategy, as the occupants of small sites moved into large community centers with defensive capabilities, including Sand Canyon Pueblo. This aggregation was part of a larger regional process as populations moved to areas—including the McElmo Dome—with good agricultural capabilities, resulting in population-resource imbalances and in some cases violence (Kohler et al., chapter 3 in this volume; Schwindt et al. 2016).

Demographic analysis concludes that the pre-AD 1250 population in the upper Sand Canyon locale was not nearly large enough to account for the post-AD 1250 population in Sand Canyon Pueblo. Thus, many households must have immigrated from elsewhere to join the Sand Canyon community (Ortman and Varien 2007; Schleher et al., chapter 14 in this volume). It is possible that those immigrants came from other parts of the larger northern San Juan region. Schleher et al. (chapter 14 in this volume) identify similarities in communities of practice in pottery production as one indicator that immigrants were most likely from the central Mesa Verde region, but specific source locations remain unknown.

Sand Canyon Pueblo is built of masonry and includes approximately 420 rooms, ninety kivas, a great kiva, and a D-shaped structure. The entire architectural complex was arranged in an arc around a plaza and spring and surrounded by a "massive" stone enclosing wall that incorporated a series of towers (Kuckelman 2010, 499). The enclosing wall was built in a single episode, and the various sets of rooms added within a few decades, indicating a planned and organized but not unitary construction (Ortman and Bradley 2002). Excavators estimate that it housed 400–600 people at the height of its occupation. The earliest construction at Sand Canyon Pueblo dates to about AD 1250, and construction continued in the 1260s until at least 1271. The latest tree-ring date is AD 1277vv, indicating some activity at the site until that year or shortly thereafter. Thus, Sand Canyon Pueblo was built, lived in, and depopulated over the course of about thirty years, and the final depopulation of Sand Canyon Pueblo was part of the final depopulation of the northern San Juan region in the early AD 1280s. Kuwanwisiwma and Bernardini (chapter 5 in this volume) support the interpretation that migrants moved into large settlements prior to the depopulation of the central Mesa Verde region.

Pot Creek Pueblo

Pot Creek Pueblo (LA260) is an ancestral Pueblo settlement in the Taos area of the northern Rio Grande region in New Mexico (figure 16.1). It was one of three large, aggregated villages founded in the Taos area during the thirteenth century AD; the other two—Taos and Picuris—are still homes to Northern Tiwa–speaking peoples today. Taos and Picuris community members recognize various cultural affiliations to Pot Creek Pueblo (Brown 1973; Fowles 2004).

Our archaeological understandings of Pot Creek Pueblo are based on field school excavations that started in the 1950s and continued until the early 2000s (Adler 2021; Arbolino 2001; Crown 1991; Fowles 2004). As was the case at Sand Canyon Pueblo—prior to the aggregation at Pot Creek Pueblo, Taos, and

Picuris—the local population mostly lived in small, dispersed settlements in the Pot Creek drainage. However, in contrast to the settlement history of Sand Canyon Pueblo, Severin Fowles's (2004) synthesis of the local settlement history established that in the early AD 1200s, prior to the major construction events at Pot Creek Pueblo, there was a tight cluster of nearly two dozen smaller unit pueblos within several hundred meters of where Pot Creek Pueblo would soon be built. By the early AD 1200s, at least 300–400 people lived in this cluster and likely comprised one part of the founding population of Pot Creek Pueblo; however, there is also evidence, detailed under "Community Social Organization," that a portion of the Pot Creek Pueblo residents came from outside the Taos area (Fowles 2005). Furthermore, Crown et al. (1996) argue that northern Rio Grande community centers were largely built by peoples who had lived in aggregated pueblos elsewhere and were very familiar with the templates for site layout. A final difference is the scale of regional populations. Extensive regional survey in the Taos area (Fowles 2004; Herold and Luebben 1968; Woosley 1986) concludes that Taos region populations probably numbered 2,000–3,000 people, smaller than the central Mesa Verde region population by a factor of ten. Also, in contrast to Sand Canyon Pueblo, there is limited evidence that violence contributed to the founding of Pot Creek Pueblo. Rather, the aggregation into Pot Creek Pueblo and other large sites following a significant period of intercommunity conflict during the Valdez phase (AD 980–1200) may have quelled the earlier cycles of conflict in the Taos region.

Pot Creek Pueblo is built of coursed adobe comprising ten separate roomblocks, each containing between twelve and thirty-five ground-floor rooms (figure 16.1). Of the estimated 284 ground-floor rooms that have been mapped, 148 have been tested or fully excavated. While parts of the village architecture reached three stories, most of the structures were one to two stories, leading to an estimated 350–450 rooms. Population estimates vary depending on what proxy one uses to go from rooms to people. Based on architectural configurations of definable households (Arbolino 2001), population estimates fall between 400 and 500 individuals at the height of the Pot Creek Pueblo occupation in the early fourteenth century AD, about the same as Sand Canyon Pueblo. Roomblocks at Pot Creek Pueblo are built in definable episodes, with the majority of construction episodes containing three or fewer rooms, indicating that most of the site growth was based on the integration of household-level groups into existing architectural complexes.

At both Sand Canyon Pueblo and Pot Creek Pueblo, hundreds of living spaces were built, used, and ultimately emptied of human occupants over a span of decades, about three at Sand Canyon Pueblo (AD 1250–1280s) and six at Pot Creek Pueblo (AD 1265–1320s). At Sand Canyon Pueblo, construction spanned about two decades. At Pot Creek Pueblo, there were two major construction episodes. Pot Creek Pueblo's first cutting date cluster is AD 1265, followed by an intense period of construction during the AD 1270s, and an isolated construction surge in the mid-AD 1280s. Construction slowed in the last decades of the thirteenth century AD, and there may have been a short-term relocation of part of the village population in the AD 1290s. The latest cutting date of AD 1319 from the great kiva at Pot Creek Pueblo indicates that people left the site in the early AD 1320s.

COMMUNITY SOCIAL ORGANIZATION

Many eastern Pueblo communities, including those at Taos and Picuris, have clearly delineated dual organizations (Fox 1967; Ortiz 1969; Parsons 1936; Ware 2014). Ortiz's (1969) detailed explanation of Tewa dual organization at Ohkay Owingeh serves as the template for Rio Grande Pueblo moiety structure, but as Fowles (2005) argues, the historical contingencies of these organizational structures must be considered as well. Evidence for dual organization is evident at both Sand Canyon Pueblo and Pot Creek Pueblo, although to different degrees.

At Sand Canyon Pueblo the architectural layout of the household clusters as well as the overall site configuration argue for multiple social organization groupings. The settlement has two separate halves divided by a small drainage, two ritual structures, a D-shaped building, and a great kiva, all suggestive of dual organization (Kuckelman 2007). However, both ritual structures are in the same (west) half of the site. Furthermore, there are also about ninety small kivas at Sand Canyon Pueblo, suggesting that ritual was organized at multiple scales, including household as well as possibly moiety- or site-wide. We suspect that the principles of dual organization were just beginning to emerge at Sand Canyon Pueblo.

Evidence for dual organization is much stronger at Pot Creek Pueblo. Severin Fowles (2013) links the foundations of dual organization found at both Taos and Picuris Pueblos to the ancestral occupation at Pot Creek Pueblo and the conjoining of historically separate peoples who occupied Pot Creek. Fowles points to architectural layout, room features, and ceramic evidence to argue that at least two groups with differing settlement histories and cultural identities occupied the village, and immigrants originated from areas to the south, in and around present-day Espanola and Santa Fe, New Mexico. He proposes that there was an early conjoining of southern groups with existing agrarian populations in the Taos area, reflected in the different layouts of late twelfth- and early thirteenth-century AD surface pueblos. Fowles (2004) associates L-shaped site configurations with the later immigrants into the Taos region and the C-shaped roomblock configurations with the autochthonous groups resident in the Taos area. Fowles (2013) dates this possible immigration from the Tewa area to sometime in the late twelfth century AD, whereas Adler (in prep) dates the immigration to the later thirteenth century. Temporal differences aside, there is consensus that the dual social organization at both Taos and Picuris Pueblos finds its roots in the joining of local and nonlocal peoples at Pot Creek Pueblo and possibly concurrently in the other Taos region community centers. Recent reinterpretations of the ancestral architecture, site layout, and presence of great kivas at Picuris Pueblo support a long history of dual organization at that settlement as well (Adler in prep).

A second important difference between Sand Canyon Pueblo and Pot Creek Pueblo is indicated by the number and distribution of small kivas and thus how they were used and what role they played in household and suprahousehold ritual activity. At Sand Canyon Pueblo, residents built one kiva for every 4–5 surface rooms; the ratio at Pot Creek Pueblo is 70–100 rooms per kiva. There is strong evidence that the Sand Canyon Pueblo small kivas were household-level facilities used for both domestic and ritual activity (Kuckelman 2010). In contrast, the small kivas at Pot Creek Pueblo would have been used by, and associated with, multihousehold ritual and social groups (Adler 1993). Both communities have several ritual structures that are much larger than these small kivas, so there may have been a more consistent use of these larger structures as community-level ritual spaces at both villages.

LEAVING TOWN: OUT-MIGRATION AND CLOSURE

The final depopulations of Sand Canyon Pueblo in the AD 1280s and Pot Creek Pueblo in the AD 1320s involve major differences in reasons for emigration as well as similarities in how people decommissioned their lived spaces. Kuckelman (2010) detailed how conditions changed in the last few years of occupation at Sand Canyon Pueblo by comparing material from general middens to what she calls "abandonment" contexts. She found a shift toward reliance on wild resources, including wild plants, cottontail, and deer, likely necessitated by decline in maize production in the late AD 1270s and the onset of the Great Drought starting in AD 1276. By this time, the two large, public buildings (the D-shaped structure and great kiva) were no longer in use. Pot Creek Pueblo occupants may have been less directly affected by the Great Drought, given the relatively high elevation (7,600 ft.) of the settlement and lower overall population density in the Taos area, though, due to the limited sampling strategies employed in early excavations at the settlement, we do not have high-resolution floral and faunal data to support this interpretation empirically.

Soon after the onset of the Great Drought, Sand Canyon Pueblo was attacked. Many rooms, mostly small kivas, were burned, and at least thirty-five people died, probably killed in the attack (Kuckelman 2010, 502, 509). The survivors did not rebuild but left Sand Canyon Pueblo and probably the region. Many rooms contained de facto refuse, indicating that they did not take much with them (Kuckelman 2010, 502). Assuming the population estimate for the site (400–600 people) is correct and that most were still resident at the site at the time of the attack, there would have been hundreds of survivors.

Although the details are complex and fill many volumes, it is clear that the northern San Juan region was almost entirely depopulated by AD 1285 and that many of the people who left moved to the northern Rio Grande (Glowacki 2015; Ortman 2012). Kuckelman's analysis of Sand Canyon Pueblo kivas shows that seventeen of twenty-four ("abandonment categories" "2, 3, and 4" in 2010, table 1) were used until the end of the site's occupation, in the AD 1270s or possibly early AD 1280s. Thus, the final depopulation of Sand Canyon Pueblo—after the attack—coincides with the final depopulation of the region. More than 12,500 tree-ring dates are reported for the northern San Juan region, and none post-dates AD 1281, indicating that the region was depopulated shortly after that date.

The survivors who left Sand Canyon Pueblo around AD 1280 would have been part of a large stream of migrants, many moving to the northern Rio Grande, where they and their descendants reorganized their society and changed much of their material culture (Ortman 2012). It is not possible to say exactly where the people who left Sand Canyon Pueblo went, or to know if they maintained their community, although genetic evidence summarized by Kuckelman (2010) indicates some similarities between Sand Canyon Pueblo and people at sites on the Pajarito Plateau and at Pecos Pueblo. It is clear that the people who left Sand Canyon Pueblo moved a long distance, likely hundreds of kilometers away. Despite that present interpretations of Pot Creek Pueblo identify immigrants as coming from the Tewa Basin to the south, it is not out of the realm of possibility that some of these migrants originated in or around the central Mesa Verde region.

In contrast to the violent end at Sand Canyon Pueblo, there are no indications of open conflict, raiding, or violent death at Pot Creek Pueblo. Furthermore, the people who left Pot Creek Pueblo stayed in the area, moving to either Picuris or Taos Pueblos, each only 16 km from Pot Creek Pueblo. It is possible others may have returned to the Tewa Basin, particularly those who appear to have immi-grated to the Taos area in the twelfth or thirteenth centuries AD. The dearth of de facto refuse in the rooms at Pot Creek Pueblo indicate a short-distance move, one in which all usable, portable items could have been taken to their new home. Oral accounts from members of Taos Pueblo and relating to Pot Creek Pueblo identify past groups such as the Water People who migrated into the area, con-joining with groups having different histories in and around the area (Fowles 2005, 2013). Pot Creek Pueblo is identified in oral traditions as Taïtona, the place of the Water People. These traditional histories agree that various peoples with different identities, and likely different locations of origin, coalesced at Taïtona, and archaeological lines of evidence discussed in the preceding sections align with those histories.

Structure Decommissioning

We end our comparison with a discussion of commonalities in structure decommissioning. Although the two settlements were depopulated amidst quite different conditions, with deadly conflict at Sand Canyon Pueblo and the out-migration of tens of thousands of people compared to no evidence of conflict and very short-distance relocation of Pot Creek Pueblo villagers, there are transregional, shared practices of leaving one's village. Specifically, at both sites there is evidence of deliberate room closure through burning.

Although an attack that left at least thirty-five dead is associated with the end of Sand Canyon Pueblo, there is evidence that the survivors did not simply flee. Rather, they deliberately burned at least some rooms at the site to establish some degree of closure before joining the migration stream that left the region. Specifically, as Kuckelman (2010, 519–520) describes, sometime after the attack the roofs of many kivas were burned. These were made of earth-covered logs and would not have burned easily or accidentally, even if touched by raiders' torches. Rather, it is more likely that they were deliberately burned either by surviving residents or by friendly nearby neighbors.

Evidence of room decommissioning by burning has been documented in various surface and subsurface structures throughout Pot Creek Pueblo. Unlike patterns at sites with well-documented destruction in which entire blocks of rooms were consumed by fire (e.g., Chodistaas Pueblo [Whittlesey and Reid 2019]), structure burning at Pot Creek Pueblo is spatially spotty. Of the nearly 150 rooms partially or completely excavated at the site, 62 show evidence of partial or complete destruction through burning (figure 16.1). Evidence for burning includes oxidization and reduction of adobe walls, charred structural timbers, and carbonized corn and other botanical materials on room floors.

A second important pattern emerging from excavations of surface architecture at Pot Creek Pueblo is that very few of the rooms appear to have been trash filled, meaning that the rooms were in use, or were viable living spaces, at the time the major occupation of the site ceased, probably sometime around AD 1320–1325. Of the rooms excavated, two signatures dominate the archaeological deposits. The first signature is a nearly complete lack of either primary or secondary deposits in the surface rooms. Although these empty rooms may have been used as storage spaces during the active occupation of the site, it is also possible that the rooms were cleaned out during and after the primary occupation of the site ceased in the early fourteenth century AD.

The second signature at Pot Creek Pueblo is the presence of large amounts of stored corn and associated domestic artifacts, commonly associated with a significant level of burning, in a number of the rooms. Subsurface architecture was also terminated through the use of fire at Pot Creek Pueblo. Four small subterranean kivas and a single great kiva have been excavated. All four kivas show evidence that their final treatment involved burning but only after having been prepared for their fiery decommissioning. The great kiva, according to Ronald Wetherington (1968), was not burned, but he also argues that construction of the great kiva was never fully completed.

All indications point to a planned decommissioning of lived spaces at Pot Creek Pueblo including the purposeful placement of items best understood as offerings in various rooms and kivas, and the intentional burning of many of these same spaces. More detailed interpretations of these contexts indicate that these final acts were not wonton destruction or the result of violent raiding. In fact, the use of fire and fire products, particularly ash, are common prophylactics used not only across Pueblo and non-Pueblo cultures in the American Southwest but also many other areas across the world (Adler in prep; Roth and Adams 2021). Specifically, ethnographic groups utilizing fire as a protectant do so to shield these spaces from witches or other malevolent individuals possessing supernatural means to defile lived spaces and create imbalance, illness, and evil throughout the worlds of the living and the dead (Darling 1998; Walker 1998).

CONCLUSIONS

When we began work at Crow Canyon Archaeological Center in the 1980s, there were precious few archaeological projects contending with questions of social agency, multiethnic community histories, or the inclusion of oral traditional perspectives from descendant populations. Research generated at the Crow Canyon Archaeological Center over the past four decades has been seminal in making these approaches part of our understandings of the past, and Crow Canyon research continues to forge new perspectives on both ancestral and descendant Indigenous peoples in the American Southwest.

In keeping with this research tradition, we have emphasized a range of interesting parallels and significant contrasts in this comparison of Pot Creek and Sand Canyon Pueblos. These two villages became large population centers in two distant regions within about a decade of one another and rapidly reached similar maximal populations of 400–500 people.

Both settlements drew from locally dispersed smaller settlements as well as migrants from elsewhere, though at Pot Creek Pueblo there is clearer evidence of both local and nonlocal peoples coalescing. Neither settlement was long lived; Pot Creek Pueblo lasted about sixty years (AD 1260–1320), several decades longer than Sand Canyon Pueblo (AD 1250–1280). Both communities apparently embraced dual organization as an overarching social organizational strategy, although such organization may have been in its early stages at Sand Canyon Pueblo. Households were also important organizational units at both settlements, but there were major differences in use of small kivas. At Sand Canyon Pueblo one or sometimes several kivas are part of nearly all household architectural units, whereas at Pot Creek Pueblo kivas are much less common and would have been shared by at least several households.

The two communities, which saw very different ends, still decommissioned their architecture in similar ways. At both, once people decided to leave, they put some or many of their lived spaces to the torch. What we might misinterpret as destruction and final desecration is better understood as part of a pan-Pueblo practice that allows one to leave home and ritual spaces by protecting these places with fire and protecting the ancestors who still occupy the village.

REFERENCES

Adler, Michael A. 1993. "Why Is a Kiva? New Interpretations of Prehistoric Social Integrative Architecture in the Northern Rio Grande Region of New Mexico." *Journal of Anthropological Research* 49 (4):319–346.

Adler, Michael A. 2021. "Fire, Ash and Sanctuary: Pyrotechnology as Protection in the Pre-Colonial Northern Rio Grande." In *Agent of Change: The Deposition and Manipulation of Ash in the Past*, edited by Barbara Roth and E. C. Adams, 76–93. New York City: Berghahn Books.

Adler, Michael A. In prep. "Tiwa Resilience: The Archaeology of Pueblo Community Persistence." Manuscript in preparation for University of Arizona Press.

Arbolino, Risa Diemond. 2001. "Agricultural Strategies and Labor Organization: An Ethnohistoric Approach to the Study of Prehistoric Farming in the Taos Area of Northern New Mexico." PhD diss., Southern Methodist University, Dallas.

Brown, Daniel. 1973. "Structural Change at Picuris Pueblo, New Mexico." PhD. diss., University of Arizona, Tucson.

Crown, Patricia. 1991. "Evaluating the Construction Sequence and Population of Pot Creek Pueblo, Northern New Mexico." *American Antiquity* 56 (2): 291–314.

Crown, Patricia, Janet D. Orcutt, and Timothy A. Kohler. 1996. "Pueblo Cultures in Transition: The Northern Rio Grande." In *The Prehistoric Pueblo World, A.D. 1150–1350*, edited by Michael Adler, 188–204. Tucson: University of Arizona Press.

Darling, Andrew J. 1998. "Mass Inhumation and the Execution of Witches in the American Southwest." *American Anthropologist* 100 (3): 732–752.

Fowles, Severin. 2004. "The Making of Made People: The Prehistoric Evolution of Hierocracy among the Northern Tiwa of New Mexico." PhD diss., University of Michigan, Ann Arbor.

Fowles, Severin. 2005. "Historical Contingency and the Prehistoric Foundations of Moiety Organization among the Eastern Pueblos." *Journal of Anthropological Research* 61 (1): 25–52.

Fowles, Severin. 2013. *An Archaeology of Doings: Secularism and the Study of Pueblo Religion.* Santa Fe, NM: School for Advanced Research Press.

Fox, Robin. 1967. *The Keresan Bridge: A Problem in Pueblo Ethnology.* New York City: Humanities Press.

Glowacki, Donna M. 2015. *Living and Leaving: A Social History of Regional Depopulation in Thirteenth-Century Mesa Verde.* Tucson: University of Arizona Press.

Herold, Laurance C., and Ralph A. Luebben. 1968. *Papers on Taos Archaeology*. Taos: Fort Burgwin Research Center.

Kuckelman, Kristin A., ed. 2007. *The Archaeology of Sand Canyon Pueblo: Intensive Excavations at a Late-Thirteenth-Century Village in Southwestern Colorado*. https://www.crowcanyon.org/ResearchReports/SandCanyon/Text/scpw_contentsvolume.asp.

Kuckelman, Kristin A. 2010. "The Depopulation of Sand Canyon Pueblo, a Large Ancestral Pueblo Village in Southwestern Colorado." *American Antiquity* 75 (3): 497–525.

Lipe, William, and Scott Ortman. 2000. "Spatial Patterning in Northern San Juan Villages, A.D. 1050–1300." *Kiva* 66 (1): 91–122.

Ortiz, Alphonso. 1969. *The Tewa World: Space, Time, Being and Becoming in a Pueblo Society*. Chicago: University of Chicago Press.

Ortman, Scott G. 2012. *Winds from the North: Tewa Origins and Historical Anthropology*. Salt Lake City: University of Utah Press.

Ortman, Scott G., and Bruce A. Bradley. "2002 Sand Canyon Pueblo: The Container in the Center." In *Seeking the Center Place: Archaeology and Ancient Communities in the Mesa Verde Region*, edited by M. D. Varien and R. H. Wilshusen, 41–78. Salt Lake City: University of Utah Press.

Ortman, Scott G., and Mark D. Varien. 2007. "Settlement Patterns in the McElmo Dome Study Area." In *The Archaeology of Sand Canyon Pueblo: Intensive Excavations at a Late-Thirteenth-Century Village in Southwestern Colorado*, edited by Kristin A. Kuckelman. https://www.crowcanyon.org/ResearchReports/SandCanyon/Text/scpw_contentsvolume.asp.

Parsons, Elsie Clews. 1936. *Taos Pueblo*. Menasha, WI: George Banta.

Roth, Barbara, and E. Charles Adams, eds. 2021. *Agent of Change: The Deposition and Manipulation of Ash in the Past*. New York City: Berghahn Books.

Schwindt, Dylan M., R. Kyle Bocinsky, Scott G. Ortman, Donna M. Glowacki, Mark D. Varien, and Timothy A. Kohler. 2016. "The Social Consequences of Climate Change in the Central Mesa Verde Region." *American Antiquity* 81 (1): 74–96.

Walker, William.1998. "Where Are the Witches in Prehistory?" *Journal of Archaeological Method and Theory* 5 (3): 245–308.

Ware, John A. 2014. *A Pueblo Social History: Kinship, Sodality, and Community in the Northern Southwest*. Santa Fe, NM: School for Advanced Research Press.

Wetherington, Ronald K. 1968. *Excavations at Pot Creek Pueblo*. Taos: Fort Burgwin Research Center.

Whittlesey, Stephanie M., and J. J. Reid. 2019. "The Rapidly Evolving Household: Episodic Change at Chodistaas and Grasshopper Pueblos, Arizona." In *Communities and Households in the Greater American Southwest: New Perspectives and Case Studies*, edited by Robert Stokes, 48–80. Boulder: University Press of Colorado.

Woosley, Anne. 1986. "Puebloan Prehistory of the Northern Rio Grande: Settlement, Population, Subsistence." *Kiva* 51 (3): 143–164.

17

Bi-Walls, Tri-Walls, and the Aztec Regional System

STEPHEN H. LEKSON

This chapter has two goals, one substantive and one methodological: to explore bi- and tri-walled structures, which can define the regional system engaged by Aztec Ruins; and to demonstrate possible complementarities of big data and smaller sets of clunkier evidence. Big data: ceramics. Clunky evidence: architecture.

Long ago, as a naive grad student snarled in the statistics of projectile points, I asked Lewis Binford: "What's a good 'sample size'?" (I was, as mentioned, naive.) Binford rolled his eyes and replied: "Big enough to look good, but small enough so you can know each one of 'em by its first name."

In this age of big data (which rejoins us toward the end of this chapter), I believe that smaller, select evidence can still do good service. For example, monumental architecture. It is possible to know all the (known) Chaco great houses by their names / numbers and (if properly permitted) visit each and every one. Great houses are big, but great houses are not big data.

I focus here on another, even less numerous forms of monumental buildings from the Chaco-Aztec era: bi-wall, tri-wall, and quadri-wall structures. These are circular buildings with concentric rows of rooms surrounding a central space the size of a small round room conventionally called a "kiva" or a tower (figure 17.1).

https://doi.org/10.5876/9781646424597.c017

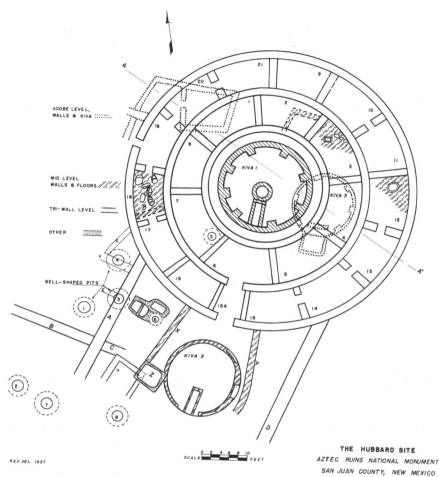

FIGURE 17.1. *The Hubbard Site, Aztec Ruins National Monument (Vivian 1959, fig. 5). Public domain.*

There is a spot of terminological confusion in the naming/numbering of these structures: Some archaeologists count the wall of the "kiva" or tower as one of the walls; others do not. Thus, one person's bi-wall might be another person's tri-wall. What probably matters is the number of concentric rings of rooms surrounding the interior space, but I've made no attempt to standardize naming/numbering to avoid confusion. Another procedural matter: Throughout, I use "Chacoan" and "Chaco-era" to refer to the spans of both Chaco Canyon (AD 850–1125) and Aztec Ruins (AD 1110–1280), which I see as a single political expression, with legs (Lekson 1999, 2015).

About forty of these are known—a small sample size—from Aztec Ruins National Monument on the east, to Aneth, Utah, on the west; and from Yellow

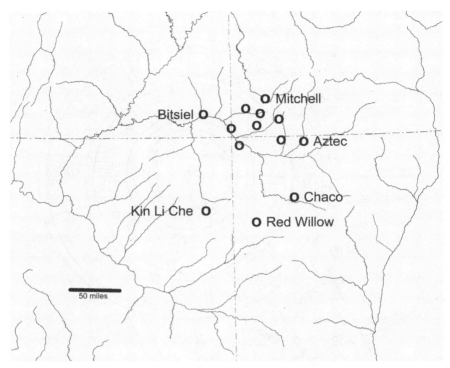

FIGURE 17.2. *Locations of bi-walls, tri-walls, and quadri-walls. Courtesy of the author.*

Jacket, Colorado, on the north, to Manuelito Canyon (about 25 km southwest of Gallup, New Mexico) on the south (figure 17.2). Donna Glowacki provides an overview of these structures (2015, 72–81; see also Kuckelman 2003). For other mentions of bi- and tri-walls, see Glowacki, chapter 12, and Potter et al., chapter 13 in this volume. Very few have been excavated; one was excavated by Crow Canyon at Yellow Jacket Pueblo (Kuckelman 2003), a dozen miles northwest of the Crow Canyon campus.

BI-WALLS AND TRI-WALLS

Only five of these structures have been excavated. The first is the tri-wall central, round area (room?) at the Hubbard Site (figure 17.1) at Aztec Ruins National Monument. It was originally constructed as a 7.2 m diameter structure, plastered, featureless, and possibly roofless. Subsequently (perhaps immediately), a shallow, 5.5 m in diameter, free-standing "kiva" (with hearth, deflector, etc.) was inserted into the space (Vivian 1959, 18). The interior walls of Hubbard tri-wall stand over 2 m tall, and the excavator estimated an original height of over 3 m (Vivian 1959, 16).

The second is the Pueblo del Arroyo tri-wall at Chaco Canyon (which the excavator, when referring to the central area of the structure, called a "McElmo

Tower") (Judd 1959, 109; see also Vivian 1959, 61–70). This structure was originally 6.4 m in diameter at ground level, fully or partially paved with flagstone, and largely dismantled. No interior features survived.

The Red Willow bi-wall, near Tohatchi, New Mexico, was excavated during a highway salvage project in the1960s (Peckham 1963). It's located a short distance northwest of a small great house (the bi-wall and great house were recorded as a single site, LA 4470). The central round room, about 7 m in diameter at grade, has floor features associated with "kivas" (i.e., hearth, deflector, etc.) but lacked a "bench" and a floor vault. The excavator estimated the structure stood one story tall (Peckham 1963, 58).

The "Great Tower" at Yellow Jacket Pueblo (figure 17.3, near the town of that name in southwestern Colorado), the fourth structure, was reexcavated by Crow Canyon (Kuckelman 2003, 30–43). A trench revealed a floor with "kiva" features (a "bench," low masonry pilasters, a central, round firebox, and a floor vault) in a 5.5 m diameter structure—a suite of features suggesting an elevated "Chaco-style kiva" (Lekson 1986, 54–59) (for reasons mysterious to me, now referred to as a "court kiva" [Windes 2014]). Unlike Hubbard, the interior wall of the concentric circle of rooms forms the wall of the kiva (Kuckelman 2003, 41); it seems likely that the kiva was an integral part of the larger bi-wall, although it could have been constructed inside the structure at a later date. The enveloping "tower" was originally two stories tall (Kuckelman 2003, 30).

Finally, a fifth "tri-wall kiva" was partially excavated at the Mitchell Springs Ruin Group, near Cortez, Colorado. It is interpreted as a Chaco-era "tower" standing over 3 m tall and enclosing a 4 m plus diameter Chaco-style kiva (with bench, hearth, and floor vault). The "tower" is surrounded by two rings of rooms attached to a great house (Dove 2021). The excavator believed that the central tower was three stories tall, surrounded by an inner ring of two-story rooms, and finally surrounded by an outermost ring of one-story rooms (Dove 2021, fig. 6). This is similar in configuration to the Holmes "tower" bi-wall above the San Juan River (figure 17.4) seen and illustrated by William H. Holmes (1876, pl. 3). The interior of Holmes's bi-wall was about 3 m in diameter. "The wall is . . . from 2 to 6 feet in height. Long lines of debris, radiating from all sites, indicate that is has been much higher, and has but recently fallen" (Holmes 1876, 9). Holmes's image—an artist's reconstruction—shows a central, two-story tower, encircled by a ring of one-story rooms.

BI-WALLS AND TRI-WALLS AS KIVAS

Although the number of excavated bi- and tri-walls is small, preserved architecture is centered on "kivas" or "kiva-like" features, including hearths and deflectors, and in some cases benches, and vaults. If our small sample is, in fact, representative, we can infer that the central, round rooms in all bi- and tri-walls are so-called

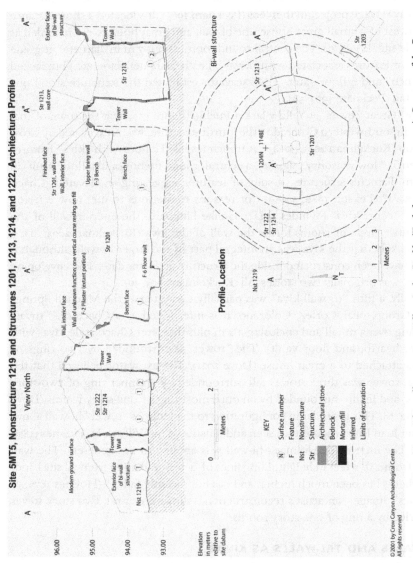

FIGURE 17.3. "Great Tower" bi-wall structure at Yellow Jacket Pueblo (Kuckelman 2003, map 27). *Courtesy of the Crow Canyon Archaeological Center.*

kivas. The appellation *kiva* does not mean they were principally ceremonial, ritual, or religious structures; it indicates primarily residential functions.

For those new to this argument, the term *kiva*, applied to round rooms in Chaco and Aztec, is an unfortunate misnomer (Lekson 1986, 50–51, 1988). In archaeological terms, *kiva* refers to a round room with a constellation of architectural features and should not of itself suggest ceremony. "For the last three decades archaeologists in the central Mesa Verde region have identified small kivas (with diameters less than 10 m) as serving a domestic function in addition to focusing some ritual activities at the level of the household, extended household, or lineage group" (Crabtree et al. 2017, 77). That is, small "kivas," like those found in bi- and tri-walls, can be reasonably assumed to indicate

Plate 3.

FIGURE 17.4. *Holmes Tower (Holmes 1876, pl. 3). Public domain.*

residential, rather than purely ceremonial, functions, although household-level rituals and ceremonies undoubtedly took place.

The rooms encircling bi- and tri-walls are small and almost uniformly featureless. The Hubbard Site is the only tri-wall with walls sufficiently tall to reveal doors. At Hubbard, only the exterior row (of the two encircling rows) had doors. That is, the interior row lacked doors, and there is enough preservation in the architecture that doors would have been preserved and detected. Only one door (15A) opened to the exterior; it was large ("3 feet wide") and there is no information on its shape, so I assume it was rectangular (from photos, it appears that this door was not preserved sufficiently to ascertain if it was T-shaped). All other doors opened between rooms in a circular, rather than radial, pattern; that is, the doors connected rooms in their tiers or concentric rows and did not open into the center or out to the exterior. These "doors are rather small, 1.7 to 2.3 feet wide and, where intact, 4 feet high with raised sills up to 1 foot above the floor level"

(Vivian 1959, 17), almost certainly storage room doors (Lekson 1986, 25–28). In light of the small size of the encircling rooms recorded in all bi- and tri-wall structures, and consistent with storage rooms at great houses, I consider Hubbard's doors indicative. The encircling rooms were probably designed for storage.

Holmes's bi-wall "tower" may have inspired Jonathan Reyman's (1985), and perhaps David Dove's (2021), suggestion that bi- and tri-walls were towers surrounded by "stepped" rings of rooms, not unlike a tiered wedding cake. This interpretation has not garnered favor, but I find Holmes's, Reyman's, and Dove's suggestions interesting and, along with Hubbard's 3 m tall walls and Yellow Jacket's two-story "Great Tower," suggestive. The central, round space of at least some bi-walls and tri-walls may have been round towers. Round towers were numerous across the Four Corners at the same time (Bredthauer 2010; Glowacki 2015, fig. 23). Free-standing towers, however, generally lack floor features beyond the occasional fire pit (Bredthauer 2010), and to my knowledge none had "kiva" features.

To summarize, bi- and tri-walls were free-standing buildings, at least initially, centered on large Chaco-style "kivas," surrounded by concentric rings of storage rooms. Some, but not all, were towers; and some tower bi- and tri-walls may have been tiered. My summary extrapolates from limited information, but that's all the information we have.

DATING BI-WALLS AND TRI-WALLS

I'm not aware of any tree-ring dates unambiguously associated with bi- or tri-walls. A date of AD 1109c, once associated with the Pueblo del Arroyo tri-wall, comes instead from late construction activities attached to the main building (inserted between the main building and the free-standing tri-wall) (Lekson 1986, 223; corrected by Windes 2010). A date of AD 1148++vv from Hubbard is of uncertain provenience and may not be from Hubbard at all (Lekson 1983, 16). A date of AD 1254+vv from the "disturbed" fill of the central space in the Yellow Jacket "Great Tower" almost certainly comes from the complex of rooms (Square Mug House) built after the construction of the tower; early excavations redeposited fill from cleared rooms in Square Mug House into previously excavated units (Kuckelman 2003).

The ceramic assemblages at all five sites suggest occupations in the early AD 1100s through the mid-to-late AD 1200s—that is, contemporary with Aztec Ruins. All feature McElmo and Mesa Verde Black-on-white ceramic types; intriguingly, including the Red Willow bi-wall, 125 km south of Aztec Ruins and 150 km south of Mesa Verde proper.

BI-WALL AND TRI-WALL FUNCTION

Encircled by rings of rooms, bi-walls and tri-walls are riddles wrapped in mysteries inside enigmas. What are they? Kristin Kuckelman (2003, 43) notes:

"Various uses have been suggested for multiwall structures, which are 'ostentatiously different from ordinary residential structures in architectural form and setting.'" Researchers have theorized that these structures were used as residences for a developing priestly class; as intercommunity ceremonial centers; as fortresses, council chambers, and places of worship; or as platform mounds. William Lipe and Scott Ortman (2000, 111) suggest that some multiwall structures could have been residences "for one or two households that had access to significantly more than the usual amount of storage space, and perhaps had stewardship of important rituals."

Lipe and Ortman (2000) recognized that small "kivas" dating to the tenth through thirteenth centuries AD were, as noted, primarily residences. Thus, the central "kiva" features of bi- and tri-walls marked residential rather than ceremonial functions. This is not to deny the presence and importance of ceremony but, rather, to emphasize that bi- and tri-walls were first and foremost residences, possibly of the "developing priestly class"—or another elite social stratum?

Kuckelman (2003, 43) concluded, "The unique design of these structures strongly suggests that they held special, possibly integrative, significance and were used for special activities that were important, exclusive, and restricted." Glowacki (2015, 72–81) groups "multiwalled structures" together with great houses as "restricted-use architecture"—correctly, I think. Both were "oriented towards small-scale interactions among people who were members of a specific group (e.g., household, lineage, or non-kin ritual group)" (72–81). I suggest those "specific groups" were elites or, more accurately, nobles—hereditary elite classes commonly part of Native North American agricultural societies (discussed in Lekson 2018, 76–83). (Note that Glowacki also included D-shaped "multiwalled structures"; these interesting buildings have no counterparts at Chaco or Aztec—unless the "D" mimics the ground plan of Pueblo Bonito? Glowacki demonstrates that their geographic distribution differs from that of bi- and tri-walls, with D-shaped buildings occurring further west.)

Whatever their function(s), I suggested two decades ago that these buildings were architectural icons of Aztec Ruins and its regional system (Lekson 1999, 103). Aztec Ruins, in the twelfth to thirteenth centuries AD, was the successor capital (sensu Rapoport 1993) after Chaco Canyon in the eleventh and early twelfth centuries AD (Lekson 1999, 2015). This historical interpretation was initially controversial but today seems to be generally accepted (e.g., Reed 2008, 2011).

THE AZTEC REGIONAL SYSTEM

Aztec Ruins was centered on free-standing tri- and quadri-walls. Like Chaco, Aztec Ruins was a planned city with multiple great houses and other features built on sites determined by a larger design (Stein 1987, fig. 4; Stein and McKenna 1988, fig. 10; republished in Lekson 1999, fig. 3.6). For more recent invaluable work on the eastern half of the landscape, see Paul Reed et al. (2010). A largely unexcavated quadri-wall (Mound F) forms the center or focus of the plan. (Note that Reed et al. 2010 interpret Mound F as a large tri-wall structure, but my observations suggest three rows of rooms in four concentric walls; only the spade will tell.) Free-standing tri-walls, northeast and northwest of the quadri-wall, create points on two axes crossing through the central quadri-wall, aligning to the great kivas of Aztec's two largest great houses: Aztec East and Aztec West. One of these tri-walls, the Hubbard Site, was excavated; the other, Mound A, remains unexcavated. Two additional small bi-walls (Mounds B and C) appear to be attached or associated with great houses in the Aztec East complex. That's five bi-, tri-, and quadri-walled circular structures at Aztec Ruins, four more than any other site. Glowacki (2015, 76), in her excellent review of multiwalled structures, concluded, "The tri-wall form is decidedly linked to Aztec and its ritual and political organization."

Archaeologists working in the San Juan area generally recognize Aztec Ruins as a second (smaller) Chaco but often downplay or discount its importance to the larger central Mesa Verde region. This omission is understandable, because we heretofore lacked evidence to delineate Aztec's regional reach, much less to evaluate its dynamics. Chaco announced itself with great houses; many of those great houses continued through Aztec's era but with significant changes in how they were used. Were they "hallmarks" of Aztec or relics of Chaco? ¿Quién sabe?

Bi- and tri-walls, I think, provide monuments on the landscape that can be reasonably linked to Aztec and only Aztec; they are one solid line of evidence to define Aztec's region. Not big data, but a small set of clunkier evidence—forty-odd multiwalled structures. Bi- and tri-walled structures in the central Mesa Verde region have been documented and analyzed by Glowacki (2015, 72–81). She noted several multiwalled structures at southern sites but concluded "multiwalled structures were a decidedly northern San Juan phenomenon" (Glowacki 2015, 75). I am particularly interested in bi- and tri-walled structures far to the south of Aztec Ruins, including structures near Tohatchi, New Mexico; Manuelito, New Mexico; and Ganado, Arizona—as far as 200 km from Aztec. In contrast, in the Mesa Verde region proper, the most distant bi-wall (near Aneth, Utah) is about 115 km from Aztec. (In my opinion, there is a high probability of more, undiscovered bi- and tri-wall structures in the north and especially in the south; the intensity of research in the northern San Juan dwarfs the work done south of Chaco, on the Navajo Nation, and Zuni Pueblo.) If, as I argue, bi- and tri-walls mark Aztec's regional extent in the north, what about those southern sites?

Clunky evidence, at last, meets big data. The Southwest Social Networks Project is an outstanding big data initiative led by Barbara Mills, Matt Peeples, and others. This remarkable project recently analyzed social networks based on ceramics in fifty-year increments in the time of Chaco and Aztec (Mills et al. 2018). To summarize one aspect of their fruitful study, two densely interconnected social networks consistently appeared, one to the north of the San Juan River and a larger network to the south, centered on Chaco but extending well into Arizona to the Mogollon Rim (figure 17.5). During the AD 1100–1150 period—Aztec's rise—a third network emerged:

> Interestingly, during the AD 1100–1150 interval, our community-detection analyses show three communities: the large northern and southern communities divided along the same lines seen in earlier intervals, and a third component (in yellow) that represents sites along the edges of these two larger communities . . . Another interesting result is that the cluster of Chaco structures near Aztec is not as central to the network as might be expected, although Aztec itself is. Aztec's ascendency as the capital of the Chaco World (e.g., Lekson 2015) is especially evident in the AD 1150–1200 interval during the "post-Chaco" period. (Mills et al. 2018, 933–936).

In figure 17.6, I impose a white polygon of the approximate distribution of bi- and tri-walled structures. Their distribution bridges northern and southern networks, including over two-thirds (but, significantly, not all—as Glowacki noted) of the northern and a much smaller proportion of the southern. And, intriguingly, the distribution of multiwalled structures encompass most of the emergent "third component." The smaller set of clunky evidence complements big data, and vice versa! They show different geographies; if bi- and tri-walls define Aztec's regional system, that system incorporated parts of both northern and southern networks, but only parts. This should not surprise us—ceramics define one set of social dynamics, and monumental architecture another. Ceramics—the big data of social network analysis—track daily interactions, craft economies, and less-frequent distant contacts, things that we today might call "social." Chacoan monuments—the relatively small number of great houses, roads, tri-walls, and so on—track interelite communication, power projection, institutional infrastructure, things that we today would call "political." (For those favoring ceramics over buildings, the "third network" provides an intriguing parallel patterning between the two.)

Aztec's political structure overarched strongly regionalized social networks—a polity encompassing varied local economies, ethnicities, languages, and so forth—much like Chaco's earlier region (see Lekson 2018, chap. 4). However, Aztec and its region were smaller and, ultimately, less successful.

Bi-walls and tri-walls, remarkably prominent at Aztec Ruins, were symbols of the new order, similar to, yet distant from, Chaco Canyon. The sole tri-wall at Chaco Canyon, at Pueblo del Arroyo, was either never completed or was razed prior to AD 1300; it played a role at Chaco but only a transitory role. With the shift of the capital north, Aztec developed new symbols of power based on traditional architectures; elements of the common "unit pueblo" transformed into habitations "ostentatiously different from ordinary residential structures" (Lipe

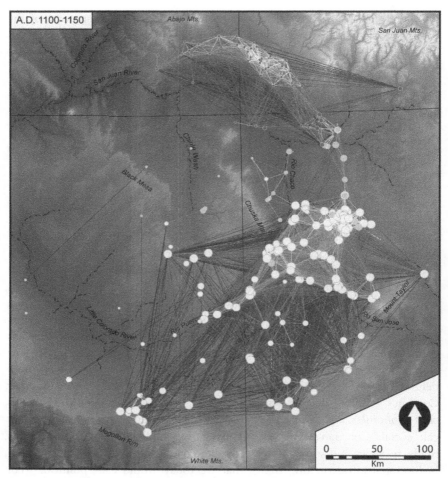

FIGURE 17.5. *Chaco great house and great kiva networks, AD 1100–1150 (Mills et al. 2018, fig. 8). Courtesy of Matthew Peeples.*

and Ortman 2001, 111). It seems likely that bi- and tri-walls located in larger settlements marked the apartments of elites or nobles. But it didn't last. With Aztec's collapse and the depopulation of the Four Corners, many of the social / political system's markers were scraped off (Lipe 2010). Architectural forms associated with Chaco and Aztec disappeared from the Pueblo region, while a few reappear far to the south in the Casas Grandes region, most notably, the T-shaped door (Lekson 1999, appendix A, 2021).

Sightings of "bi-walled structures of a different sort" in the late prehistoric and protohistoric Rio Grande (Peckham 1963, 70) stretch beyond the modulus of elasticity; the Rio Grande sites are not bi-walls as defined here. Charles

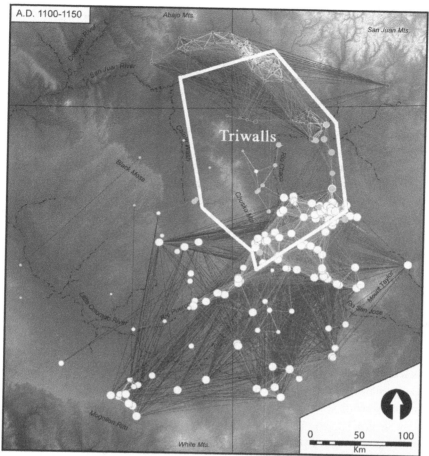

FIGURE 17.6. *Same as figure 17.5 with distribution of bi- and tri-walls (modified from Mills et al. 2018, fig. 8). Courtesy of Matthew Peeples.*

Di Peso's (1974, 208) claim for similarities between Aztec's tri-walls and Cerro de Moctezuma (the walled signal tower high above Paquimé, the Casas Grandes capital) has not survived subsequent research and mapping (Pitezel 2007). Bi-walls and tri-walls, like Aztec and Chaco, were erased from Pueblo life, along with the social/political systems they represented.

Acknowledgments. My thanks to Winston Hurst for showing me the Aneth bi-wall, westernmost of its ilk. And to Matt Peeples for permission to use his fascinating maps of social networks (figures 17.5 and 17.6). And to Cathy Cameron for her careful reading and correction of this text. All errors, of fact or of fiction, are of course my own.

REFERENCES

Bredthauer, Allison V. 2010. "A Towering Enigma: An Examination of Late Pueblo II and Pueblo III Towers in the Northern San Juan Region." MA thesis, Department of Anthropology, University of Colorado, Boulder.

Crabtree, Stefani A., R. Kyle Bocinsky, Paul L. Hooper, Susan C. Ryan, and Timothy A. Kohler. 2017. "How to Make a Polity (In the Central Mesa Verde Region)." *American Antiquity* 82 (1): 71–95.

Di Peso, Charles C. 1974. "A Comparison of Casas Grandes and Chaco Canyon Architecture." In *Casas Grandes*. Vol. 4, *Dating and Architecture*, by Charles C. Di Peso, John B. Rinaldo, and Gloria J. Fenner, 208–211. Dragoon, AZ: Amerind Foundation.

Dove, David M. 2021. "Greathouse Formation: Agricultural Intensification, Balanced Duality, and Communal Enterprise at Mitchell Springs." *Southwestern Lore* 87 (1): 5–49.

Glowacki, Donna M. 2015. *Living and Leaving: A Social History of Regional Depopulation in Thirteenth-Century Mesa Verde*. Tucson: University of Arizona Press.

Holmes, William H. 1876. "A Notice of the Ancient Remains of Southwestern Colorado Examined during the Summer of 1875." *Bulletin of the Geological and Geographical Survey of the Territories*. Vol. 2, nos. 1: 3–24. Washington, DC: Government Printing Office.

Judd, Neil M. 1959. *Pueblo del Arroyo, Chaco Canyon, New Mexico*. Smithsonian Miscellaneous Collections 138 (1). Washington, DC: Smithsonian Institution.

Kuckelman, Kristin A. 2003. "The Great Tower Complex." In "Architecture," in *The Archaeology of Yellow Jacket Pueblo (Site 5MT5): Excavations at a Large Community Center in Southwestern Colorado*, edited by Kristin A. Kuckelman, 31–43. http://www.crowcanyon.org/yellowjacket.

Lekson, Stephen H. 1983. "Dating the Hubbard Tri-Wall and Other Tri-Wall Structures." *Southwestern Lore* 49 (4): 15–23.

Lekson, Stephen H. 1986. *Great Pueblo Architecture of Chaco Canyon, New Mexico*. Albuquerque: University of New Mexico Press.

Lekson, Stephen H. 1988. "The Idea of the Kiva in Anasazi Archaeology." *Kiva* 53 (3): 213–234.

Lekson, Stephen H. 1999. *Chaco Meridian*. Walnut Creek CA: Altamira Press.

Lekson, Stephen H. 2015. *Chaco Meridian*. 2nd ed. Lanham, MD: Rowman and Littlefield.

Lekson, Stephen H. 2018. *A Study of Southwestern Archaeology*. Salt Lake City: University of Utah Press.

Lekson, Stephen H. 2021. "Cliff Dwellers of the Sierra Madre." *Archaeology* 74 (2): 57–64.

Lipe, William D. 2010. "Lost in Transit: The Central Mesa Verde Archaeological Complex." In *Leaving Mesa Verde*, edited by Timothy A. Kohler, Mark D. Varien, and Aaron M. Wright, 262–284. Tucson: University of Arizona Press.

Lipe, William D., and Scott G. Ortman. 2000. "Spatial Patterning in Northern San Juan Villages, A.D. 1050–1300." *Kiva* 66 (1): 91–122.

Mills, Barbara J., Matthew A. Peeples, Leslie D. Aragon, Benjamin A. Bellorado, Jeffery J. Clark, Evan Giomi, and Thomas C. Windes. 2018. "Evaluating Chaco Migration Scenarios Using Dynamic Social Network Analysis." *Antiquity* 92 (364): 922–939.

Peckham, Stewart. 1963. "The Red Willow Site: A Bi-Walled Kiva near Tohatchi, New Mexico." In *Highway Salvage Archaeology* Number 4: 56–72, edited by Steward Peckham. Santa Fe: Museum of New Mexico.

Pitezel, Todd. 2007. "Surveying Cerro de Moctezuma, Chihuahua, Mexico." *Kiva* 72 (3): 353–369.

Rapoport, Amos. 1993. "On the Nature of Capitals and Their Physical Expression." In *Capital Cities / Les Capitales*, edited by John Taylor, Jean G. Lengellé, and Caroline Andrew, 31–67. Ottawa: Carleton University Press.

Reed, Paul F., ed. 2008. *Chaco's Northern Prodigies: Salmon, Aztec, and the Ascendancy of the Middle San Juan Region after A.D. 1100.* Salt Lake City: University of Utah Press.

Reed, Paul F. 2011. "Chacoan Immigration or Local Emulation of the Chaco System? The Emergence of Aztec, Salmon, and Other Great House Communities in the Middle San Juan." *Kiva* 77 (2): 119–138.

Reed, Paul F., Gary M. Brown, Michael L. Brack, Lori S. Reed, Jeffrey Wharton, and Joel Gamache. 2010. *Aztec East Ruin Landscape Project.* Technical Report No. 2020-101 Center for Desert Archaeology, Tucson.

Reyman, Jonathan E. 1985. "A Reevaluation of Bi-Wall and Tri-Wall Structures in the Anasazi Area." In *Contributions to the Archaeology and Ethnohistory of Greater Mesoamerica*, edited by W. J. Folan, 293–334. Carbondale: Southern Illinois University Press.

Stein, John R. 1987. *An Archaeological Reconnaissance in the Vicinity of Aztec Ruins National Monument, New Mexico.* Santa Fe, NM: National Park Service Southwest Cultural Resources Center.

Stein, John R., and Peter J. McKenna. 1988. *An Archaeological Reconnaissance of a Late Bonito Phase Occupation near Aztec Ruins National Monument, New Mexico.* Santa Fe, NM: National Park Service Southwest Cultural Resources Center.

Vivian, R. Gordon. 1959. *The Hubbard Site and Other Tri-Wall Structures in New Mexico and Colorado.* Archaeological Research Series 5. Washington, DC: National Park Service.

Windes, Thomas C. 2010. "Dendrochronology and Structural Wood Use at Pueblo del Arroyo, Chaco Canyon, New Mexico." *Journal of Field Archaeology* 35 (1): 78–98.

Windes, Thomas C. 2014. "The Chacoan Court Kiva." *Kiva* 79 (4): 337–379.

18

Revisiting the Depopulation of the Northern Southwest with Dendrochronology

A Changing Perspective with New Dates from Cedar Mesa

BENJAMIN A. BELLORADO AND THOMAS C. WINDES

The depopulation of ancestral Pueblo people from the northern Southwest has been a fascination of archaeologists for decades. Using a suite of social and environmental models, scholars have attempted to explain the processes that led tens of thousands of people in the greater San Juan River drainage (figure 18.1) to vacate thousands of communities at the end of the thirteenth century AD. Beyond a purely academic exercise, understanding how and why this large-scale depopulation occurred can help scientists understand how human populations respond to both climatic and social turmoil and specify the impetus for local and large-scale migrations.

We focus on the overlooked, but highly valuable, perishable wood resources used at sites. Dendroarchaeological studies provide insight into the dating of construction and remodeling of structures, the local (or non-local) tree resources that were harvested and used for distinct purposes, harvesting strategies, preparation and treatment of wood, paleoenvironmental reconstructions, and the condition of the forest. In this chapter, we review previous depopulation discussions for the northern Southwest and summarize prior dendrochronological

https://doi.org/10.5876/9781646424597.c018

assessments of the timing of the depopulation in the western portion of the northern San Juan region and the greater San Juan River Basin, from the point of view of the Cedar Mesa area (figure 18.1) in the southern portion of the recently established Bears Ears National Monument. We begin by providing a synthesis of new tree-ring data from over two dozen previously unrecorded cliff dwellings from the greater Cedar Mesa area (figure 18.2). We use these data to reassess the nature and timing of the depopulation locally and the effect these data have on the depopulation of the larger region.

THE DEPOPULATION OF THE NORTHERN SAN JUAN REGION

Across much of the Colorado Plateau, the mid-to-late Pueblo II (Chaco) period (AD 1000–1140) and Pueblo III (post-Chaco) period (AD 1140–1280) were tumultuous times (Mills et al. 2018). During the beginning of this timeframe, communities organized into a large, regional system (i.e., the Chaco regional system) (Kantner and Kintigh 2006; Lekson 2006; Mills et al. 2018). By the mid-AD 1100s, this system fractured into smaller organizational entities focused at the household- and village-levels (Glowacki 2015). By the last decade of the thirteenth century AD, the entire region was depopulated and never permanently resettled by ancestral Pueblo people. To date, most prior research has attributed these changes to climatic fluctuations (Benson et al. 2007; Bocinsky 2014; Dean 1996a, 2010; Kuckelman, chapter 19 in this volume; Schwindt et al. 2016; Van West 1996), particularly in southeastern Utah, where precipitation and available farmlands are more marginal than areas to the east (Glowacki 2010; Wright 2010). However, recent research demonstrates that social factors also contributed to major changes in ancestral Pueblo societies (Glowacki 2010, 2011, 2015; Ortman et al. 2000). Donna Glowacki (2010, 202–203) argues that a key component to understanding the depopulation of the region is "a careful analysis of social and cultural intraregional variation," as a myriad of social and cultural differences fostered "the circumstances that preceded the migration." Understanding the spatial and temporal sequence of settlement distribution during this pivotal period is critical for explaining the depopulation of the region just prior to AD 1300 (Glowacki 2010). In this chapter, we review prior dendrochronological assessments for the timing of the depopulation in the greater Cedar Mesa area (figure 18.2) and provide new data from recent research that substantially refines our understanding of local- and large-scale migrations from this area and the larger region.

DENDROCHRONOLOGICAL ASSESSMENTS OF THE DEPOPULATION

Research focused on depopulation processes in the greater San Juan River drainage has been largely dependent on the compilation of large tree-ring datasets recovered from sites across the area (Dean 2010; Matson et al. 2015; Varien 1999, 2010). Researchers working with the Crow Canyon Archaeological Center

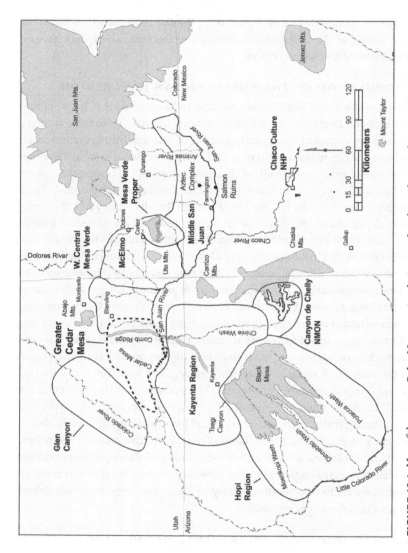

FIGURE 18.1. *Map of the greater Cedar Mesa area in relation to cultural complexes in the greater San Juan River drainage, including the Central Mesa Verde, Kayenta, Canyon de Chelly, and Middle San Juan cultural regions. Map courtesy of the Crow Canyon Archaeological Center.*

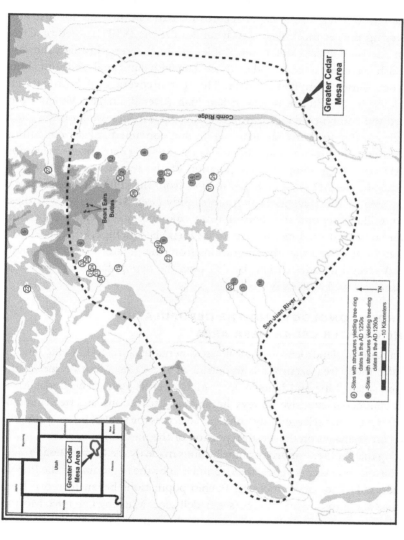

FIGURE 18.2. *Map of all the known sites in the greater Cedar Mesa (i.e., the Southern Bears Ears) area with tree-ring dates from the AD 1250s and 1260s. Site reference numbers correspond to Table 18.1. Map created by Benjamin A. Bellorado.*

have been instrumental in the generation and compilation of these datasets (Nash and Rogers 2014; Schwindt et al. 2016; Varien 1999, 2010). The regional tree-ring database at Crow Canyon began with Mark Varien's (1999) dissertation research on the northern San Juan region. To collect these data, Varien went to the Laboratory of Tree-Ring Research (LTRR) at the University of Arizona and Xeroxed all the paper records for dates in their file for his study area. During the second Village Ecodynamics Project (VEP II)—led by Crow Canyon Archaeological Center (see Kohler et al., chapter 3 in this volume)— Steve Nash was contracted to update those data with dates analyzed after about 1995, when Varien compiled his data. The spatial coverage of both datasets is restricted to sites in the northern San Juan River drainages. Varien (2010) analyzed the combined data from these prior datasets, focusing on the latest-dated sites in the northern San Juan region that contained at least ten cutting dates. Varien (2010, 23–25) found that the latest tree-ring dates from this region were AD 1281, suggesting the depopulation of the region was complete by the middle-to-late AD 1280s. The latest dates from the cliff dwellings in Tsegi Canyon area of the Kayenta region are slightly later, at AD 1286, and these sites were likely depopulated between AD 1290 and 1300 (Dean 1969, 1996b). Prior research (Matson, Lipe, and Curewitz 2015; Matson, Lipe, and Haase 1988; Varien 2010) proposed that the migrations from the greater Cedar Mesa area occurred several decades earlier; by AD 1250, the depopulation of the Cedar Mesa area was well underway.

DENDROCHRONOLOGY AND THE DEPOPULATION OF THE GREATER CEDAR MESA AREA

The majority of dendrochronological assessments of ancestral Pueblo sites in the Cedar Mesa area occurred as the result of the Cedar Mesa Project in the 1970s and 1980s (Lipe and Matson 2007; Matson et al. 1988). The Cedar Mesa Project conducted extensive surveys, limited test excavations, and tree-ring sampling efforts in several large study units spread across the landscape and primarily focused on drainages on the western portion of the mesa.

Among many other important contributions made by the Cedar Mesa Project, R. G. Matson and his colleagues (1988) found that by the beginning of the Pueblo III period (AD 1150–1200), ancestral Pueblo populations began to move from mesa tops and into canyon settings (see Bedell 2000; Matson et al. 1988; Morton 2002). This same process also took place in the central Mesa Verde region in the east (see Glowacki et al., chapter 12 in this volume). In these settings, most settlements constructed in the late AD 1100s and early 1200s were built in alcoves and along canyon shelves and bottoms, usually near reliable springs and where access to canyon bottoms and mesa tops was relatively direct. Subsistence farming likely occurred on the mesa tops, whereas other domesticated and encouraged crops were grown in well-watered canyon bottom settings (Matson 1991; Morton 2002).

Varien's (2010, table 1.2) analysis of the last decades of ancestral Pueblo occupation of the greater Cedar Mesa area included four tree-ring dated sites that yielded ten or more cutting dates at, or after, AD 1260. These sites include 42SA12785, 42SA5114, 42SA256 (see figure 18.2 and table 18.1), and the Moon House Complex, which is itself composed of three separate loci each with distinct site numbers (designated as M 1–3 [42SA5004, 42SA5005, and 42SA25380 respectively]) and is the site with the largest quantity of cutting dates ($n = 79$) and the latest dates. Richard Ahlstrom (1985) and William Bloomer (1989) determined that the largest construction events in the complex likely started about AD 1240, continued through the 1260s, and to some extent was occupied until the mid-to-late 1270s.

Since the time of Varien's (2010, table 1.2) publication—which includes data from 42SA256—Tom Windes and his Cedar Mesa Wood Project "Wood Rat" crews collected an additional seventy-five dates from the site. Each of these sites yielded samples from wooden beams in structures and work areas that dated to the AD 1250s and earlier. Windes's analysis of these data indicates that most of the AD 1260s dates were from newly constructed or remodeled rooms and features in sites that had already been occupied in the decade, or decades, prior. These late dates, however, also indicate where some of the remaining populations in the area were residing and where they continued to build a limited number of new buildings and remodeled older structures in the years leading to depopulation.

In addition to the sites above, six additional sites in the VEP III database were identified with tree-ring dates in the AD 1250s, and at least twice as many have dates in the AD 1240s (Bannister et al. 1969; Matson et al. 2015; Varien 2010). This reduced frequency of dates in the 1250s—after such a strong presence of dates in prior decades—caused Matson and his colleagues (1988) to argue that the depopulation of Natural Bridges and Cedar Mesa was well underway by this decade. These sites are distributed across the greater Cedar Mesa landscape and indicate that while small, the population of the area at the beginning of the second half of the thirteenth century AD was distributed across this long-lived cultural landscape. Matson and his colleagues (2015, 343) interpreted these data as evidence that the majority of the Natural Bridges area had been vacated by about AD 1250, that Cedar Mesa was almost completely depopulated by 1260 (Matson et al. 2015, 343), and that the Moon House Complex was one of just a few sites occupied by a small holdout population that remained in the area in the AD 1260s and early 1270s. They concede, however, that the occupation of Comb and Butler Washes, and areas further east, may have been occupied a decade or more later.

TABLE 18.1. Table of previous and newly compiled tree-ring date assemblages, date clusters (based on Ahlstrom's definition of a tree-ring date cluster [1985:60]), and site attributes for sites dating to the AD 1250s and 1260s in the greater Cedar Mesa area.

Latest Dates	Figure 18.2 Map Ref	Site No.	Original Data / Prior Study	Range of Tree-Ring Dates	Earliest Cutting Date	Latest Cutting Date	Latest Date	Latest Cluster of Dates (3 or more Dates)	Reference
Sites containing structure(s) with 1260s dates	1	42SA5004	Prior	1215–1268	1259GB	1259GB	1268+B	NA	Ahlstrom (1985); Bloomer (1989)
	2	42SA6678	New	1229–1268	1229v	1261r	1268+v	1260r–1261r	Bellorado (2020, appendix E, 2021)
	3	42SA5814	New	1149–1268	1260B	1260B	1268+vv	1250vv–1255+LB	Windes (2022, table 4)
	4	42SA5005	Prior	1143–1267	1143G	1257LGB	1267++B	1259+GB–1264+GB	Ahlstrom (1985); Bloomer (1989)
	5	42SA12785	Prior	1125–1267	1145v	1267GB	1267GB	1205v–1211v	Walker (1977)
	6	42SA6654	New	1249–1267	1249v	1267B	1267B	1257+B–1261v	Windes (2010)
	7	42SA25380	Prior	1166–1266	1204G	1259v	1266+B	1248+B–1266+B	Ahlstrom (1985); Bloomer (1989)
	8	42SA1725	New	1249–1266	1250B	1259B	1266+v	NA	Windes (2021)
	9	42SA5114	Prior	1077–1265	1208B	1259B	1265+GB	1256+B–1259B	Bedell (2000); Varien (2010)
	10	42SA5810	New	1236–1265	1265v	1265v	1265v	NA	Windes (2012, 2013, 2018a)
	11	42SA1763	New	1235–1263	1255v	1265B	1265B	1258+B–1265B	Windes (2012, 2013, 2018a)
	12	42SA34831	New	1208–1263	1240L	1263B	1263B	1257+v–1263B	Bellorado (2020, appendix E, 2021, 186–198)
	13	42SA9309	New	1182–1261	1211v	1261B	1261B	1246B–1251+B	Bellorado (2020, appendix E, 2021)
	14	42SA9310	New	1235–1260	1235B	1248B	1260+B	NA	Bellorado (2020, appendix E, 2021)
	15	42SA256	New	1040–1260	897v	1260v	1260r	1259B–1260r	Windes (2015, 2019); Varien (2010)
	16	42SA5819	New	912–1260	912v	NA	1260+vv	NA	Windes (2014, 2018a)

continued on next page

Sites containing structure(s) with 1250s dates								
17	42SA4564	Prior	1096–1259	1096v	1259B	1259B	1223vv–1228v	Varien (2010)
18	42SA5112	Prior	1046–1258	NA	NA	1258+G	1256+B–1258+G	LTRR records
19	42SA6803	New	895–1257	1143v	1257v	1257v	1250v–1250rB	Windes (2010)
20	42SA29514	New	1257	NA	NA	1257+v	NA	Windes (2013, 2014, 2018a, 2020)
21	42SA1738	New	1145–1256	1229B	1250LB	1256+vv	1247++v–1253+v	Bellorado (2015, 2020, appendix E, 2021)
22	42SA5028	New	1147–1255	NA	NA	1255vv	NA	Bellorado (2020, appendix E, 2021)
23	42SA5118	Prior	897–1255	1095B	1249G	1255+B	1234v–1239+GB	Bedell (2020, appendix E, 2000)
24	42SA6638	New	972–1254	NA	NA	1254+vv	NA	Windes (field notes)
25	42SA23690	New	1207–1254	1207B	1238B	1254+B	1245+G—1254+B	Bellorado (2020, appendix E, 2021)
26	42SA34830	New	924–1253	1055B	1248B	1253+B	1244+v—1248B	Bellorado (2015, 2020, appendix E, 2021, 52–53, 199–210)
27	42SA707	New	926–1253	1138v	1237v	1253+B	1138vv–1151+vv	Windes (field notes)
28	42SA6967	New	935–1253	1253rGB	1253rGB	1253rGB	NA	Windes (field notes)
29	42SA4580	Prior	1127–1252	1252v	1252v	1252v	1214vv—1217+vv	Varien 2010
30	42SA6683	New	1252	NA	NA	1252+v	NA	Bellorado (2020, appendix E, 2021)
31	42SA6779	New	521–1252	1053v	1250v	1252+vv	1250B—1252+vv	Bannister et al. (1969); Windes (field notes)
32	42SA6961	Prior	1153–1251	1243v	1251rGB	1251rGB	1247B—1251rGB	Bannister et al. (1969); LTRR Files; Windes (field notes)
33	42SA6819	New	1200–1250	NA	NA	1250+B	1243+v—1247+B	Windes (2014)
34	42SA6811	New	1248–1250	1250v	1250v	1250v	NA	Windes (field notes)

To this large body of existing data, we provide a suite of new tree-ring dates from sites occupied in the last decades of ancestral Pueblo occupation in southeastern Utah. We collected these data during two separate, but related, projects focused on obtaining tree-ring dates from cliff dwellings in the canyons. The Cedar Mesa Wood Project (CMWP) (Windes 2012, 2013, 2014, 2015, 2016, 2018a, 2018b, 2019, 2020, 2021, 2022) is a long-term project aimed at creating site chronologies of threatened, intact cliff dwellings across the area. The second project, the Cedar Mesa Building Murals Project (CMBMP), was a multi-year program aimed at creating an inventory of intact building murals in cliff dwellings across the area (Bellorado 2015, 2020, 2021). Between 2013 and 2017, the project focused on creating a seriation of plaster mural decoration styles by collecting and dating tree-ring samples from the wooden roofs and intramural beams of structures with murals. Fieldwork methodologies for both projects included site and structure mapping, infield artifact tallies, and sampling of available and potentially datable wooden beams. Whereas the CMWP conducted extensive tree-ring dating and condition assessments of all wooden elements at the sites visited by the project (e.g., Windes and McKenna 2001), the CMBMP used a more-focused approach that targeted beams in contexts that could help to date mural composition events.

Both projects each documented dozens of intact structures and mapped the contexts of their wooden construction members in detail (see one example in Figure 18.3). During these projects, we collected hundreds of tree-ring samples from intact structures. Once collected, the samples were analyzed at the LTRR by lab technicians and by the lead author of this chapter (see Bellorado 2020, chap. 5). Based on the results, we identified thirteen sites that had significant construction events in the AD 1250s and ten additional sites that had evidence of construction in the 1260s (figures 18.2 and 18.3 and table 18.1). One additional site, 42SA256, was revisited, and a suite of seventy-five new dates were obtained. As of the writing of this chapter, we have identified a total of eighteen sites with dates in the AD 1250s. We also identified sixteen sites with dates in the AD 1260s, some of which also have 1250s and earlier dates. Our four new latest dates consist of two near-cutting dates of AD 1267+B and 1268+v from 42SA6678, a noncutting date of 1268+vv from 42SA5814, and a cutting date of 1267B from 42SA6654 (table 18.1). These new dates place these sites as immediate contemporaries with both the Moon House Complex and 42SA12785, from which a near-cutting date of AD 1268+B from the M-2 unit (42SA5004), a noncutting date of 1267++B from the M-1 unit (42SA5005), and a cutting date of 1267GB from 42SA12785 had been reported. These dates from the Moon House Complex and 42SA12785 were previously identified as the latest dates from the greater Cedar Mesa area (Ahlstrom 1985; Bloomer 1989; Matson et al. 2015; Varien 2010).

SETTLEMENT LOCATION AND SITE ATTRIBUTES
IN THE LAST DECADES OF OCCUPATION

While late sites are distributed across the landscape (figure 18.2), the majority of the latest sites where we worked are concentrated on the eastern side of Cedar Mesa; all of these eastern sites are situated in relatively similar areas half-way between the crest of Cedar Mesa—or Elk Ridge to the west, and Comb Wash to the east. Two of these sites are located in canyon-head settings with Hovenweep-style towers (Bredthauer 2010), and the rest are scattered in canyons across the greater Cedar Mesa area. Other than 42SA12785, which is north of the Bears Ears buttes and Elk Ridge (Walker 1977), all sites with AD 1260s dates in our dataset are in the canyons of Cedar Mesa proper. Often, these latest-occupied sites appear positioned to take advantage of (1) large patches of deep soils on mesa top settings, where dryland and runoff farming would have been possible; (2) persistent springs and seeps just below canyon rims and in the bottoms of the deepest canyons; and (3) easily defendable canyon shelf and alcove locations (figure 18.3), which are hard to access.

Prior studies (Glowacki 2010; Matson et al. 2015; Wright 2010) have demonstrated that compared to settlement locations in the McElmo and central Mesa Verde areas, farming conditions were relatively marginal in the greater Cedar Mesa area. Several studies (Ahlstrom et al. 1995; Salzer 2000, Salzer and Kipfmueller 2005; Windes 2018a, 2020; Wright 2010) have shown that the AD 1250–1275 period was one of the coldest and driest quarter centuries of the entire ancestral Pueblo occupation of the larger region and that southeastern Utah was often relatively drier than other parts of the region. Thomas Windes (2020, 14) also documented that the extreme cold and hot temperatures on Cedar Mesa are more severe than places like Chaco Canyon. It should be of no surprise then that the latest settlements documented in this study are situated adjacent to some of the deepest and most productive soils available in the area, particularly since the reduced population levels would have resulted in less competition over the use of these farmlands.

Most of the latest sites were situated in defensive settings, including hard-to-reach alcoves and shelves on the walls of the deepest canyons. They were placed in locations that were difficult to reach and where access was restricted to narrow ledges that required the use of hand-and-toe holds, a series of ladders that could have been pulled up when needed, or, in one case, a wooden bridge across a deep chasm along a shelf below the canyon rim (figure 18.3). These sites often have thick enclosing walls with sealable door entries and small viewport features with directed views of access points. While secure, entry to some sites was so precarious that bringing water and other resources into them and providing access for elders and juveniles must have been difficult. These inconveniences, however, seemed to have been outweighed by the need for residences to be defendable

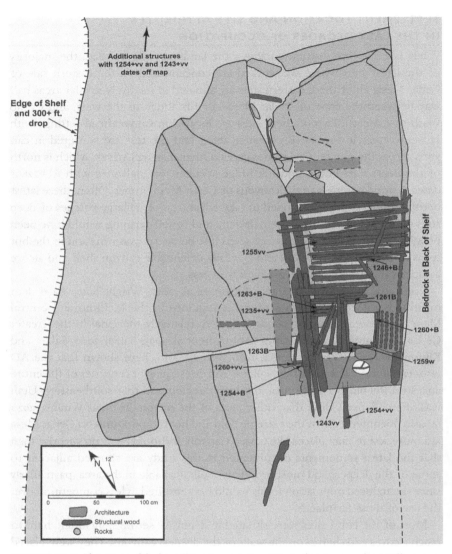

FIGURE 18.3. *Plan view of the kiva (Structure 12) at 42SA1763 showing wooden roof beams and available tree-ring dates. Map by Tom Windes, Christine Gilbertson, Cliff Evans, and Marcia Simonis, July 25, 2012. Digitized by Clay Mathers and Benjamin A. Bellorado.*

against marauders, and we interpret site placement in hard-to-access locations as evidence of pronounced social strife during the final decades of occupation.

Although these sites were hard to reach, their occupants were not hiding, as the back walls of the alcoves (above the masonry rooms) or the rooms themselves were decorated with pictographs composed of large circles that were

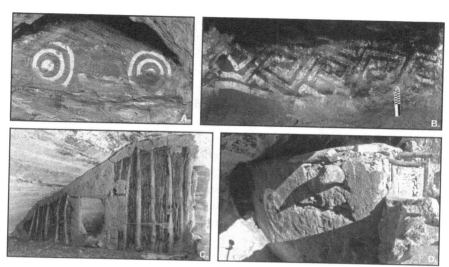

FIGURE 18.4. *Examples of (A) painted shield-like rock art above a habitation site tree-ring dated to the AD 1260s; (B) a bichrome mural with landscape elements in a kiva dated to the 1260s; (C) a second-story wall with entryway made with jacal construction tree-ring dated to the late 1240s (Bellorado 2020, 2021); and (D) a bichrome mural functioning as a winter solstice marker (Bellorado and Mills 2022, fig. 12.10). Photographs by Benjamin Bellorado.*

painted with brightly colored, bold decorations (figure 18.4a). These icons likely represented the large coiled-basketry shields that have been identified from Pueblo III period contexts (Bellorado 2020; Jolie 2018; Schaafsma 2000). These shield images appear to have symbolized both the ability of the site's occupants to defend their homes (Schaafsma 2000) and to communicate their membership in particular clans, warrior societies, or religious sodalities (Bellorado 2020). In addition to large, bold pictographs, several sites had bold, bichrome-plaster murals decorating the exterior surfaces of a few special rooms (Bellorado 2020; Ortman 2008) (figure 18.4b).

The vernacular styles of architecture documented at many of the sites in the study area with mid-to-late AD 1200s construction were composed of wet-laid, single course, masonry as well as jacal architecture (figure 18.4c). At least a few sites in the area have habitation rooms constructed with front walls of jacal with entryways, and some even have slab or masonry entrybox complexes, Kayenta-style in form (Dean 1969, 27). Jacal construction is rarely seen in the central Mesa Verde region, and entryboxes even less so, but both were common features of construction in the Kayenta region (Dean 1969, 25; Geib 2011, 319). We also documented numerous examples of cotton textile-production evidence (i.e., weaving tools, loom anchors, loom parts, and discarded raw material refuse) at these late sites, indicating that cotton textile production was a full-fledged industry across the study area (Bellorado 2015, 2020, 2021; Crabtree and Bellorado 2016). Cotton weaving was a technology and practice that also had roots in the Kayenta region (Kent 1957, 1983; Lipe 1967; Magers 1975; Teague 1998).

When considered together—and with the frequent (though low) quantities of Tsegi Orange Wares, Tusayan Corrugated Gray Wares, and Tusayan White Wares (Bellorado 2015, 2021; Lipe and Glowacki 2011; Windes 2019), as well as square kivas and flat kiva roofs—these late Pueblo III period occupants of the greater Cedar Mesa area had strong material (as well as likely ideological) connections with groups in the Kayenta region. Other types of architecture (i.e., McElmo-style masonry [large blocky sandstone coursing with thick mortar joints], T-shaped doorways, Mesa Verde Region–style towers, cribbed-roof kivas with pilasters), and Mesa Verde ceramic traditions bespeak connections with the central Mesa Verde region to the east. The designs on painted white wares in the Cedar Mesa area contain a large proportion of cotton-textile-based motifs, typical in the Kayenta region but rarer on Mesa Verde white ware tradition ceramics from the central Mesa Verde area (Bellorado 2020; Crabtree and Bellorado 2016; Ortman 2000). This unique pattern of hybridity between the Mesa Verde and Kayenta material traditions define the cultural practices and local traditions of the greater Cedar Mesa area during the thirteenth century AD. It is this distinctive suite of mixed features that were maintained by groups leaving the Cedar Mesa area during the depopulation and took hold in the areas where they immigrated. For example, Schleher et al. (chapter 14 in this volume) suggest that due to the prevalence of cotton textile-based designs on white ware pottery, at least some of the population of Sand Canyon Pueblo may have immigrated from southeastern Utah, where these design systems were more common. While the full suite of hybrid features of potential Cedar Mesa area origin have not been identified at Sand Canyon Pueblo to date, the distinct cotton-textile-based designs stand out as recognizably different from the local pattern of coiled-basketry-based design systems that were more common at the contemporaneously occupied site of Goodman Point Pueblo and across the central Mesa Verde area (Linford 2018; Ortman 2000).

IMPLICATIONS FOR THE DEPOPULATION OF CEDAR MESA AND THE LARGER REGION

The addition of newly tree-ring dated sites to the dataset of those occupied after AD 1250 illuminate a significant amount of new construction during the AD 1250s, and at least a limited amount of new construction and remodeling in the 1260s; this changes our current view of the depopulation of the Cedar Mesa area dramatically. These data demonstrate that rather than a small holdout population at the Moon House Complex, a substantial population remained in the area until the early-to-mid AD 1270s, consisting of sixteen known sites (there are likely many more). This population built its habitations in hard-to-reach, defendable locations near sizable springs and water sources and in places where both canyon bottoms and mesa tops were easily accessible.

We have not attempted to formally estimate the size of the late population in the AD 1260s, but we provide preliminary estimates for consideration here. Matson and his colleagues (2015, 334) estimated that the average size of a family unit was comprised of five individuals. Thus, if we assume that each of the sixteen sites with AD 1260s components were occupied by one to three families, then a minimum of 80 to 240 individuals could have occupied these sites (table 18.1). Based on our documentation and analysis, however, we suspect that between 45 and 73 separate habitation units were built or remodeled in these sixteen sites in the 1260s, suggesting a more reasonable but still conservative occupation estimate of at least 225 to 365 occupants during this decade. Given the frequency of late dates and the likelihood that similar sites existed in the immediate area (particularly on the eastern side of Cedar Mesa), we suspect that the population in the AD 1250s, 1260s, and 1270s was much larger than previously proposed.

Additionally, Bellorado (2020, 2021) identified a style of painted bichrome building murals inside kivas, in gallery spaces, and on the exteriors of, and above, special buildings at five of the sites dated to the AD 1260s (42SA1763, 5005, 9309, 9310, and 42SA34831) (table 18.1). This style of mural was made using a combination of red-and-white, red-and-yellow, or red-and-green bichrome designs that often depict either landscape-based design elements or cotton textile motifs, or both (figure 18.4b). Based on tree-ring dates from a total of nine structures with painted bichrome decorations in the project area, Bellorado (2020) determined that this mural style developed in the area during the mid-to-late AD 1240s or early 1250s and continued until the final depopulation of the area in the early-to-mid 1270s. Bellorado (2020, fig. 5.15) also found this style of mural was produced in structures ten to twenty years earlier in the Cedar Mesa area than the rest of the region. In lieu of available tree-ring dates at sites with few or no chronological controls, the presence of this style of mural provides evidence that structures were occupied during, or after, the AD 1250s. In addition to the nine dated structures with both painted murals and tree-ring dates, Bellorado (2020, 2021, Table 7.3) identified the presence of painted murals in fifty-two additional structures that were mostly composed of kivas and habitation rooms that likely represent individual family units at a total of forty-six sites distributed across the greater Cedar Mesa area and that were occupied after AD 1250. Since these sites often contained 1–3 contemporary habitation units, they could reasonably account for an additional 280–560 people, if not more. Since Bellorado's sample of painted structures was limited by access to sites, mural preservation, and the presence of datable wood that he sampled, there are likely many more sites with painted decorations in the area that date to the last decades of the thirteenth century AD occupation of the area. These settlements were more widely dispersed when compared to the contemporaneous large, aggregated pueblos in the west central Mesa Verde, McElmo, and Mesa Verde Proper subregions of the northern San Juan region (Glowacki 2015, fig. 3; Glowacki and Ortman 2012; Ortman et al. 2000; Varien 1999) and in the Tsegi Canyon area (Dean 1969), but they still formed integrated communities that were loosely concentrated in a variety of canyon settings.

We unequivocally demonstrate occupation until AD 1270 and maybe later, yet our data also show that the number of dates declined in the years and decades before our latest dates, just as they were also in decline in the other regions. This decrease strongly suggests that immigration and the beginning of complete depopulation began in each area before the latest date. Our data from the greater Cedar Mesa area provide new evidence that indicates depopulation of the Four Corners area began before the onset of the Great Drought, and it likely indicates migration was due to many factors, both environmental and social.

IMPLICATIONS FOR THE DEPOPULATION OF THE LARGER REGION

Data presented here allow us to make important observations about the depopulation of the broader region at the end of the thirteenth century AD. First, the population size of the greater Cedar Mesa area between AD 1260 and 1270 was larger than previously proposed, and the timing of the emigration from the area was more protracted than previously suspected. Our data support prior suggestions by Glowacki (2015, 199) that the depopulation of communities and the larger social landscape likely occurred on the scale of the household. While many groups left prior to AD 1250, those who remained lived in small settlements scattered across the area for another one to two decades before emigrating. It is unlikely that occupation could have persisted if the area did not meet some minimum population threshold; an important finding of our research is demonstrating that there were enough people remaining to meet this threshold for viability into at least the AD 1260s.

Like communities in the east, the latest Cedar Mesa occupants appear to have developed new forms of civic-ceremonial architecture and religious practices. Unlike population centers in the east where large bi-wall, tri-wall, and D-shape structures were built (see Lekson, chapter 17 in this volume), new architectural forms of civic-ceremonial architecture in the Cedar Mesa region were smaller in size. These new types of communal architecture take the form of galleries with large windows (i.e., at Moon House M-1 [42SA5005]), at least one rectilinear great kiva, and one great kiva in an alcove (Bellorado 2020), many of which were also decorated with painted bichrome kiva murals with landscape referents (figure 18.4b and d). The bichrome-style murals found in kivas, coupled with the use of jacal construction and evidence of specialized cotton weaving, are attributes that provide evidence for immigrants from the Cedar Mesa area living at aggregated sites in the central Mesa Verde region and beyond (i.e., the middle San Juan, Canyon de Chelly, and the Gallina regions) (Bellorado 2017, 2020, fig. 5.14).

Perhaps the most well-known example of these bichrome murals with cotton textile and landscape referents are found in the third story room of Cliff Palace's four-story tower (Room 11) (Bellorado 2020, fig. 5.14c; Fewkes 1911, 42; Malville and Putnam 1993, fig. 5; Nordenskiöld [1893] 1990 [1893], fig. 78; Ortman 2012, fig. 10.3y). J. McKim Malville and Claudia Putnam (1993, 94–97) proposed that this mural was used as a calendrical observation station and to mark recurring astronomical events, including summer and winter solstices. Scott Ortman (2008, 244) found several examples in the central Mesa Verde region where similar murals were painted in second- or third-story rooms where the path of the sun, moon, and stars, and surrounding landscape views would have been visible throughout much of the year.

In the Cedar Mesa area and across the region, Bellorado (2020, 2021) also found that bichrome murals were often painted in or on rooms in elevated locations where astronomical events could have been observed. Bellorado (2021, 230) documented one example in the Cedar Mesa area that was painted on the exterior of a room in a perched alcove, which blends both landscape and textile imagery, and that functioned as a winter solstice marking device. At midday, during several days surrounding the winter solstice, the low angle of the sun causes a roof beam protruding from the structure to cast a shadow across the center of a series of painted concentric circles in the mural (figure 18.4d). Just before noon, the tip of the shadow pierces the centermost of the concentric circles. Based on these observations, we suggest that across the region bichrome murals in or on rooms in elevated locations were used, in part, as astronomical observatories. Our data show that this mural style developed earlier in the southeastern Utah but that it quicky spread across the region as the depopulation of the area began. This style of mural, and its strong association with astronomical observations, may represent the material expression of one set of ritual practices, ceremonies, and cosmological beliefs that developed in the greater Cedar Mesa area and then spread across the region as the depopulation unfolded.

Kuwanwisiwma and Bernardini (chapter 5 in this volume) discuss oral histories about specific clans of Hopi ancestors that moved from the greater Cedar Mesa area (i.e., the Bears Ears area) to the central Mesa Verde region. They explain the processes whereby clans local to the Cedar Mesa area with knowledge of particular ceremonies were recruited by communities in the central Mesa Verde region and vice versa. While they do not discuss murals, weaving technologies, or architectural styles in relation to these ceremonies or the clans that owned them, the spread of these features and technologies into new areas could be viewed as be the material signatures of these or other groups, their ritual practices, and specialized ceremonies being recruited by communities across the region. Whether viewed through the lens of migration or ritual recruitment of clans into far-flung communities, the depopulation of the greater Cedar Mesa area likely resulted from a complex array of push-and-pull factors that brought specific groups, their ritual practices, and technologies into new social landscapes just before the depopulation of the greater San Juan River drainage at the end of the thirteenth century AD.

Unlike the large community centers in the east, no large, aggregated pueblos were built in Cedar Mesa at the scale of Sand Canyon or Goodman Point Pueblos, though several medium-to-large-sized canyon-head sites (by Cedar Mesa standards) with tower complexes (i.e., 42SA1725 and 42SA1721/1763) around permanent springs may have functioned in similar ways. These sites, along with at least ten other likely contemporaneous sites with towers on the eastern escarpment of Cedar Mesa (in Comb and Butler Washes) (Bredthauer 2010, fig. 4.1), represent the westernmost extent of the Hovenweep-style tower complex in the region. Alison Bredthauer (2010, 110, 211) argues that the presence of Hovenweep-style towers and their placements at the heads and rims of canyons along with their pottery indicate that the occupants of these sites had strong social and ideological ties to the central Mesa Verde area.

When groups left the area throughout the AD 1200s, they migrated into increasingly aggregated communities in the central Mesa Verde region in the east, or to the Tsegi Canyon or Canyon de Chelly areas to the south (figure 18.1). Prior research by Crow Canyon and others have provided explanatory models for push-pull factors influencing migrations. These include discussions of warfare, disease and health, human impact on the environment, and environmental change (Dean 2010; Kuckelman 2010a, 193; Kuckelman et al. 2000; Lightfoot and Kuckelman 2001; Varien 2010; Wright 2010), perhaps even impacted by worldwide changes from catastrophic volcanic eruptions (Windes 2019). Social strife—as well as changes in social structure, settlement organization, and religious practices—may have provided the impetus to leave broad areas of the larger region (Glowacki 2010, 2011, 2015).

SUMMARY

A larger population remained in the Cedar Mesa area in the late Pueblo III period than had previously been proposed. Our data indicate a population of at least several hundred people, if not over 1,000 or more, in the area during the AD 1260s. While relatively small when compared to the larger sites in other areas, these populations formed a dispersed community that shared important connections that were expressed through settlement locations, architecture, building murals, and rock art. New communities were built near access to permanent springs and in precarious settings. Placement of sites in defensible settings that contained large shield imagery beginning in the mid-to-late AD 1240s and 1250s indicates the potential that warfare and intravillage strife were pressing issues for the groups who remained in the area. The impetus for shifting settlements to canyon-head settings in the early-to-mid AD 1200s may have begun in response to increased warfare and the threat of violence, either between local and outside forces or between local canyon communities. Groups moved away to avoid these conditions, and the remaining population took refuge in precarious places. Given contemporaneity, we propose that this social strife was related to similar types of increased violence and conflict that transpired at sites to the east, including Castle Rock and Sand Canyon Pueblos in the central Mesa Verde area (Kuckelman 2010a, 193, 2010b; Kuckelman et al. 2000; Kuckelman, chapter 19 in this volume) and in the middle San Juan region at Salmon Pueblo (Akins 2008, 164).

While some of the groups from Cedar Mesa may have left the region entirely, most likely moved east or southeast to join groups living in the central Mesa Verde, even the middle San Juan (Glowacki 2015), and possibly even the San Juan Basin areas. Some groups, however, may have moved out of the greater Cedar Mesa area to the south and west to join Kayenta region communities, in the Tsegi Canyon area and beyond, with whom they already had historic ties as evidenced by the use of shared architectural traditions including jacal architecture and entryboxes (Dean 1969; Geib 2011). Evidence of migrants from the Cedar Mesa area may also include the use of pilasters in kivas in Tsegi Canyon (Dean 1967, 132), the appearance of Mesa Verde–style mug technology at Awat'ovi in the Hopi region (Smith 1971, 198, fig. 153), and the use of tchamahias made from Brushy Basin chert sourced to the greater Cedar Mesa area (Arakawa et al., chapter 15 in this volume; Wenker 1999).

CONCLUSIONS

In this chapter we have provided new and unequivocal evidence for late construction activities in the canyons of Cedar Mesa during AD 1250–1270 period at a larger scale than previously suggested in prior studies (Matson, Lipe, and Curewitz 2015; Matson, Lipe, and Haase 1988; Varien 2010). These samples come primarily from sites with defensive attributes including difficult-to-access locations along cliff ledges and around, and on top of, pinnacle outcrops. Some sites also exhibit various architectural barriers, inhibiting direct access to parts of the site. We have documented in detail the large canyon sites within several canyon systems across the greater Cedar Mesa area and the southern areas of the Manti–La Sal National Forest and have begun to refine the late chronology at the end of the occupation of this long-lived cultural landscape (see Matson, Lipe, and Curewitz 2015; Matson, Lipe, and Haase 1988). The AD 1200s was a period of great change for ancestral Pueblo people across the northern San Juan region, with much warfare, out-migration to the east and south, and final cessation of habitation over much of the region by AD 1300 (Ahlstrom et al. 1995; Duff and Wilshusen 2000; Glowacki 2015; Varien 2010). These findings are due in large part to the contributions of researchers and associates associated with the Crow Canyon Archaeological Center, especially William Lipe, R. G. Matson, Mark Varien, and Steve Nash. We hope to continue this tradition by building on existing datasets and augmenting these data with new research.

The tree-ring dates presented in this chapter add to the enormous body of dendrochronological data for the northern Southwest. While our contribution is relatively small in terms of raw numbers of new dates, these data come from a critical area within the larger region, one distinguished by some of the best preservation and some of the most remarkable examples of ancestral Pueblo material culture. As such, these data provide valuable new insights into the greater Cedar Mesa area and the larger region. Just as important, our contribution illustrates that archaeologists should not limit their perspectives on the possibilities of tree-ring research due to "an embarrassment of riches," as Stephen Nash and Christina Rogers (2014) posit. Instead, we should continue to refine existing tree-ring chronologies and cultural histories in order to gain a more in-depth understanding of regional depopulation processes at the end of the thirteenth century.

REFERENCES

Ahlstrom, Richard V. N. 1985. "The Interpretation of Archaeological Tree-Ring Dates." PhD diss., University of Arizona, Tucson.

Ahlstrom, Richard. V. N., Carla R. Van West, and Jeffrey S. Dean. 1995. "Environmental and Chronological Factors in the Mesa Verde-Northern Rio Grande Migration." *Journal of Anthropological Archaeology* 14 (2): 125–142.

Akins, Nancy J. 2008. "Human Remains Recovered from the Tower Kiva at Salmon Ruins." In *Chaco's Northern Prodigies: Salmon, Aztec, and the Ascendancy of the Middle San Juan Region after A.D. 1100*, edited by Paul F. Reed, 140–164. Salt Lake City: University of Utah Press.

Bannister, Bryant, Jeffrey S. Dean, and William J. Robinson. 1969. *Tree-Ring Dates from Utah S-W: Southern Utah Area*. Tucson: Laboratory of Tree-Ring Research, University of Arizona.

Bedell, Melanie Lynne. 2000. "Late Pueblo II and Pueblo III Cliff Dwellings and Community Patterns in Grand Gulch, Southeastern Utah." MA thesis, Washington State University, Pullman.

Bellorado, Benjamin A. 2015. "Cedar Mesa Building Murals Inventory, Documentation, and Dating Project: A Report of the Survey, Sampling, and Results of Work Conducted in 2013 and 2014." Annual Report Prepared for the Monticello District

Field Office of the BLM and the Canyonlands Natural History Association. Blanding, Utah: Edge of the Cedars Museum.

Bellorado, Benjamin A. 2017. "The Context, Dating, and Role of Painted Building Murals in Gallina Society." *Kiva* 83 (4): 471–493.

Bellorado, Benjamin A. 2020. "Leaving Footprints in the Ancient Southwest: Visible Indicators of Group Affiliation and Social Position in the Chaco and Post-Chaco Eras (A.D. 850–1300)." PhD diss., University of Arizona, Tucson.

Bellorado, Benjamin A. 2021. "The Cedar Mesa Building Murals Inventory, Documentation, and Dating Project: A Final Report on the Results of Research Conducted on Bureau of Land Management Administered Lands in Southeastern Utah between 2013 and 2017." Final report prepared for the Monticello District Field Office of the BLM and the Canyonlands Natural History Association, Edge of the Cedars Museum, Blanding, UT.

Bellorado, Benjamin A., and Barbara J. Mills. 2022. "Building Murals, Ritual Clothing, and Stages for Religious Performance in the Greater Cedar Mesa Area." In *Linda Cordell: Detail, Passion, and Innovation in Archaeology and Beyond*, edited by Maxine McBrinn and Debora Huntley, 111–122. Albuquerque, NM: Museum of New Mexico Press.

Benson, Larry V., Kenneth Lee Petersen, and John Stein. 2007. "Anasazi (Pre-Colombian Native American) Migrations during the Middle-Twelfth and Late-Thirteenth Centuries: Were They Drought Induced?" *Climatic Change* 83 (1–2): 187–213.

Bloomer, William W. 1989. "Moon House: A Pueblo III Period Cliff Dwelling Complex in Southeastern Utah." MA thesis, School of Anthropology, Washington State University, School of Anthropology, Pullman.

Bocinsky, R. Kyle. 2014. "Landscape-Based Null Models for Archaeological Inference." PhD diss., Washington State University, Pullman.

Bredthauer, Alison V. 2010. "A Towering Enigma: An Examination of Late Pueblo II and Pueblo III Towers in the Northern San Juan Region." MA thesis, University of Colorado, Boulder.

Crabtree, Stefani A., and Benjamin A. Bellorado. 2016. "Using Cross-Media Approaches to Understand an Invisible Industry: How Cotton Production Influenced Pottery Designs and Kiva Murals in Cedar Mesa." *Kiva* 82 (2): 174–200.

Dean, Jeffrey S. 1967. "Chronological Analysis of Tsegi Phase Sites in Northeastern Arizona." PhD diss., Department of Anthropology, University of Arizona, Tucson.

Dean, Jeffrey S. 1969. *Chronological Analysis of Tsegi Phase Sites in Northeastern Arizona.* Papers of the Laboratory of Tree-Ring Research, No. 3. Tucson: University of Arizona Press.

Dean, Jeffrey S. 1996a. "Demography, Environment, and Subsistence Stress." In *Evolving Complexity and Environmental Risk in the Prehistoric Southwest*, edited by Joseph A. Tainter and Bonnie Bagley Tainter, 25–56. Santa Fe Institute Studies in the Sciences of Complexity, Proceedings, Vol. 24. Reading, MA: Addison-Wesley Publishing Company.

Dean, Jeffrey S. 1996b. "Kayenta Anasazi Settlement Transformations in Northeastern Arizona, A.D. 1150–1350." In *The Prehistoric Pueblo World, A.D. 1150–1350*, edited by Michael A. Adler, 29–47. Tucson: University of Arizona Press.

Dean, Jeffrey S. 2010. "The Environmental, Demographic, and Behavioral Context of the Thirteenth-Century Depopulation of the Northern Southwest." In *Leaving Mesa Verde: Peril and Change in the Thirteenth-Century Southwest*, edited by Timothy A. Kohler, Mark D. Varien, and Aaron M. Wright, 324–345. Tucson: University of Arizona Press.

Duff, Andrew I., and Richard H. Wilshusen. 2000. "Prehistoric Population Dynamics in the Northern San Juan Region, A.D. 950–1300." *Kiva* 66 (1): 167–190.

Fewkes, Jesse Walter. 1911. "Antiquities of the Mesa Verde National Park: Cliff Palace." Bureau of American Ethnology Bulletin 51.

Geib, Phil R. 2011. *Foragers and Farmers of the Northern Kayenta Region: Excavations along the Navajo Mountain Road*. Salt Lake City: University of Utah Press.

Glowacki, Donna M. 2010. "The Social and Cultural Contexts of the Central Mesa Verde Region during the Thirteenth-Century Migrations." In *Leaving Mesa Verde: Peril and Change in the Thirteenth-Century Southwest*, edited by Timothy A. Kohler, Mark D. Varien, and Aaron M. Wright, 200–221. Tucson: University of Arizona Press.

Glowacki, Donna M. 2011. "The Role of Religion in the Depopulation of the Central Mesa Verde Region." In *Religious Transformation in the Late Pre-Hispanic Pueblo World*, edited by Donna M. Glowacki and Scott Van Keuren, 66–83. Amerind Studies in Archaeology. Tucson: University of Arizona Press.

Glowacki, Donna M. 2015. *Living and Leaving: A Social History of Regional Depopulation in Thirteenth-Century Mesa Verde*. Tucson: University of Arizona Press.

Glowacki, Donna M., and Scott G. Ortman. 2012. "Characterizing Community-Center (Village) Formation in the VEP Study Area, A.D. 600–1280." In *Emergence and Collapse of Early Villages: Models of Central Mesa Verde Archaeology*, edited by Timothy A. Kohler and Mark D. Varien, 219–246. Berkeley: University of California Press.

Jolie, Edward A. 2018. "Social Diversity in the Chaco System, A.D. 850–1140: An Analysis of Basketry Technological Style." PhD diss., Department of Anthropology, University of New Mexico, Albuquerque.

Kantner, John W., and Keith W. Kintigh. 2006. "The Chaco World." In *The Archaeology of Chaco Canyon: An Eleventh-Century Pueblo Regional Center*, edited by Stephen H. Lekson, 1st ed., 153–188. School of American Research Advanced Seminar Series. Santa Fe, NM: School of American Research Press.

Kent, Kate Peck. 1957. "The Cultivation and Weaving of Cotton in the Prehistoric Southwestern United States." *Transactions of the American Philosophical Society* 47 (3): 457–732.

Kent, Kate Peck. 1983. *Prehistoric Textiles of the Southwest*. Southwest Indian Arts Series. Santa Fe, NM: School of American Research.

Kuckelman, Kristin A. 2010a. "Catalysts of the Thirteenth-Century Depopulation of Sand Canyon Pueblo and the Central Mesa Verde Region." In *Leaving Mesa Verde: Peril and Change in the Thirteenth-Century Southwest*, edited by Timothy A. Kohler, Mark D. Varien, and Aaron M. Wright, 180–199. Tucson: University of Arizona Press.

Kuckelman, Kristin A. 2010b. "The Depopulation of Sand Canyon Pueblo, A Large Ancestral Pueblo Village in Southwestern Colorado." *American Antiquity* 75 (3): 497–525.

Kuckelman, Kristin A., Ricky R. Lightfoot, and Debra L. Martin. 2000. "Changing Patterns of Violence in the Northern San Juan Region." *Kiva* 66 (1): 147–165.

Lekson, Stephen H., ed. 2006. *The Archaeology of Chaco Canyon: An Eleventh-Century Pueblo Regional Center*. School of American Research Advanced Seminar Series. Santa Fe, NM: School of American Research Press.

Lightfoot, Ricky R., and Kristin A. Kuckelman. 2001. "A Case Study of Warfare in the Mesa Verde Region." In *Deadly Landscapes: Case Studies in Prehistoric Southwestern Warfare*, edited by Glen Rice and Steven A. LeBlanc, 51–64. Salt Lake City: University of Utah Press.

Linford, Samantha Jo. 2018. "Moieties in the Northern Rio Grande: Ceramic Design Analysis and Social Identity in Southwest Colorado and Northern New Mexico." MA thesis, Department of Anthropology, University of Colorado, Boulder.

Lipe, William D. 1967. "Anasazi Culture and Its Relationship to the Environment in the Red Rock Plateau Region, Southeastern Utah." PhD diss. microfilm on file at the Department of Anthropology, University of Michigan, Ann Arbor.

Lipe, William D., and Donna M. Glowacki. 2011. "A Late Pueblo II Period 'Surge' of Kayenta Ceramics into Southern Utah?" Paper presented at the 76th Annual Meeting of the Society for American Archaeology. Sacramento, CA.

Lipe, William D., and R. G. Matson. 2007. "The Cedar Mesa Project: 1967–2007." Electronic Document. Washington State University Library: Research Exchange. Washington State University, Pullman. Accessed January 30, 2023. https://rex.librar ies.wsu.edu/esploro/outputs/report/The-Cedar-Mesa-Project-1967-2007/99900501 031601842.

Magers, Pamela C. 1975. "The Cotton Industry at Antelope House." *Kiva* 41 (1): 39–47.

Malville, J. McKim, and Claudia Putnam. 1993. *Prehistoric Astronomy in the Southwest*. 2nd ed. Boulder, CO: Johnson Printing Company.

Matson, R. G. 1991. *The Origins of Southwestern Agriculture*. Tucson: University of Arizona Press.

Matson, R. G., William D. Lipe, and Diane Curewitz. 2015. "Dynamics of the Thirteenth-Century Depopulation of the Northern San Juan: The View from Cedar Mesa." *Kiva* 80 (3–4): 324–346.

Matson, R. G., William D. Lipe, and William Randolph Haase IV. 1988. "Adaptational Continuities and Occupational Discontinuities: The Cedar Mesa Anasazi." *Journal of Field Archaeology* 15 (3): 245–264.

Mills, Barbara J., Matthew A. Peeples, Leslie D. Aragon, Benjamin A. Bellorado, Jeffery J. Clark, Evan Giomi, and Thomas C. Windes. 2018. "Evaluating Chaco Migration Scenarios Using Dynamic Social Network Analysis." *Antiquity* 92 (346): 922–939.

Morton, Ethan E. 2002. "Late Pueblo II and Pueblo III Canyon Settlement Patterns at Cedar Mesa, Southeast Utah." MA thesis, Department of Anthropology, Washington State University, Pullman.

Nash, Stephen E., and Christina T. Rogers. 2014. "An Embarrassment of Riches: Tree-Ring Dating, the History of Archaeology, and the Interpretation of Precolumbian History at Mesa Verde National Park." In *Archaeology in the Great Basin and Southwest: Papers in Honor of Don D. Fowler*, edited by Nancy J. Parezo and Joel C. Janetski, 309–321. Salt Lake City: University of Utah Press.

Nordenskiöld, Gustaf. (1893) 1990. *The Cliff Dwellers of the Mesa Verde*. Mesa Verde National Park Visitor and Research Center Museum, CO: Mesa Verde Museum Association.

Ortman, Scott G. 2000. "Conceptual Metaphor in the Archaeological Record: Methods and an Example from the American Southwest." *American Antiquity* 65 (4): 613–645.

Ortman, Scott G. 2008. "Architectural Metaphor and Chacoan Influence in the Northern San Juan." In *Archaeology without Borders: Contact, Commerce, and Change in the U.S. Southwest and Northwestern Mexico*, edited by Laurie D. Webster and Maxine E. McBrinn, 227–255. Boulder: University Press of Colorado.

Ortman, Scott G. 2012. *Winds from the North: Tewa Origins and Historical Anthropology*. Salt Lake City: University of Utah Press.

Ortman, Scott G., Donna M. Glowacki, Melissa J. Churchill, and Kristin A. Kuckelman. 2000. "Pattern and Variation in Northern San Juan Village Histories." *Kiva* 66 (1): 123–146.

Salzer, Matthew W. 2000. "Temperature Variability and the Northern Anasazi: Possible Implications for Regional Abandonment." *Kiva* 65 (4): 295–318.

Salzer, Matthew W., and Kurt F. Kipfmueller. 2005. "Reconstructed Temperature and Precipitation on a Millennial Timescale from Tree-Rings in the Southern Colorado Plateau, U.S.A." *Climatic Change* 70 (3): 465–487.

Schaafsma, Polly. 2000. *Warrior, Shield, and Star: Imagery and Ideology of Pueblo Warfare*. Santa Fe, NM: Western Edge Press.

Schwindt, Dylan M., R. Kyle Bocinsky, Scott G. Ortman, Donna M. Glowacki, Mark D. Varien, and Timothy A. Kohler. 2016. "The Social Consequences of Climate Change in the Central Mesa Verde Region." *American Antiquity* 81 (1): 74–96. https://doi.org/10.7183/0002-7316.81.1.74.

Smith, Watson. 1971. *Painted Ceramics of the Western Mound at Awatovi*. Reports of the Awatovi Expedition. Vol. Reports of the Awatovi Expedition. No. 8 vols. Papers of the Peabody Museum of Archaeology and Ethnology, Harvard University Vol. 38. Peabody Museum of Archaeology and Ethnology, Harvard University, Cambridge.

Teague, Lynn S. 1998. *Textiles in Southwestern Prehistory*. Albuquerque: University of New Mexico Press.

Van West, Carla R. 1996. "Agricultural Potential and Carrying Capacity in Southwestern Colorado, A.D. 901–1300." In *The Prehistoric Pueblo World, A.D. 1150–1350*, edited by Michael A. Adler, 214–227. Tucson: University of Arizona Press.

Varien, Mark. 1999. *Sedentism and Mobility in a Social Landscape: Mesa Verde and Beyond*. Tucson: University of Arizona Press.

Varien, Mark D. 2010. "Depopulation of the Northern San Juan Region: Historical Review and Archaeological Context." In *Leaving Mesa Verde: Peril and Change in the Thirteenth-Century Southwest*, edited by Timothy A. Kohler, Mark D. Varien, and Aaron M. Wright, 1–33. Tucson: University of Arizona Press.

Walker, J. Terry. 1977. "A Description and Interpretation of ML 1147, An Undisturbed Archaeological Site, Manti-LaSal National Forest, Utah." MA thesis, Brigham Young University, Provo, UT.

Wenker, Chris T. 1999. "Prehistoric Puebloan Lithic Procurement and Tchamahia Production." MA thesis, Northern Arizona University, Flagstaff.

Windes, Thomas C. 2010. "Summary of Field Work at Natural Bridges National Monument in July–August 2010." Unpublished Annual Report on file. NPS Permit NABR-2010-SCI-0005. Arches and Canyonlands National Park Service Headquarters, National Park Service, Moab, UT.

Windes, Thomas C. 2012. "Report on BLM Field Work in SE Utah 2012." Unpublished Annual Report on file. Monticello Field Office, Bureau of Land Management, Monticello, UT.

Windes, Thomas C. 2013. "Report on BLM Field Work in SE Utah 2013: Dry and Slickhorn Canyons, Butler Wash, and Beef Basin." Unpublished Annual Report. BLM Wood Project #2013-U-13-BL-0707b. Monticello Field Office, Bureau of Land Management, Monticello, UT.

Windes, Thomas C. 2014. "Structural Wood Documentation and Dendrochronology in SE Utah: Report on the 2011 Field Work on Cedar Mesa in Slickhorn Canyon and in Natural Bridges National Monument." Unpublished Annual Report on file. 2011 Discovery Grant (11-5-BLM/NPS). Final Report for Canyonlands Natural History Association, Canyonlands Natural History Association, Moab, UT.

Windes, Thomas C. 2015. "Report on BLM Structural Wood Projects in SE Utah 2014: Cedar Mesa, Fable Valley, Beef Basin, and Whiskers Draw." Unpublished Annual Report on file. BLM Wood Project #2014-U-14-BL-1362. Monticello Field Office, Bureau of Land Management, Monticello, UT.

Windes, Thomas C. 2016. "Structural Wood Documentation and Dendrochronology in SE Utah: Tree-Ring and AMS Dates from Cedar Mesa." Unpublished Annual Report on file. 2016 Discovery Grant (16-05-BLM). Final Report for Canyonlands Natural History Association. Canyonlands Natural History Association, Moab, UT.

Windes, Thomas C. 2018a. "Structural Wood Documentation and Dendrochronology in SE Utah: Tree-Ring and AMS Dates from Cedar Mesa." Unpublished Annual Report on file. Canyonlands Natural History Association Project 2016 Discovery Pool Grant (#16-05-BLM). Canyonlands Natural History Association, Moab, UT.

Windes, Thomas C. 2018b. "Structural Wood Project in the Slickhorn Canyon Area, Cedar Mesa, 2018: BLM, Monticello District, SE Utah." Unpublished Annual Report on file. BLM Wood Project #MTFO18023 (Utah State Project #2018–U-18-BL-0387). Monticello Field Office, Bureau of Land Management, Monticello, UT.

Windes, Thomas C. 2019. "Report of 2016 and 2017 Field Activities on BLM Lands, Monticello District, SE Utah." Unpublished Annual Report on file. BLM Wood Project #MTFO18023 (Utah State Project #U-18-BL-0100). Monticello Field Office, Bureau of Land Management, Monticello, UT.

Windes, Thomas C. 2020. "Structural Wood Project in the Slickhorn Canyon Area, Cedar Mesa, 2020, BLM, Monticello District, SE Utah." Unpublished Annual Report on file. BLM Wood Project #MTFO20014 (Utah State Project #U20BL0143 [2020]). Monticello Field Office, Bureau of Land Management, Monticello, UT.

Windes, Thomas C. 2021. "Report on Two Utah State Lands Sites in the Tower Canyon Branch of Mule Canyon (42SA1725) and in Beef Basin (42SA222/5377), SE Utah, 2015 Wood Project Report." Unpublished Annual Report on file. Trust Lands Administration Main Office. Utah School and Institutional Trust Lands Administration, Salt Lake City, UT.

Windes, Thomas C. 2022. "Structural Wood Project in the Slickhorn Canyon Area, Cedar Mesa, 2022, BLM, Monticello District, SE Utah." Unpublished Annual Report on file. BLM Wood Project # MTFO20014 (Utah State Project # U20BL0143 [2021]). Monticello Field Office, Bureau of Land Management, Monticello, UT.

Windes, Thomas C., and Peter J. McKenna. 2001. "Going against the Grain: Wood Production in Chacoan Society." *American Antiquity* 66 (1): 119–140.

Wright, Aaron M. 2010. "The Climate of the Depopulation of the Northern Southwest." In *Leaving Mesa Verde: Peril and Change in the Thirteenth-Century Southwest*, edited by Timothy A. Kohler, Mark D. Varien, and Aaron M. Wright, 75–101. Tucson: University of Arizona Press.

19

Thirteenth-Century Villages and the Depopulation of the Northern San Juan Region by Pueblo Peoples

KRISTIN KUCKELMAN

During the initial forty years of research conducted by the Crow Canyon Archaeological Center (Crow Canyon), several excavation projects focused on a primary stated research goal of the Center: discover how and why Pueblo peoples completely and permanently ended residential settlement of the northern San Juan region late in the thirteenth century AD. Crow Canyon chose this research focus because, even as late as the mid-1980s, this depopulation was still poorly understood, which significantly obstructed a comprehensive understanding of the Pueblo past. Between 1984 and 2008, Crow Canyon thus conducted excavations at numerous sites of thirteenth-century villages (Churchill 2002; Kuckelman 2000a, 2003b, 2007, 2017; Ryan 2015a, 2015b). In this chapter, I briefly synthesize and contextualize recent findings on thirteenth-century villages in the region and focus particularly on final regional depopulation.

Approximately 250 villages were occupied in the northern San Juan region during the thirteenth century (Glowacki 2015, 46–47; Glowacki et al., chapter 12 in this volume). Multicomponent Yellow Jacket Pueblo (Kuckelman 2003a) was the largest of these. Woods Canyon (Churchill 2002), Shields (Ryan 2015b),

https://doi.org/10.5876/9781646424597.c019

and Albert Porter (Ryan 2015a) Pueblos, also multicomponent, yielded data crucial to understanding the histories of thirteenth-century villages in the region. Goodman Point, Castle Rock, and Sand Canyon Pueblos, single-component sites, were occupied for only the final few decades preceding complete regional depopulation about AD 1280, and those sites (Kuckelman 2000a, 2007, 2017d) thus yielded data specific to conditions and events just before depopulation. During the past forty years, little excavation occurred at the sites of any other thirteenth-century villages in the region. Here, I follow William Lipe and Scott Ortman's (2000, 92) definition of an ancestral Pueblo village as a settlement that contained more than fifty contemporaneous structures in proximity to each other.

In this region, the thirteenth century was a time of increased population density (Duff and Wilshusen 2000; Glowacki 2010, table 9.1, 2015; Hill et al. 2010, figs. 2.1, 2.2; Varien 2010, table 1.1), shifts in settlement patterning (see Lipe and Varien 1999), cultural development and transformation, architectural innovation, and ritual intensification (Glowacki 2015). It was the peak of Pueblo culture in this region until the system was severely impacted by the coalescence of numerous deleterious conditions and events that included deteriorating environmental conditions, population packing (Hill et al. 2010, figs. 2.1, 2.2; Varien et al. 2000, figs. 2, 3, 4), crop failure, and intercommunity warfare. The most consequential occurrence in the thirteenth century in the region was the complete and final departure of Pueblo peoples, bringing the Pueblo III period to an end about AD 1280.

Between about AD 1130 and 1180, the region had experienced a period of severe drought (Berry and Benson 2010, figs. 3.2D1, 3.4B; Burns 1983; Dean and Van West 2002, figs. 4.1, 4.3), and widespread warfare (Billman et al. 2000; Kuckelman 2016, table 6.1; Turner and Turner 1999; White 1992). The population of the region decreased during that time, but after climatic conditions improved after AD 1180 (Berry and Benson 2010, figs. 3.2W2, 3.4C), the resulting rebound in population and construction activity continued well into the thirteenth century (Glowacki 2010, table 9.1, 2015; Varien 2010, table 1.1).

AD 1200 TO 1250

The occupational histories of thirteenth-century villages in the northern San Juan followed multiple trajectories (see Ortman et al. 2000); however, some general trends can be noted. During the first half of the century, loose settlement clusters formed on rolling uplands with excellent agricultural potential. These clusters composed social, economic, and political communities, and some, such as the Goodman Point community (Coffey 2018; Ryan 2015b), included a village and a great kiva (Coffey 2018). Communities shared an ideology, a social identity, domestic water sources, and cooperative projects. The subsistence system was heavily dependent on maize crops (Decker and Tieszen 1989; Matson 2016) and on domesticated turkeys, although a variety of game and edible wild plants (see Oas and Adams, chapter 22 in this volume) supplemented these domesticates. Periods of cooler temperatures during this time (Salzer and Kipfmueller 2005) could have curtailed growing seasons and reduced crop productivity. The unprecedented consumption of turkey co-occurred with a severe reduction in mule deer as a result of overhunting (Driver 2002; Schollmeyer and Driver, chapter 21 in this volume).

The largest village during the first half of the century, and the largest Pueblo site ever recorded in the region, was Yellow Jacket Pueblo (Kuckelman 2003a), which occupied nearly 100 acres and housed as many as 1,300 residents. It is likely that during this time Yellow Jacket was a regional hub of power and influence and might thus have served as an example to dispersed communities of the advantages of aggregated settlement and stimulated other communities to follow suit. Regional population is estimated to have peaked between AD 1225 and 1260 (cf. Hill et al. 2010, figs. 2.2a, 2.2b) at nearly 35,000 residents (Varien 2010, 16–17).

AD 1250 TO 1280

By about AD 1250, serious difficulties had developed. Some models suggest that out-migration from the region predated AD 1250 (Cordell et al. 2007; Duff and Wilshusen 2000), but a large number of the remaining 35,000 residents of the region (Varien 2010, 16–17) moved from rolling uplands to construct villages in canyon settings (Varien 2010, table 1.4), many of which were located on or near the primary community spring (Lipe 1995, 153; Lipe and Ortman 2000; Lipe and Varien 1999). The population near the geographic middle of the San Juan region—that is, the central Mesa Verde portion of the region—reached its greatest density (Hill et al. 2010, figs. 2.1a, 2.2; Varien 2010, table 1.1; Varien et al. 2000, fig. 4), possibly augmented by immigration from outlying areas of the region (Glowacki 2015; Hill et al. 2010, fig. 2.1a; Varien 2010); tree-ring dates indicate that occupation of southeastern Utah by Pueblo peoples was significantly reduced by about midcentury (Bellorado and Windes, chapter 18 in this volume; Glowacki 2015).

Villages in the Hovenweep area (Winter 1975, 1976, 1977) were built on bedrock canyon rims; others, such as Sand Canyon Pueblo (Kuckelman 2007) and Goodman Point Pueblo (Kuckelman 2017d), were constructed around more heavily vegetated canyon heads, and villages at Mesa Verde proper, such as Cliff Palace (Fewkes 1911) and Long House (Cattanach 1980), were situated in large alcoves. Thus, by midcentury, most of the population of the region had resettled into fewer and larger settlements (Kohler 2010, 119) on or near some of the most agriculturally productive soils in the region (Dean 2010, 333; Glowacki 2010, 2015). The population of Yellow Jacket Pueblo dwindled (Kuckelman 2007), and Sand Canyon, with 450 to 700 residents, and Goodman Point, with 600 to 900 residents, became the two largest villages in the region (Adler and Hegmon, chapter 16, and Schleher et al., chapter 14 in this volume).

Proprietary access to springs was a key factor in this resettlement; for Pueblo families, the region was uninhabitable without springs for domestic water. The area occupied by the dispersed Goodman Point community, for example, contained numerous springs (Connolly 1992, fig. 4.2); however, at midcentury, residents constructed Goodman Point Pueblo around their most prolific spring. Some research suggests that drought in the mid-AD 1200s could have reduced the flow rate of some springs in the region (Kolm and Smith 2012, 77–79); in any case, by midcentury, proximity to the primary community spring trumped proximity to crop fields.

The new villages incorporated many defensive structures (Kuckelman 2002). Sand Canyon and Goodman Point Pueblos included massive enclosing walls that stood at least one story tall, angled loopholes for viewing the landscape outside the village, and towers (Kuckelman 2007, 2017d). The defensive aspects of towers are well documented (Farmer 1957; Hibben 1948; Kuckelman 2000b; Lancaster and Pinkley 1954, 44–47; Mackey and Green 1979; Schulman 1950; Wilcox and Haas 1994, 218). Towers at Sand Canyon Pueblo abutted the outside face of the village-enclosing wall but could be accessed only from inside the village.

The aggregation of population, in and of itself, might have been one goal of the midcentury resettlement. Aggregation is a highly effective defensive strategy (Crown et al. 1996, 200–201; Haas and Creamer 1996, 209–210; Kidder 1924; LeBlanc 1999; Reid et al. 1996; Tuggle and Reid 2001), and a correlation has been reported between population aggregation and conflict (Haas and Creamer 1996; Wilcox and Haas 1994). The placement of new villages in defensible locations and the construction of defensive architectural features suggest social turmoil and credible threat of attack.

By midcentury, Pueblo families had become even more heavily dependent on maize crops for many of their calories (Decker and Tieszen 1989; Matson 2016) and on domesticated turkeys for animal protein; turkeys were also fed maize (McCaffery et al. 2014; Munro 1994; Nott 2010; Rawlings and Driver 2010; Schollmeyer and Driver, chapter 21 in this volume). Wild resources had been reduced (Adams and Bowyer 2002, 123; Dean and Van West 2002, 97; Driver 2002, 158–160, Johnson et al. 2005; Kohler 2004; Kohler et al. 2007) by a millennium of exploitation. The survival of Pueblo residents thus depended on the success of maize crops. However, multiple environmental downturns that included disrupted precipitation patterns (Dean 1996; Dean and Funkhouser 1995; Van West and Dean 2000; Wright 2010), cooler temperatures (Adams and Petersen 1999; Petersen 1988, 1994; Salzer 2000; Wright 2010, fig. 4.3), and periodic droughts (Dean and Van West 2002) had descended upon the region. These conditions developed when the Pueblo population in the central portion of the region reached its greatest density (Hill et al. 2010, figs. 2.1a, 2.2; Kohler et al. 2007; Varien 2010; Varien et al. 2007), which would have limited the ability of families to relocate farmsteads and fields (Cordell et al. 2007, 385–386) and would have reduced wild plant and animal resources already diminished by periodic droughts and centuries of exploitation.

By midcentury, violence in the northern Southwest had begun to escalate (Haas 1990; Haas and Creamer 1996; LeBlanc 1998, 1999; LeBlanc and Rice 2001; Lightfoot and Kuckelman 2001; Morris 1939, 42; Schaafsma 2000; Wilcox and Haas 1994, 236). Many lines of indirect evidence—defensible settlement locations, defensive architecture, population aggregation, traditional narratives, warfare imagery, and structural burning—have been discussed elsewhere (see Kuckelman 2002, 2012, 2014; Lightfoot and Kuckelman 2001). Direct evidence has been found in the form of both antemortem and lethal-level perimortem trauma on human remains (Cattanach 1980, 145–146; Kuckelman 2010b; Kuckelman et al. 2002, table 3; Kuckelman and Martin 2007, table 12; Lambert 1999; Street 2001, 198), and the remains of some individuals exhibit multiple antemortem cranial fractures (Kuckelman 2017b; Kuckelman et al. 2002, table 3) that would have been inflicted between midcentury and final regional depopulation. Such violence is likely to have been a factor in decisions to construct defensive villages with proprietary access to domestic water.

FINAL DEPOPULATION

The so-called Great Drought, which descended on the Southwest by at least AD 1276 and persisted for decades (Berry and Benson 2010, figs. 3.2D2, 3.4D; Dean and Van West 2002; Douglass 1929), dealt the final blow to Pueblo occupation of the region. Evidence of the effects of the Great Drought on Pueblo peoples has proved challenging to detect in the archaeological record; robust assemblages of food refuse that could be firmly dated to the final few years of regional occupation have been lacking until recently. However, Crow Canyon excavations at Sand Canyon (Kuckelman 2007), Goodman Point (Kuckelman 2016, 2017d, 2020), and Castle Rock (Kuckelman, ed. 2000) Pueblos yielded abundant food remains that reveal evidence of subsistence stress. The remains of food consumed during most of the time the villages were occupied, found in midden deposits, were compared to remains of final meals consumed just before the villages were depopulated, found in abandonment contexts. The results (Hoffman et al. 2010, Kuckelman 2008, 2010a, 2010b, 2016) reflect dramatic dietary shifts indicative of famine just before village and regional depopulation—remains of turkeys and crop foods dominate midden samples, whereas remains on floors and in cooking features are mostly wild plant foods (including nonpreferred foods) and the skeletal remains of various wild animals. Corroborating evidence was reported by Robert Muir (1999); the variety of taxa represented in the faunal assemblage from Sand Canyon Pueblo is less than expected for midden contexts and greater than expected for other contexts. Multiple independent data thus indicate that just before depopulation, Pueblo farmers became predominantly hunters and gatherers, presumably because of crop failure and an associated reduction in turkey flocks.

The occupations of the two largest villages in the region—Goodman Point and Sand Canyon Pueblos—as well as smaller pueblos such as Castle Rock and probably at least some of the Mesa Verde cliff dwellings, ended in attacks in which many people perished, sometime within a few years after the onset of the Great Drought. Direct evidence of these attacks was left on the remains of men, women, and children that were left unburied on prehistoric ground surface, on structure floors, and on structure roofs at sites of villages excavated by Crow Canyon (Kuckelman 2010b; Kuckelman 2017d; Kuckelman et al. 2002) and at sites of other villages, including Mesa Verde cliff dwellings (Cattanach 1980, 415; Fewkes 1909, 24; Kuckelman et al. 2017; Kuckelman and Martin 2007, table 12; Lambert 1999, 141; Morris 1939, 82; Street 2001, 198) and Ruin 6 (Morris 1939). Some remains exhibit perimortem cranial depression fractures and other traumatic injuries (Kuckelman 2012, 126); multiple individuals who perished had survived previous cranial trauma (Kuckelman 2017b; Kuckelman et al. 2002, table 3). At Goodman Point Pueblo, weathered human remains found in the roof-fall debris of multistory structures (towers) reveal that during attacks, such structures were used as refuges and perhaps for active defense (Kuckelman 2017a). Evidence of trophy taking and anthropophagy associated with these warfare events has been reported elsewhere (Kuckelman 2010b, 2017b, 2020; Kuckelman et al. 2002; Lambert 1999, 141).

No compelling archaeological data indicate the presence of any culture group other than Pueblo peoples in the northern San Juan region at any time either before or during the thirteenth century AD (see Kuckelman 2002, 2014; Kuckelman et al. 2002; LeBlanc 1998, 1999; Lipe 1995, 161–162; Lipe and Varien 1999, 341; Wilcox and Haas 1994). It is likely that Pueblo warriors from the largest villages in the region—Sand Canyon and Goodman Point Pueblos—were among the aggressors. Human remains at Goodman Point Pueblo that predate the final attack of that village appear to be evidence of "perpetrator" actions against enemy settlements (Kuckelman 2020), whereas no such evidence has been reported for other pueblos occupied late in the thirteenth century. It is possible that more-distant groups of Pueblo warriors, such as those in the middle San Juan region of northwestern New Mexico, invaded villages in the central Mesa Verde area. Regardless of who perpetrated which attack, neither victors nor anyone else settled in the defeated pueblos.

Perhaps surprisingly, hydrologic data suggest that a scarcity of domestic water is unlikely to have been a factor in final depopulation. Recent simulation studies indicate that the flow rates of different springs in this area varied widely (Kolm and Smith 2012, 77) but do not indicate a significant decrease in flow rate late in the thirteenth century (Kolm and Smith 2012, 82–83; Smith et al. 2006). Further, recent studies on the spring at Goodman Point Pueblo (Wright Paleohydrological Institute 2011) suggest that flow rates would have been adequate for the needs of the community throughout the Pueblo occupation of the region (Kuckelman 2017c), even during droughts. It is also important to note that occupation of the region continued during the severely droughty fifty-year period of the mid-AD 1100s (Kohler et al. 2007; Varien 2010), which would have been all but impossible had most springs ceased to issue water. Thus, the major effect of the Great Drought was famine rather than a shortage of domestic water.

Of the nearly 15,000 tree-ring dates that have been obtained for the northern San Juan region, the latest fifteen, which fall into the span AD 1278 through 1281, are from cliff dwellings at Mesa Verde. Thus, during regional depopulation, Mesa Verde cliff dwellings might have been among the final strongholds. Unfortunately, nonprofessional digging of the uppermost, crucial deposits in many cliff dwellings in the late 1800s destroyed much of the record of the final days of residence of those settlements (see Kuckelman 2016).

CONCLUSIONS

In the past four decades, Crow Canyon archaeologists and colleagues generated significant new data regarding thirteenth-century villages in the northern San Juan: population density peaked and then waned, settlement patterns shifted, defensive architecture proliferated, dependence on maize and turkey increased to precarious levels, and disastrous environmental conditions that resulted in famine and intense interpueblo warfare were key factors in permanent depopulation in the final quarter of the thirteenth century. Numerous researchers have documented a correlation between stressful environmental conditions and violence (Ferguson 1997, 340–341; Hsiang et al. 2013, 7; Keeley 1996, 139, 140; Lambert 1997, 78; Mackey and Green 1979, 153; Milner et al. 1991; O'Shea and Bridges 1989). A coincident escalation of warfare in other areas of the Southwest (Rice and LeBlanc 2001) as well as in other areas of the continent (Lightfoot and Kuckelman 2001, 64) is more characteristic of widespread environmental deterioration than of localized tensions among Pueblos.

Thus, recent research into the final depopulation of the northern San Juan indicates that myriad environmental challenges, warfare, and other social disruptions were powerful deterrents to continued occupation of the region. However, springs continued to issue domestic water, and food in the form of reduced crops and some wild plant and animal resources would have been available, so it is unlikely that the region became completely uninhabitable by Pueblo peoples. Why didn't occupation continue at reduced density? The answer may lie in the fundamental community-based fabric of Pueblo society. That is, after many residents were killed or emigrated, remaining population levels were socially and ritually nonviable; both Timothy Kohler (2010) and Donna Glowacki (2010,

2015) point out that social coherence would have been difficult to maintain under conditions of low population density. Most emigration from the region thus stemmed from famine associated with devastating environmental conditions and from warfare, but complete depopulation resulted from the associated non-viable population levels.

Acknowledgments. I would like to thank Crow Canyon for the opportunity to contribute to this fortieth anniversary volume and to Debra Martin for generously sharing her osteological data on human remains from Mesa Verde National Park.

REFERENCES

Adams, Karen R., and Vandy E. Bowyer. 2002. "Sustainable Landscape: Thirteenth-Century Food and Fuel Use in the Sand Canyon Locality." In *Seeking the Center Place: Archaeology and Ancient Communities in the Mesa Verde Region*, edited by Mark D. Varien and Richard H. Wilshusen, 123–142. Salt Lake City: University of Utah Press.

Adams, Karen R., and Kenneth L. Petersen. 1999. "Environment." In *Colorado Prehistory: A Context for the Southern Colorado River Basin*, edited by William D. Lipe, Mark D. Varien, and Richard R. Wilshusen, 14–50. Colorado Council of Professional Archaeologists, Denver.

Berry, Michael S., and Larry V. Benson. 2010. "Tree-Ring Dates and Demographic Change in the Southern Colorado Plateau and Rio Grande Regions." In *Leaving Mesa Verde: Peril and Change in the Thirteenth-Century Southwest*, edited by Timothy A. Kohler, Mark D. Varien, and Aaron M. Wright, 53–74. Tucson: University of Arizona Press.

Billman, Brian R., Patricia M. Lambert, and Banks L. Leonard. 2000. "Cannibalism, Warfare, and Drought in the Mesa Verde Region During the Twelfth Century AD." *American Antiquity* 65 (1): 145–178.

Burns, Barney T. 1983. "Simulated Anasazi Storage Behavior Using Crop Yields Reconstructed from Tree Rings: A.D. 652–1968." Ann Arbor, MI: University Microfilms International.

Cattanach, George S., Jr. 1980. *Long House: Mesa Verde National Park, Colorado*. Washington, DC: National Park Service.

Churchill, Melissa J., ed. 2002. *The Archaeology of Woods Canyon Pueblo: A Canyon-Rim Village in Southwestern Colorado*. Cortez, CO: Crow Canyon Archaeological Center. https://www.crowcanyon.org/resources/the_archaeology_of_woods_canyon _pueblo_a_canyon_rim_village_in_southwestern_colorado/.

Coffey, Grant D., ed. 2018. *The Goodman Point Archaeological Project: Goodman Point Community Testing*. Cortez, CO: Crow Canyon Archaeological Center. Accessed January 23, 2021. https://core.tdar.org/document/447957/the-goodman-point -archaeological-project-community-testing (tDAR id: 447957), https://doi.org/10 .6067/XCV8447957.

Connolly, Marjorie R. 1992. "The Goodman Point Historic Land-Use Study." In *The Sand Canyon Archaeological Project: A Progress Report*, edited by William D. Lipe, 33–44. Crow Canyon Archaeological Center, Occasional Papers, no. 2. Cortez, CO: Crow Canyon Archaeological Center. Available: https://institute.crowcanyon.org /occasional_papers/Sand_Canyon_Progress_Report.pdf.

Cordell, Linda S., Carla R. Van West, Jeffrey S. Dean, and Deborah A. Muenchrath. 2007. Mesa Verde Settlement History and Relocation. *Kiva* 72 (4): 379–405.

Crown, Patricia L., Janet D. Orcutt, and Timothy A. Kohler. 1996. "Pueblo Cultures in Transition: The Northern Rio Grande." In *The Prehistoric Pueblo World, A.D. 1150–1350*, edited by Michael A. Adler, 188–204. Tucson: University of Arizona Press.

Dean, Jeffrey S. 1996. "Demography, Environment, and Subsistence Stress." In *Evolving Complexity and Environmental Risk in the Prehistoric Southwest*, edited by Joseph A. Tainter and Bonnie B. Tainter, 25–56. Santa Fe Institute Studies in the Sciences of Complexity, Proceedings, vol. 24. Reading, MA: Addison-Wesley Publishing Company.

Dean, Jeffrey S. 2010. "The Environmental, Demographic, and Behavioral Context of the Thirteenth-Century Depopulation of the Northern Southwest." In *Leaving Mesa Verde: Peril and Change in the Thirteenth-Century Southwest*, edited by Timothy A. Kohler, Mark D. Varien, and Aaron M. Wright, 324–345. Tucson: University of Arizona Press.

Dean, Jeffrey S., and Gary S. Funkhouser. 1995. "Dendroclimatic Reconstructions for the Southern Colorado Plateau." In *Proceedings of the Workshop, Climate Change in the Four Corners and Adjacent Regions: Implications for Environmental Restoration and Land-Use Planning*, edited by W. Joseph Waugh, Kenneth L. Petersen, Peter E. Wigand, B. D. Louthan, and R. D. Walker, 85–104. Grand Junction, CO: U.S. Department of Energy, Grand Junction Projects Office.

Dean, Jeffrey S., and Carla R. Van West. 2002. "Environment-Behavior Relationships in Southwestern Colorado." In *Seeking the Center Place: Archaeology and Ancient Communities in the Mesa Verde Region*, edited by Mark D. Varien and Richard H. Wilshusen, 81–99. Salt Lake City: University of Utah Press.

Decker, Kenneth W., and Larry L. Tieszen. 1989. "Isotopic Reconstructions of Mesa Verde Diet from Basketmaker III to Pueblo III." *Kiva* 55 (1): 33–47.

Douglass, A. E. 1929. "The Secret of the Southwest Solved by Talkative Tree Rings." *National Geographic Magazine* 56:736–770.

Driver, Jonathan C. 2002. "Faunal Variation and Change in the Northern San Juan Region." In *Seeking the Center Place: Archaeology and Ancient Communities in the Mesa Verde Region*, edited by Mark D. Varien and Richard H. Wilshusen, 143–160. Salt Lake City: University of Utah Press.

Duff, Andrew I., and Richard H. Wilshusen. 2000. "Prehistoric Population Dynamics in the Northern San Juan Region, A.D. 950–1300." *Kiva* 66 (1): 167–190.

Farmer, Malcolm F. 1957. "A Suggested Typology of Defensive Systems of the Southwest." *Southwestern Journal of Anthropology* 13:249–266.

Ferguson, R. Brian. 1997. "Violence and War in Prehistory." In *Troubled Times: Violence and Warfare in the Past*, edited by Debra L. Martin and David W. Frayer, 321–355. Amsterdam: Gordon and Breach.

Fewkes, Jesse W. 1909. *Antiquities of the Mesa Verde National Park: Spruce Tree House*. Bureau of American Ethnology Bulletin, no. 41. Washington, DC: Smithsonian Institution.

Fewkes, Jesse W. 1911. *Antiquities of the Mesa Verde National Park: Cliff Palace*. Bureau of American Ethnology Bulletin, no. 51. Washington, DC: Smithsonian Institution.

Glowacki, Donna M. 2010. "The Social and Cultural Contexts of the Central Mesa Verde Region during the Thirteenth-Century Migrations." In *Leaving Mesa Verde: Peril and Change in the Thirteenth-Century Southwest*, edited by Timothy A. Kohler, Mark D. Varien, and Aaron M. Wright, 200–221. Tucson: University of Arizona Press.

Glowacki, Donna M. 2015. *Living and Leaving: A Social History of Regional Depopulation in Thirteenth-Century Mesa Verde*. Tucson: University of Arizona Press.

Haas, Jonathan. 1990. "Warfare and Evolution of Tribal Polities in the Prehistoric Southwest." In *The Anthropology of War*, edited by Jonathan Haas, 171–189. Cambridge: Cambridge University Press.

Haas, Jonathan, and Winifred Creamer. 1996. "The Role of Warfare in the Pueblo III Period." In *The Prehistoric Pueblo World, A.D. 1150–1350*, edited by Michael A. Adler, 205–213. Tucson: University of Arizona Press.

Hibben, Frank C. 1948. "The Gallina Architectural Forms." *American Antiquity* 14:32–36.

Hill, J. Brett, Jeffery J. Clark, William H. Doelle, and Patrick D. Lyons. 2010. "Depopulation of the Northern Southwest: A Macroregional Perspective." In *Leaving Mesa Verde: Peril and Change in the Thirteenth-Century Southwest*, edited by Timothy A. Kohler, Mark D. Varien, and Aaron M. Wright, 34–52. Tucson: University of Arizona Press.

Hoffman, Amy, Kristin Kuckelman, Lisa Nagaoka, and Steve Wolverton. 2010. "Dietary Uses of Animal Resources Prior to the Pueblo III Depopulation of the Mesa Verde Region." Poster presented at the 75th Annual Meeting of the Society for American Archaeology, St. Louis.

Hsiang, Solomon M., Marshall Burke, and Edward Miguel. 2013. "Quantifying the Influence of Climate on Human Conflict." *Sciencexpress* 341 (6151). Accessed January 16, 2021. www.sciencemag.org.

Johnson, C. David, Timothy A. Kohler, and Jason Cowan. 2005. "Modeling Historical Ecology, Thinking about Contemporary Systems." *American Anthropologist* 107:96–107.

Keeley, Lawrence H. 1996. *War before Civilization*. New York: Oxford University Press.

Kidder, A. V. 1924. *An Introduction to the Study of Southwestern Archaeology with a Preliminary Account of the Excavations at Pecos*. Papers of the Phillips Academy Southwestern Expedition, no. 1. New Haven, CT: Yale University Press.

Kohler, Timothy A. 2004. "Pre-Hispanic Human Impact on Upland North American Southwestern Environments: Evolutionary Ecological Perspectives." In *The Archaeology of Global Change: The Impact of Humans on Their Environment*, edited by Charles L. Redman, Steven R. James, Paul R. Fish, and J. Daniel Rogers, 224–242. Washington, DC: Smithsonian Books.

Kohler, Timothy A. 2010. "A New Paleoproductivity Reconstruction for Southwestern Colorado, and Its Implications for Understanding Thirteenth-Century Depopulation." In *Leaving Mesa Verde: Peril and Change in the Thirteenth-Century Southwest*, edited by Timothy A. Kohler, Mark D. Varien, and Aaron M. Wright, 102–127. Tucson: University of Arizona Press.

Kohler, Timothy A., C. David Johnson, Mark Varien, Scott Ortman, Robert Reynolds, Ziad Kobti, Jason Cowan, Kenneth Kolm, Schaun Smith, and Lorene Yap. 2007. "Settlement Ecodynamics in the Prehispanic Central Mesa Verde Region." In *The Model-Based Archaeology of Socionatural Systems*, edited by Timothy A. Kohler and Sander E. van der Leeuw, 61–104. Santa Fe, NM: School for Advanced Research Press.

Kolm, Kenneth E., and Schaun M. Smith. 2012. "Modeling Paleohydrological System Structure and Function." In *Emergence and Collapse of Early Villages*, edited by Timothy A. Kohler and Mark D. Varien, 73–83. Berkeley: University of California Press.

Kuckelman, Kristin A., ed. 2000a. *The Archaeology of Castle Rock Pueblo: A Late-Thirteenth-Century Village in Southwestern Colorado*. Cortez, CO: Crow Canyon Archaeological Center. https://www.crowcanyon.org/resources/the_archaeology_of_castle_rock_pueblo_a_thirteenth_century_village_in_southwestern_colorado/.

Kuckelman, Kristin A. 2000b. "Architecture." In *The Archaeology of Castle Rock Pueblo: A Late-Thirteenth-Century Village in Southwestern Colorado*. Cortez, CO: Crow Canyon Archaeological Center. https://www.crowcanyon.org/resources/the_archaeology_of_castle_rock_pueblo_a_thirteenth_century_village_in_southwestern_colorado/.

Kuckelman, Kristin A. 2002. "Thirteenth-Century Warfare in the Mesa Verde Region." In *Seeking the Center Place: Archaeology and Ancient Communities in the Mesa Verde Region*, edited by Mark D. Varien and Richard H. Wilshusen, 233–253. Salt Lake City: University of Utah Press.

Kuckelman, Kristin A., ed. 2003a. *The Archaeology of Yellow Jacket Pueblo (Site 5MT5): Excavations at a Large Community Center in Southwestern Colorado*. Cortez, CO: Crow Canyon Archaeological Center. http://www.crowcanyon.org/yellowjacket.

Kuckelman, Kristin A. 2003b. "Population Estimates." In *The Archaeology of Yellow Jacket Pueblo (Site 5MT5): Excavations at a Large Community Center in Southwestern Colorado*, edited by Kristin A. Kuckelman. Cortez, CO: Crow Canyon Archaeological Center. http://www.crowcanyon.org/yellowjacket.

Kuckelman, Kristin A., ed. 2007. *The Archaeology of Sand Canyon Pueblo: Intensive Excavations at a Late-Thirteenth-Century Village in Southwestern Colorado*. Cortez, CO: Crow Canyon Archaeological Center. http://www.crowcanyon.org/sandcanyon.

Kuckelman, Kristin A. 2008. "An Agent-Centered Case Study of the Depopulation of Sand Canyon Pueblo." In *The Social Construction of Communities: Agency, Structure, and Identity in the Prehispanic Southwest*, edited by Mark D. Varien and James M. Potter, 109–121. New York: AltaMira Press.

Kuckelman, Kristin A. 2010a. "Catalysts of the Thirteenth-Century Depopulation of Sand Canyon Pueblo and the Central Mesa Verde Region." In *Leaving Mesa Verde: Peril and Change in the Thirteenth-Century Southwest*, edited by Timothy A. Kohler, Mark D. Varien, and Aaron M. Wright, 180–199. Tucson: University of Arizona Press.

Kuckelman, Kristin A. 2010b. "The Depopulation of Sand Canyon Pueblo, a Large Ancestral Pueblo Village in Southwestern Colorado." *American Antiquity* 75 (3): 497–525.

Kuckelman, Kristin A. 2012. "Bioarchaeological Signatures of Strife in Terminal Pueblo III Settlements in the Northern San Juan." In *The Bioarchaeology of Violence*, edited by Debra L. Martin, Ryan P. Harrod, and Ventura R. Pérez, 121–138. Gainesville: University Press of Florida.

Kuckelman, Kristin A. 2014. "Identifying Causes of the Thirteenth-Century Depopulation of the Northern Southwest." *Bulletin of the Texas Archeological Society* 85 (2014): 205–224.

Kuckelman, Kristin A. 2016. "Cycles of Subsistence Stress, Warfare, and Population Movement in the Northern San Juan." In *The Archaeology of Food and Warfare: Food Insecurity in Prehistory*, edited by Amber M. VanDerwarker and Gregory D. Wilson, 107–132. New York: Springer.

Kuckelman, Kristin A. 2017a. "Architecture." In *The Goodman Point Archaeological Project: Goodman Point Pueblo Excavations*. Cortez, CO: Crow Canyon Archaeological Center. Accessed January 13, 2021. Available: https://core.tdar.org/document/446779/the-goodman-point-archaeological-project-goodman-point-pueblo-excavations.

Kuckelman, Kristin A. 2017b. "Cranial Trauma and Victimization among Ancestral Pueblo Farmers of the Northern San Juan Region." In *Broken Bones, Broken Bodies: Bioarchaeological and Forensic Approaches for Accumulative Trauma and Violence*, edited by Caryn E. Tegtmeyer and Debra L. Martin, 43–59. New York: Lexington Books.

Kuckelman, Kristin A. 2017c. "Paleohydrology." In *The Goodman Point Archaeological Project: Goodman Point Pueblo Excavations*. Cortez, Colorado: Crow Canyon Archaeological Center. Accessed January 26, 2021. Available: https://core.tdar.org/document/446779/the-goodman-point-archaeological-project-goodman-point-pueblo-excavations.

Kuckelman, Kristin A., ed. 2017d. *The Goodman Point Archaeological Project: Goodman Point Pueblo Excavations*. Cortez, CO: Crow Canyon Archaeological Center. Available: https://core.tdar.org/document/446779/the-goodman-point-archaeological-project-goodman-point-pueblo-excavations, accessed January 13, 2021.

Kuckelman, Kristin A. 2020. "Ritual Modification of Human Remains in the Context of Social Turmoil among Ancestral Pueblo Peoples of the Northern San Juan." In *The

Poetics of Processing: Memory Formation, Identity, and the Handling of the Dead, edited by Anna J. Osterholtz, 66–84. Louisville: University Press of Colorado.

Kuckelman, Kristin A., John J. Crandall, and Debra L. Martin. 2017. "Caught in a Cataclysm: Effects of Pueblo Warfare on Noncombatants in the Northern Southwest." In *Bioarchaeology of Women and Children in Times of War: Case Studies from the Americas*, edited by Debra L. Martin and Caryn Tegtmeyer, 93–110. Cham, Switzerland: Springer.

Kuckelman, Kristin A., Ricky R. Lightfoot, and Debra L. Martin. 2002. "The Bioarchaeology and Taphonomy of Violence at Castle Rock and Sand Canyon Pueblos, Southwestern Colorado." *American Antiquity* 67:486–513.

Kuckelman, Kristin A., and Debra L. Martin. 2007. "Human Skeletal Remains." In *The Archaeology of Sand Canyon Pueblo: Intensive Excavations at a Late-Thirteenth-Century Village in Southwestern Colorado*, edited by Kristin A. Kuckelman. Cortez, Colorado: Crow Canyon Archaeological Center. Accessed January 14, 2021. http://www.crowcanyon.org/sandcanyon.

Lambert, Patricia M. 1997. "Patterns of Violence in Prehistoric Hunter-Gatherer Societies of Coastal Southern California." In *Troubled Times: Violence and Warfare in the Past*, edited by Debra L. Martin and David W. Frayer, 77–109. Amsterdam: Gordon and Breach.

Lambert, Patricia M. 1999. "Human Skeletal Remains." In *The Puebloan Occupation of the Ute Mountain Piedmont. Vol. 5: Environmental and Bioarchaeological Studies*, edited by Brian R. Billman, 111–161. Soil Systems Publications in Archaeology, no. 22. Phoenix: Soil Systems.

Lancaster, James A., and Jean M. Pinkley. 1954. "Excavation of Site 16 of Three Pueblo II Mesa-Top Ruins." In *Archaeological Excavations in Mesa Verde National Park, Colorado, 1950*, authored by James A. Lancaster, Jean M. Pinkley, Philip F. van Cleave, and Don Watson, 23–86. Archeological Research Series, no. 2. Washington, DC: National Park Service.

LeBlanc, Steven A. 1998. "Settlement and Consequences of Warfare during the Late Pueblo III and Pueblo IV Periods." In *Migration and Reorganization: The Pueblo IV Period in the American Southwest*, edited by Katherine A. Spielmann, 115–135. Anthropological Papers No. 51. Tempe: Arizona State University.

LeBlanc, Steven A. 1999. *Prehistoric Warfare in the American Southwest*. Salt Lake City: University of Utah Press.

LeBlanc, Steven A., and Glen E Rice. 2001. "Southwestern Warfare: The Value of Case Studies." In *Deadly Landscapes: Case Studies in Prehistoric Southwestern Warfare*, edited by Glen E. Rice and Steven A. LeBlanc, 1–18. Salt Lake City: University of Utah Press.

Lightfoot, Ricky R., and Kristin A. Kuckelman. 2001. "A Case of Warfare in the Mesa Verde Region." In *Deadly Landscapes: Case Studies in Prehistoric Southwestern Warfare*, edited by Glen E. Rice and Steven A. LeBlanc, 51–64. Salt Lake City: University of Utah Press.

Lipe, William D. 1995. "The Depopulation of the Northern San Juan: Conditions in the Turbulent 1200s." *Journal of Anthropological Archaeology* 14:143–169.

Lipe, William D., and Scott G. Ortman. 2000. "Spatial Patterning in Northern San Juan Villages, A.D. 1050–1300." *Kiva* 66 (1): 91–122.

Lipe, William D., and Mark D. Varien. 1999. "Pueblo III (A.D. 1150–1300)." In *Colorado Prehistory: A Context for the Southern Colorado River Basin*, edited by William D. Lipe, Mark D. Varien, and Richard H. Wilshusen, 290–352. Denver: Colorado Council of Professional Archaeologists.

Mackey, James, and R. C. Green. 1979. "Largo-Gallina Towers: An Explanation." *American Antiquity* 44:144–154.

Matson, R. G. 2016. "The Nutritional Context of the Pueblo III Depopulation of the Northern San Juan: Too Much Maize?" *Journal of Archaeological Science Reports* 5 (2016): 622–641.

McCaffery, Harlan, Robert H. Tykot, Kathy D. Gore, and Beau R. DeBoer. 2014. "Stable Isotope Analysis of Turkey (*Meleagris gallopavo*) Diet from Pueblo II and Pueblo III Sites, Middle San Juan Region, Northwest New Mexico." *American Antiquity* 79 (2): 337–352.

Milner, George R., Eve Anderson, and Virginia G. Smith. 1991. "Warfare in Late Prehistoric West-Central Illinois." *American Antiquity* 56:581–603.

Morris, Earl H. 1939. *Archaeological Studies in the La Plata District, Southwestern Colorado and Northwestern New Mexico*. Publication, no. 519. Washington, DC: Carnegie Institution of Washington.

Muir, Robert J. 1999. "Zooarchaeology of Sand Canyon Pueblo, Colorado." PhD diss., Department of Archaeology, Simon Fraser University, Burnaby, BC.

Munro, Natalie D. 1994. "An Investigation of Anasazi Turkey Production in Southwestern Colorado." MA thesis, Department of Archaeology, Simon Fraser University, Burnaby, BC.

Nott, Breanne M. 2010. "Documenting Domestication: Molecular and Palynological Analysis of Ancient Turkey Coprolites from the American Southwest." MS thesis, School of Biological Sciences, Washington State University, Pullman.

Ortman, Scott G., Donna M. Glowacki, Melissa J. Churchill, and Kristin A. Kuckelman. 2000. "Pattern and Variation in Northern San Juan Village Histories." *Kiva* 66 (1): 123–146.

O'Shea, John M., and Patricia S. Bridges. 1989. "The Sargent Site Ossuary (25CU28), Custer County, Nebraska." *Plains Anthropologist* 34 (123): 7–21.

Petersen, Kenneth L. 1988. *Climate and the Dolores River Anasazi: A Paleoenvironmental Reconstruction from a 10,000-Year Pollen Record, La Plata Mountains, Southwestern*

Colorado. University of Utah Anthropological Papers, no. 113. Salt Lake City: University of Utah Press.

Petersen, Kenneth L. 1994. "A Warm and Wet Little Climatic Optimum and a Cold and Dry Little Ice Age in the Southern Rocky Mountains, U.S.A." *Climatic Change* 26:243–269.

Rawlings, Tiffany A., and Jonathan C. Driver. 2010. "Paleodiet of Domestic Turkey, Shields Pueblo (5MT2307), Colorado: Isotopic Analysis and Its Implications for Care of a Household Domesticate." *Journal of Archaeological Science* 37 (10): 2433–2441.

Reid, J. Jefferson, John R. Welch, Barbara K. Montgomery, and Maria N. Zedeño. 1996. "A Demographic Overview of the Late Pueblo III Period in the Mountains of East-Central Arizona." In *The Prehistoric Pueblo World, A.D. 1150–1350*, edited by Michael A. Adler, 73–85. Tucson: University of Arizona Press.

Rice, Glen A., and Steven LeBlanc, eds. 2001. *Deadly Landscapes: Case Studies in Prehistoric Southwestern Warfare*. Salt Lake City: University of Utah Press.

Ryan, Susan C., ed. 2015a. "The Archaeology of Albert Porter Pueblo (Site 5MT123): Excavations at a Great House Community Center in Southwestern Colorado." Cortez, CO: Crow Canyon Archaeological Center. https://www.crowcanyon.org/resources/the_archaeology_of_albert_porter_pueblo_site_5mt123_excavations_at_a_great_house_community_center_in_southwestern_colorado/.

Ryan, Susan C., ed. 2015b. "The Archaeology of Shields Pueblo (Site 5MT3807): Excavations at a Mesa-Top Community Center in Southwestern Colorado." Cortez, CO: Crow Canyon Archaeological Center. http://www.crowcanyon.org/shieldspueblo.

Salzer, Matthew W. 2000. "Temperature Variability and the Northern Anasazi: Possible Implications for Regional Abandonment." *Kiva* 65:295–318.

Salzer, Matthew W., and Kurt F. Kipfmueller. 2005. "Reconstructed Temperature and Precipitation on a Millennial Timescale from Tree-Rings in the Southern Colorado Plateau, USA." *Climatic Change* 70:465–487.

Schaafsma, Polly. 2000. *Warrior, Shield, and Star: Imagery and Ideology of Pueblo Warfare*. Santa Fe, NM: Western Edge Press.

Schulman, Albert. 1950. "Pre-Columbian Towers in the Southwest." *American Antiquity* 15:288–297.

Smith, Schaun M., Kenneth E. Kolm, and John E. McCray. 2006. "Drought Effects on Prehistoric Settlements: Paleohydrologic Modeling of Spring Discharge, Canyon of the Ancients National Monument, Southwest Colorado." Geological Society of America, September 18–20; GSA Specialty Meeting Abstracts with Programs, Abstract No. 109045, ISSN1556-4800. No. 3.

Street, David J. 2001. "The Dendrochronology of Long House: An Anasazi Cliff Dwelling in Mesa Verde National Park, Colorado, USA." PhD diss., University of Sheffield, Sheffield, UK.

Tuggle, H. D., and J. Jefferson Reid. 2001. "Conflict and Defense in the Grasshopper Region of East-Central Arizona." In *Deadly Landscapes: Case Studies in Prehistoric Southwestern Warfare*, edited by Glen E. Rice and Steven A. LeBlanc, 85–107. Salt Lake City: University of Utah Press.

Turner, Christy G., II, and Jacqueline A. Turner. 1999. *Man Corn: Cannibalism and Violence in the Prehistoric American Southwest*. Salt Lake City: University of Utah Press.

Van West, Carla R., and Jeffrey S. Dean. 2000. "Environmental Characteristics of the A.D. 900–1300 Period in the Central Mesa Verde Region." *Kiva* 66:19–44.

Varien, Mark D. 2010. "Depopulation of the Northern San Juan Region: Historical Review and Archaeological Context." In *Leaving Mesa Verde: Peril and Change in the Thirteenth-Century Southwest*, edited by Timothy A. Kohler, Mark D. Varien, and Aaron M. Wright, 1–33. Tucson: University of Arizona Press.

Varien, Mark D., Scott G. Ortman, Timothy A. Kohler, Donna M. Glowacki, and C. David Johnson. 2007. "Historical Ecology in the Mesa Verde Region: Results from the Village Ecodynamics Project." *American Antiquity* 72 (2): 273–299.

Varien, Mark D., Carla R. Van West, and G. Stuart Patterson. 2000. "Competition, Cooperation, and Conflict: Agricultural Production and Community Catchments in the Central Mesa Verde Region." *Kiva* 66 (1): 45–65.

White, Tim D. 1992. *Prehistoric Cannibalism at Mancos 5MTUMR-2346*. Princeton, NJ: Princeton University Press.

Wilcox, David R., and Jonathan Haas. 1994. "The Scream of the Butterfly: Competition and Conflict in the Prehistoric Southwest." In *Themes in Southwest Prehistory*, edited by George J. Gumerman, 211–238. Santa Fe, NM: School of American Research Press.

Winter, Joseph C. 1975. *Hovenweep 1974*. Archeology Report no. 1. San Jose, CA: Department of Anthropology, San José State University.

Winter, Joseph C. 1976. *Hovenweep 1975*. Archeology Report no. 2. San Jose, CA: Department of Anthropology, San José State University.

Winter, Joseph C. 1977. *Hovenweep 1976*. Archeological Report no. 3. San Jose, CA: Department of Anthropology, San José State University.

Wright, Aaron M. 2010. "The Climate of the Depopulation of the Northern Southwest." In *Leaving Mesa Verde: Peril and Change in the Thirteenth-Century Southwest*, edited by Timothy A. Kohler, Mark D. Varien, and Aaron M. Wright, 75–101. Tucson: University of Arizona Press.

Wright Paleohydrological Institute. 2011. *Goodman Point Paleohydrology, Hovenweep National Monument*. Denver: Wright Water Engineers. Accessed January 23, 2021. www.wrightpaleo.com.

PART V

Human-Environment Relationship Research

20

The Exploitation of Rodents in the Mesa Verde Region

SHAW BADENHORST, JONATHAN C. DRIVER,
AND STEVE WOLVERTON

Bones of rodents are recovered from most archaeological sites in the American Southwest, but their complex taphonomic history means they receive less attention than other small mammal taxa, such as cottontails and jackrabbits, that are widely accepted by archaeologists as having been hunted by Indigenous communities. Here we examine the role of rodents in the diet of ancestral Pueblo people, with a focus on data from numerous Crow Canyon Archaeological Center projects in the central Mesa Verde region.

ETHNOGRAPHY, ARCHAEOLOGY, TAPHONOMY

Rodents were hunted and eaten in many Indigenous communities in the American Southwest (Gnabasik 1981; Szuter 1991). Woodrats (*Neotoma* sp.) and terrestrial squirrels (e.g., prairie dogs, ground squirrels) were the taxa most often noted by ethnographers. Rodents were sometimes the bycatch of communal hunts for lagomorphs, but there were also specific hunting methods for rodents. Rodents were clearly acceptable as food, and they seem to have been consumed routinely.

https://doi.org/10.5876/9781646424597.c020

Direct archaeological evidence for rodent exploitation includes the following: rodent bones in human coprolites (Clary 1987, 786–787), patterned burning on cranial and limb bones resulting from roasting carcasses over a fire (Badenhorst 2008; Driver 1985, 1991; Henshilwood 1997; Shaffer 1992a; Vigne and Marinval-Vigne 1983), and population structure data (Speth 2000). While these indications are rare in rodents, they are also rare in other small mammals that are widely assumed to have been hunted for food, such as cottontail rabbits.

Some analysts have downplayed the role of rodents in diets because of uncertainty as to how they became part of faunal assemblages. Rodents may have been deposited on sites without human intervention because (a) they may have been commensal—living and dying on humanly occupied sites—but not exploited; (b) rodents are attracted to depopulated sites for food and shelter (Lanoë et al. 2020); (c) rodent bones may be remains of the prey of carnivores and raptors that denned or roosted at depopulated sites. Another analytical problem is that recovery methods may produce unrepresentative samples (Shaffer 1992b), hindering taphonomic assessment. Direct dating of small mammal bones at one Southwest site, the Robinson Site (LA46326), showed that some rodents are contemporary with human occupation of the site, whereas rodent skeletons from burrows are later (Driver 1991).

THEORETICAL CONSIDERATIONS

A widely used concept in subsistence studies in the American Southwest is the "garden hunting" hypothesis, originally developed to explain faunal assemblages in archaeological sites of tropical horticulturalists (Linares 1976). Many Southwest zooarchaeologists have cited this hypothesis and suggested that fields and gardens attracted animals that could then be hunted. The cited benefits of garden hunting include a more concentrated prey biomass than would occur naturally, efficient use of time and labor by combining hunting with agricultural activities, and protection of crops by removing competitor pests. Reviews of the concept can be found in R. M. Dean (2007, 2017), J. C. Driver (2011), J. C. Driver and S. Badenhorst (2017), R. D. Leonard (1989), S. W. Neusius (1996), and C. R. Szuter (1991).

One problem in transferring the garden hunting hypothesis to the American Southwest is that it is not grounded explicitly in theory. As Leonard (1989) noted, most of the species that would be attracted to Southwest gardens could also be found in surrounding natural habitats, and there was generally no change in selection of animal species in the shift from foraging to agriculture. This is quite different from the situation described by O. F. Linares (1976), who wanted to explain the absence from archaeological assemblages in Panama of many species that would have been available in tropical forests outside the gardens. For the American Southwest, the garden hunting hypothesis fits well with ecologically oriented archaeological thinking of the 1970s, with its emphasis on systems theory, scheduling, homeostasis, and Indigenous land-management practices. However, it does not tell us under what conditions people would choose to hunt in gardens, nor does it provide any basis for making and testing predictions about archaeological signatures for garden hunting when the range of species does not change.

We use optimal foraging theory (OFT), particularly logic from the patch choice model to address this issue (Charnov et al. 1976; Stephens and Krebs 1986). Use of OFT in zooarchaeology has generally emphasized prey body size as an indicator of foraging efficiency, because large prey typically provides the highest returns per foraging costs. The prey choice model holds that if the abundance of large prey declines, there will be a shift toward greater incorporation of medium and small prey animals in the diet (Broughton 1994; Nagaoka 2001, 2002), a phenomenon seen in the San Juan Drainage Basin generally and the central Mesa Verde region in particular (Badenhorst and Driver 2009; Driver 2002; Schollmeyer and Driver 2013, Schollmeyer and Driver, chapter 21 in this volume).

The prey choice model does not examine the cost of ignoring low-ranked resources that could be obtained in the same location as high-ranked resources. In contrast, the patch choice model suggests that foragers will remain in a patch (any given area of space) as long as the resource return for that patch is greater than the average return for all patches. In the northern San Juan / Mesa Verde region, farming became increasingly important over time from the late Basketmaker periods through the Pueblo periods (Kohler et al. 2008). L. J. Ellyson et al. (2019, 64) argue that this practice led to an increase in the importance of the "food production foraging patch," or what others term garden hunting (e.g., Schollmeyer and Driver 2012).

As gardens and fields became increasingly important, people would have spent greater amounts of time and energy there. If small game became sufficiently available to the point that they were an easy-to-acquire, routinely encountered animal resource within gardens, the logic of the patch choice model holds that foragers would have shifted to hunting in those patches if the average returns became higher than more distant wild game patches. R. M. Dean (2017) makes the same case for southern Arizona Hohokam communities.

We test this hypothesis for the central Mesa Verde region using data from sites excavated over many decades by Crow Canyon. Because the garden hunting hypothesis suggests that rodents should be targeted as pests (see Sundjordet 2017), and because the addition of rodents to the list of resources extractable from the garden patch would increase the productivity of the patch, the hypothesis that we test is that there should be increased use of rodents over time in the central Mesa Verde region.

Small mammals are common in the central Mesa Verde region. Mesa Verde National Park hosts 3 species of Leporidae (cottontails and jack rabbits), 13

TABLE 20.1. Examples of population densities and nutritional value of small and large game.

Taxon	Density	Calories /100g	Protein /100g	Fat /100g	Return cal/hr.
Deer	<4/ km², arid habitats	145	23.7	1.3	18–31k
Turkey	30/ km², wild, Midwestern turkey	163	25.7	1.1	NA
Turkey	Domestic	146	23.5	1.5	NA
Jackrabbit	0.1–280/ha	153	21.9	2.4	13–15k
Cottontail	1.6–16.3/ha	144	21.8	2.4	9–10k
Prairie dog	28–50/ha	149	21.4	3.2	NA
Ground squirrel	20–50/ha	300	NA	NA	5–6k
Gopher	2.5–37/ha	325	NA	NA	NA

Note: Calories, protein, and fat expressed as grams per 100g. Return rate rounded to nearest thousand calories per hour. Data from Baker et al. (2003), Best (1996), Chapman and Willner (1978), Cully et al. (1997), Simms (1985), Smith (1991), Vangilder and Kurzejeski (1995), White (1953), Yensen and Sherman (2003). Nutritional data from USDA National Nutrient Database. NA = Not Applicable

species of Cricetidae (voles, woodrats, and mice), 1 species of Geomyidae (pocket gophers), 3 species of Heteromyidae (kangaroo rats and pocket mice), and 15 species of Sciuridae (ground squirrels, chipmunks and prairie dogs). Nutritional and ecological characteristics of some taxa are listed in table 20.1, and comparisons to larger game are also made.

METHODS

Crow Canyon projects have recovered fauna from numerous sites and different time periods in the central Mesa Verde region (table 20.2). Field methods have been consistent, and recording protocols have largely followed the methods established by Driver and his students (Driver 2005).

Rather than present rodent number of identified specimens (NISP) as a percentage of the whole assemblage, we have quantified rodents as a percentage of the rodent plus lagomorph assemblage, in two ways. First, we look at all rodents that are smaller than beaver or porcupine, designated "R" in table 20.2. Second, because it seems most likely that preferred rodent prey would have been larger species, and because the recovery and identification of smaller species (mice and voles) seemed quite variable, we have also calculated the ratio of rodents to lagomorphs only for Sciuridae (ground squirrels, chipmunks, and prairie dogs), Geomyidae (pocket gophers) and *Neotoma* sp. (wood rats), designated "MR" in table 20.2.

RESULTS

Whether there is an increase in use of rodents relative to lagomorphs through time is difficult to assess. We do not see such clear temporal patterns as the

TABLE 20.2. Number of identified specimens (NISP) data on all rodents (R), medium rodents (MR), and lagomorphs (LAG), and percentages of rodents in the (R+LAG) and (MR+LAG) assemblages.

CCAC Project	Assemblage	R	MR	LAG	R%	MR%
Basketmaker Communities	BIII	195	106	453	30.1	19.0
Basketmaker Communities	PI–III	27	27	109	19.9	19.9
Albert Porter Pueblo	PII	163	126	876	15.7	12.6
Albert Porter Pueblo	PII/PIII	177	125	1,314	11.9	8.7
Albert Porter Pueblo	PIII	578	327	1,973	22.7	14.2
Shields Pueblo	Early PI	81	81	148	35.4	35.4
Shields Pueblo	Mid PII	113	104	354	24.2	22.7
Shields Pueblo	Late PII	573	540	3,936	12.7	12.1
Shields Pueblo	Early PIII	522	479	2,383	18.0	16.7
Shields Pueblo	Late PIII	78	69	541	12.6	11.3
Goodman Point Community Testing	PII–PIII	555	484	1,597	25.8	23.3
Goodman Point Pueblo	PIII	1,157	896	3,520	24.7	20.3
Woods Pueblo	PIII	96	87	228	29.6	27.6
Yellowjacket Pueblo	PIII	549	400	1,485	27.0	21.2
Castle Rock Pueblo	PIII	359	293	1,004	26.3	22.6
Site Testing Program	PIII	783	665	1,360	36.5	32.8
Sand Canyon Pueblo	PIII	2,302	1,521	2,936	43.9	34.1

Note: All data, except for those from Goodman Point Pueblo and Goodman Point Community Testing (Ellyson 2014; Hoffman 2011; Winstead 2015), are from https://www.crowcanyon.org/index.php/access-our-research/site-reports-databases and accessed December 14, 2020.

decline in artiodactyls and the increase in turkeys documented by Driver (2002) and K. G. Schollmeyer and Driver (2013, Schollmeyer and Driver, chapter 21 in this volume) for the Mesa Verde region and by Badenhorst and Driver (2009) for the wider San Juan Drainage Basin.

Some Pueblo III period sites, such as Sand Canyon Pueblo (Muir 2007) and the hamlets sampled in the Site Testing Program (Driver et al. 1999), do have relatively high percentages of rodents when compared to earlier sites, such as those in the Basketmaker Communities Project (Cates 2020). However, this pattern is not evident at other Pueblo III period sites, such as Goodman Point, Yellow Jacket (Muir and Driver 2003), Albert Porter (Badenhorst and Driver 2015), or Shields Pueblo (Rawlings and Driver 2015). Given the relatively high percentages in some Pueblo period III sites, it is possible that some communities focused more time and energy on garden hunting, but this was clearly not universal, because other Pueblo III period sites have rodent percentages that are relatively low.

DISCUSSION AND CONCLUSION

There may be several methodological reasons for our failure to find any strong evidence of increased use of rodents through time. First, we are not measuring absolute abundance but only abundance in relation to other taxa—in this case lagomorphs. It is therefore possible that the actual consumption of rodents increased through time, though at the same rate as increased consumption of lagomorphs. This would result in consistent rodent-to-lagomorph ratios, even if actual abundances increased.

Second, a more thorough taphonomic study of rodent remains is required. It is possible that some site locations are more attractive to rodents, resulting in a larger portion of the rodent assemblage resulting from nonhuman accumulation processes. Such variation might obscure trends in numbers of rodents hunted by people.

Third, the distance of fields to residences (Varien 1999) may influence the representation of rodent remains in faunal assemblages. If fields were close, people may have brought rodents back to prepare and consume. But when fields were more distant, more rodents may have been prepared and consumed away from these larger villages. If rodent pests killed in agricultural areas were consumed there, we would not be able to detect increased reliance on garden hunting by excavating residential sites. Most of the sites in our sample are residences, and some are larger than others, and this may account for some of the variation noted in our samples.

We cannot show that rodents increased in importance through time in the Mesa Verde region, but methodological issues described make it difficult to provide a thorough assessment of the garden hunting hypothesis. An alternative hypothesis is that ancestral Puebloan peoples increased the productivity of the "garden patch" by growing more maize and feeding it to domestic turkeys, whose bone collagen signals a high input of C_4 plants (Rawlings and Driver 2010). This would have created a more reliable source of meat (and also feathers). Interestingly, turkey is the only species that seems to have been introduced to the ancestral Puebloan diet after the "garden patch" was established, and that humanly created niche would have been vital to its survival.

The rise of turkey production may have obviated the need for intensification of garden hunting. This suggestion is consistent with what we see in early agricultural communities elsewhere in the world. For example, after large mammals were domesticated in the Near East, there was a gradual decline in the use of wild game in preceramic Neolithic communities (Vigne 2008, fig. 4), and the introduction of domestic crops and mammals as part of the "Neolithic package" in Atlantic Europe resulted in a rapid transition away from hunting and fishing (Vigne 2008, 188). This review leaves us with questions unanswered and new hypotheses to test. We encourage others to look more closely at rodent remains from sites in the Mesa Verde region.

Acknowledgments. We thank the many staff from Crow Canyon Archaeological Center for their support over many years.

REFERENCES

Badenhorst, S. 2008. "The Zooarchaeology of Great House Sites in the San Juan Basin of the American Southwest." PhD diss., Simon Fraser University, Burnaby, BC.

Badenhorst, S., and J. C. Driver. 2009. "Faunal Changes in Farming Communities from Basketmaker II to Pueblo III (A.D. 1–1300) in the San Juan Basin of the American Southwest." *Journal of Archaeological Science* 36 (9): 1832–1841.

Badenhorst, S., and J. C. Driver. 2015. "Faunal Remains." In *The Archaeology of Albert Porter Pueblo (Site 5MT123): Excavations at a Great House Community Center in Southwestern Colorado*, edited by S. C. Ryan. https://www.crowcanyon.org/resources/the_archaeology_of_albert_porter_pueblo_site_5mt123_excavations_at_a_great_house_community_center_in_southwestern_colorado/.

Baker, R. J., R. D. Bradley, and L. R. McAliley Jr, 2003. "Pocket Gophers." In *Wild Mammals of North America: Biology, Management, and Conservation.* 2nd ed. edited by G. A. Feldhamer, B. C. Thompson, and J. A. Chapman, 276–287. Baltimore: Johns Hopkins University Press.

Best, T. 1996. "Lepus californicus." *Mammalian Species* 530 (May): 1–10.

Broughton, J. M. 1994. "Declines in Mammalian Foraging Efficiency during the Late Holocene, San Francisco Bay, California." *Journal of Anthropological Archaeology* 13 (4): 371–371.

Cates, K. M. 2020. "Faunal Remains." In *The Basketmaker Communities Project*, edited by S. R. Diederichs, 586–644. Accessed March 9, 2021. Manuscript on file. Cortez: Crow Canyon Archaeological Center.

Chapman, J. A., and G. R. Willner. 1978. "Sylvilagus audubonii." *Mammalian Species* 106 (September): 1–4.

Charnov, E. L., G. H. Orians, and K. Hyatt. 1976. "Ecological Implications of Resource Depression." *American Naturalist* 110 (972): 247–259.

Clary, K. H. 1987. "Coprolites from Pueblo Alto." In *Investigations at the Pueblo Alto Complex, Chaco Canyon, New Mexico, 1975–1979.* Vol. 3, pt. 2, *Artifactual and Biological Analyses*, edited by F. J. Mathien and T. C. Windes, 785–788. Santa Fe, NM: National Park Service.

Cully, J. F., A. M. Barnes, T. J. Quan, G. Maupin, and J. F. J. Cully. 1997. "Dynamics of Plague in a Gunnison's Prairie Dog Colony Complex from New Mexico." *Journal of Wildlife Diseases* 33 (4): 706–719.

Dean, R. M. 2007. "Hunting Intensification and the Hohokam 'Collapse.'" *Journal of Anthropological Archaeology* 26 (1): 109–132. https://doi.org/10.1016/j.jaa.2006.03.010.

Dean, R. M. 2017. "Fauna and the Emergence of Intensive Agricultural Economies in the United States Southwest." In *The Oxford Handbook of Zooarchaeology*, edited by U. Albarella, M. Rizzetto, H. Russ, K. Vickers, and S. Viner-Daniels, 509–524. Oxford: Oxford University Press. https://doi.org/10.1093/oxfordhb/9780199686476.013.36.

Driver, J. C. 1985. "Zooarchaeology of Six Prehistoric Sites in the Sierra Blanca Region, New Mexico." *Research Reports of Archaeology Contribution 12*. Ann Arbor: Museum of Anthropology, University of Michigan.

Driver, J. C. 1991. "Assemblage Formation at the Robinson Site." In *Mogollon V*, edited by P. H. Beckett, 197–206. Las Cruces, NM: COAS.

Driver, J. C. 2002. "Faunal Variation and Change in the Northern San Juan Region." In *Seeking the Center Place: Archaeology and Ancient Communities in the Mesa Verde Region*, edited by M. D. Varien and R. H. Wilshusen, 143–160. Salt Lake City: University of Utah Press.

Driver, J. C. 2005. "Manual for Description of Vertebrate Remains." 7th ed. Manuscript on file. Cortez, CO: Crow Canyon Archaeological Center.

Driver, J. C. 2011. "Human Impacts on Animal populations in the American Southwest." In *Movement, Connectivity and Landscape Change in the Ancient Southwest*, edited by M. C. Nelson and C. Strawhacker, 179–198. Boulder: University Press of Colorado.

Driver, J. C., and S. Badenhorst. 2017. "Hunting by Farmers: Ecological Implications." In *Economic Zooarchaeology*, edited by P. Rowley-Conwy, D. Serjeantson, and P. Halstead, 165–172. Oxford: Oxbow Books.

Driver, J. C., M. J. Brand, L. Lester, and N. D. Munro. 1999. "Faunal Studies." In *The Sand Canyon Archaeological Project: Site Testing*, edited by M. D. Varien. https://www.crowcanyon.org/resources/the_sand_canyon_archaeological_project_site_testing/.

Ellyson, L. J. 2014. "Resource Intensification of Small Game Use at Goodman Point, Southwestern Colorado." MA thesis, University of North Texas, Denton.

Ellyson, L. J., L. Nagaoka, and S. Wolverton. 2019. "Animal Resource Use Related to Socioenvironmental Change among Mesa Verde farmers." *Journal of Anthropological Research* 75 (3): 361–392.

Gnabasik, V. R. 1981. "Faunal Utilization by the Pueblo Indians." MA thesis, Eastern New Mexico University, Portales.

Henshilwood, C. S. 1997. "Identifying the Collector: Evidence for Human Processing of the Cape Dune Mole-Rat, Bathyergus suillus, from Blombos Cave, Southern Cape, South Africa." *Journal of Archaeological Science* 24 (7): 659–662.

Hoffman, A. S. 2011. "Faunal Exploitation during the Depopulation of the Mesa Verde Region (AD 1300): A Case Study of Goodman Point Pueblo (5MT604)." MA thesis, University of North Texas, Denton.

Kohler, T. A., M. D. Varien, A. M. Wright, and K. A. Kuckelman. 2008. "Mesa Verde Migrations: New Archaeological Research and Computer Simulation Suggest Why

Ancestral Puebloans Deserted the Northern Southwest United States." *American Scientist* 96 (2): 146–153.

Lanoë, F. B., J. D. Reuther, C. E. Holmes, and B. A. Potter. 2020. "Small Mammals and Paleovironmental Context of the Terminal Pleistocene and Early Holocene Human Occupation of Central Alaska." *Geoarchaeology* 35 (October): 164–176. https://doi.org/10.1002/gea.21768.

Leonard, R. D. 1989. *Anasazi Faunal Exploitation: Prehistoric Subsistence on Northern Black Mesa, Arizona.* Carbondale: Centre for Archaeological Investigations, Southern Illinois University at Carbondale, Occasional Paper 13.

Linares, O. F. 1976. "'Garden Hunting' in the American Tropics." *Human Ecology* 4 (4): 331–349.

Muir, R. J. 2007. "Faunal Remains." In *The Archaeology of Sand Canyon Pueblo: Intensive Excavations at a Late-Thirteenth-Century Village in Southwestern Colorado*, edited by K. A. Kuckelman. http://www.crowcanyon.org/sandcanyon.

Muir, R. J., and J. C. Driver. 2003. "Faunal Remains." In *The Archaeology of Yellow Jacket Pueblo (Site 5MT5): Excavations at a Large Community Center in Southwestern Colorado*, edited by K. A. Kuckelman. http://www.crowcanyon.org/yellowjacket.

Nagaoka, L. 2001. "Using Diversity Indices to Measure Changes in Prey Choice at the Shag River Mouth Site, Southern New Zealand." *International Journal of Osteoarchaeology* 11 (1–2): 101–111.

Nagaoka, L. 2002. "The Effects of Resource Depression on Foraging Efficiency, Diet Breadth, and Patch Use in Southern New Zealand." *Journal of Anthropological Archaeology* 21 (4): 419–442.

Neusius, S. W. 1996. "Game Procurement among Temperate Horticulturalists: The Case for Garden Hunting by the Dolores Anasazi." In *Case Studies in Environmental Archaeology*, edited by E. J. Reitz, L. A. Newsom, and S. J. Scudder, 273–288. New York: Plenum Press.

Rawlings, T. A., and J. C. Driver. 2010. "Paleodiet of Domestic Turkey, Shields Pueblo (5MT3807), Colorado: Isotopic Analysis and Its Implications for Care of a Household Domesticate." *Journal of Archaeological Science* 37 (10): 2433–2441.

Rawlings, T., and J. C. Driver. 2015. "Faunal Remains from Shields Pueblo." In *The Archaeology of Shields Pueblo (Site 5MT3807): Excavations at a Mesa-Top Community Center in Southwestern Colorado*, edited by S. C. Ryan. http://www.crowcanyon.org/shields pueblo.

Schollmeyer, K. G., and J. C. Driver. 2012. "The Past, Present, and Future of Small Terrestrial Mammals in Human Diets." In *Conservation Biology and Applied Zooarchaeology*, edited by S. Wolverton and R. L. Lyman, 179–207. Tucson: University of Arizona Press.

Schollmeyer, K. G., and J. C. Driver. 2013. "Settlement Patterns, Source-Sink Dynamics, and Artiodactyl Hunting in the Prehistoric U.S. Southwest." *Journal of Archaeological Method and Theory* 20 (September): 448–478.

Shaffer, B. S. 1992a. "Interpretation of Gopher Remains from Southwestern Archaeological Assemblages." *American Antiquity* 57 (4): 683–691.

Shaffer, B. S. 1992b. "Quarter-Inch Screening: Understanding Biases in Recovery of Vertebrate Faunal Remains." *American Antiquity* 57 (1): 129–136.

Simms, S. R. 1985. "Acquisition Cost and Nutritional Data on Great Basin Resources." *Journal of California and Great Basin Anthropology* 7 (1): 117–126.

Smith, W. P. 1991. "Odocoileus virginianus." *Mammalian Species* 388 (September): 1–13.

Speth, J. D. 2000. "Boiling vs. Baking and Roasting: A Taphonomic Approach to the Recognition of Cooking Techniques in Small Mammals." In *Animal Bones, Human Societies*, edited by P. A. Rowley-Conwy, 89–105. Oxford: Oxbow Books.

Stephens, D. W., and J. R. Krebs. 1986. *Foraging Theory*. Princeton, NJ: Princeton University Press.

Sundjordet, S. 2017. "Let Them Plant Their Own: Implications of Interactive Crop-Loss Processes during Drought in Hopi Maize Fields." *Journal of Ethnobiology* 37 (2): 241–259.

Szuter, C. R. 1991. *Hunting by Prehistoric Horticulturalists in the American Southwest*. New York: Garland Publishing.

Vangilder, L., and E. Kurzejeski. 1995. "Population Ecology of the Eastern Wild Turkey in Northern Missouri." *Wildlife Monographs* 130 (October): 3–50.

Varien, M. D. 1999. *Sedentism and Mobility in a Social Landscape: Mesa Verde and Beyond*. Tucson: University of Arizona Press.

Vigne, J-D. 2008. "Zooarchaeological Aspects of the Neolithic Diet Transition in the Near East and Europe, and Their Putative Relationships with the Neolithic Demographic Transition." In The *Neolithic Demographic Transition and Its Consequences*, eds. J-P. Bocquet-Appel and O. Bar-Yosef, 179–205. Dordrecht, Netherlands: Springer. https://doi.org/10.1007/978-1-4020-8539-0_8.

Vigne, J-D., and M-C. Marinval-Vigne. 1983. "Methode pour la mise en evidence de la consummation du petit gibier." In *Animals and Archaeology: 1. Hunters and Their Prey*, edited by J. Clutton-Brock and C. Grigson, 239–242. Oxford: British Archaeological Reports International Series.

Winstead, C. 2015. "The Use of Faunal Remains for Identifying Shifts in Pit Structure Function in the Mesa Verde Region: A Case Study from Goodman Point." MA thesis, University of North Texas, Denton.

White, T. E. 1953. "A Method for Calculating the Dietary Percentage of Various Food Animals Utilized by Aboriginal Peoples." *American Antiquity* 18 (4): 396–398.

Yensen, E., and P. W. Sherman. 2003. "Ground Squirrels." In *Wild Mammals of North America: Biology, Management, and Conservation*, edited by G. A. Feldhamer, B. C. Thompson, and J. A. Chapman, 211–231. 2nd ed. Baltimore: Johns Hopkins University Press.

21

Fine-Grained Chronology Reveals Human Impacts on Animal Populations in the Mesa Verde Region of the American Southwest

KAREN GUST SCHOLLMEYER AND JONATHAN C. DRIVER

Historical disciplines are increasingly realizing their potential to contribute long-term data to contemporary issues in many fields. However, the temporal resolution of archaeological datasets is often on a scale of centuries, making them less useful for fine-grained understandings of cultural and environmental change. The work of Crow Canyon Archaeological Center (CCAC) in the central Mesa Verde region is an exception, with unusually fine-grained temporal resolution on faunal datasets from archaeological assemblages collected over four decades. These data provide a long-term record of human use of animals at a time scale that allows us to examine direct and indirect human impacts on animal populations and associated subsistence strategies.

In the US Southwest, Holocene mammal extinctions were rare until the arrival of Europeans. However, some mammal taxa are very rare in archaeological sites, whereas others are nearly ubiquitous. This pattern may result in part from an "extinction filter" effect, under which fauna present in a study area include only those taxa able to survive the impacts of prior human hunting and landscape alteration within that area (e.g., Cowlishaw et al. 2005). Unusually fine-grained

https://doi.org/10.5876/9781646424597.c021

temporal data allow us to examine the impacts of human hunting and land use on these taxa over time and show how local changes in human population density and distribution influenced the relative abundance of local animals.

In this study, several patterns seen among modern subsistence hunters are shown to have operated in the past, sometimes on a scale of many centuries. Artiodactyls, the largest-bodied and slowest-reproducing game animals in the area, became substantially less available around large villages by AD 1060, and remained scarce for two centuries despite changes in human settlement patterns. Artiodactyls were never regionally extirpated, suggesting that reserve areas with little human hunting pressure helped these animal populations remain viable for centuries despite intense localized hunting. Domesticated turkeys became important after these initial impacts on large game and remained a major food source for the growing human population also from the mid-eleventh century, despite the labor required to feed them. Lagomorphs were an important source of meat throughout the time periods considered in this chapter and do not show evidence for sudden changes in use related to human hunting and anthropogenic landscape change. However, a long-term increase in the ratio of cottontail to jackrabbit can be seen.

CHRONOLOGY

In the central Mesa Verde region, dendrochronological dates and frequent temporal changes in pottery styles allow bone assemblages from some archaeological sites to be dated to periods as short as forty years (Ortman et al. 2007), an unusually precise range for archaeological materials. Thanks to intense archaeological survey, almost all community centers of fifty or more rooms have probably been recorded (see Glowacki et al., chapter 12 this volume). Within the large, systematically surveyed portion of the study area, all surviving archaeological sites of one or more rooms have probably been recorded (Schwindt et al. 2016; Varien et al. 2007). This unusual precision allows us to examine faunal assemblages from different stages of human residence within the region, including the first substantial permanent villages, changes in population density, and the final years of residence by pre-Hispanic Pueblo farmers.

The earliest evidence of sedentary farmers in the area is from the Basketmaker III period (AD 500–750), when a pulse of immigration established the first substantial sedentary human population (Diederichs 2020; Schleher et al., chapter 10 in this volume; Schwindt et al. 2016; Varien et al. 2007). Most people lived in dispersed single-family residences, but this period also saw the establishment of small, multihousehold villages. In this chapter we generally focus on the most precisely dated assemblages from the region. However, because we lack a sample of precisely dated Basketmaker III period sites, we have included data from aggregated faunal assemblages from mid-Basketmaker III period (AD 575–660) and late Basketmaker III period (AD 660–750) contexts from a recent CCAC project (Cates 2020).

During the Pueblo I period (AD 750–900), migrants from the east and west arrived, eventually coalescing into villages of over 100 households (Johnson et al. 2005). Many of these villages were short lived, with occupations of forty or fewer years (Wilshusen 1999). Around AD 880 a large-scale southward emigration began (Judge 1989, 216). We report data from three Pueblo I period assemblages.

During the early Pueblo II period (AD 900–1060) the regional human population was low, with residence in widely dispersed households, sometimes loosely clustered into a dispersed community (Lipe and Varien 1999a; Throgmorton et al., chapter 11 in this volume). Another episode of immigration occurred in the late Pueblo II period (AD 1060–1140). As local populations increased, residences became increasingly aggregated into clusters around community centers built in the style of Chaco Canyon to the south. Our study includes faunal assemblages from four villages from the early Pueblo II period and three villages from the more populous late Pueblo II period (table 21.1), allowing us to contrast the resources used by farmers during both a more dispersed and a more aggregated period of settlement.

The early Pueblo III period (AD 1140–1225) began with decades of widespread drought (Ryan 2010). Rapid population growth commenced with the end of the drought around AD 1180, and farmers built increasingly aggregated clusters of residences on mesa tops (Lipe and Varien 1999b). Population growth continued during the late Pueblo III period (AD 1225–1300), reaching a peak between AD 1225 and 1260 (Schwindt et al. 2016; Varien et al. 2007). Community centers became larger and more numerous, with most people living in tightly aggregated villages. Most villages were located in or near canyons rather than on mesa tops. Faunal assemblages are drawn from two early Pueblo III period villages and five late Pueblo III period villages (table 21.1). These assemblages provide information about resource use by the largest and most aggregated human populations to have lived in the area.

The end of the Pueblo III period saw a dramatic depopulation around AD 1260. Shortly after AD 1280, residential use of the region by Pueblo people ended (Schwindt et al. 2016; Varien et al. 2007). Our study includes one assemblage from Sand Canyon Pueblo that was deposited in the final few years of occupation, likely in the late 1270s.

INDICES AND CHANGES IN ANIMAL ABUNDANCE

Numerous processes can influence the relative abundance of animal bones from different taxa in an archaeological assemblage, including taphonomic, anthropogenic, and nonanthropogenic environmental factors (Schollmeyer and Driver 2013). We are most interested here in anthropogenic influences, and in taxon

TABLE 21.1. Assemblage size and date ranges for faunal data used in this study.

Period	Site	Date Range (AD)	NISP	Reference
Mid-Basketmaker III	Aggregated data: Basketmaker Communities project	575–660	743	Cates (2020)
Late Basketmaker III	Aggregated data: Basketmaker Communities project	660–750	887	Cates (2020)
Pueblo I	Shields Pueblo (5MT3807)	725–920	445	Rawlings and Driver (2015)
	Little Cahone (5MT8838)	725–800	432	Akins (1988)
	Duckfoot site (5MT3868)	840–880	5,710	Walker (1993)
Early Pueblo II	Stix and Leaves Pueblo (5MT11555)	920–980	16,926	Bradley (2010)
	Dobbins Stockade (5MT8827)	1020–1060	138	Akins (1988)
	Norton House (5MT8839)	1020–1060	176	Akins (1988)
	Shields Pueblo (5MT3807)	1020–1060	1,846	Rawlings and Driver (2015)
Late Pueblo II	Shields Pueblo (5MT3807)	1060–1140	12,913	Rawlings and Driver (2015)
	Albert Porter Pueblo (5MT123)	1060–1140	2,820	Badenhorst and Driver (2015)
	Yellow Jacket Pueblo (5MT5)	1060–1140	426	Muir and Driver (2003)
Early Pueblo III	Shields Pueblo (5MT3807)	1140–1225	11,974	Rawlings and Driver (2015)
	Albert Porter Pueblo (5MT123)	1140–1225	7,746	Badenhorst and Driver (2015)
Late Pueblo III	Shields Pueblo (5MT3807)	1225–1280	2,234	Rawlings and Driver (2015)
	Albert Porter Pueblo (5MT123)	1225–1280	1,549	Badenhorst and Driver (2015)
	Sand Canyon Pueblo (5MT765) Secondary refuse	1250–1275	3,968	Kuckelman (2010); Muir (2007)
	Castle Rock Pueblo (5MT1825)	1256–1285	4,224	Driver (2000)
Terminal Pueblo III	Sand Canyon Pueblo (5MT765) Abandonment	Immediate preabandonment late 1270s	2,674	Kuckelman (2010); Muir (2007)

variability related to the resilience of taxa to those influences. We attempt to mitigate the effects of taphonomic variation by examining statistically significant trends across multiple bone assemblages, which should cancel out biases in taphonomy, sampling, and analysis associated with individual assemblages. We control for spatial environmental variation by focusing on a consistent area, the Montezuma Valley, over time. Nonanthropogenic environmental variation from climatic variability over time has been well studied in the area (Varien et al. 2007) and does not appear to be a substantial influence on the patterns discussed here. We compare the relative proportions of several orders and genera of animals in these archaeological assemblages using the number of identified specimens (NISP) identified to that order, genus, or lower taxonomic level. Comparing proportions highlights changes in the relative abundance of different types of animals over time, and how those changes are related to shifts in the size and distribution of the local human population.

Artiodactyls

Artiodactyls are the primary large-bodied prey taxa in the Southwest and are generally preferred by hunters for economic and social reasons, a pattern documented by both conservation biology studies (e.g., Cowlishaw et al. 2005; Peres and Nascimento 2006) and anthropological ones (e.g., Kent 1989; Lupo 2007). Thus, changes in artiodactyl representation relative to other taxa are often inferred to reflect changes in the local availability of these animals to hunters (e.g., Grayson 1991). When other factors (such as climate change) are controlled, such changes in local availability are likely related to human hunting and/or to anthropogenic habitat changes. Southwestern archaeologists commonly assess changes in artiodactyl relative abundance by using the artiodactyl index (artiodactyls/[artiodactyls+lagomorphs]) as a means of comparing assemblages. Artiodactyls present in archaeological assemblages in the study area are primarily deer (*Odocoileus hemionus* and *O. virginianus*) and pronghorn (*Antilocapra americana*), with smaller numbers of elk (*Cervus canadensis*) and bighorn sheep (*Ovis canadensis*).

Meleagris Gallopavo

Most turkey (*Meleagris gallopavo*) specimens represent domesticated animals (Speller et al. 2010). Before the Pueblo II period, turkey remains are rare in the area. Where they do occur, they are often burials of whole, articulated animals interpreted as birds used for ritual feathers rather than food (e.g., Cates 2020). In later periods, domesticated turkeys are widespread in trash deposits and were heavily provisioned with maize (Rawlings and Driver 2010). The effort put into raising and feeding these animals has been argued by some researchers to be an attempt to gain additional protein and fat resources in the face of declining artiodactyl availability (Badenhorst and Driver 2009; Spielmann and Angstadt-Leto 1996), an argument we return to in "Results." The turkey index (turkey/[turkey+lagomorphs]) is commonly used for comparisons in the Southwest.

Lagomorphs

Lagomorphs (jackrabbits [*Lepus*] and cottontails [*Sylvilagus*] in the study area) provide information concerning both human hunting and habitat. The ratio of jackrabbits to cottontails varies across the US Southwest. On the Colorado Plateau, increases in human population size, settlement aggregation, and intensification of farming activities are correlated with increases in the proportion of cottontails relative to jackrabbits, likely due to associated habitat modification (Driver and Woiderski 2008). The lagomorph index, widely used for comparisons of the ratio of jackrabbits to cottontails, is most commonly calculated as (*Sylvilagus*/[*Sylvilagus*+*Lepus*]).

RESULTS

Artiodactyl index values decrease consistently from AD 725 to AD 1225 (table 21.2). Fisher's exact tests comparing artiodactyl and lagomorph number of identified specimens (NISP) between consecutive periods show a significant difference between the Pueblo I and early Pueblo II periods ($p = 0.04$), between the early and late Pueblo II periods ($p = 0$) and between the late Pueblo II period and early Pueblo III ($p = 0$). These figures indicate substantial anthropogenic impacts on local artiodactyl populations occurred by AD 1060, considerably earlier than previously suggested (Driver 2002).

The early, late, and terminal Pueblo III period assemblages show another interesting pattern. Artiodactyl relative abundance is uniformly low from AD 1180 to AD 1225, but the late AD 1270s assemblage has a significantly higher artiodactyl index (Fisher's exact $p = 0$). Kristin Kuckelman (2010, and chapter 19 in this volume) attributes this to a possible failure of maize crops that forced people to other foods shortly before the abandonment of this pueblo. However, it has also been argued that sufficient maize could have been grown to meet the needs of the population (Ermigiotti et al., chapter 4 in this volume). Several researchers have suggested hunting in distant areas was generally unsafe during the Pueblo III period (Driver 2002; Lipe 1995), and there is substantial evidence for interpersonal violence during this time (Kuckelman 2016; Kohler et al., chapter 3 in this volume). If these conditions were the case, the need for supplemental food in the last decades of this period at Sand Canyon Pueblo must have been very great, forcing people to hunt in distant places despite the danger. Alternatively, the overall reduction in regional human population in later Pueblo III period times may have taken hunting pressure off artiodactyls, making them more available to those people who did not leave the region.

TABLE 21.2. NISP, index values, and the results of Fisher's exact analysis of changes between time periods.

	Mid-BIII	Late BIII	Pueblo I	Early PII	Late PII	Early PIII	Late PIII	Terminal PIII
Lepus NISP	46	69	376	4,652	833	642	140	Unavailable
Sylvilagus NISP	96	107	1,219	6,428	3,851	3,324	1,279	Unavailable
Lagomorph NISP	147	178	2,020	12,978	4,758	4,074	1,478	1,560
Artiodactyl NISP	16	13	338	1,935	442	171	48	348
Turkey NISP	n/a	n/a	42	322	942	2,865	744	374
Artiodactyl Index (AI)	0.10	0.07	0.14	0.13	0.09	0.04	0.03	0.18
Turkey Index (TI)	n/a	n/a	0.02	0.02	0.17	0.41	0.33	0.24
Lagomorph Index (LI)	0.68	0.61	0.76	0.58	0.82	0.84	0.90	0.96
Fisher's Exact Artiodactyl vs. Lagomorph NISP		0.20	0.10	0.04	0.00	0.00	0.07	0.00
Fisher's Exact Turkey vs. Lagomorph NISP				0.20	0.00	0.00	0.00	0.00
People/km^2	1.4	1.4	1-4-4.6	1.2-3.2	6.3-9.5	10.3-10.5	14.3	10.9-0

Note: "Lagomorph NISP" is sum of *Lepus*, *Sylvilagus*, and specimens identified only as "lagomorph." Estimated human population densities for the McElmo subregion from Schwindt et al. (2016).

Turkey index values also show considerable variability over time (table 21.2). We did not calculate the turkey index for Basketmaker III period assemblages, because most turkey specimens come from a single buried individual. A statistically significant increase occurs in the turkey index from very low to moderate levels between the early and late Pueblo II periods (Fisher's exact $p = 0$), and another significant increase from moderate to high levels between the late Pueblo II and early Pueblo III periods ($p = 0$). It is notable that statistically significant declines in the artiodactyl index take place across these same intervals. From its peak in the early Pueblo III period, the turkey index declines significantly in the late Pueblo III period (Fisher's exact $p = 0$) and again between late Pueblo III period and the terminal Pueblo III period deposits from Sand Canyon Pueblo ($p = 0$). This decline may be related to the crop failures suggested by Kuckelman (2010) but could also be a response to increased access to preferred artiodactyls.

The lagomorph index remains fairly stable over time, with an overall trend to an increased cottontail-to-jackrabbit ratio from the Basketmaker III period through the terminal Pueblo III period (table 21.2). Lagomorphs were sufficiently resilient to predation to remain an important food source. The relative increase in cottontail to jackrabbit could result from resource depression of jackrabbits relative to cottontails, or from habitat modification (Driver and Woiderski 2008).

DISCUSSION

We suggest that both gradual and abrupt changes in subsistence practices are documented in the faunal record. The lagomorph index shows a gradual trend toward greater use of cottontails relative to jackrabbits. We propose that this change relates to a regional change in habitat brought about by farming and deforestation that created more favorable habitat for cottontails (see Driver and Woiderski 2008). The constant availability of lagomorphs demonstrates their resilience to predation. Zooarchaeological data do not allow us to calculate absolute quantities of animals procured, so it is difficult to determine whether the consistently high proportion of lagomorphs means an ample supply of food. However, lagomorphs remained easily accessible relative to other taxa for a long period of time, suggesting they were at least relatively resilient at this time scale. The fact that use of rodents does not increase through time (see Badenhorst et al., chapter 20 in this volume) supports the interpretation of lagomorphs as a consistently available source of food.

Artiodactyl usage was never especially high, but there was a significant and rapid decline in access to artiodactyls beginning in the late Pueblo II period and continuing in the Pueblo III period (AD 1060 to 1260). It is notable that this decline begins in the mid-eleventh century AD, when human population levels in the McElmo subregion (from which most of our assemblages are derived) experienced rapid growth (Schwindt et al. 2016), accompanied by aggregation of people around larger villages. As human populations grew throughout Pueblo III period times (Schwindt et al. 2016), artiodactyl usage declined even further (table 21.2). Archaeologists have traditionally viewed reductions in local artiodactyl populations as a gradual process, but our analysis shows substantial changes would have taken place within one or two human generations in the central Mesa Verde region after the establishment of larger villages during the late Pueblo II period. The archaeological data emphasize both how readily local reductions in access to certain taxa can occur with large-bodied, relatively slow-reproducing prey in an arid environment, and how long-lasting these initial impacts can be. Local large mammal access did not rebound until human populations declined in the late thirteenth century AD.

The use of turkey as food increased suddenly in the late Pueblo II period and became even more important in the Pueblo III period. Several researchers have suggested that turkey domestication in this area represents a response to declining protein and fat availability from large mammals as those resources became increasingly rare (Badenhorst and Driver 2009; Spielmann and Angstadt-Leto 1996), and the evidence from these assemblages supports that interpretation.

Modern studies indicate that as alternative meat sources (fish and domesticated animals) become more accessible, consumption of wild game can decline (e.g., Wilkie et al. 2005). Turkey production was probably quite labor intensive, since these animals were so heavily provisioned with maize grown by farmers, and substantial use of these domesticated animals does not occur until after access to local artiodactyls declines.

Although artiodactyls became increasingly rare over time, they continued to be available in small numbers. Some of this continued access may have been via long-distance hunting trips to areas outside a village's usual hunting territory, a pattern analogous to the long-distance hunts for large mammals documented in modern studies of areas with localized depletion of some taxa (e.g., Peres and Nascimento 2006). Individual villages varied in their access to large game, a pattern we argue elsewhere may be related to source-sink dynamics and the role of high-elevation habitats in providing animals that migrated into the heavily hunted areas around some villages (Schollmeyer and Driver 2013). The presence of refugia may have been instrumental in the regional persistence of these animals despite high hunting pressure in the areas around villages. The importance of refugia for both the persistence of animal populations and continued hunting opportunities has been highlighted in a number of contemporary studies, particularly in the tropics (e.g., Naranjo and Bodmer 2007).

Acknowledgments. We thank S. Ortman and the researchers and staff of the Crow Canyon Archaeological Center for their collaboration and support. This research was funded by the Social Sciences and Humanities Research Council (Canada), and additional support was provided by Simon Fraser University and the Arizona State University School of Human Evolution and Social Change. Datasets used in this chapter may be accessed online via the Digital Archaeological Record, http://core.tdar.org/ and at www.crowcanyon.org for sites excavated by CCAC.

REFERENCES

Akins, Nancy J. 1988. "Faunal Assemblages from the South Canal Sites." In *Archaeological Investigations on South Canal*, edited by Kristin A. Kuckelman and James N. Morris, 529–548. Four Corners Archaeological Project, Report Number 11. Cortez, CO: Complete Archaeological Service Associates.

Badenhorst, Shaw, and Jonathan C. Driver. 2009. "Faunal Changes in Farming Communities from Basketmaker II to Pueblo III (A.D. 1–1300) in the San Juan Basin of the American Southwest." *Journal of Archaeological Science* 36 (9): 1832–1841.

Badenhorst, Shaw, and Jonathan C. Driver. 2015. "Faunal Remains." In *The Archaeology of Albert Porter Pueblo (Site 5MT123): Excavations at a Great House Community Center in Southwestern Colorado*, edited by Susan C. Ryan, 448–475. https://www.crowcanyon.org/ResearchReports/AlbertPorter/Albert_Porter_Pueblo_Final.pdf.

Bradley, Bruce. 2010. *Report of Archaeological Research Conducted at Stix and Leaves Pueblo (5MT11555), Montezuma County, Colorado.* Unpublished report accessed through ResearchGate, January 25, 2021. https://www.researchgate.net/.

Cates, Kari M. 2020. "Faunal Remains." In *The Basketmaker Communities Project*, edited by Shanna R. Diederichs, 513–584. Accessed March 4, 2021. https://www.crowcanyon .org/resources/the_basketmaker_communities_project_2020_final_interpretive _report/.

Cowlishaw, Guy, Samantha Mendelson, and J. Marcus Rowcliffe. 2005. "Evidence for Post-depletion Sustainability in a Mature Bushmeat Market." *Journal of Applied Ecology* 42 (3): 460–468.

Diederichs, Shanna R., ed. 2020. *The Basketmaker Communities Project.* https://www .crowcanyon.org/resources/the_basketmaker_communities_project_2020_final _interpretive_report/.

Driver, Jonathan C. 2000. "Faunal Remains." In *The Archaeology of Castle Rock Pueblo: A Thirteenth-Century Village in Southwestern Colorado*, edited by Kristin A. Kuckelman. http://crowcanyon.org/ResearchReports/CastleRock/Text/crpw_faunalremains.asp.

Driver, Jonathan C. 2002. "Faunal Variation and Change in the Northern San Juan Region." In *Seeking the Center Place: Archaeology and Ancient Communities in the Mesa Verde Region*, edited by Mark D. Varien and Richard H. Wilshusen, 143–160. Salt Lake City: University of Utah Press.

Driver, Jonathan C., and Joshua R. Woiderski. 2008. "Interpretation of the 'Lagomorph Index' in the American Southwest." *Quaternary International* 185 (1): 3–11.

Grayson, Donald K. 1991. "Alpine Faunas from the White Mountains, California: Adaptive Change in the Late Prehistoric Great Basin?" *Journal of Archaeological Science* 18 (4): 483–506.

Johnson, C. David, Timothy A. Kohler, and Jason Cowan. 2005. "Modeling Historical Ecology, Thinking about Contemporary Systems." *American Anthropologist* 107 (1): 96–107.

Judge, James. 1989. "Chaco Canyon—San Juan Basin." In *Dynamics of Southwest Prehistory*, edited by Linda S. Cordell and George J. Gumerman, 209–262. Washington, DC: Smithsonian Institution Press.

Kent, Susan. 1989. "Cross-cultural Perceptions of Farmers as Hunters and the Value of Meat." In *Farmers as Hunters: The Implications of Sedentism*, edited by Susan Kent, 1–17. Cambridge: Cambridge University Press.

Kuckelman, Kristin A. 2010. "The Depopulation of Sand Canyon Pueblo: A Large Ancestral Pueblo Village in Southwestern Colorado." *American Antiquity* 75 (3): 497–525.

Kuckelman, Kristin A. 2016. "Cycles of Subsistence Stress, Warfare, and Population Movement in the Northern San Juan." In *The Archaeology of Food and Warfare*, edited by A. VanDerwarker and G. Wilson. Cham: Springer. https://doi.org/10.1007/978-3 -319-18506-4_6.

Lipe, William D. 1995. "The Depopulation of the Northern San Juan: Conditions in the Turbulent 1200s." *Journal of Anthropological Archaeology* 14 (2): 143–169.

Lipe, William D., and Mark D. Varien. 1999a. "Pueblo II (A.D. 900–1150)." In *Colorado Prehistory: A Context for the Southern Colorado River Basin*, edited by William D. Lipe, Mark D. Varien, and Richard H. Wilshusen, 242–289. Denver: Colorado Council of Professional Archaeologists.

Lipe, William D., and Mark D. Varien. 1999b. "Pueblo III (A.D. 1150–1300)." In *Colorado Prehistory: A Context for the Southern Colorado River Basin*, edited by William D. Lipe, Mark D. Varien, and Richard H. Wilshusen, 290–352. Denver: Colorado Council of Professional Archaeologists.

Lupo, Karen D. 2007. "Evolutionary Foraging Models in Zooarchaeological Analysis: Recent Applications and Future Challenges." *Journal of Archaeological Research* 15:143–189.

Muir, Robert J. 2007. "Faunal Remains." In *The Archaeology of Sand Canyon Pueblo: Intensive Excavations at a Late-Thirteenth-Century Village in Southwestern Colorado*, edited by Kristin A. Kuckelman. http://www.crowcanyon.org/sandcanyon.

Muir, Robert J., and Jonathan C. Driver. 2003. "Faunal Remains." In *The Archaeology of Yellow Jacket Pueblo (Site 5MT5): Excavations at a Large Community Center in Southwestern Colorado*, edited by Kristin A. Kuckelman. http://www.crowcanyon.org/yellowjacket.

Naranjo, Eduardo J., and Richard E. Bodmer. 2007. "Source-Sink Systems and Conservation of Hunted Ungulates in the Lacandon Forest, Mexico." *Biological Conservation* 138 (3-4): 412–420.

Ortman, Scott G., Mark D. Varien, and T. Lee Gripp. 2007. "Empirical Bayesian Methods for Archaeological Survey Data: An Application from the Mesa Verde Region." *American Antiquity* 72 (2): 241–272.

Peres, Carlos A., and Hilton S. Nascimento. 2006. "Impact of Game Hunting by the Kayapó of South-Eastern Amazonia: Implications for Wildlife Conservation in Tropical Forest Indigenous Reserves." *Biodiversity and Conservation* 15 (8): 2627–2653.

Rawlings, Tiffany A., and Jonathan C. Driver. 2010. "Paleodiet of Domestic Turkey, Shields Pueblo (5MT3807), Colorado: Isotopic Analysis and Its Implications for Care of a Household Domesticate." *Journal of Archaeological Science* 37 (10): 2433–2441.

Rawlings, Tiffany A., and Jonathan C. Driver. 2015. "Faunal Remains from Shields Pueblo." In *The Archaeology of Shields Pueblo (Site 5MT3807): Excavations at a Mesa-Top Community Center in Southwestern Colorado*, edited by Susan C. Ryan, 186–221. https://www.crowcanyon.org/ResearchReports/Shields/Shields_Pueblo_Final.pdf.

Ryan, Susan. 2010. "The Occupational History of Albert Porter Pueblo during the A.D. 1130–1180 Drought." *Kiva* 75 (3): 303–325. https://doi.org/10.1179/kiv.2010.75.3.001.

Schollmeyer, Karen Gust, and Jonathan C. Driver. 2013. "Settlement Patterns, Source-Sink Dynamics, and Artiodactyl Hunting in the Prehistoric U.S. Southwest." *Journal of Archaeological Method and Theory* 20:448–487.

Schwindt, D., R. Bocinsky, S. Ortman, D. Glowacki, M. Varien, and T. Kohler. 2016. "The Social Consequences of Climate Change in the Central Mesa Verde Region." *American Antiquity* 81 (1): 74–96. https://doi.org/10.7183/0002-7316.81.1.74.

Speller, Camilla F., Brian M. Kemp, Scott D. Wyatt, Cara Monroe, William D. Lipe, Ursula M. Arndt, and Dongya Y. Yang. 2010. "Ancient Mitochondrial DNA Analysis Reveals Complexity of Indigenous North American Turkey Domestication." *Proceedings of the National Academy of Sciences* 107 (7): 2807–2812. https://doi.org/10.1073/pnas.0909724107.

Spielmann, Katherine A., and Eric Angstadt-Leto. 1996. "Hunting, Gathering and Health in the Prehistoric Southwest." In *Evolving Complexity and Environmental Risk in the Prehistoric Southwest*, edited by Joseph A. Tainter and Bonnie Bagley Tainter, 79–106. Reading, MA: Addison-Wesley.

Varien, Mark D., Scott G. Ortman, Timothy A. Kohler, Donna M. Glowacki, and C. David Johnson. 2007. "Historical Ecology in the Mesa Verde Region: Results from the Village Ecodynamics Project." *American Antiquity* 72 (2): 273–299.

Walker, Danny N. 1993. "Faunal Remains." In *The Duckfoot Site*. Vol. 1, *Descriptive Archaeology*, edited by Ricky R. Lightfoot and Mary C. Etzkorn, 239–252. Cortez, Colorado: Occasional Papers, no. 3, Crow Canyon Archaeological Center. https://institute.crowcanyon.org/occasional_papers/Duckfoot_Vol1.pdf.

Wilkie, David S., Malcolm Starkey, Kate Abernethy, Ernestine Nstame Effa, Paul Telfer, and Ricardo Godoy. 2005. "Role of Prices and Wealth in Consumer Demand for Bushmeat in Gabon, Central Africa." *Conservation Biology* 19 (1): 268–274.

Wilshusen, Richard H. 1999. "Pueblo I (A.D. 750–900)." In *Colorado Prehistory: A Context for the Southern Colorado River Basin*, edited by William D. Lipe, Mark D. Varien, and Richard H. Wilshusen, 196–241. Denver: Colorado Council of Professional Archaeologists.

22

Forty Years of Archaeobotany at Crow Canyon and 850 Years of Plant Use in the Central Mesa Verde Region

SARAH E. OAS AND KAREN R. ADAMS

In this chapter we synthesize forty years of archaeobotanical analyses in the central Mesa Verde region by Crow Canyon Archaeological Center that document 850 years of domesticated and wild plant usage during the Basketmaker III (AD 500–750) period through the late Pueblo III (AD 1225–1280) period (CCAC 2021). This is one of the largest studies of consistently acquired, examined, and reported archaeological plant sample assemblages to assess stability and change in human-plant relationships over eight centuries of time. We discuss long-term patterns of ancestral Pueblo foodways and emphasize the importance of maintaining mixed, diverse agricultural and wild plant subsistence strategies. Through combining archaeological and ethnobotanical research, this chapter provides insights into the history of a range of foods, fuels, and other economically important plants of ancestral Pueblo and other Native peoples from the Four Corners region of the US Southwest. In doing so we highlight a range of pre-Hispanic crops and gathered foods, some of which had fallen out of favor and use by the time ethnographers began recording historic plant use data in the late nineteenth and early twentieth centuries.

https://doi.org/10.5876/9781646424597.c022

BACKGROUND

In this chapter we draw primarily on the Crow Canyon Archaeological Center database of macrobotanical remains analyzed from over 1,500 flotation samples recovered from forty-three settlements in the central Mesa Verde (table 22.1). To address changes in plant use through time, we focus on 1,305 flotation samples that were assigned to one of nine chronological culture periods ranging from AD 500–1280. Flotation samples capture very small plant parts invisible to excavators. To address temporal changes in plant use, we rely on presence-absence, or ubiquity, calculations. The underlying assumption with ubiquity analysis is that the frequency at which one encounters certain plant taxon in an archaeological site provides a relative measure of the level of use / importance of the plant to an ancient culture (Adams 2004; Popper 1988).

As ubiquity calculations assume all samples in a group are independent (Popper 1988, 61), we further consolidated sample counts in cases where discrete archaeological features were heavily sampled. For example, a hearth feature sampled and analyzed as eight 1-liter flotation samples was only counted as a single sample after the results were combined. Intensive sampling of features increases chances for discovery of rare taxa and reinforces patterns of commonly utilized resources. As such, ubiquity values in this chapter are calculated from a total of 1,016 "Independent Feature" samples (table 22.1). In table 22.1, sample counts are subdivided into deposit types to allow for comparisons between plants recovered from thermal features that likely represent the last few uses of the feature, and from midden and other secondary deposit contexts (e.g., Schiffer 1987, 58–64) that provide insights into the wider range of plant preparation and discard practices accumulated over longer time periods.

Details concerning the sampling and identification methods of archaeological plant remains are accessible in the Crow Canyon Archaeological Center archaeobotanical manuals available online (Adams 2004; Adams and Murray 2004). All taxonomic nomenclature and common names used in this chapter follow *A Utah Flora* (Welsh et al. 1987), with updated scientific nomenclature drawn from the PLANTS Database (USDA NRCS 2021). For a complete list of all charred plants and plant parts identified in analyzed flotation and macrofossil remains, see Oas and Adams (2021a).

The Central Mesa Verde Environment

The biotic communities of the Greater Southwest, including the United States and Mexico, offer a wide range of useful plant resources (Brown 1982a). In the central Mesa Verde region, two widespread communities include the Great Basin Conifer Woodland (Brown 1982b, 52–57) and Great Basin Desertscrub lands (Turner 1982, 145–155). Some plant resources within these communities that would be of interest to human groups are listed in table 22.2. Within the

TABLE 22.1. Analyzed archaeobotanical samples by period and context.

| Period | Dates (AD) | Total Samples | Independent Feature Samples | | | | References |
			Thermal	Midden and Secondary	Other	Total	
Early Basketmaker III	500–660	144	11	25	74	110	Adams (2020)
Late Basketmaker III	660–750	59	5	6	37	48	Adams (2020)
Pueblo I	750–920	120	19	7	71	97	Adams (1993, 2015a, 2015b, 2020)
Early PII	980–1060	46	1	26	10	37	Adams (2015a, 2015b, 2018, 2020)
Late PII	1060–1140	88	13	31	23	67	Adams (2015a, 2015b), Murray and Jackman-Craig (2003)
Early PIII	1140–1225	167	25	99	11	135	Adams (1999, 2015a, 2015b), Rainey and Jezik (2002)
Middle PIII	1210–1240	48	4	23	17	44	Adams (1999)
Late PIII	1225–1280	297	75	98	52	225	Adams (1999, 2015a, 2015b, 2018), Adams et al. (2007), Rainey and Jezik (2002)
Terminal PIII	1255–1280	336	53	148	52	253	Adams (1999, 2015a, 2015b, 2018), Adams and Brown (2000)
Total		1,305	206	463	347	1,016	

Source: Table by authors.

TABLE 22.2. Environmental traits and some useful plant resources in the major biotic communities of the central Mesa Verde area.

Biotic Community	Environmental Traits	Trees	Shrubs	Perennials	Annuals	Reference
Great Basin Conifer Woodland	1500–2300 m amsl; annual precipitation averages 250–500 mm, spread through the year; growing season averages 215 days	Juniper (*Juniperus*) and pine (*Pinus*) species are common	Saltbush (*Atriplex*), sagebrush (*Artemisia*), yucca (*Yucca* spp.), sumac (*Rhus*), rabbitbrush (*Chrysothamnus*), mountain mahogany (*Cercocarpus*), oak (*Quercus*)	Cacti (*Opuntia, Echinocereus, Mammillaria*), grasses	Beeweed (*Cleome*), goosefoot (*Chenopodium*), mallow (*Sphaeralcea*), pigweed (*Amaranthus*), sunflower (*Helianthus*)	Brown (1982b, 52–57)
Great Basin Desert Scrub	1200–2200 m amsl; annual precipitation averages less than 250 mm; strong winter rains in the west, shifting to summer rains in the east	Restricted to drainages and basins	Sagebrush species (*Artemisia tridentata; A. bigelovii; A. arbuscula*)	Cacti (*Opuntia, Echinocereus, Ferocactus, Mammillaria*), sedge (*Cyperus*), grasses	Wild mints (*Salvia*), wild beans (*Phaseolus*)	Turner (1982, 145–155)

region, there are additional biotic communities (Brown 1982a) that would also offer a diversity of plant resources requiring travel or trade.

RESULTS

Based on the analyses of routinely collected flotation samples, and on the record of larger plant macrofossils retrieved by hand during excavation (see Oas and Adams 2021a), the subsistence record indicates the following. Across all time periods, a total of five domesticated crops, including four Mesoamerican domesticates—maize (*Zea mays*), beans (*Phaseolus* sp.), squash (*Cucurbita* sp.), and gourds (*Lagenaria* sp.)—and one Indigenous US Southwestern domesticate, little barley (*Hordeum pusillum*) were identified. An additional seventy wild plants were also identified (2021a). Reproductive plant parts, most likely deposited as part of food preparation and cooking activities, suggest fifty-six of these domesticated and wild plants were consumed as foods and/or medicines based on both archaeological context and the historic ethnographic record. In addition, we present evidence of nonreproductive remains of thirty wild plants likely used for fuelwood, construction, and a variety of other economic and/or ritual activities.

Top-Ranking Plant Foods

Figure 22.1a presents ubiquity information for the top five ranked plants foods. For complete ranking and ubiquity data for the top ten ranked plant foods, see Oas and Adams (2021b). Domesticated maize is the most frequently recovered food in all periods examined, suggesting it was the most important food source through time. From the Pueblo I period (AD 750–920) onward, a mixture of whole maize ears, cob, and kernel remains provide row-number and kernel endosperm data (e.g., Adams 2015a, 2015b, 2018; Adams et al. 2007) that can be used to understand ancient maize varieties. Overall, farmers in the central Mesa Verde region consistently maintained a diverse range of maize varieties, with 8–16 kernel rows that resemble previously described ancient varieties of 10–16 rowed flinty and 12–14 pop/flinty maize from the Mesa Verde region called "Pima-Papago" (Adams 1994, 277). Floury endosperm maize may belong to the *Maís de ocho* landrace, an eight-rowed maize of easy-to-grind floury maize that was adopted in the northern Southwest by at least AD 500 (e.g., Galinat 1970) and that previous research suggests was widely grown across the northern US Southwest by the thirteenth century AD (Oas 2019, 115–118).

Other top-ranked plants (listed in descending order) include pigweed (*Amaranthus* sp.), goosefoot (*Chenopodium* sp.), groundcherry (*Physalis* sp.), purslane (*Portulaca* sp.), grasses (Poaceae), prickly pear (*Opuntia* sp.), ricegrass (*Achnatherum hymenoides*), sagebrush (*Artemisia* sp.), tansy mustard (*Descurainia* sp.), and bulrush (*Scirpus* sp.) (see Oas and Adams 2021b). That the second through fourth top ranking plant foods are weedy species indicate these

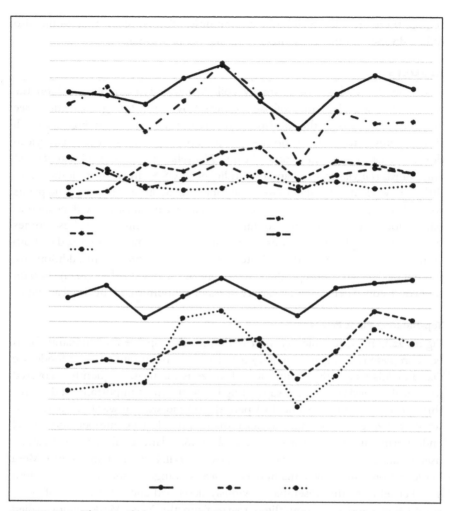

FIGURE 22.1. *Ubiquity of (a) top five ranked foods and (b) top three ranked fuelwoods from all sampled contexts during the Basketmaker III period–Pueblo III period and terminal Pueblo III period thermal features. Courtesy of the Crow Canyon Archaeological Center.*

rapid-growing plants were consistently important foods that were tolerated and perhaps even encouraged to grow in agricultural fields, kitchen gardens, and other disturbed areas such as trash heaps and pathways. Other highly ranked slower-growing perennial plant foods, such as rice grass and prickly pear, speak to the long-standing importance of collecting foods that ripened throughout the year and found in a range of microenvironments (e.g., arid, riparian). These resources could offset shortfalls in domesticated crop harvests and supply foods in the early spring, when crops were not yet ripe and food stores from the previous harvest were in low supply.

Top-Ranking Fuelwoods

Across all time periods, a total of at least twenty-seven fuelwood species were identified (Oas and Adams 2021a). Juniper (*Juniperus* sp.) is consistently the highest-ranking fuel resource whose high ubiquities suggest continual preference and access as fuelwoods in every time period. Pinyon pine (*Pinus edulis*) and sagebrush follow as typically the second- and third-most highly ubiquitous fuelwoods (figure 22.1b). These are major components of the extensive pinyon-juniper woodland and sagebrush/bitterbrush shrublands present in the region. Other top-ranking fuelwoods (Oas and Adams 2021b) include serviceberry (*Amelanchier* sp.)/peraphyllum (*Peraphyllum* sp.), mountain mahogany (*Cercocarpus* sp.), saltbush (*Atriplex* sp.), oak (*Quercus* sp.), bitterbrush (*Purshia* sp.), rabbitbrush (*Ericameria* sp.), and poplar (*Populus* sp.)/willow (*Salix* sp.)—all woody plants present in the modern vegetation communities.

DISCUSSION

The archaeobotanical results presented here for the most ubiquitous/top-ranking foods from over forty sites in central Mesa Verde region occupied from AD 500–1280 are well supported by previous studies of coprolites (e.g., Minnis 1989) and bone chemistry in the northern San Juan region (e.g., Matson 2016). Due to a range of morphological and cultural factors (see Gasser and Adams 1981, 183–184), domesticated beans do not rank in this macrobotanical record. However, they were likely important crops, and studies of coprolites from the Basketmaker III period to the Pueblo III period rank both squash and beans among the most frequently recovered foods (Minnis 1989).

Changes through Time in Food and Fuelwood

There are several changes in the rankings of foods and fuelwoods from the Basketmaker III period to the Pueblo III. The top-ranked foods in the Basketmaker III period are somewhat different from later periods. Tansy mustard ranks highest (third and fourth) in early and late Basketmaker III period samples and drops to eighth or is unranked thereafter (Oas and Adams 2021b). This late winter / early spring resource may have experienced reduced populations due to repeated harvesting during the extended Pueblo occupation of the region. Spiderling (*Boerhaavia* sp.) only ranks in the early Basketmaker III period (Oas and Adams 2021b) and is thought to be a nonlocal food. Along with a little barley caryopsis (grain) recovered from the late Basketmaker III period, spiderling and little barley suggest connections existed in the Basketmaker III period between the central Mesa Verde region and Hohokam peoples living hundreds of miles to the Southwest (Graham et al. 2017; also see Schleher et al., chapter 10 in this volume). In contrast, physalis and prickly pear rank higher in Pueblo I period through terminal Pueblo III period samples.

Juniper wood ubiquities suggest there may have been some decrease in juniper fuelwood availability in two periods: (1) the Pueblo I and (2) the early-mid Pueblo III periods (AD 1140–1240). The lowest recorded juniper ubiquity (73%) is during the Pueblo I period, which supports previous regional assessments of anthropogenic pinyon-juniper woodland reductions (Kohler and Matthews 1988). A second downward trend in pinyon ubiquity can be seen in a drop in pinyon ubiquities from 87 percent in the early Pueblo III period (AD 1140–1225) to 75 percent in middle Pueblo III period samples (AD 1225–1240) (figure 22.1b). Pinyon pine ranks as the second-most-common fuelwood in every period but the early (AD 980–1060) and late Pueblo II periods (AD 1060–1225). There is a major increase in sagebrush wood ubiquity in the early Pueblo II period to 73 percent, and the late Pueblo II period has the highest-recorded sagebrush ubiquity of 78 percent. This high sagebrush ubiquity suggests the Pueblo II period was characterized by an increasingly open, agricultural landscape with perhaps some overall reduction in pinyon-juniper woodlands surrounding settlements. Finally, sagebrush ubiquities drop to 56 percent in the early Pueblo III period and reach a low of 16 percent in the middle Pueblo III; these are periods where juniper and pinyon pine ubiquities also decrease, suggesting fuelwood scarcity was more widespread during the late twelfth and early thirteenth centuries AD.

Periods of Food Abundance and Stress

Ubiquities of maize and other weedy wild plant food data suggest certain periods were characterized by an abundance of crops and other preferred foods. The Pueblo II period appears to have largely been one with remarkably successful maize agriculture with some of the highest maize ubiquities. The highest ubiquity for kernel/embryo parts (42%) occurs in the late Pueblo II period (Oas and Adams 2021b).

Macrobotanical evidence also suggests farmers may have experienced several periods of food stress in the central Mesa Verde region. There are three periods in which maize is ranked second and goosefoot/amaranth rank as the most frequently recovered food: (1) the late Basketmaker III (AD 660–750); (2) the late Pueblo II; and (3) the early Pueblo III periods. These weedy species were likely relied on in times of crop shortfalls. While additional work is needed to address temporal and contextual patterns in plant food diversity/richness, previous studies have noted increases in the number of wild food species in samples from late Basketmaker III, late Pueblo II, and early Pueblo III period settlements (Adams 2015a, 321; 2015b, 104; 2020, 603). While some of these species may represent overlapping medicinal and/or ceremonial uses, the greater range of plants identified in samples from these periods supports arguments that communities engaged with and collected a broader range of plant foods due to diminished harvests or possibly increasing population pressures on existing resources.

Decreases in maize ubiquity in the middle Pueblo III and terminal Pueblo III periods (AD 1255–1280) thermal samples provide some additional evidence for food stress. The middle Pueblo III period has the lowest maize ubiquities of any period, and the ubiquities of nearly all other top-ranked wild foods also decrease (figure 22.1a). While relatively low sample numbers may be a factor, consistently lower ubiquities of the most highly ranked food plants suggest some degree of food stress was experienced by communities during this period. As this period falls between both the prolonged drought of AD 1130–1180 (e.g., Ryan 2010) and the "Great Drought" between AD 1276 and 1299 (e.g., Schwindt et al. 2016), the low ubiquities may indicate that the recovery from agricultural downfalls in the late Pueblo II / early Pueblo III periods was slow and/or that population increases and social unrest were additional factors adding to food insecurity. In the terminal Pueblo III period, maize recovery rates from thermal features (64%) are lower than in midden contexts (79%) (Oas and Adams 2021b), indicating less maize was available when the last meals were being prepared (also see Kuckelman, chapter 19 in this volume).

Overall, it is difficult to confidently assess precisely how certain foods grew into or fell out of use through time and what factors best explain these trends. Possible influences include changes in climate (i.e., wet-cold/warm-hot conditions that would affect the productivity of various crops/wild plants) and anthropogenic shifts in local vegetation due to agricultural expansion and continuous harvesting of foods and fuels over multiple generations. Climatic conditions and the changing local, occupied landscapes would each factor into the decisions agricultural communities made about the relative costs and benefits of gathering and processing different foods. Other social factors include changes in mobility (e.g., residential mobility, restricted movements due to warfare or social boundaries [see Arakawa et al., chapter 15 in this volume]), exchange networks, and settlement that would alter how often communities encountered and/or could access certain foods. Additional social factors might include more subtle changes in the social value placed on acquiring and preparing various foods/medicines to express or reinforce particular social identifies (e.g., Chacoan, Hohokam) and/or to participate in public feasts/ceremonials.

CONCLUSIONS AND FUTURE RESEARCH

Overall, from AD 500 to 1280, our research suggests there is little change in the top-ranked foods (or fuels). The subsistence economy consisted of a mixture of maize agriculture supplemented by other crops and a wide range of preferred encouraged and/or gathered wild plants established by the early Basketmaker

III period. This pattern persists through periods of climatic and social instability until the point of regional depopulation. The Crow Canyon plant database is the largest and most consistently analyzed source of ancient plant remains for the Greater Southwest. These data offer a remarkable opportunity for future research exploring issues of food and fuel use across multiple temporal and spatial scales. Future work, particularly studies exploring issues of plant diversity and richness, will be beneficial.

REFERENCES

Adams, Karen R. 1993. "Carbonized Plant Remains." In *The Duckfoot Site*. Vol. 1, *Descriptive Archaeology*, edited by Ricky R. Lightfoot and Mary C. Etzkorn, 195–220. Occasional Papers, No. 3. Cortez, CO: Crow Canyon Archaeological Center.

Adams, Karen R. 1994. "A Regional Synthesis of *Zea mays* in the Prehistoric American Southwest." In *Corn and Culture in the Prehistoric New World*, edited by Sissel Johannessen and Christine A. Hastorf, 273–302. Boulder, CO: Westview Press.

Adams, Karen R. 1999. "Macrobotanical Remains." In *The Sand Canyon Archaeological Project: Site Testing*, edited by Mark D. Varien. https://www.crowcanyon.org/resources/the_sand_canyon_archaeological_project_site_testing/.

Adams, Karen R. 2004. "Archaeobotanical Analysis: Principles and Methods." http://www.crowcanyon.org/plantmethods.

Adams, Karen R. 2015a. "Plant Use." In *The Archaeology of Albert Porter Pueblo (Site 5MT123): Excavations at a Great House Community Center in Southwestern Colorado*, edited by Susan C. Ryan, 313–402. Cortez, CO: Crow Canyon Archaeological Center.

Adams, Karen R. 2015b. "Plant Use at Shields Pueblo." In *The Archaeology of Shields Pueblo (Site 5MT3807): Excavations at a Mesa-Top Community Center in Southwestern Colorado*, edited by Susan C. Ryan, 97–143. Cortez, CO: Crow Canyon Archaeological Center.

Adams, Karen R. 2018. "Archaeobotanical Remains." In *The Goodman Point Archaeological Project: Goodman Point Community Testing*, edited by Grant D. Coffey, 319–388. Cortez, CO: Crow Canyon Archaeological Center.

Adams, Karen R. 2020. "Archaeobotanical Remains." In *The Basketmaker Communities Project*, edited by Shanna R. Diederichs, 585–642. Cortez, CO: Crow Canyon Archaeological Center.

Adams, Karen R., and Malaina L. Brown. 2020. "Plant Evidence." In *The Archaeology of Castle Rock Pueblo: Intensive Excavations at a Late-Thirteenth-Century Village in Southwestern Colorado*, edited by Kristin A. Kuckelman. https://www.crowcanyon.org/resources/the_archaeology_of_castle_rock_pueblo_a_thirteenth_century_village_in_southwestern_colorado/.

Adams, Karen R., Kristin A. Kuckelman, and Vandy E. Bowyer. 2007. "Archaeobotanical Remains." In *The Archaeology of Sand Canyon Pueblo: Intensive Excavations at a*

Late-Thirteenth-Century Village in Southwestern Colorado, edited by Kristin A. Kuckelman. https://www.crowcanyon.org/resources/the_archaeology_of_castle_rock_pueblo_a_thirteenth_century_village_in_southwestern_colorado/.

Adams, Karen R., and Shawn S. Murray. 2004. "Identification Criteria for Plant Remains Recovered from Archaeological Sites in the Central Mesa Verde Region." https://www.crowcanyon.org/resources/identification_criteria_for_plant_remains_recovered_from_archaeological_sites_in_the_central_mesa_verde_region/.

Brown, David E., ed. 1982a. *Biotic Communities of the American Southwest: United States and Mexico*. Special issue of *Desert Plants* 4. Tucson: University of Arizona.

Brown, David E. 1982b. "Great Basin Conifer Woodland." In *Biotic Communities of the American Southwest: United States and Mexico*, edited by David E. Brown, 52–57. Special issue of *Desert Plants* 4. Tucson: University of Arizona.

Crow Canyon Archaeological Center (CCAC). 2021. *The Crow Canyon Archaeological Center Research Database*. http://www.crowcanyon.org/researchdatabase. https://www.crowcanyon.org/researchreports/researchdatabase/database_home.asp.

Galinat, Walton C. 1970. *The Cupule and its Role in the Origin and Evolution of Maize*. Agricultural Experiment Station Bulletin 585. Amherst: University of Massachusetts.

Gasser, Robert E., and E. Charles Adams. 1981. "Aspects of Deterioration of Plant Remains in Archaeological Sites: The Walpi Archaeological Project." *Journal of Ethnobiology* 1:182–192.

Graham, Ana F., Karen R. Adams, Susan J. Smith, and Terence M. Murphy. 2017. "A New Record of Domesticated Little Barley (*Hordeum pusillum* Nutt.) in Colorado: Travel, Trade, or Independent Domestication." *Kiva* 83 (4): 414–442.

Kohler, Timothy A., and Meredith H. Matthews. 1988. "Long-Term Anasazi Land Use and Forest Reduction: A Case Study from Southwest Colorado." *American Antiquity* 53 (3): 537–564.

Matson, R. G. 2016. "The Nutritional Context of the Pueblo III Depopulation of the Northern San Juan: Too Much Maize?" *Journal of Archaeological Science* 5 (February): 622–631.

Minnis, Paul E. 1989. "Prehistoric Diet in the Northern Southwest: Macroplant Remains from Four Corners Feces." *American Antiquity* 54 (3): 543–563.

Murray, Shawn S., and Nicole D. Jackman-Craig. 2003. "Archaeobotanical Remains." In *The Archaeology of Yellow Jacket Pueblo*, edited by Kristin A. Kuckelman. https://www.crowcanyon.org/projects/yellow_jacket_pueblo/.

Oas, Sarah E. 2019. "Cibola Breadstuff: Foodways and Social Transformation in the Cibola Region A.D. 1150–1400." PhD diss., Arizona State University, Tempe.

Oas, Sarah E., and Karen R. Adams. 2021a. "CCAC Synthetic Archaeobotany Table: All Charred Plant Taxa and Parts Identified." (tDAR id: 4594.92), https://doi.org/10.48512/XCV8459492.

Oas, Sarah E., and Karen R. Adams. 2021b. "CCAC Synthetic Archaeobotany Table: Top Plant Ranking and Ubiquity Data" (tDAR id: 459493), https://doi.org/10.48512/XCV8459493.

Popper, Virginia S. 1988. "Selecting Quantitative Measurements in Paleoethnobotany." In *Current Paleoethnobotany: Analytical Methods and Cultural Interpretations of Archaeological Plant Remains*, edited by Christine A. Hastorf and Virginia S. Popper, 53–71. Chicago: University of Chicago.

Rainey, Katharine D., and Sandra Jezik. 2002. "Archaeobotanical Remains." In *The Archaeology of Woods Canyon Pueblo: A Canyon-Rim Village in Southwestern Colorado*, edited by Melissa J. Churchill. https://www.crowcanyon.org/resources/the_archaeology_of_woods_canyon_pueblo_a_canyon_rim_village_in_southwestern_colorado/.

Ryan, Susan C. 2010. "The Occupational History of Albert Porter Pueblo during the A.D. 1130–1180 Drought." *Kiva* 75 (3): 303–325.

Schiffer, Michael B. 1987. *Formation Processes of the Archaeological Record*. Albuquerque: University of New Mexico Press.

Schwindt, Dylan M., R. Kyle Bocinsky, Scott G. Ortman, Donna M. Glowacki, Mark D. Varien, and Timothy A. Kohler. 2016. "The Social Consequences of Climate Change in the Central Mesa Verde Region." *American Antiquity* 81 (1): 74–96.

Turner, Raymond M. 1982. "Great Basin Desertscrub." In *Biotic Communities of the American Southwest: United States and Mexico*, edited by D. E. Brown, 145–155. Special issue of *Desert Plants* 4. Tucson: University of Arizona.

United States Department of Agriculture Natural Resource Conservation Service (USDA NRCS). 2021. The PLANTS Database. Accessed May 3, 2021. http://plants.sc.egov.usda.gov.

Welsh, Stanley L., N. Duane Atwood, Sherel Goodrich, and Larry C. Higgins, eds. 1987. *A Utah Flora*. Great Basin Naturalist Memoirs, No. 9. Provo, UT: Brigham Young University.

23

"Old Pots Make Me Think New Thoughts"

Reciprocity, Privilege, and the Practice of Southwestern Archaeology

ELIZABETH PERRY

For forty years, the Crow Canyon Archaeological Center has conducted research and educated students and the public about ancestral Pueblo and other Indigenous cultures in the Southwest. Often what people learn at Crow Canyon is their first impression of Indigenous cultures, frequently delivered by a non-Native person. Dr. Joseph Suina of Cochiti Pueblo, who has spent his career generously educating non-Native people, reminds us that representing Native people and communities as existing only in the past is demonstrably harmful to Native people in the present (Suina, chapter 7 in this volume). The work of Indigenous Futurist–inspired artists such as Amanda Beardsley (https://iaia .edu/event/amanda-beardsley-future-vibes-exhibit/) shines light on the one-dimensional picture of Indigenous cultures that may be painted by non-Native anthropologists who are trained in universities to reconstruct and describe the lives of ancestral Native people without a deep understanding of the social, economic, and personal challenges faced by their descendants in the present and future. New thoughts imagine an archaeological discipline that recognizes the

https://doi.org/10.5876/9781646424597.c023

privilege of non-Native practitioners and an imperative for them to reciprocate by being useful to Native people in combating injustice and racism.

The focus of archaeological research and education performed by Crow Canyon since its inception is of precolonial, ancestral Pueblo cultures. The development and maintenance of social networks; the Neolithic transition; the way people make choices about settlement organization across a landscape; the conditions under which communities aggregate and disperse; the motivation for social conflict and violence; the roles of ritual, religion, social power, and social integration—all have been investigated by archaeologists drawing on the data-rich and well-preserved material culture record of the northern Southwest.

The result of such research has immense relevance for immediate challenges facing humanity. It is widely accepted that the practices of Indigenous societies—past and present—may contain guidance that contributes solutions to intractable contemporary challenges in societies throughout the world. Indigenous history and cultural practices have contributed tremendously to non-Native public knowledge, non-Native academic research, and the careers of non-Native scholars (Suina, chapter 7 in this volume). Archaeology practiced by non-Native scholars has not produced equal benefits for the living descendants of ancestral cultures and in some cases continues to perpetuate representations of Indigenous people that are harmful to individuals and communities and the pursuit of social justice and sovereignty. The expressed desire among non-Native archaeologists to demonstrate the contemporary social relevance of their research to an audience beyond their academic peers is necessary, but not sufficient, for furthering an archaeological practice that reciprocates what the discipline has taken from Indigenous people in service to the profession. Social relevance is not the same thing as social justice!

Scott Ortman (chapter 6 in this volume) recommends that practitioners discard the distinctions between archaeological and Native approaches to ancestral sites in pursuit of "an integrated approach that combines systematic observation and analysis of past behavior with a concern for wholeness, unity, spirit, and the future." It is our sincere desire that such an approach represents the norm in the discipline by the time this volume is published. Partnership with Indigenous coinvestigators and sincere integration of traditional knowledge are together a minimum requirement for the future of an ethical discipline. As Joseph Suina (chapter 7 in this volume) poignantly expresses in the title of his contribution, the descendants of Pueblo ancestors continue to be engaged in the work of "Protecting Pueblo Culture from the Western World." It is our desire at Crow Canyon to use our skills and knowledge to assist with this process. We recognize that delivering on this commitment will involve a significant shift from many of the basic principles and assumptions we learned in the process of obtaining a Western education in archaeology.

TRANSFORMATION OF THE DISCIPLINE

As a private, not-for-profit research and educational organization, Crow Canyon is in a unique position to influence transformation in the field. With the resources, expertise, and partnerships to design and execute large, multivocal research projects, educational programs, and Indigenous partnerships, we can establish new values and standards of practice for our work that are consistent with Indigenous efforts toward decolonization. Critical among such standards is a commitment to authentic reciprocity with Indigenous partners and communities. In this transformation, our values and practices would not only reflect integration of Indigenous and Western approaches to precolonial history and collaboration with Native scholars but also dictate that our work explicitly benefit Indigenous people and communities. A frequently asked question in our webinar lecture series at Crow Canyon is: "Why are you telling this story instead of a Native person?" The answer to this question, which is often uncomfortable to presenters, is privilege. Colonialism spawned the study of Native people by non-Native people, and that legacy continues to this day. A thoughtful consideration of this fact begs the questions: Is there ever a noncolonialist way to study the histories of other cultures? Does advancing knowledge of the human past only benefit the dominant culture? Does it ever benefit Indigenous people to have non-Native people involved in this practice? The transformation we seek involves facing these questions and incorporating them into practices that (1) commit to reciprocating the contributions of Indigenous people to the discipline and careers of non-Natives; (2) actively acknowledge our privilege and the atrocities of colonialism that gave rise to our field of study; (3) seek to achieve social justice outcomes in our work; and (4) recognize the high social and cultural costs of excavation to descendant communities.

CROW CANYON'S MISSION AND SOCIAL JUSTICE

As noted by Ryan (this volume) in the introductory chapter 1, the mission of the Crow Canyon Archaeological Center is to empower present and future generations by making the human past accessible and relevant through archaeological research, experiential education, and American Indian knowledge. The essence of Crow Canyon's mission is to draw on knowledge of the past as a vehicle for empowerment, on the premise that for history to be empowering people must be able to access it and it must be relevant to the challenges of the present and the future. This guiding philosophy reflects our belief that the study of the human past is intrinsically worthwhile, contributes to an informed and sustainable world, and produces leaders who engage in critical thinking. Our mission statement is the launching point for action. What measurably beneficial results can be achieved by making the human past accessible and relevant for Indigenous people and communities?

It matters who is making the past accessible to students and the public. While Crow Canyon has invited Native people to participate in our mission work since our inception, and created the Native American Advisory Group in 1995, there have been only a handful of full-time Indigenous employees and trustees in the last forty years. There are few contributions from Native scholars in this volume. Transformation in the practice of archaeology requires authentic Indigenous representation, without putting the onus on Native people to fix our problems. It is up to us to change our approach to mission delivery in a way that creates desirable opportunities for Native people that are compatible with individual commitments to community and culture. Theresa Pasqual, a longtime advisor to Crow Canyon from the Pueblo of Acoma, has explained to us that the movement to seek and train Indigenous Archaeologists to counter non-Native influence in writing history and managing archaeological sites didn't entirely solve the problem. Balancing the actions required of people in their home communities against their work in Western academic, government, and business settings is tremendously challenging. There are at least three ways that Crow Canyon can take action to ameliorate these challenges.

First is a commitment to work with Native candidates for our staff and board to craft culturally suitable expectations for participation in projects and programs. Organizations regularly make accommodations to recruit and retain non-Native experts on their staff. Shifting workplan models can create opportunities for Native staff to succeed without making extraordinary sacrifices to family and community. Alaska Native Corporations, led by entirely Native Boards, employ both Native and non-Native staff yet adjust typical paid time off policies to accommodate the need for subsistence leave among Native employees. Traditional subsistence practices at different times of the year continue to be important for cultural continuity and providing traditional foods to families and communities. These Native-led organizations don't force employees to choose between a lucrative and largely "Western" influenced job and participating in important cultural practices.

A second way Crow Canyon can be useful came up during a College Field School class taught by Pasqual. We posed the question: "Is it ever useful to Indigenous people to have non-Natives studying their history?" The question led to the exchange of nervous glances among largely non-Native college students majoring in anthropology. Pasqual explained that a certain form of advocacy by non-Native scholars has the potential to be useful. Tribes in the Southwest have an ongoing need to be heard and taken seriously by federal agencies with respect to matters of cultural affiliation, traditional lands, and repatriation. Non-Native experts in Native precolonial history are often at the table with agency decision makers and Tribal representatives. Using our standing to validate the legitimacy of Native perspectives can be helpful, but it is more helpful to step back and quietly promote the importance of the agency hearing from the Tribal representatives first. Most of Native history taught in schools and universities was not written by Native people; yet there is an abundance of Indigenous scholarship to be cited, supported, and highlighted in any study of Indigenous history—particularly the reevaluation of long-held positions in archaeology by descendant scholars.

Knowing when to step back is a cultural competency. A third way that Crow Canyon can take meaningful action to reciprocate what we have received from Indigenous knowledge is to make Native cultural competency a prerequisite for working at or holding a board position at Crow Canyon and a necessary component of our educational programs that serve students and the public. Native American (Comanche) activist LaDonna Harris founded an organization called Americans for Indian Opportunity (AIO) in 1970 that brings Indigenous values to bear on contemporary challenges. Now led by her daughter Laura Harris, AIO teaches Native cultural competencies to non-Native organizations and people. Their mission is to "advance, from an Indigenous worldview, the cultural, political, and economic rights of Indigenous peoples in the United States and around the world (https://aio.org/mission/)." It is our belief that furthering cultural competency and cultural understanding combats racism. Actively modeling and teaching antiracist behavior in the context of teaching Native precolonial history and culture amplify our mission and the potential to have a positive impact on Indigenous rights.

FUTURE DIRECTIONS AT CROW CANYON: ORGANIZATIONAL HISTORY, RESEARCH, EDUCATION, AND AMERICAN INDIAN INITIATIVES

As Susan Ryan explains in her introductory chapter, "It is our hope that future directions presented here will guide Southwestern archaeology and public education beyond current practices—particularly regarding Indigenous archaeology practices and Indigenous partnerships—and provide strategic directions, to guide Crow Canyon into the mid-twenty-first century and beyond." The authors in this volume have provided a roadmap pointing us toward the future of impactful work at this unique and "forever" organization.

The organizational history described by Lightfoot and Lipe, in chapter 2, and Kohler, Lightfoot, Varien, and Lipe, in chapter 3, explains the beginnings of large-scale, longitudinal archaeological research involving numerous scholars that persisted and evolved throughout the last forty years, culminating in one of the largest archaeological datasets in North America (Ryan, chapter 1 in this volume). Our vision is to deploy Crow Canyon's history in service to the future. We have a moral imperative to extend the impact of forty years of data collected from the ancestors and descendants of the Indigenous people of the Southwest.

Our database is free and accessible to the public, and many scholars have used it to address relevant research questions and develop educational curricula. We will continue to develop partnerships and associations with external stakeholders who draw on our database to expand knowledge of the history of this landscape, while we continue to mine this rich dataset internally with the goal of reciprocity. As Suina notes in chapter 7, "Modern-day Pueblo interest in the scientific explanation of their ancestors is greater than ever before." While not all Pueblos share this interest, Crow Canyon is uniquely positioned to provide support.

The chapters in the community and regional research and human-environment relationship studies sections of this volume explore topics that are relevant in our discipline and world affairs and have potential to contribute meaningfully to current priorities of many Indigenous communities and interest groups. Research into how social cohesion was achieved among diverse migrants by ancestral people (Schleher, Diederichs, Hughes, and Lyle, chapter 10) and into the long and deliberate process of integration into regional systems (Throgmorton, Wilshusen, and Coffey, chapter 11) contributes ancient perspectives to modern challenges. Such research also demonstrates the extraordinary ingenuity, creativity, and nuance of the direct ancestors of contemporary Pueblo people who have continuously drawn on such qualities to maintain cultural continuity in the face of deliberate attempts by non-Natives to eradicate Indigenous people and cultures. The long-term research described by Glowacki, Coffey, and Varien (chapter 12) on community center organization and change expands understanding of the sophistication and geographic reach of the ancestral Pueblo villages in the central Mesa Verde region "and the important social, religious, economic, and political roles they played in Pueblo life and history in the region." There is a tremendous amount of research in this volume that shines light on the complex combinations of social, political, environmental, and demographic factors, including significant fear and violence, that influenced the critical decision making and strategy development of ancestral Pueblo people (Potter, Varien, Coffey, and Bocinsky, chapter 13; Schleher, Linford, Coffey, Kuckelman, Ortman, Till, Varien, and Merewether, chapter 14; Arakawa, Merewether, and Hughes, chapter 15; Adler and Hegmon, chapter 16; Lekson, chapter 17; Bellorado and Windes, chapter 18; Kuckelman, chapter 19; Badenhorst, Driver, and Wolverton, chapter 20; Schollmeyer and Driver, chapter 21; Oas and Adams, chapter 22).

These authors are aware of the tremendous ingenuity, resilience, complexity, and value of Pueblo communities and culture in the past, present, and future, and they recognize the unbroken link between precolonial and modern Pueblo people. Regrettably, not all the public shares this recognition. Institutional racism and false representation of Indigenous history that privilege colonial narratives and downplay the significance of precolonial cultures continue to influence public perception. To teach Indigenous history accurately, let alone in equal measure to European history, is to expose the brutality of colonialism and the failed attempts to erase some of the most unique cultures in the world. The same qualities of the ancestral Pueblo described in this volume contribute to the persistence and revitalization of Indigenous culture and current claims for sovereignty and the return of Native lands and resources.

The future direction of research at Crow Canyon will involve evaluating how the data we possess can be used to overcome the obstacles created by colonialism. This points directly to the value and future potential of education and public archaeology. The history of education at Crow Canyon described by Franklin shows the value of engaging research and education simultaneously within one organization. Experiential education, inquiry pedagogy, and situated learning are practiced in the context of active research, drawing students and "citizen scientists" into the process of knowledge creation through the scientific method, multivocal perspectives, and oral traditions of descendant communities. The "affective lens" that Franklin introduced to Crow Canyon will continue to drive the future of our educational programs because of the demonstrated power of emotion to shift perception. The goals expressed by Patterson, Franklin, and Hammond, in chapter 9, to foster a greater understanding of our shared humanity in young learners is critical to teaching antiracist behaviors.

The future direction of American Indian initiatives is about reciprocity. Suina aptly notes in chapter 7 that ancestral Pueblo culture makes up most of our work at Crow Canyon—we would not exist without it. The Pueblo Farming Project—described in chapter 4 by Ermigiotti, Varien, Coffey, Bocinsky, Kuwanwisiwma, and Koyiyumptewa—arose from asking our Pueblo partners what interested them most that Crow Canyon could investigate, and the answer was corn farming. This project and collaborations such as the one between Kuwanwisiwma and Bernardini, in chapter 5, set the stage for future endeavors that are mutually beneficial and characterized by equal partnership—a necessary condition for Indigenous sovereignty (Suina, chapter 7 in this volume). Similarly, Ortman, in chapter 6, suggests starting inquiries into the past with an Indigenous perspective, which will benefit Western scientists who have learned to value Indigenous ways of knowing. At Crow Canyon, we intend to ensure that Indigenous people also benefit from our adoption of their lens. Hypervigilance is warranted to ensure that "adoption" does not become "appropriation" with no tangible benefit to Indigenous goals for equality and sovereignty. Adopting Indigenous perspectives to guide scientific inquiry should have a deliberate goal of legitimizing oral history and Indigenous values such that they are not treated as "less than" in policy making. Ultimately, Crow Canyon will embrace the guidance of Suina "to begin building a trusting relationship that can only come about by sitting together and sharing concerns and dreams."

CONCLUSION: SOCIAL RELEVANCE IS NOT SOCIAL JUSTICE

Crow Canyon's mission is founded on the assumption that if knowledge of our shared human past is accessible and relevant to people, that knowledge is empowering. In our next forty years, our work is to direct that knowledge in ways that contribute meaningfully and measurably to Indigenous social justice. The practice of archaeology originated from colonialism and the oppression of Indigenous people by our European ancestors. If we are to continue to practice this discipline, the next revolution in archaeology must be about reciprocity and reparation. Relevance is not enough—archaeology can be relevant and still reproduce the conditions of injustice. Given the history of the discipline, and the fact that some archaeological scholarship still represents Indigenous cultures as "dead," we believe we have a moral imperative to use the skills and knowledge we were privileged to obtain to teach and disseminate accurate histories of Native people to reduce ignorance, racism, and the harms that come from misrepresentation.

You don't need to look far to find academic and popular writing today about how Indigenous values, traditional lifeways, subsistence practices, and sociocultural frameworks hold the solutions to global catastrophes created by non-Native societies. Climate change, food insecurity, immigration, social conflict, and other challenges have all been faced by Indigenous cultures, and their solutions are largely unique and different from Western solutions. The ongoing effects of colonialism constrain traditional solutions in contemporary Native communities, even as we seek to appropriate those solutions for global use. While on the one hand it seems positive that Indigenous lifeways are increasingly valued by the Western world, there is danger in valuing the Native lifeway but not the Native person, just as archaeologists have valued the sites of the ancestors but not their descendants. The future of archaeology at Crow Canyon is recognition of privilege, reparation for the behavior of the founders of our discipline, and reciprocity for the benefits we have received from Indigenous people past and present.

Locators followed by *f* indicate figures, followed by *n* indicate endnotes, and followed by *t* indicate tables.

environmental archaeology, 21–22, 96
Ericameria sp., 353
Escalante Ruin, 240
ethics, 24; curriculum implementation, 139–41

famine, 166, 311, 313
Farley, Paul, 29
farmsteads, relocation of, 311
Far View Group, 169, 173, 175
faunal assemblages, 9, 241, 338t; changes
   through time, 340–43; human impacts on,
   335–36; recovery of, 337, 339
Fewkes, Jesse Walter, 72, 73; on Yucca House,
   206–7
fields, relocation of, 311
5MT2350, 170, 171f
5MT8899, 174f
5MT20921, 214
Flannery, Kent, 29
flotation samples, 348, 351
Flute Ceremony, 76, 77
Flute Clan, 77
food: ancestral Puebloan, 347, 351–54; insecu-
   rity/stress, 167, 354–55; wild, 310, 330, 339–42
Fort Lewis College, and Morris 25, 189
42SA5004, 290
42SA5814, 290
42SA6678, 290
42SA12785, 290, 291
Fossett, Peggy, 31
Fossett, Steve, 31
Foundation for Illinois Archaeology, 15–16
fuelwoods, 353, 354

Ganado, bi- and tri-walled structures at, 276
garden hunting, 9, 326–27
gender, knowledge and, 106
Gillota-Johnson site, 67
Gnatsville, 174f
Goodman Point Archaeological Project, 56
Goodman Point Pueblo/community, 8, 22, 173,
   176, 198, 223f, 241, 308, 309, 310, 311, 312, 329;
   description, 224–26; pottery at, 222, 227–34;
   and Sand Canyon, 94, 194
goosefoot (*Chenopodium* sp.), 351, 354
Gould, Ronald, 16
gourds (*Lagenaria* sp.), 351
Government Mountain obsidian, 153
grasses (Poaceae), 351
Grass Mesa, 166
Greasewood Clan, 73–74, 77; migrations, 76, 78
Great Drought, and depopulation, 262, 311

Great Gambler, 92
great houses, 8, 177, 240, 276, 278f; eleventh
   century, 175–76; Long Tenth Century, 167–68,
   173
great kivas, 157, 262, 264, 278f; in community
   centers, 192, 194; Dillard site, 150–52; Long
   Tenth Century, 170, 172
Great Sage Plain, 169
Green Lizard site, 35–36
Greyeyes, Willie, 87
Grinnell College, 207
Grinnell site, 217
groundcherry (*Physalis* sp.), 351, 354
growing season, maize, 61–62

Hampton Ruin, 198
Harlan Great Kiva, 228
Harris, LaDonna, 363
Harris, Laura, 363
Haynie site, 125f, 167–68, 173, 240
Heath, Meg, 21
Hedley Site Complex, 187, 198
historical thinking, 122
history: accurate Pueblo, 364–65; conceptual-
   izing, 122–23
History Colorado State Historical Fund, 185,
   206
Holmes, W. H., Yucca House, 206
Holmes Tower, 273f, 274
Homol'ovi, 78
Hopi, 113; and Cedar Mesa, 297–98; history,
   74–75; maize and, 53, 55, 57–58; and Mesa
   Verde region, 7, 67, 72–74, 75–80, 80–81n8,
   81n11; Pueblo Farming Project, 56, 115; resis-
   tance, 110–11
Hopi Cultural Preservation Office (HCPO), 55;
   and Pueblo Farming Project, 56–57
Hordeum pusillum, 351, 353
Hovenweep National Monument, 58, 185, 309
Hubbard Site, 269f, 270; tri-walled structure at,
   273–74, 276
Huber, Edgar, and Green Lizard site, 35–36
human past, conceptualizing, 122–23
human remains, evidence of violence, 166, 207,
   217–18, 311, 312
hunting, 9, 336, 340

ICR. *See* Indian Camp Ranch
igneous minette, Cowboy Wash, 216
immersive experiences: Pithouse Learning
   Center, 126–27; teaching tools, 127–28
immigration, Ute Piedmont, 217

Indian Camp Ranch (ICR): Basketmaker
Communities Project, 148, 149–50; great
kiva, 150–52; lithics, 153–54; multicultural
communities, 152–53; pottery, 154–57; social
integration, 157–59
Indian Non-intercourse Act, 113
Indian Relocation Act (Public Law 959), 111
Indian Termination, 111
Indigenous societies, 360. *See also* Native
Americans; Pueblo people
information management, DAP, 31
Insights into the Ancient Ones (Berger and
Berger), 17
Institute for Scholarship in the Liberal Arts
(Notre Dame), 185
Interdisciplinary Supplemental Education
Programs, Inc. (I-SEP), 6, 15, 19, 23, 24, 30;
curricula, 123–24; establishment of, 16–17;
programs offered by, 17–18
Inter-governmental Panel on Climate Change
(IPCC), 88
Introduction to Dendrochronology, 136–37
IPCC. *See* Inter-governmental Panel on
Climate Change
I-SEP. *See* Interdisciplinary Supplemental
Education Programs, Inc.

jacal construction, Cedar Mesa, 293, 297
jackrabbits (*Lepus* sp.), 340, 341, 342
jasper, red, 153, 242, 246, 250
Jemez, 56
Jemez Mountains obsidian, 153
Jennings, Jesse, 31
juniper (*Juniperus* sp.), 353, 354

Kane, Al, 29, 30
Katsina Clan, 77, 81n9
Kayenta region, and Cedar Mesa, 293, 294
Keres, 72
kinship terms, Tanoan, 94–95
kivas, 217, 262, 264; bi- and tri-wall structures,
271, 273–74; isolated, 213–14
knowledge, 96, 112, 113, 129; in ancestral sites,
89–90; constructing public, 120–22; and
Spanish colonialism, 107–8; Western and
Pueblo, 106–7
Knowledge Keepers, 105
knowledge making, 41
Kobti, Ziad, 39

laboratory standards, Dolores Archaeological
Project, 29

Lagenaria sp., 351
Lagomorph index, 340, 341–42
lagomorphs, 336, 340; accessibility of, 341–42;
Mesa Verde region, 327–28; regional use of,
328–29
land forms, 86; and agriculture, 59–60
landowners, collaboration with, 185
landscape, 86, 177; care for, 95–96
land use, 9; changes in, 336–37
La Plata Archaeology Consultants, 208
learning, 132; inquiry-based, 134–35, 136–38
Lee Scott site, 16
Lehi, Malcolm, 87
Lepus sp., 340, 341, 342
Lévi-Strauss, Claude, 93
lithic assemblages, 239, 241, 251; debitage,
247–49, 249f; Cowboy Wash, 215–16; Indian
Camp Ranch, 153–54; McElmo–Yellow
Jacket district, 242–47; sociopolitical organi-
zation and, 249–50
Lizard Clan, 77
Lomayestewa, Lee Wayne, 55f
Long House, 309
Long Tenth Century (LTC), 8, 165–66; great
houses, 175–76; at Haynie site, 167–68; settle-
ment patterns, 168–75
Lopez-Whiteskunk, Regina, 95
Lowry Pueblo, 92
LTC. *See* Long Tenth Century
Luebben, Ralph, 207
Lupine Ridge site, 228

Màasaw, 75, 76
MAÍS. *See* Maize of American Indigenous
Societies
maize (*Zea mays*), 53, 351, 354, 355; dependency,
310, 313; experimental farming, 58–66; Hopi
kinship with, 57–58, 75; varieties of, 55, 56
maize gardens: experimental, 7, 53, 58–59;
Pueblo Farming Project, 56–57, 60–61. *See
also* Pueblo Farming Project
Maize of American Indigenous Societies
(MAÍS), 59
Mancos Black-on-white, 173, 175
Mancos Corrugated, 175
Manuelito, bi-and tri-walled structures, 276
mapping, 137, 185, 198
Martin Site 1, 174f
Masa Negra (5MT4477), 170
matrilineal moieties, Tanoan, 95
McElmo Black-on-white, 213, 230, 274
McElmo Intensification, 192

McElmo Towers, 270–71

McElmo–Yellow Jacket district, lithic analyses, 243–45

MCG. *See* Mike Coffey Garden

McPhee Pueblo (5MT4475), 166, 170, 171*f*

megadrought, modern, 66

Meleagris gallopavo. See turkeys

memory aids, ancestral sites as, 86–87

Mesa Verde Black-on-white, 211, 213, 230, 274

Mesa Verde loess, 59–60

Mesa Verde National Park (MVNP), 58, 73, 173, 174*f*, 183, 309, 312; community centers, 188, 192, 194; lithic assemblages, 250, 252*n*6; small mammals, 327–28

Mesa Verde region, 3–4, 28*f*, 91, 153, 186*f*; drought, 66–67; dual community structure, 93–95; Hopi traditions, 7, 72–73, 76–80; ninth and tenth century, 166–67

Mexico, and Pueblos, 108

migrations, migrants, 8, 240, 263; from Cedar Mesa, 296–97, 299; Hopi clan, 72–73, 75–80; summer and winter people, 93–94

Mike Coffey Garden (MCG), 40, 60, 61; productivity of, 65–67; soil moisture and yields, 62, 63, 64–65

Mitchell Springs Ruin Group, 169, 271; great house, 173, 175*f*; Long Tenth Century, 169, 172

Montezuma Valley, 169, 171, 194

monumental architecture, 268. *See also* bi-walled structures; great houses; great kivas; tri-walled structures

Moon House Complex: bichrome murals, 296–97; defensible location, 294–95; dendrochronology, 287, 290

Moqui Springs Pueblo (5MTUMR2803), 8, 204, 206, 208, 209*f*, 210*t*, 218; description of, 211–13; isolated kivas, 214, 217

Morefield Canyon Great House Village, 194

More Than Planting a Seed (film), 55

Morley, Sylvanus, 35

Morris 25, 189

Morris 40, 170, 173

Morrison Formation, stone from, 244–45, 246

Motisinom, 75, 76, 79

mountain mahogany (*Cercocarpus* sp.), 353

Musangnuvi, 79

Mustoe site, 16

NAAG. *See* Native American Advisory Group

NAGPRA. *See* Native American Graves Protection and Repatriation Act

Naranjo, Tito, 92, 94

Narbona Pass chert, 153, 242, 246, 250

National Geographic Society, 185

National Historic Preservation Act, 84

National Park Service, 206

National Science Foundation, 37, 188

Native American Advisory Group (NAAG), 22, 128, 129–30, 140, 362

Native American Graves Protection and Repatriation Act (NAGPRA), 22–23, 56, 83

Native Americans, 5–6, 140, 359; history, 364–65; as partners, 5–6, 96–97

Neolithic (Agricultural) Demographic Transition, 39

Northern Rio Grande Pueblos, 263; settlement patterns, 259–60

Núutungkwisinom, 75, 80*n*1, 80*n*5

oak (*Quercus* sp.), 353

obsidian, 153, 242, 244, 250, 251*n*1

Occasional Papers of the Crow Canyon Archaeological Center, 31

Odocoileus spp., 339

OFT. *See* optimal foraging theory

Ohkay Owingeh, 56

oil and gas development, archaeological survey, 38

Old San Juan Pueblo (Áyibú'oke'ówinge), flood story, 86–87

optimal foraging theory (OFT), 327

Opuntia sp., 351, 354

oral histories, 91, 92, 263; on Cedar Mesa, 297–98

Orayvi, 79, 80*n*6

Ortiz, Alfonso, 22

Ovis canadensis, 339

Pajarito Plateau, 263

Palatkwapi society, 77, 80*n*1, 81*n*9

PaleoWest LLC, 183, 189, 206, 208, 209

Pamöstukwi (Fog Mountain), 78

paper excavation, simulated, 137–38

Pasqual, Theresa, 362

Paul's Old Garden (POG), 60, 61; soil moisture and yields, 62, 63, 64

PBL. *See* Problem or Project Based Learning

Pecos Pueblo, 263

Peraphyllum (*Peraphyllum* sp.), 353

Petty Ray Geophysical 8507 Project, 208

Phaseolus sp., 58, 351

Phillips, Philip, 29

photography, 112

Treaty of Guadalupe Hidalgo, 108
tri-walled structures, 268–69, 279f; Aztec
    Ruins, 275–76; distribution of, 276–77; exca-
    vation of, 270–71; function of, 274–75; as
    kivas, 273–74
trust, knowledge and, 106–7
Tsama, 94
Tsegi Canyon, 299
T-shaped doorways, 76
turkeys (*Meleagris gallopavo*), 9, 330, 339–40;
    dependence on, 310, 313, 336; use of, 341,
    342–43
Two Horn ceremonies, 77

Udick, Lynn, 31
UMUILAP. *See* Ute Mountain Ute Irrigated
    Lands Archaeology Project
United States: Indian policies, 108–14
US Forest Service, 185
University of Colorado, Boulder, 209
University of North Texas, 64
University of Notre Dame, 183
Upper Cross Canyon cluster, Long Tenth
    Century, 169, 170, 172, 173, 176
Ute Mountain Ute Irrigated Lands
    Archaeology Project (UMUILAP), 208
Ute Mountain Ute Tribal Historic Preservation
    Office (THPO), 183, 189, 206
Ute Mountain Ute Tribal Park, 17, 76, 78
Ute Mountain Ute Tribe, 17, 24, 189; cultural
    resource work for, 208–9
Ute people, 78
Ute Piedmont, 204, 205f; violence, 217–18

Van West, Carla, 22, 35, 39
Village Ecodynamics Project (VEP), 37–39, 40,
    166, 188, 240, 286, 287; community centers,
    188, 190; community structures, 214–18;
    website content, 138–39
Village Mapping Project, 187
villages, 8, 94; aggregated, 170–72, 258–59; lay-
    outs, 194, 196; thirteenth-century, 308–9

violence, 8, 36, 66, 78, 262, 311, 312; ninth and
    tenth centuries, 166, 167; Pueblo III commu-
    nities, 35, 217–18, 299
Vygotsky, Lev, 121

Wallace Ruin, great house at, 173, 240
Wàlpi, 79
warfare, 308. *See also* violence
Warrior Twins, 78, 81n13
Washington State University (WSU), 18–19, 183
water, access to, 312–13
water control features, 58, 86
webquest, simulated excavations, 138
website content, 138–39
weedy plants, 351–52, 354
Wetherill, Richard, 207
Wetherill Loam, 60
Wetherill Mesa, 250
White House, 92
Wichita State University, 16
Wild Horse Canyon obsidian, 153
Willey, Gordon, 29
willow (*Salix* sp.), 353
winter people, 93, 94
wisdom, in ancestral sites, 89–90
Woods Canyon Pueblo, 187, 241, 242, 307
Wupatki, 78

Yaya't (Hopi Magician Society), 77
Yellow Jacket Pueblo (5MT5), 79, 187, 198, 241,
    307, 309, 329; bi- and tri-walled structures,
    269–70; Great Tower, 271, 272f, 274; lithic
    assemblage, 242–43
YouTube channel, 138
Yucca House, 8, 198, 204, 210t, 217, 218; descrip-
    tion of, 213–14; Fewkes on, 206–7
Yucca House Mapping Project, 207
Yucca House National Monument, 206; survey,
    207–8

Zea mays. See maize
Zuni, 56, 78, 113; Shalako, 111–12

KAREN R. ADAMS, Crow Canyon Archaeological Center, *agave@dakotacom.net*

MICHAEL ADLER, Southern Methodist University, *madler@mail.smu.edu*

FUMI ARAKAWA, New Mexico State University, *farakawa@nmsu.edu*

SHAW BADENHORST, University of the Witwatersrand, *Shaw.Badenhorst@wits.ac.za*

BENJAMIN A. BELLORADO, Crow Canyon Archaeological Center, *bbelorado@crowcanyon.org*

WESLEY BERNARDINI, University of Redlands, *Wesley_Bernardini@redlands.edu*

R. KYLE BOCINSKY, University of Montana, *kbocinsky@crowcanyon.org*

GRANT D. COFFEY, Crow Canyon Archaeological Center, *gcoffey@crowcanyon.org*

SHANNA DIEDERICHS, Woods Canyon Archaeological Center, *shanna@woodscanyon.net*

JONATHAN C. DRIVER, Simon Fraser University, *driver@sfu.ca*

PAUL ERMIGIOTTI, Crow Canyon Archaeological Center, *permigiotti@crowcanyon.org*

M. ELAINE FRANKLIN, North Carolina State University, *mefrankl@ncsu.edu*

DONNA M. GLOWACKI, University of Notre Dame, *Donna.M.Glowacki.3@nd.edu*

REBECCA HAMMOND, Crow Canyon Archaeological Center, *rhammond@crowcanyon.org*

MICHELLE HEGMON, Arizona State University, *mhegmon@asu.edu*

KATE HUGHES, Crow Canyon Archaeological Center, *khughes@crowcanyon.org*

TIMOTHY A. KOHLER, Washington State University, *tako@wsu.edu*

STEWART B. KOYIYUMPTEWA, Hopi Cultural Preservation Office, *skoyiyumptewa@hopi.nsn.us*

KRISTIN KUCKELMAN, Crow Canyon Archaeological Center, *kaktrowel@yahoo.com*

LEIGH KUWANWISIWMA, Hopi Cultural Preservation Office, *LKuwanwisiwma@Hopi.nsn.us*

STEPHEN H. LEKSON, University of Colorado, *Lekson@colorado.edu*

RICKY R. LIGHTFOOT, Crow Canyon Archaeological Center, *rickylightfoot@hotmail.com*

SAMANTHA LINFORD, Los Alamos National Laboratory, *linford.samantha@gmail.com*

WILLIAM D. LIPE, Washington State University, *lipe@wsu.edu*

ROBIN LYLE, Crow Canyon Archaeological Center, *rlyle@crowcanyon.org*

JAMIE MEREWETHER, Crow Canyon Archaeological Center, *jmerewether@crowcanyon.org*

SARAH E. OAS, Arizona State University, *seoas@asu.edu*

SCOTT ORTMAN, University of Colorado, *scott.ortman@colorado.edu*

WINONA J. PATTERSON, Farmington High School, *winona.patterson@gmail.com*

ELIZABETH PERRY, Crow Canyon Archaeological Center, *lperry@crowcanyon.org*

JAMES M. POTTER, PaleoWest, *jpotter@paleowest.com*

SUSAN C. RYAN, Crow Canyon Archaeological Center, *sryan@crowcanyon.org*

KARI SCHLEHER, University of New Mexico, *kschlehe@unm.edu*

KAREN GUST SCHOLLMEYER, Archaeology Southwest, *karen@archaeologysouthwest.org*

JOSEPH H. SUINA, University of New Mexico, *jsuina@unm.edu*

KELLAM THROGMORTON, Crow Canyon Archaeological Center, *kthrogmorton@crowcanyon.org*

JONATHAN TILL, Edge of the Cedars State Park Museum, *jtill@utah.gov*

MARK D. VARIEN, Crow Canyon Archaeological Center, *mvarien@crowcanyon.org*

RICHARD WILSHUSEN, Colorado State University, *rhw1883@gmail.com*

THOMAS C. WINDES, University of New Mexico, *windes@unm.edu*

STEVE WOLVERTON, University of North Texas, *Steven.Wolverton@unt.edu*